Fool for Christ
The Political Thought of J.S. Woodsworth

James Shaver Woodsworth (1874–1942) stands as one of the half-dozen most important national political figures in twentieth-century Canadian history. Allen Mills acknowledges his outstanding achievements while providing a critical account of the Woodsworth legacy and revising the received opinion of him as a man of unbending conviction and ever-coherent principle.

A product of western Canada's pioneer society and a stern Methodist household, Woodsworth grew up to make his way into social service and political action. A member of parliament for over twenty years, he rejected the traditional forms of political activity, seeking a new politics and a new political party. The latter turned out to be the Co-operative Commonwealth Federation founded in 1932. Its first leader was Woodsworth himself.

In a crucial period between the World Wars, Woodsworth helped define the character of the modern Canadian, non-Marxist Left and of many of Canada's important economic and social institutions. Among them are the welfare state, the Bank of Canada, and Canada's internationalist role in the contemporary world.

Through Mills's work we come to understand a man whose legacy persists to this day.

ALLEN MILLS is Associate Professor of Political Science, University of Winnipeg.

FOOL FOR CHRIST

THE POLITICAL THOUGHT OF J S WOODSWORTH

Allen Mills

UNIVERSITY OF TORONTO PRESS
Toronto Buffalo London

© University of Toronto Press 1991
Toronto Buffalo London
Printed in Canada

ISBN 0-8020-2787-3 (cloth)
ISBN 0-8020-6842-1 (paper)

Printed on acid-free paper

Canadian Cataloguing in Publication Data

Mills, Allen George, 1945-
    Fool for Christ: the political thought of
    J.S.Woodsworth

    Includes bibliographical references.
    ISBN 0-8020-2787-3 (bound). - ISBN 0-8020-6842-1 (pbk.)

    1. Woodsworth, J.S. (James Shaver), 1874–1942.
    2. Woodsworth, J.S. (James Shaver), 1874–1942. –
    Political and social views. 3. Canada – Politics
    and government – 1921–1930.* 4. Canada – Politics
    and government – 1930–1935.* I. Title.

    FC581.W66M5 1991   971.062'092   C90-095576-7
    F1034.W66M5 1991

This book has been published with the help of a grant from the Social
Science Federation of Canada, using funds provided by the Social Sciences
and Humanities Research Council of Canada, and with assistance from the
Canada Council and the Ontario Arts Council under their block grant
programs.

For Laura, Jocelyn, and Reuben

Contents

Preface

Birkinshaw? Maud asked herself. The name sounded familiar; but it took her a moment or two to identify it with that of the labour leader in the House of Commons who, almost against his wish, had, at the end of the war, been elected by the radical elements of a western city. He had, since, by his fearlessness and intellectual integrity, combined with an extraordinary gentleness of manner and a careful courtesy to political opponents, become something of a national figure and a national storm-centre.

Frederick Philip Grove, *The Master of the Mill*

It is almost fifty years since James Shaver Woodsworth died and over thirty years since Kenneth McNaught published his biography of him. Since then there has been little reassessment of his life and legend. At the same time a myth of Woodsworth has grown up on the Canadian Left. (No doubt the two events are related.) About ten years ago at NDP conventions, youthful delegates of a radical disposition could be seen sporting buttons which featured the face of Woodsworth crowned by the encouraging slogan, 'Woodsworth Lives.' He had, apparently, come to embody the ideal traditions of the CCF/NDP: a man of impeccable political credentials, unexampled tactical sense, and unsullied political principle. That many of those celebrating Woodsworth were greatly influenced by Marxism shows how much myth can embroider reality, for Woodsworth was, of course, a militant anti-Marxist, who once put the Ontario section of the CCF into 'receivership' because of its association with the Communists.

Discovering the 'real' Woodsworth requires putting aside myth; it also requires getting beyond the hagiography which masquerades as biography and which was no doubt both cause and consequence of the myth. The adulation began while Woodsworth was still alive. In 1934 Olive Ziegler wrote *Woodsworth: Social Pioneer* and, even without the benefit of his stand on the war in 1939, she saw him as a super-human force: 'It requires spiritual insight to cut below the surface of contemporary politics to the bed-rock of eternal principles; vision to see a new system taking shape on the ruins of the old; the creative imagination of the artist to embody that mental picture in outward and visible forms. It requires something of the courage of the pioneer to attempt to bring that new system into operation, to enter upon new and untried ways, and to meet the obstacles of old, unconventional modes of thought.'[1]

In his review of Ziegler's book, Stanley Knowles talked of Woodsworth as a 'prophet' and 'pioneer,' a man of profound conviction who gave unsparingly of himself for the greater good: 'A cause into which so much of sacrifice and devotion has been poured must be in line with the very destiny of man itself, with the very stars in their courses on its side.'[2] At the memorial service for Woodsworth in Vancouver in March 1942, his old colleague William Irvine concluded his peroration as follows: 'Woodsworth has achieved immortality. His spirit will be always with us while our actions merit his presence. And by that I do not mean some mystic shadowy ghost. I meant that wherever courage takes a stand to the death in human interest, wherever justice struggles to be born, wherever the banner of human freedom is unfurled, Woodsworth will preside over the scene. He identified himself with human progress. His spirit was the spirit of progress. He is as immortal as progress itself.'[3] In his speech to the inaugural meeting of the Woodsworth Memorial Foundation in October 1944 the sceptical Frank Underhill, predictably, used less other-worldly language but still found Woodsworth to have been 'the most completely honest man that I have ever known; and the most completely selfless man, free from merely personal ambition, never indulging in selfish intrigues or struggles for personal power.'[4]

Understandably, Grace MacInnis's biography of her father, *J.S. Woodsworth: A Man to Remember* (Toronto 1953), is an admiring work. It is a better piece of history-writing than has been generally acknowledged but it lays no claim to being an academic, objective account. It overlooks some crucial matters, such as Woodsworth's early nativism, and does not confront a number of other crucial, perplexing issues and events. What it does show is that Woodsworth's private life was prosaically conventional and therefore not very interesting. Like his father's, Woodsworth's life was given over completely to a career which involved endless travel. Inordinate responsibilities were passed on to his wife, who performed heroically in raising six children, alone, in not always commodious circumstances. 'James,' as Lucy called him, would come home thoroughly tired out and so he spent less time than he might have with his children, especially the youngest two, Bruce and Howard, who were still young when he was in his earliest years in Parliament. In private, Woodsworth was a distant, patriarchal figure tempered with a kindliness that stern but honest fathers sometimes possess.

Kenneth McNaught's *A Prophet in Politics* (Toronto 1959), though written by an admirer of Woodsworth, was also the first academic consideration of the subject. It remains a fine instance of historical technique: thorough, readable, and enlightening. McNaught was the first to notice that Woodsworth was a complicated, even sometimes contradictory, figure, not just the cardboard saint who strode above mere mortals. He makes him into a sort of liberal-socialist or social democrat, a latter-day devotee of the paragon of nineteenth-century English liberalism, John Stuart Mill. McNaught wrote at the height of the Cold War and it is not unreasonable to hold that a consideration for him was to make Woodsworth agreeable to an age that was not just purblindly anti-Marxist but anti-socialist too. Thus emphasizing the confluence of liberalism and socialism, he claims that Woodsworth's thought was, *inter alia*, common-sensical, experiential, sceptical, moderate, pragmatic, individualistic, libertarian, and undogmatic. In the end, however, McNaught maintains that Woodsworth's great significance lies in his moralism, exemplified by his lonely opposition to the declaration of war in 1939. This makes Woodsworth the great 'protestant,' a man of resolute conviction, the prophet in politics.[5]

McNaught was, I believe, too ready to 'domesticate' Woodsworth to the political climate of the 1950s. Certainly there were decidedly liberal properties in Woodsworth's thought, although not always of the kind that McNaught avers and, of course, he was anti-Marxist and anti-Communist. But there was another side to him that McNaught overlooks or downplays, such as the extent to which he was in the 1920s and 1930s a democratic 'revolutionary,' at least in rhetoric, and an apologist of much in the Soviet Union's experiment with planning. McNaught also passes over a good deal of Woodsworth's controversial nativism and his flirting with eugenic theories and says little about his stand on the Spanish Civil War, a stand that shows the depths of his pacifism and isolationism.

Despite these reservations, *A Prophet in Politics* has much to offer. My intention is not so much to replicate it, and to provide another chronology of Woodsworth's political life and of the personal relationships within it, but to offer an analysis of his political theory. I proceed in this direction not just because I cleave to the old-fashioned notion that ideas matter, but because the importance of ideas was indeed Woodsworth's own perspective on his life and politics. It might also be noted that only on one occasion did Woodsworth exercise political power; much the rest of the time he simply preached ideas. I do attempt to fill in some biographical voids; for example, using the Sissons Papers I have expanded upon some of the personal details of Woodsworth's life as a young clergyman and social activist. But, in essence, my study is an *intellectual* biography. I trust that it is a *critical* one as well. I am not sure that a biographer can sustain the project of living with someone such as Woodsworth for ten years as I have, at least imaginatively, if he or she has little regard for the person in question. Yet this does not mean that a biographer should be uncritical. Michael Holroyd's definition of the activity of the literary biographer catches something of the appropriate balance between empathy and distance. I hope that I have attained an equal balance: 'Biographies of writers are written in collaboration with the posthumous subject of the biography. What is seen or overlooked, known and forgotten, comes to be shared between them. It is, like the process of reading itself, an "intimacy between strangers." The literary biographer must use, but may rearrange, the biographee's experiences, sometimes making heard what is unspoken or showing what has been hidden. But he may not go outside this pact. The line he tries to follow points towards empathy without veering off into sentimentality and maintains a detachment that stops short of incompatibility.'[6]

Acknowledgments

My interest in intellectual history and political theory was first aroused at Trinity College, Dublin, by Dr David Thornley and Professor T.W. Moody. At the University of Western Ontario, Dr Sid Noel encouraged me to give a Canadian direction to my interests. For this I thank him; regretfully, my expression of gratitude will not, I'm afraid, be sufficient to win him the Order of Canada. Richard Veatch at the University of Winnipeg shared with me his immense knowledge of inter-war internationalism. Others to whom I am intellectually indebted are: Thelma Oliver, Gerry Friesen, John Milloy, Brian Keenan, Mildred and Harry Gutkin, Carl Wenaas, Peter Ferris, Bill Blaikie, Jim Silver, Ed Broadbent, and Ramsay Cook.

The University of Winnipeg provided me with research funds. I thank its director of research, Herb Mays, and the university's historian, Gerry Bedford. Linda Gladstone and Rita Campbell were excellent typists and word-processors. Regrettably the sexual division of labour continues but I do wish to report that my wife, Laura, typed and proof-read not one word of this book. This is probably why I took so long to complete it.

The Woodsworth family were generous with their time and attention. All five surviving children of James and Lucy Woodsworth, especially Bruce Woodsworth, gave me interviews and were most liberal with their information and insights.

The National Archives of Canada, the Provincial Archives of Manitoba, the Western Canada Pictorial Index, and the Legislative Library of Manitoba were very helpful. Finally, the staff at the University of Toronto Press were endlessly encouraging. Gerry Hallowell was wise, frank, and punctual, and Laura Macleod was as perfect an editorial assistant as I imagine there can be. Her only failing seems to be that she is a supporter of the Edmonton Oilers. Curtis Fahey took a gawky manuscript and made it much less so. I thank him deeply.

ALLEN MILLS

All Peoples' Mission Picnic, c. 1910. Woodsworth is second from right.

Senior Stick, Wesley College, Winnipeg, 1896

The Woodsworth family just before leaving Winnipeg for British
Columbia in April 1917. In the back row (left to right) are Esther
(Woodsworth's mother), Lucy (his wife), Edith (his sister), and
Woodsworth; in front are Grace, Belva, Ralph, Charles; the small child
is Bruce, and Howard is missing.

J.S. Woodsworth in front of the Centre Block, Ottawa, c. 1933

Delivering a speech at the YMCA, Winnipeg, c. 1933

Delegates to the 1934 CCF convention on the steps of legislature in
Winnipeg. In the front row are Robert Gardiner (on the left), Dr Lorna
Cotton, J.S. Woodsworth, Beatrice Brigden, an unknown delegate, and
S.J. Farmer; behind them are Clarence Fines (on the left), Graham Spry
(with moustache), Angus MacInnis to the left of William Irvine (with the
bowtie), M.J. Coldwell, E.J. Garland, and Woodrow Lloyd (fourth,
third, and second from the right respectively).

J.S. Woodsworth and his wife Lucy in 1939

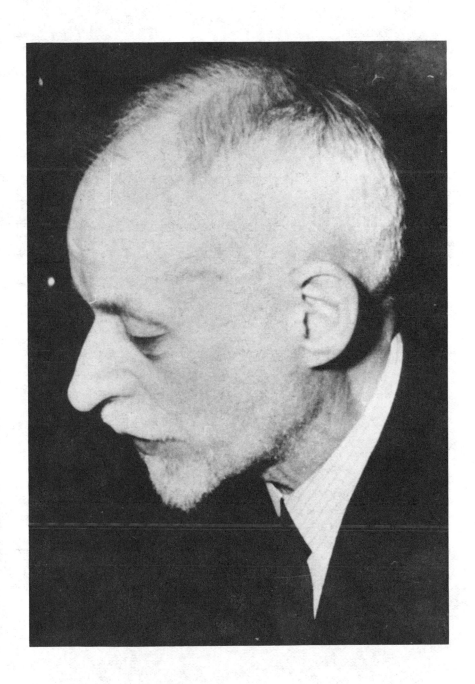

J.S. Woodsworth in the late 1930s

Winnipeg Free Press, 20 July 1933

Winnipeg Free Press, 25 July 1933

FOOL FOR CHRIST

For I think that God hath set forth us the apostles last, as it were appointed to death: for we are made a spectacle unto the world, and to angels, and to men. We are fools for Christ's sake ...

1 Corinthians 4:9–10

1

Son of the Church: 1874–1909

We returned to our places, these Kingdoms,
But no longer at ease here, in the old dispensation,
With an alien people clutching their gods.
I should be glad of another death.

T.S. Eliot

I

'The Great Lone Land' seemed to him empty and wild.[1] Empty because there were few white settlers; wild because what inhabitants
lived there were Indians. The immigration of large numbers of whites
from Ontario to Manitoba had begun to transform the social complex-
ion of the prairies. But in the great land beyond Manitoba, in the
territories reaching westward to the Rockies, there was still nothing
but Indians, increasingly living on reserves, with a few garrisons of
white settlers and, here and there, a lonely, intrepid missionary.

The Reverend James Woodsworth had come west in 1882 to Portage
la Prairie as pastor to a small Methodist congregation. Part of that early
influx of Ontarians that so greatly shaped the new province, he
brought with him his wife, Esther Josephine, and a young family, the
eldest of which was their eight-year-old son, also called James. James
Sr was of an established Ontarian, Methodist family whose roots went
back to Yorkshire, in England. Esther was the daughter of Peter and
Esther Shaver, descendants of Dutch immigrants to New England who
had fled north to British North America after the American revolution
to settle as farmers in Etobicoke. It was there in the Shaver home,

called 'Applewood,' near Toronto, that James Shaver Woodsworth had been born in July 1874.

His mother, like many women then, was pious, hard-working, uncomplaining, and probably too devoted to her husband and children. She not only looked after six children, in circumstances of frontier rudeness, but did so with her husband absent from the household much of the time. The newness of the society around instilled a simplicity and classlessness in her social demeanour. Her door was always open; the neighbours came and went; the children played in the great, unformed outdoors; and now and then Indians came begging. The household was religious and other-worldly. There was no swearing and no dancing, smoking, card-playing, or drinking. Sundays were spent quietly, with a minimum of physical work, attending church, reading the Bible, and singing hymns around the melodeon. The mother's influence was a large one: 'From the first it was his mother's great hope that James should enter the Methodist ministry, and from her he received some of his most basic convictions: a deep belief in order and efficiency, a determination to follow the dictates of conscience, and a definite concept of leadership.'[2]

James, *père*, was equally influential.[3] Of a strict religiousness, too, he was courageous, uncomplicated, practical, hard-working, and possessed of an irrepressible sense of humour. Grace MacInnis considered his most obvious quality to have been his 'palpable sincerity.'[4] The son of a Toronto building contractor and lay preacher, James was essentially an administrator of missions. In 1885, after three years in Portage la Prairie, he took on the daunting post of superintendent of missions for the Manitoba and North-West Conference of the Methodist Church. From the new family home in Brandon he ranged far afield. At the beginning he was responsible for the Indian reserves on Lake Winnipeg from Selkirk to Berens River and Norway House; and, in the west, the reserves stretching from the Blackfoot reserve in southern Alberta up through Red Deer to Athabasca. During his lifetime he would see the territory between filled with churches, in places such as Moose Jaw and Yorkton. After 1894, when British Columbia was added to his charges, he would travel as far as the islands of the Pacific coast. His capacity for travel was, apparently, bottomless. By every imaginable means, including once bareback on a donkey, he travelled an average of 32,000 kilometres a year, not just visiting his western charges but also journeying through eastern Canada for three months each winter on church business and, after 1894, making periodic trips to Britain and Ireland to recruit probationers for western Canadian missions and churches. He somehow found time for other activities. After 1884 he was involved in the planning of a new Methodist college in Winnipeg, Wesley College, and, from 1888 until his death in 1917, served on its board of directors.[5]

In 1917 James Woodsworth's memoirs, *Thirty Years in the Canadian North-West*, were published. They were, like his son's early writings, an odd and sometimes ill-organized pastiche of diary, sermon, letter, and travelogue. J.S. Woodsworth handled the final editing of his father's book and claimed to have altered it in ways that he believed improved it.[6] The book offers an indispensable insight into the mind of an enormously important figure in the history of the Canadian West; as well, it provides convincing proof that, in his early beliefs, James Shaver Woodsworth was very much the son of his father.

James Woodsworth was a kindly, genial individual; liberal in many of his political views but, in the last analysis, of a stern religious orthodoxy and unbending conviction. He was a traditional, evangelical Methodist whose life's work was to confront the *tabula rasa*, the great 'nothingness' of late nineteenth-century western Canada. To amend or accommodate an already established social hierarchy was not his intention. He came to build a new society, to fill a social void; he came to create, *ex nihilo*, a copy of Ontario on the prairies. It would be Protestant and puritanical, British in loyalties, English-speaking, individualistic, and freedom-loving but also, significantly, given to the pursuit of modernity and all its works.

By the time of his arrival in the West the shape of the future – at least as far as the Indians were concerned – was already apparent.[7] Indian title to the land had been extinguished between 1871 and 1877 in a series of treaties which were part of a larger plan of confining, domesticating, and segregating the Indians on reserves. Disease killed many, as did hunger brought on by the extinction of the buffalo and the failure, by the end of the 1880s, of the government's strategy of promoting self-sufficiency through agricultural development. On top of all this, the state used emergency rations as a means of inducing those recalcitrant Indians still alive to come under the reserve and treaty systems. In his travels James Woodsworth commented on many of these issues. Yet he never questioned Ottawa's policies. Quite the reverse; he blamed the Indians:

August 26th. (1889) – Drove to the 'Farm,' where Mr. Ross is in charge as Government Farm Instructor. One of his duties is to supply the Indians with rations ...

Yarn, twine, and farming implements are all furnished by the Government. The Indians farm and are allowed the proceeds. Those who do not work are not supposed to receive rations. It seemed to us that with such a liberal allowance from the Government, and opportunities for self-help by farming and hunting, the people ought to be well off. But they are always for 'more, more.'

It may be a question whether a too liberal paternalism on the part of both State and Church has not been a mistaken kindness, the effect being to pauperize instead of to produce independence of character.[8]

Woodsworth embodied a liberalism that had yet to make its fateful, later compromise with a hedonistic account of human nature and a relativist ethic. He believed in liberty but it was to be a manly, Christian liberty; men were free but they should also be virtuous and righteous. He was, then, Victorian, Christian, liberal, and Anglo-Canadian: a Christian whig and an Upper Canadian radical. To his mind the Indians were pagan, savage, and heathen. Characterized by 'animism' and the practice of self-mutilation, their religion was primitive and ignorant; and as practitioners of a hunting-and-gathering way of life, they were culturally and economically inferior to a scientific and technologically 'advanced' people, which was, of course, how he saw his own society. It thus fell to him and his compatriots to civilize, assimilate, proselytize, anglicize, and indeed Canadianize these unfortunate souls. Those in the path of progress should be firmly moved aside. Certainly they would receive the ministrations of the church and the solace of the true after-life, but they must not stand in the way of development. Resisters would learn the errors of their ways: 'During the year 1885 the country was greatly disturbed by what has been generally termed the "Second Riel rebellion." Many Indians and half-breeds in the territories of Assiniboia and Saskatchewan – now the Provinces of Saskatchewan and Alberta – took to the warpath and attacked the whites ... Many lives were lost during this unfortunate disturbance. On the other hand much good resulted. Disaffected half-breeds and rebellious Indians were taught a salutary lesson; they learned something of the strength of British rule, and likewise experienced something of its clemency and righteousness.'[9] Once the ground was cleared the settlers would come – farmers in the country and workers in the towns. The Canadian West stood at the crossroads of the planet: 'The geographical position of Canada, especially that of the West, invests with strategical importance its relation to the United States, to Europe, and to the Orient. It is claimed that the journey from Australia to Liverpool can be accomplished in shorter time by way of Canada than by way of the Suez. How much more quickly will this be accomplished when the Hudson's Bay route will bring Winnipeg as near Liverpool as Montreal now is! ... It would appear as if Western Canada is destined to become one of the busiest and most important of the highways of the world.'[10]

Thus, at the end of it all, an uncouth, primitive society would be transformed into something resembling the sophisticated small towns of southern Ontario:

Port Simpson is a place of unusual interest, especially to the Methodist Church. The transformation which has been effected in a short period of time is almost incredible. When Thomas Crosby went among the people about thirty years before the time of our visit, this was a pagan village, built after the old style, – large wooden houses without either grace or conveniences. Now it is a modern town, with good houses, many of them well furnished, even to sewing machines and musical instruments. The town is equipped with a good fire-hall and efficient brigade. They rejoice in the possession of at least two brass bands and a rifle corps. Our church is a substantial building, with a seating capacity for 800 people.[11]

Woodsworth, however, was not a believer in economic and technological development, *simpliciter*. He was a Protestant and Anglo-Saxon nationalist, and a white man as well. In *Thirty Years in the Canadian North-West* he anticipated a glorious economic future. But he also worried about some of the possible disagreeable features of the settlement of the West. Some immigrants, he felt, might be neither sufficiently virtuous nor of the correct political or racial type:

In these latter days we are beginning to realize that even the severity of our climate has its compensations. Attention is called to this by the following clipping from a recent issue of the Toronto Daily Globe (Feb., 1912):

'Dr. George R. Parkin has been talking to the Royal Geographical Society of Great Britain about the relation of climate to national character. One of the features of the address was a reference to the value of "thirty below" in relieving Canada of the negro problem and in keeping out the lazy and improvident white ...'[12]

Personally I am of opinion that if the Church or churches as organizations are not called on to interest themselves as to the character of immigration, Christian people should watch this great movement, lest peoples of various nationalities, with various and conflicting moral and religious beliefs, and social sentiments, should come more rapidly than true assimilation can take place. I am not convinced that the principal object in view should be so much the rapid filling up of this great country, as the securing of such a quality of material that a type of national life may be produced equal in its intelligence, as well as in its moral and religious fibre to any on the face of the earth; a nation whose foundations are laid in righteousness, whose people are the Lord's, and whose pre-eminence because of righteous principles and conduct will ensure its prosperity and long-continued existence.[13]

Clearly the germ of the social gospel as well as the nativism of J.S. Woodsworth derived from his father.

From the evidence of *Thirty Years in the Canadian North-West*, on at least three occasions and possibly on a fourth, the father took his eldest son with him on his travels. Their most extensive journey together was for five weeks in August–September 1889.[14] From Brandon they went to Calgary and Banff, and then to the Morley Mission on the Stony Indian reserve in the Bow River valley, a mission established in 1871 by one of those redoubtable Methodist missionaries of that time, the Reverend John McDougall. The latter fixed them up with the not always encouraging arrangement of a buckboard pulled by half-wild horses. Travelling to Edmonton, father and son experienced the numinous grandeur of the vast, silent land: 'Sometimes when overtaken by night we camped in some place where grass and water were convenient. We had no tent, occasionally the shelter of a "bluff," but our robes and blankets both under and over us, we slept as only they can who have the whole out-of-doors, and that the boundless prairie, to breathe in.'[15] On the reserves at Stony and Battle River, they learned of the decimation of the Indian population through disease. At Battle River they met 'Old Grasshopper,' said to be one hundred and four years of age. He made a deep impression on young James, who would remember him some ten years later, in England, in 1900: 'It is said that in the long ago when all the Indians were pagan, Grasshopper had made a vow that he would kill ten men before he died. He had redeemed his pledge to the extent of seven when the law and Christianity interfered with such sanguinary pursuits ... While we were at supper at Mr. Ross the old man opened the door and looked in, flourished a beef-bone and spoke with animation, then quietly disappeared, Mr. Ross explaining that the old man complained that he had had too large a share of bone in his meat allowance.'[16] By early September they had reached White Fish Lake reserve, some hundred kilometres northeast of Edmonton. There they sided with the local chief, Pakan, in his desire to keep Roman Catholic priests from preaching and teaching on the reserve. Memories and fears of 1885 were still alive: 'September 2nd. – Left White Fish Lake and drove to Saddle Lake, a distance of forty miles ... A Church of England missionary was stationed here for a while, but left in 1885. Our Society bought the buildings. During the rebellion a certain rebel Indian was delegated to kill the missionary (Mr. I.). When the Indian entered the house, his heart failed him. He said to Mr. I., "You run away, and I will say you were gone when I came here."'[17] Woodsworth was very proud of Methodism's role in the rebellion:

It is a notable fact, and very gratifying, especially to the Methodist Church, that the Indians under her care were united in their loyalty to Queen and country. They were frequently and persistently urged by the rebels to join their ranks, but as persistently refused. At White Fish Lake our Indians were greatly annoyed by agents from Big Bear and Poundmaker visiting Pakan's camp and exciting the young men to rebellion. After several civil but determined refusals these agents persisted, so as a final answer to their importunities one of Pakan's men shot the messenger. Pakan took the man before General Strange as soon as the latter came to Victoria and stated the whole case. After hearing it the General slapped him on the back and fully justified the act.[18]

The Indians had received swift, rough treatment but not of a kind that, after reflection, Woodsworth deemed inappropriate.

II

Surprisingly little is known of J.S. Woodsworth's boyhood and adolescence. But the main lineaments are clear. His youth was lived on the frontier and in a home where a rigorous Methodism prevailed. It was an isolated, demanding existence, whose adversities were made bearable only by the family's strong sense of self-reliance and religious purpose. The frequent absences of his father led James to assume many parental responsibilities. He was, much of the time, *in loco patris*. His mother deferred to his judgment and he was responsible for overseeing and disciplining his three brothers and two sisters, responsibilities he sometimes undertook with excessive zeal.[19]

Frontier isolation ended for Woodsworth in 1891 when he came to Winnipeg to attend Wesley College. Whether he knew it or not, he was now poised at the edge of many new worlds. Even with a population of only 50,000 Winnipeg was very different from what he had been used to. The town had expanded rapidly in the last twenty years as a railway centre and staging point for the settlement of the new farming areas of southern Manitoba. And in the next twenty-five years immigration into Winnipeg would mushroom, transforming it into not just a service centre and entrepôt but also into a city of significant industrial and manufacturing activity. There thus developed within it an industrial working class. To many churchmen, in Manitoba as elsewhere, this new economic presence raised serious questions about the church's role in modern society.

Intellectual change was also abroad in the early 1890s. The controversial claims of Charles Darwin in *The Origin of Species* and *The Descent of Man* had caused many to question traditional Christian conceptions of nature, time, and human beings' place in the world. The new science moved in step with the new historical analysis of the Bible. The higher criticism, as it was known, viewed the biblical documents as historical records like any others and subject to the same rigorous academic standards of textual criticism and interpretative understanding. Its proponents quickly concluded that the conventional Protestant belief in the inerrancy and infallibility of the Bible was an unsustainable proposition. Whether called a 'collapse of orthodoxy,' as Richard Allen puts it, or a 'crisis of belief,' to use Ramsay Cook's phrase, these insurgent ideas helped produce the distinctive account of the Christian's duty to society known as the 'social gospel.'[20] In its heyday, before the First World War, the latter encompassed a broad range of political positions. The most radical of these held that the Christian's main obligation was not spiritual quests, the conversion of the heathen, or the attainment of other-worldly bliss, but the more mundane and practical task of building the Kingdom of God on earth through collective, structural social change. It sought to replace traditional theology with the newer intellectual disciplines of psychology, genetics, and sociology; and, politically, it rejected established ideas in favour of socialism.

The social gospel movement was on the rise in all the Protestant churches in western Europe and North America in the 1880s and 1890s. In Canada it most affected the Presbyterians and Methodists. At Queen's University in 1893 Principal George Munro Grant instituted an annual theological alumni conference at which social and political issues were constant topics of discussion. It was at these meetings that Salem Bland began to explore political and social matters. Also at Queen's was the Scottish idealist, John Watson, a professor of moral philosophy who taught Bland and, earlier, had been a pupil of Edward Caird in Britain. J.S. Woodsworth, too, would sit at Caird's feet at Oxford in 1899 as would George John Blewett two years later. The latter would come to Wesley in 1901 as professor of church history and remain there until 1906.[21] The writings of his tragically short life, particularly his two books, *The Study of Nature* (1907) and *The Christian View of the World* (1912), constituted perhaps the most philosophically sophisticated explication of the social gospel in Canada in his day. Bland, the eventual author of *The New Christianity* (1920), would be appointed to Wesley in 1903 as professor of New Testament exegesis and remain there until his dismissal in 1917. Woodsworth would become a firm friend and accomplice of both of them, especially after his return to Winnipeg in 1902. After 1898 his travels would take him to Victoria College, Toronto, where he was influenced by the modernist theologian Nathaniel Burwash, and then to Oxford and the lectures of Caird and A.M. Fairbairn. These last two were Scots. Caird was greatly influenced by Hegel and Kant. Part of the surge of interest in idealism in Britain at the end of the century, he used the theory of evolution in his *The Evolution of Religion* (1893) to argue that a single religious principle was manifested in all the world's religions. Fairbairn became acquainted with the new, German historical criticism of the Bible in the 1860s. In general, his theology was broad and liberal.

Toronto and Oxford were, of course, in the future. For now, Woodsworth's involvement in the invigorating world of progressive ideas took the more modest form of undergoing an undergraduate training in arts and science. In 1891 Wesley College was not yet a dynamic centre of the social gospel; Woodsworth made only one specific mention of a liberating theological influence while at Wesley and this had to do with Dr John Mark King, principal at nearby Manitoba College, who was by no means a radical social gospeller.[22] Essentially Woodsworth was impressed by King's inquiring intellectual attitude. What Wesley *did* provide was a modern and broadly based curriculum. The faculty was almost to a man composed of ordained Methodist ministers, born in southern Ontario and graduates of Victoria College. They taught the best of the intellectual tradition of the West: in English literature, Chaucer, Shakespeare, Pope, and Wordsworth; in French, Corneille, Racine, and Molière; in German, Schiller and Goethe. Greek and Latin were part of the curriculum but so were the natural sciences. Woodsworth's area of specialization was mental and moral science, an old-fashioned term for philosophy and psychology but including, in his case, economics and politics. The required reading included Locke, Kant, Paley, Janet, John Stuart Mill, Bagehot, and Sidgwick. Life at Wesley was many-sided. Woodsworth threw himself into student affairs and the football team and happily indulged in student pranks and innocent soirées, usually under the watchful eye of an elder from Winnipeg's Methodist elite:

On Friday night we had a fine supper given by Mr and Mrs J.W. Sifton ... [The seniors], there are only six of us, decided to appear in white ties, but someone had found out and the freshmen appeared in white ties too. [However] the senior students all got ahead of the freshies in taking a lady to the table. You see there were only a limited number and so it would not have done to have Freshmen with ladies and Seniors without ... Professor Cochrane put his foot on [bouncing] so far as doing it in the classroom was concerned. The 'meds' have a splendid apparatus. They use the canvas blanket that the 'stiffs' or bodies are carried around in.[23]

Received invitation from a 'Friday Evening Club.' Instead of dances, topics were introduced, and each gentleman had to find a lady to discuss a topic with. While music played the topic must be pursued; when music stopped one changed partners.[24]

In his letters home (the absence of the father meant that he wrote to each parent separately) Woodsworth counselled his mother on many matters. He was especially concerned to prevent her from overworking:

Now while I think of it, have you disposed of that clothing left in your care? You will find quite a bundle of it including some bedding in the hay loft ... You really ought to get rid of it while the cold weather lasts for spring will soon be here and the opportunity lost. Then too this is a good season of the year to sort

over those old barrels of clothes. If you can't do better give them to the Indians ...
If you want any further information as to the whereabouts of anything around
the house or any further suggestions I shall be pleased to furnish them ...[25]

It is not right for you to wear yourself out as you are doing. You always try to
impress on us the idea that we should not overwork ... Now why will you not
do the same? As you sometimes say life is not intended not to have enjoyment
and why should you try to make an exception in your case?[26]

Woodsworth graduated in 1896. His time at Wesley had been re-
warding: he was elected senior stick (president of the student body) of
Wesley and won the university bronze medal in mental and moral
science. Between 1896 and 1898 he was a probationer minister in the
small community of Napinkee, to the southwest of Brandon. There he
became reacquainted with the hazards and loneliness of the prairie trail
and the extremities of rural poverty. He also faced, in his pastoral
work, the tragedy of crushing illness and premature death. His letters
continued to advise his mother to take life more easily and to rely more
on the children for household chores.

Dedicated at birth to God as the first-born son of parents who had
lost their earlier children,[27] Woodsworth's inevitable progress towards
ordination required that he receive an education in theology. In 1898
he enrolled in divinity at Victoria College in Toronto. He lived on
Avenue Road with his cousin, Charlie Sissons, who would later become editor of the *Canadian Forum*, biographer of Egerton Ryerson, and
a professor of classics. At Victoria, Woodsworth was exposed more
fully to the higher criticism in theology and came face-to-face with
urban poverty and Christian social activism at the Fred Victor Mission.
Thus the social gospel, first imparted obliquely by his father, and the
'liberal' approach to theology, as Woodsworth himself put it, first
acquired in Winnipeg from Dr King,[28] were intellectual perspectives
that were confirmed for him in his year in Toronto.[29] With encouragement from Chancellor Burwash at Victoria and his parents, the latter
also providing financial support, Woodsworth spent a year at Oxford
to broaden his experience and outlook even more.

Woodsworth's time in Britain, from late October 1899 to June 1900,
demonstrated again his unusual self-reliance and self-confidence. Although there were a few distant relatives and he had introductions
to some local Methodists, he knew no one. He did have permission
to attend Caird's lectures at Balliol and Fairbairn's at Mansfield.

However, in not matriculating into Oxford University, he denied himself the friendships possible through full association with a college and its tutors. Nor was Woodsworth especially robust. The chronic bronchial problem that produced growths in his throat and recurring colds added uncertainty to his life. Particularly, his independence showed through in his willingness to come to terms with cultures that were somewhat strange and unfamiliar.

The fresh-faced, bearded young man who had arrived in Liverpool in October 1899 was a sincere, serious, sometimes priggish innocent from a new and distant world. He himself quickly recognized his lack of experience of a society with such entrenched historical traditions. In one of his earliest letters he vented frustration at his inability to discover 'the particulars of the rules and customs' of Oxford's university life. There were, it seemed, no such things as 'handbooks': 'Indeed it appears very complicated. Like some of the old castles and houses it is the growth of ages and has all kinds of queer corners. Each new part has had to be adapted to the old and can only be understood when connected with it.'[30]

If Britain was sometimes steeped in an incomprehensible antiquity, it was not completely *terra incognita*. Although from the Canadian prairies, Woodsworth had been raised with the view that he was a legitimate heir to all things British. Eventually he would come to see Britain as different and strange in all sorts of unexpected ways, but on first arriving there it was like coming home. Of course, Woodsworth's perspective on British history was not without its biases; his was a liberal, dissenting understanding of the British past, what has come to be called the whig view. Religiously, Britain was not the land of medieval Catholicism and high-church Anglicanism but of courageous reformers, Protestants in spirit or in fact: Wycliffe, Latimer, Ridley, and Wesley. Edinburgh was not the city of Mary Queen of Scots but of the covenanters.[31] The Reformation and the Puritan revolution, he believed, had consolidated a tradition of political freedom and dissent which by the late nineteenth century was embodied in the Liberal Party. Woodsworth took obvious pride in writing home that he had visited the House of Commons and observed the actual place where Gladstone had 'sat for so many years.'[32] He also went to see Gladstone's home at Hawarden in Cheshire.

On literary and aesthetic grounds, too, for he always had a deep appreciation of art and literature, Woodsworth's arrival in Britain had the aspect of a return to his cultural roots. He exulted over his visits to

Stratford-upon-Avon and Kenilworth as much as he did over his visits to Wesley's birthplace at Epworth or the Martyrs' Memorial in Oxford. In another of his letters he spoke of the intoxicating beauty of Oxford: 'Milton must have seen Oxford when he gave his idea of Paradise. Today as I sat amid the most beautiful shrubbery and trees surrounded by the ivy banked walls with the blackened old towers seen through the soft hazy air and heard the chimes and thought of some of the historic associations I felt simply lost. The whole was almost over-powering to anyone who had any sense whatever of the aesthetic.'[33] A visit to Cambridge in January 1900 produced a similar reaction. He saw Wordsworth's rooms and those of Byron, Macaulay, and Thackeray. He also visited the rooms of Arthur Hallam, whom Tennyson had immortalized in 'In Memoriam,' and saw the rough draft of the poem itself. The conclusion of the letter describing this visit summed up his reaction to British life and culture: 'Now tell me wouldn't you like to come and live where they make history and poetry.'[34]

Woodsworth, then, was deeply moved by Britain's gloriously culti-vated, liberal, and Protestant past, and was a fervent admirer of it as well. (On one occasion he did criticize the non-conformist tradition, lamenting the destruction of works of art in Scotland by Oliver Crom-well and the Puritans.) Yet his time in Britain also convinced him that he was different. Sometimes he felt unaccepted because the English viewed him as a colonial, although he never came close to feeling the sort of rejection by the English claimed by some English Canadians of his generation – Frank Underhill is an example – and which was so much a part of their eventual sense of *Canadian* nationalism.[35] Woods-worth felt more positively. His visit gave him a sense of being *Cana-dian*, but as powerful was the confirmation he received of his identity as a *British* Canadian. In sharpening his sense of who he was, he was not led to cut away the influence of British culture. But, equally, the discovery in himself of differing traditions, in the end, prompted him to affirm the qualities of his own country and to aspire to new ideals on its behalf: 'I think I am gaining an idea of a culture deeper than scholarship which many of us have utterly ignored. I do not want to accept all I see – I do not despise what we have at home in Canada – I would not exchange Canada for England. But my ideals for Canada are being raised.'[36] His sense of otherness as a Canadian derived from what he now recognized were the distinctive attitudes he had brought from the New World, and also from the attitudes and expectations of British people. In British eyes he was, to repeat, a citizen of the colonies. Less disparagingly and somewhat romantically, he was also the denizen of a land of snow, where wild animals roamed and Indians practised their exotic and terrifying ways. To his brother Harold, Woodsworth wrote of an invitation to talk to a Sunday-school class in the countryside near Oxford. It would, he said, be very difficult to resist taking advantage of the curiosity and preconceptions of his audience. He was tempted to tell the story of the visit to their home of three blacks: '[They] slept in our spare bed and used so much hair oil that mother could never get the pillow cases "washed white" again.'[37] Or there were the stories he could tell about the Indians:

At that time we were surrounded by Indian tribes. One day my mother was working in the kitchen – there were no men in the house. But as she looked up from her work she saw the ugly face of a great *Red* Indian peering at her through the window ... On another day she heard the soft patter of Indian feet and the door was cautiously pushed open and the sad face of an Indian woman appeared. Poor child of the plains! Her child was sick and hungry. Her little papoose! She had come to her little 'white sister' for help. She told the story in the beautiful sign language which the 'colonists' soon learn to understand. She knew the white sister had a little pap-poose [Harold]. So you see my dear children, that the Red Indians *too* have hearts ... Another story [was that] of the Red Indian who had vowed to kill seven men and had already killed four: Well one night as we sat in a wooden house the door was flung open and there stood before us the emaciated form of an old but powerfully built Indian. He was in a rage and was flourishing an immense bone from which he had partly torn the flesh. He advanced into the night ... It was Grasshopper himself ... So on I go. Wouldn't I be a daisy lecturer! Will import you as a specimen of the boys of the Wild West.[38]

These private thoughts, though perhaps never given public expression, reveal not just how English children then viewed Canadians, but also the extent to which the nativism of the father had successfully rubbed off on the son. Although he would later moderate his views, J.S. Woodsworth never completely shed his early awkwardness and insensitivity towards blacks and Indians, and, later, eastern Europeans. His stories about the Indians are particularly interesting since they reveal a popular attitude at the time, that Indians were sinister, alien, and violent.[39] The story of Grasshopper is, of course, a retelling of the one that appeared in his father's memoirs.[40] There, while it is clear that Grasshopper had had a ferocious past, in old age he had mellowed so that his brandishing of a bone was a pathetic protest against the lack of meat. In the son's version, Grasshopper has become more violent and personifies the myth of the irrational, perhaps cannibalistic, and certainly animal-like savage.

Woodsworth had his own preconceptions of the British. He was especially taken aback by English Methodists. The latter viewed fox-hunting as a sin; Woodsworth, son of the frontier, prided himself on his prowess at goose-hunting, even if it was something he was forbidden to undertake on Sundays. He was also perplexed by the tolerance they showed towards drinking and smoking.[41] His comments on drink show him as somewhat of an unyielding puritan: 'Of course temperance is not nearly so advanced here as it is with us. Tonight after service one of the officials asked me if I would have anything to drink before the return drive. *Possibly* he may have meant a hot drink of tea or coffee. *Probably* he meant a glass of beer. That a man is a Methodist or even a Methodist preacher is not a sure sign that he is a teetotaller.'[42] He was also offended by the courting habits of 'certain classes.' In broad daylight people actually walked with their arms around each other: 'Then in the evening along the walks the benches are filled with young people happy in each other's arms. You would have to resort to extreme measures to induce them to suspend kissing operations. It seemed very ridiculous at first but nothing startles me now.'[43] Indeed the lack of personal decorum and public order was one of the more emphatic themes running through his letters from Britain. While he was there the Boer War was under way. He intimated that he sided with the Boers but mainly he was undecided. When he did express strong views they were in criticism of the noisy celebrations that broke out when Britain's cause was victorious, particularly after the relief of Ladysmith: 'Tonight doubtless it is just as bad but I have had enough with two nights. A very saturnalia seems to be the order. Indeed the inclinations of vulgarity, intemperence and immorality are disgusting.'[44] At about the same time he wrote:'"Patriotic" songs are all right but when hundreds of half drunken men are destroying property and the police powerless it seems hardly correct to sing "Britons never shall be slaves."'[45]

Woodsworth's respect for order made him sympathetic towards things German. In June 1900 he made a short trip to Cologne, the Rhineland, and Heidelberg:

There does not seem to be that degraded element which is everywhere in evidence in the great cities of England. Even the lowest classes – the costers – are far superior to their English brethren ... Of course there is a military air about everything. The guards or conductors on the RR are dressed much as officers. As you know the RRs are the property of the government ... Today at Duisberg I saw a fine company of German soldiers. They appeared to be lancers ... As they rode along the high stone paved streets one almost imagined that he was back in the days of chivalry again. The Germans do of course retain the old idea of 'honor.' (Germans) are a way ahead of Englishmen. The presence of large numbers of soldiers gives a lively appearance to a crowd ... These people are very polite. The English are boorish as compared to them.[46]

Woodsworth's visit to Britain and Europe was in his estimation a great success. He now had to make decisions about his future. Ordination was a foregone conclusion but he was having second thoughts about the exact form of his ministerial service. His year at Victoria had whetted his interest in the higher criticism and the social gospel and this had been reinforced at Oxford by the lectures of Caird and Fairbairn. Politically, too, his world view was proceeding in provocative, original directions. In the Christmas vacation in 1899 he had lived for a while at Mansfield House, a settlement house in London's East End, and learned something of the mass poverty, alcoholism, and general social disrepair of big cities. And the Boer War had made him think about international affairs. Yet, having weighed things up, he concluded for now that his interests lay not in a practical direction but in an academic one. The influence of Blewett at Victoria and Caird at Oxford had convinced him to consider the project of constructing an ethical system that would incorporate the insights of all the world's religions. Woodsworth claimed that he was gifted not as a preacher or as a church administrator but as a 'teacher.'[47] He also worried about the bronchial ailment which required that he be close to a medical specialist. These considerations, he felt, pointed to an academic career in a church-based college, ideally in western Canada. To his father he conceded that by Oxford's standards he was unqualified to fill such a position, but by those of Canada he was not. He asked him to talk over the matter 'quietly' with a few members of the board at Wesley.[48]

Woodsworth was, therefore, in a state of intellectual transition. But if one part of his life was undergoing radical change, another part travelled in traditional channels. Notwithstanding his sympathy for London's poor, he still retained the Arminian belief of Methodists that individuals were personally responsible for working out their own salvation, so that moral failure had to be attributed not to society or circumstance but only to oneself.[49] And even after his years at Wesley, Victoria, and Oxford he could still be dogmatic, condescending, and hidebound when confronted by radical critics of the established social order. Woodsworth recounted having met a student from Ruskin Hall, the labour college at Oxford. The 'poor fellow's' unforgivable fault was that he was not just a radical but a Methodist radical, a 'queer combination':

I do pity poor fellows like this man. He has had practically no schooling. In some way he has obtained money to keep him at Ruskin Hall for a few months. So he has come up expecting great things. Now take a man of 35 or 40 from the English middle classes. Place him in a socialistic hot bed. Give him adventurers for companions. Surround him with an atmosphere of atheism and general antagonism to all existing institutions, educational, church and state, and you are pretty sure to develop some very strange views.

   History and socialism are the great subjects taught; but they are taught from a very false standpoint and the result is the narrowest bigotry which believes itself generous and impartial. Mr. Herbert Spencer is the great high priest and prophet of the faith as delivered to the inquiring but ... prejudiced students of Ruskin Hall. Now my private opinion is that Spencer's 'Synthetic Philosophy' is largely 'Conglomerate Rubbish.' He makes the most inaccurate statements and sweeping generalisations. He calmly takes for granted the most disputed positions and even in argument thus begs the question. But what can working men know of logic? ... I do think though it is unfortunate that uneducated men who are eagerly searching for knowledge should have no place to go for help but to such writers and teachers. No wonder it is almost impossible for such men to keep their religion ...[50]

III

Woodsworth's depreciation of the queer, Methodist radical was ironic because, by 1903, he had become just such a person himself. The apparent rapidity of this transformation belies its actual complexity and gradualness. Already by 1900, when he had uttered the above condemnation, the battlements of his Methodist faith were being undermined. His predilection for theological modernism and social action had led him to doubt Methodism's evangelical doctrines, puritanical practices, and political quietism and conservatism. Yet it was the increasingly dead hand of his childhood Methodist faith that predominated, for the time being. On his return from Britain he was ordained a Methodist minister, thus fulfilling his parents' long-held hope for him. He was stationed first at Carievale in Assiniboia and after that, from 1901 to 1902, at Keewatin, near Rat Portage, later Kenora, in northern Ontario.

No sooner was he ordained than anxieties and discontents came welling up.[51] He was happy to be involved in the practical world, but pastoral work was often repetitive and tedious. And, although he was quite capable of appreciating nature, he preferred working among city people, particularly the young and students. Working people in Keewatin were uninterested in intellectual things, while city people vacationing at the nearby lakes disappointed him: 'There is a superficiality and sham about many of them. There are few whom one would really wish to regard as friends.'[52] It didn't help matters that at Keewatin his salary was only $500 a year and that he was devoid of female companionship. All in all, his prospects seemed bleak.

To all sorts of personal discontents were added intellectual doubts. Woodsworth's reading in his earliest years after ordination continued to be a mélange of unusual authors – from paternalistic radicals such as Ruskin and Carlyle to such Christian socialists and social gospellers as F.D. Maurice, Charles Kingsley, and Josiah Strong. Other favourite authors included higher critics such as Hans Wendt; Charles Darwin and Benjamin Kidd, both evolutionary thinkers in their different ways; and such liberals as W.E.H. Lecky and W.T. Shead. There was no unity of view among them, except that they were all unconventional and helped undermine received Methodist doctrines. According to Woodsworth himself, he was being increasingly driven to a 'rationalistic' account of Christianity. He questioned the inerrancy of the Bible, the historicity of the New Testament miracles, and the divinity of Christ. Only the sympathy and understanding of his parents, close by in Brandon, kept him from a breakdown. Everything was in flux:

I have been drifting steadily towards a kind of rationalistic view of religion. Many of the old positions – at any rate as stated – must go. But where things will end I do not know. I have to hold everything in a merely tentative manner. However, as I have a firm hold on the eternal verities – on the personal love and guidance of God, I do not feel that I need fear the issue – except in so far as it gives grief or disappointment to my friends. But here comes in another question. When I am not *sure*, and when in any case I cannot hold to the literal meaning of some of our doctrines, am I justified in remaining in an office in which I am supposed to subscribe to them? ... Then independently of dogma – for indeed that does not affect materially either my spiritual life or work, I often feel very much disheartened with my work – doubtful as to its efficiency – in fact disgusted with the whole work of the Church.[53]

Certainly this was a strong indictment of an institution in which Woodsworth had only recently become an ordained minister and about whose workings he had, after all, known for a long time. Clearly he had made the wrong decision in choosing to enter the ministry. In many respects his religious experience had been a hollow and superficial one, a second-hand habit passed down by his parents. Woodsworth's early religious commitment was mainly a belief in good works, or what was then called 'personal purity.' The Methodist call to sacrifice, duty, and charity was a compelling and consciously embraced imperative in his life at this time and, in one form or another, would remain so until he died. But if his sense of discipleship was never lacking, the same could not be said of his spiritual experience of God. To Woodsworth, God was present in nature and in the world but mainly he was *out there* and at a distance. This perspective anticipated his later, discrepant mixture of *de facto* atheism, deism, and pantheism. The young Woodsworth rarely expressed his faith in a manner that was personal, contemplative, or spiritual. God from on high called him to a life of duty; He rarely provided him with emotional or spiritual succour. The presence of a wife might have brought some, more earthly, consolation but Woodsworth's love for his cousin Clara was unrequited. He bemoaned the absence of a wife but stoically wondered whether, under the circumstances, it might not be a mixed blessing:

My position sometimes seems almost unbearable. I am again in the woods – deeper than ever – and see no daylight ahead ... But for one thing I am profoundly thankful. Since before Christmas I have been thanking God that I have no wife. It is bitter, so bitter to bring grief to my home. Bitter to shut myself out from the possibility, however remote that possibility, of ever winning one whom I still love. Hard to give up my life work. But I am so glad, that no wife is involved in my (shall I say it) appalling apostasy ... I cannot bear to remain in a position in which my very presence is a tacit acknowledgement of concurrence. Of course even now I would not answer satisfactorily a point blank question – but then no one suspects my orthodoxy ... Next Sunday I preach from 'Dead to sin-alive to God' – that allows me to avoid the resurrection question and yet preach a doctrine that I heartily believe. Am I even by my silence Jesuitical?[54]

To extricate himself from his dreadful predicament, Woodsworth determined upon a two-fold course of action. He would resign the ministry; and – despite his earlier doubts about the wisdom of marriage for someone in his position – he would seek a wife. In June 1902 he travelled to the annual Methodist conference with every intention of submitting his resignation. As fate would have it, he had been appointed to the Stationing Committee. This required that he attend the conference several days before it began, and in this period Woodsworth was talked out of resigning.[55] In an odd turn of events, instead of leaving the church, he stayed on and was promoted. He was offered the position of assistant-pastor at Grace Church in central Winnipeg, a church of some prestige and wealth. All at once Woodsworth escaped backwoods isolation, was given the opportunity of working with young people in a setting close to Wesley College, and saw his salary double to $1,000.

The matter of a wife produced a number of odd twists and turns before coming to a satisfactory conclusion. In his student days at Victoria in 1898–9, Woodsworth had lived not just with his cousin, Charlie Sissons, but with two other students. One was his paternal cousin, Clara Woodsworth, daughter of Richard. (Sissons remembered her as 'very attractive ... with her wavy hair and fine eyes.')[56] The other was Lucy Staples. Lucy, of average height and with an open, handsome face, came of impeccable Ontario and Methodist stock.[57] Born in 1874 on a farm in Bethany, near Peterborough, in Durham County, she was descended from emigrants from the southeast of Ireland. She was educated in Lindsay and Ottawa, had studied literature, history, and languages at Victoria College, and had been president of the women's literary society there. In the house on Avenue Road in that fateful year firm attractions had been ignited. James had fallen in love with Clara and Charlie with Lucy. The difficulty was that, in both cases, the admiration was not returned. The stuffy, repressed conventions of the time threw a veil of reticence over these matters. Only years later, in February 1902, in a predictably cryptic manner, did Sissons reveal to Woodsworth his unrequited love for Lucy.[58] This induced Woodsworth to confess his own unfulfilled love for Clara, or 'Miss W.' as he called her. In August, Woodsworth declared that he had 'practically buried that hope of the last three or four years.'[59] Five months later he talked as freely about affairs of the heart as he had ever done: 'Last summer ended my hopes of any ... relationship with Miss W. As I saw absolutely no response and possibility of response it seemed as if my love – partly selfish I suppose – returned to myself. Yes returned – not "dried up." Through Miss W. I learned that I had such an emotion ... I feel more and more the need of a wife – the first time I have made such a confession. It almost startles me.'[60]

In the same letter Woodsworth also revealed that, having recently met one of her relatives, he was intending to write to Lucy. By June matters had advanced enough for him to be able to tell Sissons that Lucy, now teaching in a high school in Lindsay, had replied and encouraged him, and so he had resolved to visit her. Woodsworth knew that etiquette and friendship dictated that he proceed carefully. Yet no matter how hard he tried, his actions were never sufficiently adroit and sensitive to prevent embarrassing and painful outcomes.

First, he visited Sissons in early September in Chatham. In a conversation in a rowboat on the Thames, Sissons revealed that there was no hope that his love for Lucy would be reciprocated.[61] Many years later he recalled that Woodsworth was very clear on the reason for his trip: 'In the fall of 1903 he visited me in Chatham and as we rowed on the lazy Thames informed me of the purpose of his visit east. He was about to call on another member of the group of four at 56 Avenue Road, Miss Lucy Staples, who was teaching moderns in the Lindsay Collegiate Institute, and ask her to marry him.'[62] Woodsworth, much closer to the time, claimed that his intentions had been more opaque: 'You suggest that I may have noticed a coldness in your attitude after the talk on the river when you divined in some measure my purpose. Not at all. And I did not dream that you would "divine my purpose." It could hardly then be called a purpose. All was too vague.'[63] Yet Woodsworth did admit to having been gratified when he heard that Sissons's prospects were non-existent: 'Yes I was glad to hear from you that your affection had never been fully returned, and to learn that you really realized that it could not be. The way was thus clear – that was all. And yet I did not feel in any sense guilty of being a spy – or did not cease to really sympathize with you in your disappointment. Had you still had hope – Well, I might have gone to Lindsay; but I should have come away again – and that would have been the end of it.'[64]

Woodsworth proceeded to Lindsay, and he and Lucy got along famously. After a week he proposed marriage and she accepted. He intended to visit Sissons on the way home but a mix-up in railway schedules prevented him. In St Paul, he wrote a long, detailed letter to his cousin. Woodsworth bubbled over with happiness: 'Charlie, it is a wonderful experience to look deep into a woman's eyes and know that you are loved. My heart was full of pure thankfulness.' On passing through Toronto, he had, he said, told Clara his good news: 'Clara could not wait long for the news and when I told her, hugged me and danced for joy. She is a beautiful girl. I think I love her more than ever; though in a different way. How strange. It was she who came to help me choose an engagement ring. Strange. Isn't it all strange?' Woodsworth ended the letter with a show of concern for Sissons. The ecstasy and self-absorption of the moment produced in him sympathy, perhaps, but also a sort of insensitivity and supercilious preachiness:

And now Charlie, I am not forgetful of you. Lucy's first thought or almost her first thought was about you. She had not thought to care for anyone – at least till after you were married. She felt so sorry that she had brought you such trouble. And now I think I know you; and yet I hope you will not feel one twinge of bitterness because we are so happy. Charlie, I am perfectly convinced that one day happiness will come to you. But, my dear boy, prove yourself first; don't precipitate matters. You are young. Several years will make a wonderful difference. What do I mean? I dare not suggest more. I do not know what may happen. But I believe a higher 'destiny' is in our lives. If we are only *true*, all things are going to work together for our good.

Charlie, I owe you a good deal for a suggestion made some time ago. I did not think it meant much to me then; but it has already been germinating. And in the joy which has come into our lives, we – for I think Lucy will join me in this – can with almost prophetic assurance encourage you by the message that all is for the best, and will be for you as it has been for us. I see possibilities. These may not become actual. But *God is good and is in our lives.* I wish that I could feel your handshake; but I think it's all right or I could not have written this.[65]

All was *not* right. Sissons's reply, evidently, expressed a deep disquiet. At least Woodsworth had the grace to recognize his mistake: 'And forgive me Charlie for mentioning your "future" in my last letter. I don't know why I did it. I think that I thought that all the world must be in love, and that right away. And I longed to see others as happy as I was. The thought was inevitable – the expression of it in poor taste.'[66]

The wedding took place ten months later on 7 September 1904 in

Bethany. Clara Woodsworth was the bridesmaid and Charlie Sissons the best man. Looking back on the wedding some sixty years later Sissons was able to see humour in an event that, at the time, must have caused him anguish: 'The wedding was a quiet affair; just a few relatives and neighbours were present at the spacious farm house set in the midst of rolling hills and well-tilled fields ... Miss Clara Woodsworth was bridesmaid. We four returned to Toronto together, and the porter in the pullman, misled we supposed by James's beard, made a mistake as to bride and groom and plied the wrong couple with pillows and service, which we accepted for the moment with complacency.'[67] Later, in April 1909, James and Lucy named their first-born son after Sissons.[68] (Two daughters had been born earlier.)

Lucy brought impressive qualities to the marriage. If her husband could be undemonstrative and formal, she was warm and outgoing. Some might argue that she submerged her life in her husband's; others might claim that she willingly cooperated in his endeavours so that they became hers, too. Raising six children was not easy. After Woodsworth's move to All Peoples' Mission in 1907, she had to care for the children largely by herself since her 'wandering husband' was frequently in distant places lecturing and raising money. She had a fine mind and was a brilliant teacher. She foresook a career of her own to raise a family and provide the domestic stability to which Woodsworth could return after his endless, enervating travels. As he lay resting on the davenport, she would read to him from a variety of books: Wells's *The Outline of History*, the Bible, and *Pilgrim's Progress*. Sometimes he read to her but, in essence, his needs were the ones that predominated. Without her love and support his frenetic life would have been impossible.

IV

After a honeymoon spent in the Muskokas, Woodsworth brought his new wife home to Winnipeg and proudly introduced her to the congregation at Grace Church. The next year was probably the most contented time of his life. His duties as assistant to the Reverend R.P. Bowles involved mainly working with young people and organizing a literary discussion group. But Bowles's absences and invitations from other churches allowed Woodsworth ample opportunity to preach. A hard-backed exercise book in the *Woodsworth Papers* contains the outlines of a series of sermons he delivered between December 1903 and October 1904.[69] Its importance cannot be over-estimated. It is the only continuous, extensive documentation extant of the theological and political outlook of the young Woodsworth.

The Woodsworth of the Grace Church sermons was a self-confessed Christian socialist whose world view was increasingly questioning in tone and developmental and progressive in content. He did retain, however, a strong sense of the Methodist call to a life of good works and personal purity. For him, the human soul would always be a battleground of the flesh and the spirit, between sensuality and pleasure on the one hand and duty and self-abnegation on the other. A sermon on the importance of self-denial underlined that, even with his growing concern for social questions and new ideas, he remained true to long-established Methodist doctrines and practices: 'A full stomach does not conduce to clear thinking, and may not perhaps be the best condition for the highest spiritual experiences. Kneeling has no necessary connection with prayer. Logically, I suppose you ought to be able to pray just as well leaning back in an arm chair as on your knees on the floor. But most of us can pray better kneeling. The attitude of humility is helpful to a devout frame of mind. So by fasting – by denying ourselves – our thoughts may be turned to the deeper needs of our spiritual life.'[70]

Human nature may have been for him the seat of the passions and appetites and, as he put it, of a 'voluptuousness [that was] effeminate, epicurene and sensual,' but his Christian spirituality did not require an anchorite-like withdrawal from the world and society. On the contrary, participating in the wider world and serving others were integral parts of the redemption and fulfilment of the individual Christian. God called his disciples to engage in the actual and the practical. His immanence meant that society must be 'transformed': 'It is not the contemplative life that appeals to us today. It is the *strenuous* life. As Christians we realize that the world must be conquered for Christ ... '[71] Nor was the church's social message to be one of purely individual improvement:

It is right to help the sick; it is right to do away with filth and over crowding and to provide sunlight and good air and good food. We have tried to provide for the poor. Yet have we tried to alter the social conditions that lead to poverty? ... You can't separate a man from his surroundings and deal separately with each ...[72]

Christianity is not merely individualistic, it is socialistic ... The work of the church is not merely to save men; it is to redeem, to transform society. Jesus said very little about saving souls – he spoke often about the establishment of the kingdom.[73]

Part of this theory of the interconnectedness of individual righteousness and social service was an evolutionary account of the history of the church. Christian history was the story of the pursuit of the 'heavenly' and the 'ideal,' all in the face of the obstructiveness and procrastination of the established church. Church politics, as with the secular type, were essentially clashes between conservatives and reformers. But over time the persistence of the innovator brought an ever-greater attaining of the Christian ideal: 'I believe in a progressive revelation ... I believe in development. The old forms must pass away. If the spirit would live, it must clothe itself continually in new forms.'[74] The embodiment of these new forms in the modern era had, of course, been the Protestant churches. (Woodsworth disputed the Roman Catholic Church's claim to primacy and infallibility.) Succeeding waves of reformers, first during the Reformation and then the Methodists of the eighteenth and early nineteenth centuries, had challenged Christians to recognize the fundamentals of their faith: that it was anti-dogmatic, anti-ecclesiastical, anti-hierarchical, anti-sacerdotal, and anti-denominational; that, in brief, true religion was 'ethical' and not 'ceremonial.'

At first sight Woodsworth's crusading reformism looks suspiciously like a schismatic, religious anti-formalism. (Much of his thought requires just such an interpretation.) His radicalism, however, was tempered by a recognition of the importance, to some limited extent, of tradition and history. He specifically mentioned the Protestant principle of freedom of conscience and the early Methodist belief in 'personal experience' as instances of past traditions that the church should not dispense with. He brought the same perspective to his early disquisitions on the character of secular political change. In a sermon entitled 'Our Attitude to the Past' he chastised North Americans for their diminished and dismissive view of history.[75] In Canada, he observed, there were no conservatives, for in a new land there was nothing to conserve. Farming operations were often 'experimental,' business ventures frequently 'speculative,' and personal views 'tentative'; there prevailed in North America a lack of stability, an 'unstable equilibrium,' 'a certain restlessness in our life and thought,' a lack of a historical perspective. Canadians should respect and preserve whatever traditions they did possess: 'So we might study the British constitution. It is the growth of centuries. It is the outcome of fierce struggles and bloody wars. It is the record of a thousand reforms, the combined, consolidated wisdom of many generations ... Our forefathers fought against tyranny in a hundred forms ... But an uneducated people – a people untrained in self-government – may become the tool of a demagogue.'[76] For Woodsworth, while reformers must keep their eyes on the ideal or the heavenly, change should conform to the pattern of gradually amending and moderating existing forms. If institutions were to be replaced this should occur gradually; the ideal should be realized only in the actual: only by slow degrees would mankind 'approximate' to its ideals.

Already by 1903–4 Woodsworth was convinced that socialism was the incarnation of the ideal in his own day. The main contemporary intellectual stimulus of this conviction was his reading of the social gospel. The nineteenth-century English divine F.W. Robertson was one person he specifically mentioned as having affected him greatly at this time.[77] Blewett and Bland, professors at Wesley since 1901 and 1903 respectively, were almost certainly others.[78] As well, there was his direct experience of British slums, lumber towns such as Rat Portage and immigrant communities in Winnipeg's North End. In fact, his 'socialism' during these years subsisted quite satisfactorily without either academic or practical influences. At bottom it found all it needed in the words of the New Testament; that is, with a little help from the ubiquitous and ever-serviceable Thomas Carlyle. In the sermon 'Spiritual Laws and Business Life,' Woodsworth's application of the simple dicta of the Gospels to contemporary commercial practices was sufficient to lead him to what he believed was socialism.[79] There was, he contended, a marked discrepancy between a market conception of value and the Christian notion of distributive justice. It could always be asked of the employer: Even in a free market, does the worker receive a fair wage? Also, he claimed, Christianity held to the notion of 'gratuitous service,' of doing something for nothing. Christ placed men and women under an obligation to bear the infirmities of the weak: 'I am here to condemn as unchristian the spirit that refuses to acknowledge the responsibilities which are involved in power. No Christian lives to himself. His abilities, his wealth, his business are all held in trust and must be used in the master's service ... The Christian is often called upon to do things that won't pay and to keep out of things that will pay. Business interests must be subordinate to higher things.'[80] Nor was money the true test of human value. The intrinsic value of the human person was a principle fundamentally at variance with the instrumentalist ethic of a commercial system: 'The real value of men ought to determine the relationship between the employer and employees. Carlyle speaks bitterly about the cash nexus ... The employee records his time on an automatic machine when he enters the shop. The machine doesn't even say good morning. (That would be an improvement and might easily be arranged.) As he passes out he presses his button again. He is known by a number as the convicts in a penitentiary. At the end of the week he receives his check, the only thing he cares about.'[81]

Newer forms of thought and intellectual perspectives were, of course, infiltrating his world view and mixing with his Christian presuppositions. Woodsworth was aware of the growing popularity in his day of social Darwinism, although he explicitly rejected one account of it: namely, that human affairs were governed by the survival of the fittest. He argued a different conclusion: that the evolution of society was instead leading to greater cooperation and interdependence. This brought him to pronounce upon the moral responsibilities of the new 'corporations' of labour and capital. His youthful socialism betrayed a charming innocence as it strained after an even-handedness of approach towards the two great classes of modern industry:

Our law must be applied to the relation between capital and labour and, to our surprise, we find in our law a recognition of the fundamental teachings of socialism – 'The strong to bear ...' Apply this to capitalists. Combines and trusts and monopolies not abolished if economically advantageous but to be used not as a means of oppression but for the bettering of the conditions of the people. (Let the Standard Oil Co use its monopoly to lower not raise the price of oil ... Has it not done that?)

And the Trades and Labour Unions. Not to use their powers to disorganize trade and secure an unjust share of the profits but to further the interests of the whole business world. An instance is on record ... where a delegation from the employees waited on the manager. They said – we have figured out the cost of the articles we manufacture. We think you ought to get 50¢ each and we ought to have the rest. The manager did some figuring with them and showed that he was getting less than 50¢. The delegation retired in confusion. Next day they again waited on the manager. I thought that matter was settled he said. No we don't consider it settled the spokesman said. We still think you ought to have 50 cents and we have come to ask you to reduce our wages. You laugh ... but true or not it illustrates the true spirit. The very fact that it seems to be improbable shows how far our business concerns are from being run according to the laws of Christian love.[82]

Establishing a moral relationship between capital and labour was one application of Christianity. There were others. National and local politics were to be cleansed of the influence of mercenary and supine leaders and their political machines. The church should concern itself with drink, prostitution, and poverty. A growing concern of Woodsworth's was immigration and the incursion of 'hordes' of uneducated, unchristian foreigners. The church's job must be to 'Canadianize' and 'Christianize' them. It was precisely during his time at Grace Church that he conceived of writing a book on this subject. Already in 1904 he had a title for it: 'Strangers within our gate.'[83] Finally, Woodsworth was exercised over the evils of nationalism and war and what is today called under-development: 'A nation too has duties and responsibilities in the brotherhood of nations ... The civilized nations have a heavy responsibility toward the uncivilized world. The greatest wars have been fought for territory and for national aggrandizement, not for liberty and righteousness. We are proud of being Britain's yet Britain has by no means been blameless in this regard ... War is opposed to Christian teaching.'[84]

The sermons of the Grace Church period illuminate an interesting stage in the young radical's development. Propositions crucial to Woodsworth's later world view have by now been put in place: that Christianity was a practical, this-worldly religion; that the church must ever evolve and become more ecumenical; that social change should take on a collective form; and that war and imperialism were categorical evils. Although he identified himself as a socialist, his economic doctrine was not especially heterodox. He abhorred market-based notions of right and fairness and envisaged a system of wage and labour relations infused with an ethos of Christianity. But it was a socialism devoid of any significant interference in private property. It was a definition not unlike that of earlier English Christian socialists such as Maurice and Kingsley, for whom socialism depended not on common ownership but on cooperation, duty, and benevolence, and it was similar to ideas found in such contemporaneous authors as Arnold Toynbee Sr and Andrew Carnegie. Indeed in *The Gospel of Wealth and Other Timely Truths* (1900), the latter proposed a sliding scale whereby wages would be adjusted upwards and downwards, depending on the profit-levels of the moment, something that was very similar to Woodsworth's notion of the workers handing back the surplus of inflated wages. Woodsworth's socialism was still in a nascent condition.

V

The early years at Grace Church were happy ones but they were immensely busy. As well as the work of the church, he and Lucy were occupied with bringing up a young family. (Their first child, Grace, was born in July 1905 and their second, Belva, in May 1907.) Lucy was frequently ill and bedridden in these years, requiring the help of a nurse. They did not have a permanent residence and there were the constant comings-and-goings of visitors and relatives. Matters seemed at their worst in the late summer of 1905 when Woodsworth helped his parents move house from Brandon to Winnipeg:

This past month has been the most disturbed ... hand-to-mouth sort of existence that I have ever spent. Lucy is ill. What turn things would take we hardly knew. There is a nurse in the house. Mary, my sister, was not strong and nearly played out. The washer women etc. foreigners – needed constant direction. Edith was trying to do some studying. Constant interruptions from outside. Then came housecleaning and moving.[85]

In my last letter I think I told you something of our 'distracted summer.' Well the settling was a fitting climax. I had a weeks heavy work with men at Brandon. Then we had to board for some weeks. Father and mother came and joined the girls with some friends. The house was not finished when it should have been. Then we began to gather 'the stuff' from various parts. What a jumble! The car load after delays arrived in a rainstorm. Wpg mud! Then the struggles with workmen: window cleaners, scrub women, gas men, electric light men, plumbers, carpet men, curtain hangers, painters, telephone people. It's like a nightmare.[86]

A characteristic Woodsworth exhibited early on was his tendency to live life at a frantic pace. Once he was committed to a task, the effort he expended on its behalf was total, and his eventual exhaustion only left him craving a fresh start on something else. By December 1905 he was again expressing dissatisfaction with his situation.[87] He was not finding it easy to work with Dr W.A. Sparling, Bowles's successor at Grace;

his health was giving him trouble; and he was casting longing glances at a charge in British Columbia or possibly, in the mission field in the far East. The time had come to move on. Early in 1906 his health was sufficiently poor to cause him to spend a year without station. His father was planning to visit Europe and, in the autumn, Woodsworth, with Lucy and his sister, Mary, accompanied him on a tour of the British Isles and the Continent. Woodsworth went on, alone, to Italy, Egypt, and Palestine. Visiting the Holy Land, he was moved to express his newer, progressive understanding of the Gospel:

While in Palestine I decided that, come what might, I must be true to my convictions of truth. It seemed to me that, in the Church, I was in a false position. As a minister I was supposed to believe and to teach doctrines which either I had ceased to believe or which expressed very inadequately my real beliefs.[88]

As, from a vantage point on the Mount of Olives I looked across to Jerusalem and tried to adjust my beliefs and manner of life in accordance with realities, there came to me with new force the words of Robertson of Brighton 'the sacrifice of Jesus must be completed and repeated in the life of each true believer.'
    The very heart of the teaching of Jesus was the setting up of the Kingdom of God on earth. The vision splendid has sent forth an increasing group to attempt the task of 'Christianizing the Social Order.'[89]

The representing of his own spiritual travail as analogous to that of Christ underlines the degree to which Woodsworth conceived of his life in terms of Christ-like heroism and sacrifice. It was, no doubt, while he was in Palestine that he acquired a life-sized, grotesque crown of thorns, which survives in a faded hat-box in his papers in the National Archives of Canada in Ottawa. On his way home Woodsworth received word from Charlie Sissons that a position might be available for him supplying the Methodist church in Revelstoke, British Columbia, where Charlie was now teaching. Woodsworth resisted the suggestion at first. By now Lucy was pregnant with their second child and was in no condition, he felt, to travel a great distance. He was also sensitive to any suggestion that he might have obtained a position through pressure exerted by his relatives.
    In fact, the intimacy of his family's connections with the Methodist Church in Canada presented him with a constant dilemma. The problem was that his father probably knew every Methodist minister and

church leader in western Canada and many others elsewhere. The son's relations with his parents were close at this time, as indeed they continued to be to the end of their lives. In 1900 he had asked his father's help in obtaining a lectureship at Wesley, where the latter was on the board. His request then was without effect. There is no evidence that his family's connections brought about his stationing at such an advantageous position as Grace Church in 1902, but one wonders whether it was of no consequence either. His father was chairman of the board of All Peoples' Mission in 1907 when he was appointed superintendent there. And to what extent was the church's mild response to his two attempts at resignation in 1902 and 1907 affected by the knowledge that he was James Woodsworth's son? Later, in 1912, when he sought a lecturing position at Victoria College, Woodsworth *fils* encouraged the assistance of Sissons, Blewett, and Bowles, if they deemed him competent, that is.[90] Now, in October 1906, faced with the prospect of a stationing at Revelstoke, he expressed concern over likely charges of nepotism: 'Well don't push the thing at all. If that is my place the way will open up. I would rather be shut out of a suitable place than shove myself into an unsuitable. Then I'm against "family compacts" and wouldn't like to have the people think that my father and cousin "managed things."'[91]

Woodsworth eventually changed his mind on the Revelstoke position. The original offer, he had believed, was to begin the following June and last for a full year, at least. On learning that it was to be for only six months and that it was to begin immediately, he accepted. In his new charge he was again in the sort of community that he had been a part of in Keewatin: railway men and mill workers. He laboured unstintingly on behalf of his congregation and he was beseeched to remain. This was impossible because he had now decided to leave the ministry, again. His resignation attempt this time would be both more determined and more public than that in 1902. He resolved that he would not be talked out of it and that he would present the church with a detailed, public explanation of the hope that was no longer in him. In June 1907, at a meeting of conference held in Carman, Manitoba, he submitted a long, elaborate letter of resignation.[92] In it he began by arguing that candidates to the ministry were required to subscribe to a number of specific beliefs and rules. A crucial number of these, he confessed, he no longer accepted. In particular he could not support the General Rules of Methodist Discipline that prohibited drinking, gambling, dancing, and attendance at theatres and horse-racing. There were also many items of Christian doctrine about which he held profound doubts, the most important of these being the authority of the Bible, the atonement, the virgin birth, and the resurrection and divinity of Christ. He continued with what we can recognize as an exemplary statement of the theoretical essentials of fundamentalism: that words and doctrines have definite, fixed meanings, that their sense was not infinitely elastic and amendable so that, if their basic meaning could not be adhered to, holders of religious office had no recourse but to resign:

I was required to state that I believed and would preach certain definitely-specified doctrines. Some may say that it is necessary only that I believe the essential underlying truths. But who is to determine what are the essential underlying truths? Words have well-recognized meanings. We cannot play fast and loose with them. Again, it may be objected that if one is held down hard and fast to the letter of the law, there is no room for the development of doctrine. Precisely! But the fact still remains that, as a candidate for the ministry, I was required to state that I believed and would preach certain specified doctrines. I am bound to require all candidates to make a similar statement. So long as I hold the office to which such statements admitted me, and to which I would not, to-day, receive admission without making the same statements, I am bound in common honesty to continue to believe and to preach these doctrines. So soon as I am unable to 'sincerely and fully believe them' and to 'fully and faithfully preach them,' it seems to me that but one course is open.[93]

Convincing his colleagues to accept this reasoning was, however, the difficult task. His letter of resignation was moved through a maze of committees and general meetings and, in the end, Conference decided, on the recommendation of a subcommittee, that 'there [was] nothing in his doctrinal beliefs and adhesion to our discipline to warrant his separation from the ministry of the Methodist Church and therefore [we] recommend that his resignation be not accepted and his character be now passed.'[94]

Several aspects of this unsuccessful resignation are worth noting. First, there was a decidedly undulating quality in Woodsworth's expression of his Christian beliefs. In a trough of doubt and despondency at Keewatin in 1902, his faith or, at least his buoyant expression of it, was renewed in the year before and after his marriage. This was especially evident in his proclaiming of God's goodness and purposes in his letters to Sissons at that time. Then by 1906–7 unbelief and despair had returned. Secondly, in his letter of resignation in 1907, Woodsworth referred to a number of items of Christian belief and practice that he no longer believed. Yet some of these he had categorically asserted as being definitely true in public sermons as recently as 1904: specifically, the need for personal religious experience and the utility of fasting. (His rejection of the prohibition against drinking, dancing, and gaming is also curious. Woodsworth, to the day he died, never believed in the morality of these activities.) To be sure, Woods worth was capable of changing his mind between 1904 and 1907. But in that case, he changed his mind relatively quickly or was capable of exhibiting an enthusiasm of public expression which belied the tenuousness of his private beliefs. Probably both tendencies were present in him.

Finally, the resoluteness of his intention to resign can be queried. Woodsworth was sensitive to his parents' wishes that he remain in the church; also, as McNaught argues, he had, no doubt, a deep emotional attachment to the church so that leaving it was difficult.[95] But he did wish to resign, he did embarrass his parents anyway in publicizing his intentions, and he did assert dogmatically that honesty required his resignation. In the end he was not supported in this by the official church. The two unsuccessful resignation attempts may underline the exceptional tolerance that the Methodist Church was capable of exhibiting at that time. But, equally, they also show the extent of Woodsworth's willingness to abandon his own assessment of the situation and to substitute for it that of others whose views he had earlier rejected. If he had been a man of stern, unbending principle, he could have chosen to resign anyway, even though Conference did not think this was necessary. Indeed it might be argued that the very 'individualism' of his moral viewpoint required him to do so. For, according to this view, institutions invariably express fallible judgments because that is the nature of collectivities; only the judgments of 'lonely' individuals are likely to be right and true. Thus there was, perhaps, an element of abdication of responsibility and what existentialists call 'bad faith' in Woodsworth's final resolve to go along with Conference: 'So I bowed to the decision of Conf. I feel myself free to be myself and to work for the alteration of the formal standards. Of course in a sense I will be a marked man. Really though even some of the most orthodox have been the most urgent that I should remain. Well I hope I have done the right thing. I have tried to do so. From the legal standpoint my skirts are clear ... From the standpoint of the living Church there seems to be no doubt that I can work in harmony.'[96]

Before he left Conference Woodsworth became aware of an opening at All Peoples' Mission in Winnipeg. It was exactly the sort of practical work he craved for and was undoubtedly a reason for his decision not to leave the church. Father and son returned from Conference together. Sometime in the next month his father told him: 'You have your opportunity. This is the most difficult work in Canada.'[97]

When Woodsworth took over its superintendency, All Peoples' was part mission and part charitable institution. In 1907 its administration, financing, and work were ill-organized. Woodsworth did much to correct these problems. Under him the mission expanded both the size and type of its operations so that it became much more of a settlement house *cum* social-welfare agency. Its work included many aspects: kindergarten, language and home-keeping school, and centre of political education and agitation. Pre-eminently Woodsworth saw its function as ministering to the social needs of the thousands of immigrants then crowding into the north of the city. An interesting question is to establish the sort of intellectual sensibility he displayed towards non-Anglo-Saxons.

Woodsworth spoke little about Canadian Indians in his early life or later on. However, in 1907 there appeared two revealing references. In late 1906 his brother Joe had been working somewhere, 'buried in the wilds ... in ranch country,' probably in the interior of British Columbia or, more likely, Alberta. In August 1907 he described to Sissons some of Joe's adventures: 'If he gets out safely he will have had a great summer's outing. The Indians he reports as unspeakably vile physically and morally.'[98] When Joe did safely emerge, Woodsworth reported: 'Joe had a summer with no end of adventures among the Indians. He was glad to get out to civilization again.'[99] He evinced a similar attitude towards eastern European immigrants. His task at All Peoples' was to bring them within the pale of civilization. It can, of course, be argued that he did at least embrace the plight of the aliens: that is, he did try to help them, according to his lights. But in seeking to improve their lot he was, in his own mind, seeking the betterment of his inferiors. The foreigners were a 'problem'; they were arriving in too large numbers and their customs, unless altered, were likely to be a dead-weight upon the superior standards of the Anglo-Canadian way of life. And, for all his theological radicalism, Woodsworth had not lost

all belief in an old-fashioned Protestant sectarianism. At All Peoples'
Mission he developed a scheme of 'Protestantizing' Polish Catholics by
an intriguing strategy of boring-from-within:

A short time ago the only Independent [Polish] Church building in Winnipeg
was sold for the mortgage. We have bought it. What do you think of a
Methodist Church with altar and crucifixes and candles and holy water and
confessional, etc. A Methodist Catholic Church. Well, its a ticklish business
but we intend to make the attempt to keep the congregation with the Church.
They claim to have about 200 families in the parish. An old priest has been
ministering to them. We will permit them to carry on their services in much
their own way. We don't appear in the matter. Simply give them the privilege
to continue to use the Church they built but which is now controlled by us.
Then our man will preach the gospel to them, distribute the Bible among them
and induce them to send their children to the Public Schools. Our hope is that
if the light is given and the truth implemented that the useless forms will
slough off. Independence from Rome is not necessarily Reformation but
affords the opportunity for Reformation. Of course we can't tell how things
will work out but the people regard us as their friends. Already the Reformation is beginning. Balijrodzki is taking down the pictures of the Polish saint
and changing the name of the Church from that of St. Mary of ——— (Polish
tradition) to the Church of Our Saviour, at the same time getting rid of the
statue of the Virgin. This is a big step. They ask why. He explains. They are
thinking about it and talking about it. These illiterate peasants have never
questioned before. Do you know in the R.C. Ch. they have a patron saint of the
farmers dressed up, the people put dollar bills in the pocket of the saint's
clothes in order that they may have good crops! The ignorance and superstitu-
tion is 'a corker.' The whole idea is instead of pounding the R.C. Ch. from
outside to foster and direct the reform movements which are taking place
within the Church.[100]

During his early years at All Peoples' Woodsworth, while an intellectual pioneer on some issues, was uncompromisingly traditional on all
matters involving his own and his society's identity. He was decidedly
an Anglo-Canadian and a Protestant. He took to the polyglot population of north Winnipeg the new secular message of sociology and social
administration. He also took the desiderata of an older nativism. This
was especially clear after he published *Strangers within Our Gates* in
1909.

2

Setting Sail, 1909–1921

Cut the hawsers – haul out – shake every sail! ...
Steer for the deep waters only ...
For we are bound where mariner has not yet dared to go,
And we will risk the ship, ourselves and all ...
O daring joy, but safe! are they not all the seas of God?
O farther, farther, farther sail!

Walt Whitman

I

Measured at least by frequency of public utterance, Whitman's stanza from 'Passage to India' in *Leaves of Grass* was Woodsworth's most beloved piece of poetry. It conveys well the mixture of innocent abandon and impetuous optimism that marked his life between 1909 and 1921. In these years he moved away from the Methodist Church, continuing in the more secular direction that had begun with his decision to become superintendent of All Peoples' Mission in 1907. In 1913 he would became director of the Canadian Welfare League, and three years later the head of the Bureau of Social Research. In these two latter occupations he was in essence a social planner and welfare administrator, a member of the new helping professions that would become so crucial to the operation of the twentieth-century liberal democratic state.

These appointments, although outside the pattern of the normal career of a Methodist minister, did not take him beyond the social gospel. Woodsworth had not yet abandoned the church and things theological. In fact, in the years before the First World War, if he had any explicit scheme of social change at all, he placed the church at the centre of it. Taken over by reformers, the Protestant churches in Canada, he believed, could constitute the vanguard of political change. The extent of his involvement with the church – and his hopes for it – at this time meant that Woodsworth had little association with political parties and said little about the day-to-day world of national and local politics. Thus contemporary political leaders such as Borden, Laurier, Roblin, and Norris were all but absent from his universe. Such facts are salutary because they correct an understandable tendency to think of him as destined to make of politics his life's work. When he did so, after 1921, it was only after many other alternatives had been rejected or closed off. Woodsworth was not heroically intended for Parliament. Indeed there is evidence that for him a political career was a last resort.

The doubts that had prompted his early unsuccessful decisions in 1902 and 1907 to resign the ministry were held unresolved and in abeyance during his time at All Peoples' Mission. But they would return to haunt him. He had already drunk deeply of the wells of modern thought; he was not an especially spiritual person, in the mystical sense of that word; and he was a person of sometimes extreme personal honesty. Whatever their relative weight, these factors together must eventually have brought a final rupture with the church. Woodsworth was, after all, the consummate Protestant and not just because he was more a man of action than of contemplation. Raised in a tradition of non-sacerdotal, religious dissent, he felt constrained to shed association with any group that offended his lofty standards. He was unimpressed by the notion of traditional institutions, secular or religious, as the embodiment of authority, custom, splendour, or mystery: 'With him, to outgrow an idea was to outgrow at the same time the mode of living based on that idea. He had the courage, always, to leave the old familiar environment for the new, untried adventure.'[1]

In fact, Woodsworth's first major act of leave-taking, his departure from the Bureau of Social Research in early 1917, was not of his own choosing though, of course, it had everything to do with his outspokenness. In December 1916 he had written a letter to the *Manitoba Free Press* criticizing the federal government's policy of national registration and what he believed would be its inevitable concomitant, conscription of manpower for war purposes. The bureau was publicly funded and Woodsworth was quickly fired by the Manitoba government. There followed five years of change and uncertainty, during which he made yet one more attempt to pursue the life of a simple Methodist minister, this time in a small, isolated settlement on Howe Sound, north of Vancouver. By now he and Lucy had a large family (to their first three children were added Ralph in 1910, Bruce in 1914, and Howard in 1916), and amidst the magical, arcadian surroundings of Gibson's Landing the family seemed to have found a suitable place to live their lives. Indeed Gibson's Landing fast became their inspirational home. (In later life they returned there for vacations and two of the children would retire to live in the immediate area.) Unfortunately, although it was mainly a community of foreign loggers, the village did have its local Methodist élite who after a year of the new clergyman petitioned the British Columbia Stationing Committee not to appoint Woodsworth there again.[2] It was, then, a decision of no little disruption to the family when he finally resigned from the ministry in June 1918 and, without means of employment in Gibson's Landing, moved to Vancouver.

He now embarked on an intense immersion in labour politics, which in its eventual political effect would go far beyond anything that derived from his earlier association with the Winnipeg Trades and Labor Council as a representative of the Ministerial Association after 1910. In Vancouver he worked on the docks, became a member of a union, and lived for a while with Ernest Winch, the union leader. In early 1918 the Federated Labor Party (FLP) had been formed and Woodsworth quickly became one of its earliest supporters and major publicists. He also became an organizer for the Non-Partisan League in Alberta. On a speaking tour of the prairies in the spring of 1919, news came of the Winnipeg General Strike. After his participation in the strike and his brush with the authorities he returned to the coast. He continued to speak for the FLP but this was unpaid work. In August he was passed over for the position of permanent organizer and secretary of the Winnipeg branch of the Dominion Labor Party (DLP).[3] The following year he returned to Winnipeg and began work for William Ivens's Labor Church; later, in 1920, he ran as an FLP candidate for the provincial legislature in British Columbia. After his defeat he had three offers of a job: as secretary of a labour organization in Prince Rupert, as editor of a labour paper in Nova Scotia, and as organizer of a people's forum – a service designed to provide popular debates and entertainment for the working class – in Winnipeg. He opted for the last, although it hardly guaranteed him much security. In a letter of July

1921 to Charlie Sissons, by now a professor of classics at Victoria College in Toronto, Woodsworth expressed disappointment over the direction of his life. What he wanted was a career that was not so precarious: 'Some talk to me of politics but I'd rather teach than enter upon a political career.'[4] He pressed him to let him know of 'any opening in University work' that he might hear of. Nothing came along. Almost as a last resort Woodsworth entered upon a career in politics. In August, he joined the Independent Labor Party of Manitoba and was its successful candidate in the national election in December.

What was Woodsworth's intellectual outlook between 1909 and 1921? Clearly, his mind was ranging over a rapidly changing historical landscape and, not unexpectedly, there were developments and refinements. As striking, however, was the continuity of metaphysical belief, a continuity epitomized by a deep philosophical optimism and a historical conceit that, as he put it, 'we are on the eve of a new social and moral movement akin to the Reformation or other of the great movements of history.'[5] At the heart of his world view was a set of assumptions to do with historical progress, technology, and evolution.

Woodsworth's view of human history made much of the role of technological and economic factors and, in general, postulated movement in a progressive direction. He was an early believer in Darwinian theories of natural selection and, of course, rejected any literal, non-mythical account of the origins of life as contained in the first chapters of Genesis. Mainly he posited a technological account of the rise of human society. Certain techno-economic modes of production, he claimed, had generated a sequence of social stages: hunting, pastoral, agricultural, hand work, and machine. Each of these in turn had produced distinctive, dominant thought-forms. Suffusing the whole process was the spirit of progress. Woodsworth alluded only rarely to the necessary conditions that constituted historical progress; to a great degree he assumed them as a given of his world view, thus reflecting the effect upon him of optimistic notions derived from Victorian liberalism, Anglo-Canadian nationalism, and Christian eschatological ideas regarding the 'end of time.' However, it is clear that, for him, the essential characteristics of progress were the increasing capacity of technology and parliamentary government to provide, respectively, the means of economic sufficiency and political freedom.

According to this view, human behaviour and thought could never be static. Subject principally to techno-economic forms but also to cultural, genetic, and environmental influences, conceptions of human nature, God, and the good were never final but always subject to change. It was a frankly teleological, relativist, and determinist account of history and human ideas. Woodsworth denied that he was a historical 'fatalist'; he claimed to allow a role to human will and volition and indeed he was not as historically determinist as such contemporaries as Salem Bland and William Irvine, and Marxists in the Socialist Party of Canada. But he did believe that history moved in law-like ways open to human comprehension and that the highest duty of humanity was to attune itself to the inherent purposes of history.

Fortunately, these purposes, especially in the present age, were benevolent and exalted. Here he adapted to his use the teleology of Christian eschatology, the communitarian account of social Darwinism, and the technocracy of science. Human society in the present epoch was, Woodsworth argued, on the threshold of technological perfection and material sufficiency for all. What was historically imminent generated its correlative account of morality and politics. The age called forth an ethic of unity, solidarity, and cooperation, and made imperative the political hegemony of the technical expert and social administrator.

II

To help the Methodist church come to grips with the issue of immigration, Woodsworth in 1909 wrote *Strangers within Our Gates*. It is a perplexing and frustrating book. To some later critics it is a work of nativism, Anglo-Canadian nationalism, and near-racism. Marilyn Barber, for example, faults Woodsworth for having subsumed the individual immigrant into the group, a turn of phrase that might be a delicate way of saying that he engaged in racial typing; she also criticizes him for having subordinated the gospel of love to the gospel of nationalism.[6] Curiously, Woodsworth's principal biographers, MacInnis and McNaught, largely omit mention of the book and its argument. This is regrettable because *Strangers within Our Gates* provides a lengthy and elaborate elucidation of the thinking of its author not just on the subjects of race and immigration but on other matters as well.

It is evident from *Strangers within Our Gates* that Woodsworth was highly uncomfortable with the issues of race and immigration, and that from this there derived a fair measure of illiberality, bad judgment, and contradiction. Woodsworth was a Canadian nationalist; he was also at heart an anglophile. During his stay in Britain in 1899–1900, as noted, he exulted in making contact with his cultural roots. Also, he was always proud of his Loyalist background, and his grandfather's sword, raised in anger in 1837 against William Lyon Mackenzie's insurrection, was later prominently displayed on the wall of his home in Winnipeg; in spite of his vaunted pursuit of an uniquely Canadian version of socialism, for most of his political life he followed the example of the British Labour Party; and even in his later years he was to confess that he felt more English in spirit than Canadian.[7] This admiration of things British derived from his early immersion in the values of British imperialism and Victorian whiggism.

To his dying days, Woodsworth was uneasy with a multi-ethnic conception of the Canadian identity. It was, of course, the arrival of large numbers of non-British immigrants after 1896 that raised the possibility that Canada would cease to be a British nation. Woodsworth's tackling of this prickly question provides the basic drama of *Strangers within Our Gates*, a drama heightened by the fact that in this early work he was already being pulled in an opposite intellectual direction by his universalist beliefs in brotherhood and cultural pluralism. The latter, in time, greatly tempered his original Anglo-Canadian nativism but they never prevailed over it. This was in keeping with the overall bias of his intellectual outlook, which emphasized such themes as unity, centralization, and uniformity.

If racism is defined as a theory that claims that qualitative distinctions exist between groups on the basis of physical characteristics, Woodsworth in *Strangers within Our Gates* should not be called racist. His co-author, A.R. Ford, might have been and Woodsworth must share some guilt by association. (Even here care must be taken. Woodsworth often collaborated with and publicized the views of people with whom he disagreed. While director of the Bureau of Social Research, in his report in 1917 on Ukrainian settlements on the prairies, he published an extreme criticism of socialism at a time when he himself was an avowed socialist.) Admittedly, Woodsworth did quote, with seeming approval, the views of John R. Commons that African blacks were 'unstable, indifferent to suffering, and easily aroused to ferocity by the sight of blood ... They exhibit certain qualities which are associated with their descendants in this country, namely, aversion to silence and solitude, love of rhythm, excitability, and lack of reserve. All travellers speak of their impulsiveness, strong sexual passion and lack of will power.'[8] More directly, Woodsworth himself invited the charge of racism by his use of loose language as, for example, in his characterization of the behaviour of 'the Negro' as a consequence of 'blood.'[9] And often his descriptions of the typical behaviour of other 'racial' groups were insensitive and tendentious.

But mainly he employed the term 'race' to denote a particular cultural or ethnic and not a physical type, and usually it was language that he took to be the touchstone of the distinctive group identity in question.[10] Other less important factors were climate, terrain, religion, customs, and so on. In the contemporary world, then, 'racial' groups exhibited marked differences of culture. Superimposed on this theory were assumptions about what constituted the criteria of the progress and civilizing of the human species, so that if racial groups differed from each other, some must be more civilized than others. In short, there was a hierarchy of culture. (Clearly, Woodsworth was no cultural relativist; he did not believe that racial differences were morally moot or insignificant.) Woodsworth's account of race, then, was sociological and ecological in method. It was not because of any inherent superiority that the British people embodied the hallmarks of civilization; rather it was because of the 'adventitious' circumstances of the Protestant religion, a northern climate, and an individualistic culture. Yet Woodsworth also used an older ethical language, one that intimated that those with civilization 'deserved' their superiority and those without it were somehow blameworthy. There was evident moral disdain in his calling those beyond the pale, 'savage,' 'pagan,' 'superstitious,' and 'barbaric.'

Canadians, as a British people, he claimed, had inherited the wherewithal of civilization: parliamentary democracy, religious freedom, intellectual dissent, scientific inventiveness, and the independent spirit of a freeholder-yeoman class of farmers. Not just English-speaking Canadians but northern peoples in general showed similar qualities. Germans, Scandinavians, and the descendants of an earlier wave of British emigration, the Americans, were the most desirable class of immigrants to Canada. Unacceptable were the eastern and southern Europeans, largely because they had been raised to be politically deferential, religiously superstitious, and economically backward. Worse still were Orientals and Hindus, who undercut the wages of white Canadian workers and refused to become assimilated. Blacks, like Orientals and Hindus, should be excluded altogether, partly because the colour of their skin made it unlikely they would integrate with Canadian society, but mainly, he claimed, because centuries of 'slavery' and 'savagery' had rendered them unsuitable for democratic citizenship. Some 'inferior,' non-Anglo Saxon peoples were, however, acceptable. Jews, for example, showed agreeable traits; they were hard-working, ambitious, individualistic, temperate, and religious. Subject to the right environmental influences they could conform to the preferred type.

Still unresolved was the question of how to deal with those groups already in Canada who, because they lived in colonies and group settlements, had so far resisted assimilation. Woodsworth's argument in this regard makes it clear that, while he emphasized the need for national unity and cultural conformity, the unified nation that was to emerge was to be composed of liberal individualists. He recommended that existing independent and often self-sufficient colonies and group settlements such as those of the Mennonites and Ukrainians, preserving as they did a unique and 'un-Canadian' way of life, should be undermined and in time dissolved altogether. A corporate, organic way-of-life did not *ipso facto* recommend itself to Woodsworth. Nor did a people preserving traditional customs necessarily draw his admiration. The assimilative and regulative power of the state and its delegated private agencies was to be brought to bear on these groups through school attendance laws, independent trade unions, special national churches and, where expedient, Protestant evangelism. What would in time emerge was a unified nation of English-speaking, freedom-loving, Protestant-minded individualists: ambitious, self-reliant, hardworking, abstemious, lovers of family, and intellectually innovative. *Strangers within Our Gates* preached the need for a sociological and normative unity of individualist values; individuality and conformity were both present in its recommendations.

Another important aspect of Woodsworth's argument for assimilation and cultural conformity had to do with the necessity of sociological and normative unity for the preservation of democracy. His view, simply, was that heterogeneity produced political disintegration and corruption. (This claim was, incidentally, separate from though related to another argument: that immigrants, raised in a political culture of dependency, such as Czarist Russia or Habsburg Austro-Hungary, could not readily become efficacious and active democratic citizens.) To Woodsworth, linguistic diversity and social isolation made impossible the public and inter-personal communication essential to democracy. An inability to speak the dominant language isolated minorities in 'ghettos' where sectional passions and localist outlooks predominated. A heterogeneous people lacked a means of 'cooperation for the public

welfare.' Finally, he argued, immigrant minorities, shut out of participation in a common way-of-life, were easily held hostage by unscru-
pulous political operators and go-betweens:

When the elections come, the services of the aforesaid disreputable fellow are
again required. With his knowledge of English and the foreign tongues he
commands the situation. The party must have him and must depend upon
him. Big promises and a little money will go a long way. He 'fixes' a few of the
leaders in the settlement. Then, on election day, the beer and whiskey flow
freely. The election is won! ... Peoples emerging from serfdom, accustomed to
despotism, untrained in the principles of representative government, without
patriotism – such peoples are utterly unfit to be trusted with the ballot ...
    Our democratic institutions are the outcome of centuries of conflict by which
to some extent we have been fitted for self-government. It is as absurd as it is
dangerous to grant to every newly arrived immigrant the full privilege of
citizenship ... The next reform should look to the restriction rather than the
extension of the franchise.[11]

Among nearly all the races there are political clubs. The political parties find it
in their interest to maintain newspapers in the various leading languages. The
non-English are frequently settled in 'colonies' so that they have virtually the
balance of power. Canada's future lies with her immigrants. Another word of
warning from the United States: 'The heterogeneity of these races tends to
promote passion, localism and despotism, and to make impossible free cooperation for the public welfare.'[12]

   Strangers within Our Gates was an untidy work, put together too
quickly, as Woodsworth admitted, so that it evinced a good deal of
contradiction. Having expatiated on the importance of preserving an
Anglo-Canadian identity, and after being cold to the possibility of
further immigration by most racial groups, Woodsworth wondered
whether the ultimate answer might not be some pan-Canadian identity
large enough to accommodate all immigrants and their unique ways of
life and identities.[13] Moreover, far from being inferior, immigrants, he
continued, might well be superior to native-born Canadians since they
had shown laudable courage and ingenuity by their very decision to
leave their homeland.[14] Also, English Canadians should rise above
their 'arrogant superiority and exclusiveness ... perhaps characteristic
of the English race.'[15] Finally, having built an argument for the exclusion of Orientals, on the grounds that they refused to integrate,

Woodsworth in other parts of the book undermined his own contentions. Here he quotes approvingly from an annual report of the Methodist Missionary Society: 'The Orientals are here, and a time will come when they will be here in large numbers ... Shall we regard and treat them as barbarians, a menace to society, to be mobbed, boycotted, driven out of the country? That was only to proclaim that we are barbarians ourselves, utterly unworthy of the freedom of which we boast so much ... These strangers from the Far East are human beings like ourselves, of the 'one blood,' and just as capable, under proper leadership of rising in the scale of civilization and becoming a useful element in our cosmopolitan population as are immigrants from other countries.'[16]

Woodsworth was capable of sympathetic understanding of the plight of the non-Anglo-Saxon immigrant. But what was never in doubt was the priority he gave to assimilation and uniformity over the competing claims of heterogeneity and pluralism: 'We must learn that the world is wide,' he wrote in *Strangers within Our Gates*, 'and that there are a great many other types than our own, and some just as good, though different. Other languages, customs and religions have their value. Again, we must not expect the foreigners at once to abandon the old in favour of the new. Such a course would show only weakness of character. Loyalty to the old is the best guarantee to the new ...' He then went on to quote an American writer, J.C. Monaghan: 'The people who come to us and have no love of the land left behind will be wanting in one of a strong man's best characteristics. *I would not be understood as advocating a continuance of the separate schools, papers, churches, etc. If the assimilation is to go on rapidly, every school, paper and church in which a foreign tongue figures is in some measure a hindrance.*'[17] Monaghan's sentiments perfectly expressed Woodsworth's. They go to the heart of the argument of *Strangers within Our Gates* and, later, even after some amendment, they remained the burden of his conception of Canada's 'racial' identity.

In 1913 Woodsworth returned to the racial question in a series of fourteen articles, entitled 'Canadians of Tomorrow,' in the *Manitoba Free Press*. In *Strangers within Our Gates* he had emphasized the importance of unity in support of an Anglo-Canadian national identity. By 1913 it is evident that he was trying to embrace a more pluralistic account of the country's character. Yet this new emphasis was not undertaken without deep inner turmoil and by no means did it result in the abandonment of his concern for unity. Woodsworth began with a highly revealing anecdote about meeting a foreign-born census-taker, no doubt two years earlier in 1911: '"Vat nationality you?" I looked down, I'm afraid somewhat contemptuously, at my little foreign interlocutor. Here was a question concerning which I had no hesitation. Though living in the midst of Poles and Ruthenians and Germans and Jews I did not forget that I was of the old Canadian Loyalist stock. I fancy I was several inches taller as I proudly proclaimed my nationality – "Canadian." "Canadian," repeated the census enumerator, with a puzzled expression. "Canadian – not many of dem kind in dis country!" Yes, we laugh. But those words are prophetic and the time of their fulfilment is not far distant.'[18]

Woodsworth then gave what can only be described as a lament for the Anglo-Canadian nation. European immigrants were coming in excessively large numbers and, with their high birthrate, they would 'swamp' native-born Canadians. Traditions were changing: 'In the cities the single family house [was] being replaced by the tenement – a European abomination imported via New York.' Immigrants were not interested in temperance, so 'the quiet Canadian Sunday of our childhood' was becoming a thing of the past. Non-British immigrants did not appreciate the importance of the British connection in Canada's imperial policy; they brought corruption to politics; and, because so many of them were Catholics, continued immigration would tip the balance against the Protestant church. After this threnody, it could surely be expected that Woodsworth would recommend the sort of solution he had advocated in *Strangers within Our Gates*. But against the grain of his argument, he concluded: 'Our British-Canadian ideal has been that of a homogenous people with a common language and common "mores" ... But now with our heterogeneous immigration we must frankly recognize that the old ideal is incapable of realization, and that for good or ill Canada is to be the home of a composite race or of mixed races. If true unity is attained it will come not because of a common past nor through the coercion of majorities but in the varied experiences of a common life and the participation in a great vivifying common hope. Assuredly, the future is full of dangers, but the simpler quieter life is impossible. Destiny drives us onwards.'[19] Woodsworth ended by quoting again Whitman's poem about cutting the hawsers and pursuing the daring joy of adventurous initiatives.

The shifting logic and emotion of his argument uncovers something of Woodworth's nature. He began with regret, proceeded to frank historical realism, and, finally, used the latter as a springboard for an idealistic leap into the future. Perhaps his theory of history led him to these labile twists. It was as if the course of history must never be grudgingly accepted but always enthusiastically celebrated. Woodsworth was a complicated man. He did have a deep attachment to Canada's pre-industrial past. But he was, even more, a carefree upholder of history's progressive purposes. Ironically, though a self-confessed social critic, he could be quite complacent in his view of what was happening in his society. He believed so strongly in the progress inherent in change that, for him, whatever change brought about must be for the best and the fulfilment of an historical ideal.

In any event, the old Anglo-Canadian vision of the nation was, for Woodsworth, obsolescent, even if it was at times gently hankered after. The various European immigrants (he had not changed his mind about the total unsuitability of Orientals and blacks) should be granted respect and sympathy. They brought enterprise and culture; they were the bearers of European civilization and the Judeo-Christian inheritance. They should be accorded fair wages and decent public services. And, far from being expunged, their cultural uniqueness should be encouraged: 'Mere imitativeness is a sign of weakness, not of strength. The most imitative thing on two legs is the monkey! The man that can on the slightest provocation divest himself of old customs, dissociate himself from old traditions, give up old ideals, exchange his religion and forget the old home-land – that man will surely not become the best Canadian citizen ... Our true attitude then ought to be that of respect and intelligent sympathy.'[20]

If there was to be a multiplying of diversity, a blooming of a hundred flowers, what remained of Woodsworth's idea of national unity? Clearly, he had rejected the earlier Anglo-Canadian conception. But had this been put behind him in order to embrace a multi-ethnic model? The answer is no. In his *Free Press* articles of 1913, at the same time as he celebrated ethnic heterogeneity he drew satisfaction from the coming of a new, 'united Canadian people.'[21] He told of a meeting at the People's Forum in Winnipeg addressed by a number of immigrant speakers: 'What Europe had failed to do in a thousand years was being done under our very eyes. Racial, linguistic, national, social, political, and religious prejudices were being broken down. These diverse peoples were being welded and fused into a united Canadian people ... And here is Canada's contribution to world affairs. If on this continent we can learn how diverse people may live together in peace we will contribute a thousand fold more to the world's peace than by either building a "tin pot navy" or contributing the money for three British Dreadnoughts.'[22]

Strangers within Our Gates, to repeat, was emphatic about the need for national uniformity. In *My Neighbor* (1911), even more than in *Strangers within Our Gates*, Woodsworth had preached the importance of integration. In that work he had announced his discovery of the city as an organism, a web of interdependent part, and thus had begun his life-long preoccupation with the ideal of 'cooperation.' Of course, schemes of cooperation and social unity do not disallow the possibility of joint action by discordant, discrepant parts.[23] This, however, was not how Woodsworth understood such ideas as cooperation and unity. Although his *Free Press* articles gave greater recognition to cultural and ethnic pluralism, his thinking was shot through still with the language and aspirations of conformity and assimilation.

It is here that the fundamental antinomy in Woodsworth's view of the national question is evident. At the moment of the initial triumph of pluralism, he continues to make the case for unity. The paradox is more perplexing again, because his argument for unity and cooperation is frequently predicated upon a frank assertion of the evils of diversity and pluralism. That is, the case for social coherence is stated so strongly that it precludes his holding both principles in some relation of balance or counterpoint. As Woodsworth usually saw it, diversity of any kind – social, economic, religious, ethnic, or political – was likely to be disruptive, sectional, prejudiced, or self-serving.[24] What most struck him before 1914 and in the early years of the First World War were the deeply fissiparous tendencies at work in Canadian society: ethnic ghettos, religious denominations, segregated fraternal organizations, sectional political parties, and egotistical individualism:

'In this country,' said a settler, whose nationality it was not difficult to discover, 'we're something like [h]ash – something of everything all mixed together.' Each community is a heterogeneous aggregation with little coherency and no active unifying principle at work.[25]

We have been inexperienced and we have been too busy each with his own affairs to bother much about the common welfare ... Our British ancestry, our Protestant traditions, our frontier training, have developed a sturdy independence but have left us decidedly short on those elements which are essential to the co-operation involved in our complex modern life which finds its highest expression in the city.[26]

The solutions were to be integrative, society-wide, inclusive, and cosmopolitan: social settlements, community centres, public schools, ecumenical churches, cooperative political parties, and peoples' forums. These would instantiate and inculcate the new, pan-Canadian ideal.[27]

Thus Woodsworth's other important conviction, namely cultural and ethnic pluralism, was clearly subordinated to his emphasis on unity. To confirm this interpretation, it is necessary to explain more exactly what it was he was guaranteeing the immigrant when he talked glowingly of tolerance and acceptance of cultural differences.

To Woodsworth immigration would always require government controls of some kind.[28] Undesirables must be kept out: the frankly immoral, the economically destitute, the insane and chronically infirm, and the orphaned. Also, Orientals and blacks should be excluded, for the most part. While all European races should be allowed entry, the volume should be regulated, and immigrants going on the land given preference. Once in Canada, all immigrants ought to enjoy full rights of citizenship, not just official rights such as rights to naturalization and the franchise, but those informal rights as well that ensured a living wage, access to decent social services, and entry to trade unions. Immigrants must be encouraged to retain such cultural traditions as their art and music.[29] Finally, native-born Canadians should show tolerance and benevolence.[30] *This* is what Woodsworth understood by a policy of pluralism.

Clearly it did not mean support of residential segregation. Established ethnic communities should be broken up and integrated into a wider, 'Canadian' way of life.[31] The most telling indictment Woodsworth made of ethnic segregation was that it prevented the development of a capacity to think in moral, that is, public-spirited, terms:

The establishment of sound and suitable public institutions, the development of high political ideals and a 'social conscience' would not have been easy in a country which consisted of scattered communities of people trained in individualistic habits of thought and activity. The presence of alien and unassimilated elements have aggravated the difficulty and tended to retard the development of a sense of community fellowship, or corporate responsibility, and of devotion to a social ideal. The general indifference to the conduct of public affairs, the lack of adequate means for the expression of disinterested public opinion, the difficulty of united action, has afforded an opportunity for the baser elements in our public life to gain a position of influence that has degraded the public life and service of Canada ...[32]

The [People's] Forum breaks down the artificial barriers that so seriously divide our communities. It takes people out of their own little circles. It broadens their interests and makes them sympathetic toward those who hold views different from their own. It helps to create a common interest, to develop a community spirit and thus to prepare the way for a more disinterested and efficient citizenship.[33]

Immigrants should be encouraged to sustain their uniqueness, but they must do so detached from a corporate way-of-life with its historically derived commonalities of ethnicity, culture, and language. Moreover, they should be required to send their children to English-speaking schools, preferably public ones; and they themselves should be encouraged to attend adult classes that would teach the English language, Canadian civics, hygiene, temperance, farming techniques, and homemaking.[34] Some recognition should be given to minority languages but not at the expense of English: 'I can see no reasons why under proper safe-guards provision should not be made for the teaching of other than the English language. We do this in our universities, where we recognize the cultural value of the various European languages. Why should it not be done at the age when children can most readily learn a second language. But, this should be done in such a way that it would not interfere with the unifying influences of the school. English should be the language of our schools, and should be taught thoroughly.'[35]

In addition to a vast and growing state apparatus, a number of newly created private agencies would provide the requisite services to the immigrant: social welfare agencies, social settlements, non-denominational churches, people's forums, consolidated school districts, and community centres. All of these would, of course, be potent instruments of assimilation. Partly Woodsworth recognized this; partly he deluded himself. Essentially he convinced himself that the new 'unifying' institutions, because of their inclusive, public-spirited, and community-wide nature, were somehow culturally neutral. Woodsworth, in an article published in 1917, showed that he understood very well the hegemonic and assimilative role of such traditional agencies as the established churches and fraternal organizations: 'If better-class Canadians venture into the [immigrant] district it is in the role of "uplifters." They come as outsiders to impose their particular brand of religion or patriotism or social institutions upon an alien community.'[36] What he overlooked was the fact that ostensibly ecumenical, community-wide, and progressive organizations could be as much agents of conformity as the older 'sectarian' ones.

Woodsworth's belief that racial types were not normally the result of physiological differences did not mean he was incapable of thinking in physical and biological categories. In 1916, while director of the Bureau of Social Research, he published a series of five articles on 'mental defectives,' in which he enunciated a genetically and physiologically based theory of the origins of mental illness.

Woodsworth's premises were derived from two American psychologists, W.E. Fernald and Henry Goddard.[37] Fernald was the author in 1893 of *The History of the Treatment of the Feeble-minded*. Goddard was one of the leading clinical psychologists of his generation. Director of the psychological laboratory at the Training School for Feebleminded Children at Vineland, New Jersey, he was the first to apply Alfred Binet's IQ tests in the United States in 1908. Later he traced the family tree of one person to show the persistent, inherited nature of mental illness.[38] In 1912 Goddard was one of the first psychologists to be invited by the American Public Health Service to Ellis Island to make use of IQ tests on immigrants. His results, he believed, showed that 83 per cent of Jewish, 80 per cent of Hungarian, 79 per cent of Italian, and 87 per cent of Russian immigrants were feeble-minded.[39] (In a 1919 lecture he used the evidence of psychological testing to disprove arguments for social equality.) Although Woodsworth did not use these sources to justify a genetic account of racial differences, his strange intellectual influences and his familiarity with the literature of eugenics are, at least, to be noted. With Fernald's and Goddard's help Woodsworth claimed that there was a fundamental distinction between insanity and mental defectiveness. The former was a worse condition and encompassed, to use the terminology of the times, idiots, imbeciles, and morons. Although not as extreme, paradoxically, the condition of defectives was less easily improved because their minds were incomplete rather than diseased, which was the predicament of the insane: 'With an insane man the mental machinery is out of order and he may be set right. The mental defective never had a full equipment of mental machinery and no amount of treatment or education can give it to him.'[40] Mental defectiveness might be the result of accidental or environmental factors but mostly it was the consequence of heredity. Woodsworth quoted Fernald: '"The hereditary cases are the most numerous. The recent intensive study of the family histories of large numbers of the feeble-minded by Goddard, Davenport and Tredgold show that in at least 80 per cent of their cases the mental defect had been preceded by other cases of defect in the immediate family line. Goddard finds that 65 per cent of his institutional cases had one or both parents actually feeble-minded. It is believed that this hereditary defect is the result of protoplasmic defect in the germ plasm of the family stock."'[41] A little earlier, in April 1916, Woodsworth was reported in *The Voice* as having made the same point: 'Early in the 19th century, a soldier in New England formed a union with a feeble-minded girl, by whom he had several children, all infected with their mother's weakness. About 450 descendants of this union had been traced at the present time, Mr. Woodsworth said. And they were nearly all criminals, paupers, prostitutes, or feeble-minded persons. The soldier afterwards married a Quaker girl of good family and sound mind. Of this marriage 350 descendants had been traced. Almost without exception they were successful business men, educators, lawyers, professional men and prosperous farmers.'[42]

With mental defectives apparently reproducing themselves with some abandon and with the First World War taking away the prime of Canada's 'normal' manhood, Woodsworth was worried about the prospect of national race suicide. Action by government was imperative; mental defectives should be isolated in large public institutions. There would be a financial cost in this, Woodsworth admitted, but by no means as much as the hidden social and economic costs of inaction. For it was a central part of his argument that a close connection existed between criminal and generally anti-social behaviour on the one hand and mental defectiveness on the other. Mental defectives, in effect, possessed the minds of children. They were incapable of acknowledging rules or honouring duties; they had no sense of moral responsibility. They were gullible and unemployable; they easily fell into a life of prostitution, theft, drunkenness, promiscuity, indigence, and exploitation. Woodsworth did not hazard a precise measure of the proportion of crime that owed its origin to mental defectives, although he did assert that 'some of the authorities believe that a very considerable proportion of those frequently convicted of certain offences [were] feeble-minded' and that perhaps as many as half of known prostitutes suffered from mental defectiveness.[43] There were other hidden social costs. Lack of isolated facilities to treat mental defectives meant that their presence in schools and hospitals frequently diverted these institution from their normal purposes. Partly to 'treat' them but more, perhaps, to prevent promiscuous copulation, mental defectives should be segregated and supervised in large custodial institutions. Largeness of scale would promote economy and also allow a variety of smaller institutions to take account of special needs: 'The newer state institutions [in the United States] have followed the colony plan of organization, combining a custodial department, training school, industrial department and farm. The institutional lines during the past 20 years have adopted the cottage or detached type of construction, allowing for classification according to age, sex, mental and physical condition, and grade of inmates. It is to be noted that the larger states are now providing separate institutions for epileptics, for children, and for adult women.'[44]

Woodsworth made two other recommendations. First, there should be a tighter immigration policy. His claim was not that mental defectiveness was specific to or concentrated in particular racial groups but only that the social costs of the immigration of mental defectives was so great that none of them should be allowed into the country. This would entail improving medical examinations and locating medical centres closer to the port of origin of immigrants. In these last proposals Woodsworth acknowledged his debt to Dr J.D. Page, chief medical officer of the port of Quebec. He also explicitly supported another of the latter's recommendations: that monies from poll taxes imposed on Chinese immigrants be used specifically to improve the system of medical examinations.

Secondly, Woodsworth advocated that, for Canadians and immigrants already landed in the country, marriage certificates be issued only after a thorough medical examination. Discussing the possibility of sterilization, he stated that 'any policy that will accomplish this [preventing more of the unfit from coming into existence] is in the end economic.'[45] That is, he had no difficulty, in principle, with the policy of sterilization. Yet, on this occasion, his view, expressed in somewhat clinical language, was that, in the present state of public opinion, 'sterilization was not practicable.'

Several motifs spring out from Woodsworth's account of mental illness. One is his insatiable, modernist confidence in the methods of science to discern the roots of social pathology and prescribe remedial treatment. There is also his predilection for large, centralized custodial and therapeutic institutions separate from society. Perhaps most emphatically present is his use of a new ethical language that would bear the weight of his new medical-biological model of mental illness. It was neither 'moral delinquency' nor 'moral depravity' that caused crime but mental incapacity or, as with the 'mentally healthy' criminal, 'lack of proper training.' For both groups the appropriate response of the state should be 'treatment' rather than retribution or punishment.[46] In the new world that was dawning, medical experts and social administrators would be the true legislators of mankind. A scientifically derived, morally neutral, world view would supersede the ancient Christian language of right and wrong.

III

Between 1909 and 1921, Woodsworth's religious perspective underwent extensive change. Perhaps in no other area of his life at this time did he travel so far, so quickly. Before 1909 Woodsworth had been a quintessential social gospeller. His decision to work at All Peoples' Mission was the living out of this theological commitment, as was his subsequent association with the Canadian Welfare League and the Bureau of Social Research. As the years passed, his outlook became more secular and avowedly political. When he finally left the Methodist Church in 1918, the reasons he cited were not the religious ones he had advanced in 1907 but rather such obviously political issues as war, pacifism, and the dominance of the church's affairs by a wealthy, business élite.[47] Immediately after the war, Woodsworth participated in the Labor Church in Winnipeg but, after that experiment failed, he was largely devoid of connection with any organized congregation. He did have some association with the Unitarian church in Ottawa after he moved there in 1922. When he brought his family back to Winnipeg in 1925, however, he failed to attend any church, instead holding an informal Sunday service in his own home for his family, a practice he had begun several years earlier. Some of his children were still young and, understandably, they occasionally considered these sessions, which could last for two hours, to be tedious and unendurable.[48]

Simultaneous and commensurate with his fading religious commitment, there took place a decline in his hopes for the Protestant church as a mobilizer of social and political change. Before 1910, as was made clear in Strangers within Our Gates, Woodsworth had been very much a Protestant as well as an Anglo-Canadian nationalist, viewing the

Protestant tradition as an integral part of the whig inheritance of English Canada and therefore something that sustained a dynamic, scientific, and freedom-loving people. In this early period he saw the Protestant churches as bearers of religious truth to a superstitious Catholicism and an unbelieving Judaism.[49] As his political vision grew, this emphasis changed radically, although not yet in a way that diminished the historic and doctrinal significance of the Protestant churches. Indeed he now came to assert that the latter's *raison d'être* lay not in the conversion of individuals and the protection of the Anglo-Saxon nation but in transforming the whole of society and politics.[50] This period of his thinking lasted roughly from 1910 to 1914. After 1914 he came to be unalterably disillusioned by the political and institutional conservatism and sectarian denominationalism of the Protestant churches, asserting that the Holy Spirit had abandoned them and fixed its dwelling-place in community-wide, welfare organizations such as social settlements, public schools, people's forums, trade unions, and farmers' movements.[51] Beginning in 1918, therefore, Woodsworth justified his dedication to work amidst 'secular' agencies less and less in religious terms, and it was as a secular-minded citizen of a modern, cosmopolitan culture that he served in Parliament after 1921. Yet, even as it was a declining influence, the continuance in his thought of religious metaphors and symbolism in the years just before, during, and after the First World War cannot be overlooked. Christianity also provided Woodsworth with his most persistent self-images, those of the crusader and the martyr.

Nowhere is this indebtedness better exemplified than in his use of apocalyptic imagery.[52] In an article in 1916 Woodsworth talked of having had a vision of the twentieth-century holy city. It had happened in Montreal. One night, weary of 'statistics' and 'problems,' he had, as he put it, gone out 'into the streets' and made his 'way toward the mountain.' Before him, from the top of Mount Royal, stretched the whole city. He caught a vision of Montreal as a 'vast city, the metropolis of a country as populous as the United States.' With 'the haunting music of "The Holy City"' in his ears, there 'came back to me a sacred evening hour when from the Mount of Olives I had looked across to old Jerusalem. It was doubtless near the very spot from which Jesus had beheld the city and wept over it. Two thousand years had passed – two thousand years of Christian teaching and effort and still the people of Jerusalem were living in poverty and ignorance and vice. Had the work of Jesus then been a failure? ... No!. His work had to be repeated by each of his disciples. His work had to be carried a step further – a step nearer completion – by each generation.'[53]

This utopian conception, owing perhaps as much to Edward Bellamy as to Jesus Christ, became for Woodsworth an ideal standard against which to measure the city of the present with its poverty, homelessness, and prostitution. It was now the duty of his generation 'to make our dreams come true': 'I thought I could discern the indistinct outlines of the work-places of the future. To these men and women went forth in the morning, not like "dumb driven cattle," but eagerly as the artist to his studio or the child to its play. They worked thruout [sic] the day, not as masters and slaves, not as jealous rivals, but as partners in a common enterprise. ... They returned in the evening each having contributed according to his ability to the welfare of the community; each as a matter of course enjoying his full share of the opportunities which the community offered.'[54]

On other occasions Woodsworth larded his speeches and writings with apocalyptic imagery of a sudden incursion into time of transcendent, spiritual forces, which would be the fulfillment of history. Such imagery, combined with his more secularly derived progressive view of history, provided him with his potent belief in the immanence of change and the incipience of social perfection. Often he described Jesus as a sort of revolutionary: the son of a carpenter, the friend of the poor and 'the common people who heard him gladly,' he was (here Woodsworth used Eugene Debs's words), 'the master proletarian revolutionist, the sower of the social whirlwind ... the martyred Christ of the working class.'[55]

Woodsworth recognized that apocalyptic and eschatological language could readily sanction revolutionary and violent politics.[56] From deep conviction, also Christian in origin, he was a pacifist; and, influenced by nineteenth-century accounts of history, particularly the Darwinian one, he was also very much an evolutionist.[57] So how exactly was the creation of the holy city to be accomplished? It was to be done peacefully, that much was clear. But would it be achieved slowly or rapidly, with a sudden rupture of tradition, or gradually and in a manner that incorporated useful elements of the past? Predictably, because Woodsworth's first 'political' project centred on the church as the primary agent of change, he first addressed these issues in his reflections on the need for reform within the church.

For Woodsworth the problem of change was at heart one of the relationship of forms to ideas.[58] The utility of any institutional form, be it a church, a creed, a custom, or a habit, derived from the clarity of the 'idea' or intellectual purpose that inhered within it; institutions could command popular loyalty only insofar as they were expressive of valid, discernible ideas. Otherwise, they were lifeless and ethically meaningless. Change occurred principally through the efforts of 'idealists,' such as prophets, poets, and religious and political leaders.[59] Examples were John the Baptist, St Francis of Assisi, Wycliffe, Savonarola, Knox, Cromwell, Tennyson, and, of course, Jesus Christ. The reaction of moribund institutions towards such individuals was, customarily, irrational, so the advocate of change must expect social rejection, persecution, and perhaps death. After Whitman and Tennyson, Woodsworth quoted most often from James Russell Lowell's 'The Present Crisis': 'Truth forever on the scaffold, wrong forever on the throne/ Yet that scaffold sways the future, and, behind the dim unknown,/Standeth God within the shadow keeping watch above his own.' The fate of the reformer, then, was to become a suffering servant of change. This he endured to ensure that new ideas would in time become embodied in new institutions. The difficulty, Woodsworth recognized, was that imagining novel ideas was not easy since everything the human race knew derived from already established thought-forms and institutions. Yet change mediated by the old forms would never be effectual. The problem was one of putting new wine into old bottles:

What should be our attitude to the old institutions? We respect them of course because of the place they have occupied. Naturally we recognize with reluctance that they are no longer adequate to the new needs. What shall we do with them? Some sort of compromise suggests itself. "Put the new wine into the old bottles – preserve the old forms ..."

Following this policy we attempt to read new meanings into old words and phrases. Up to a certain point this seems not only justifiable, but necessary. We proceed from the known to the unknown. Thus words are constantly taking on new connotations. But if the changes are not carefully explained and clearly understood, those responsible for the altered meanings are not ingenuous and the truths are confusing.

In like manner the attempt has been made in all ages to put a new significance into old forms and ceremonies. While it is right to recognize the good in the old and to appreciate that good, there is a danger that the new may be absorbed by the old. The early church christianized many pagan customs and has paid the penalty of being more or less paganized. Every new life seems to develop its own forms. At its peril it endues itself in forms that are the outgrowth of another or earlier form of life. So with the attempt to regenerate old institutions. There is a subtle temptation to adopt this method in order to make rapid or visible progress. But there comes a time when the old machine must be scraped [sic], and if a new machine stands ready one need not bemoan the workmanship of the scrap iron ... We must face the use of new bottles – new institutions, new methods, a new social order.[60]

Radical reform ought to make as clean a break as possible with the past, its metaphysics, and its institutions; radical change must aspire to transcend the existing particularities and contingencies of culture and history. It was this perspective that caused Woodsworth in 1914 to reject the established churches altogether and, since he still held to some version of the social gospel, to advocate new kinds of churches.[61] Already, he claimed, there existed a new ideal of religion, one that was social, practical, scientific, progressive, and democratic. Before 1914, he held that the established churches could be successfully brought to conform to this ideal; after, he concluded that they could not. To Woodsworth the unsatisfactory predicament of the established denominations was that they were embedded in history and culture.[62] This had led them to a sectional and indeed sectarian conception of Christianity, a religion of creed, ceremony, and ecclesiastical structures. They partook too much of established cultural and economic forms; in the case of the Protestant churches in Canada, they embodied the conventions of English Canadianism and the economics of the bourgeois, middle class. (The transformative ideal of solidarity, unity, and cooperation was, as it turned out, not so much a new conception as a return to the original universalist and ecumenical ethic of the Christian church before institutional rot had, presumably, set in with Constantine's embrace of Christianity in the fourth century.)[63] A new church should cast off all historical and cultural accretions and seek to distinguish between the essential and the non-essential in religion. It should learn to 'discover what, stripped of all externals, true religion and undefiled' essentially was.[64]

William Ivens's labour-church movement in Winnipeg after 1918 provided Woodsworth with an example close at hand of the new religion. After closer examination of it, however, he became less sure that new wine could easily be put into completely new bottles.[65] There were, he said, two tendencies in the Labor Church. One was Marxist, and saw all religion as 'superstition and the purpose of the new church as the inculcating of Marxian economic doctrine.' In contrast, the majority of members wanted to retain some of the traditional forms – christening, prayer, blessings – and invest them with new meanings: 'We still use some of the old forms, even though we recognize that they do not adequately or even correctly express our idea. This is not camouflage. They are the forms of expression with which we are familiar and we have not yet developed new ones. So, at banquets, toasts are still drunk, even though only water is used. We have not yet evolved a "prohibition" method of expressing good fellowship! ... As one age runs into another, so old ideas and institutions are not suddenly and absolutely changed, but are modified and transformed and, then, parts of them incorporated into the new.'[66]

In sum, Woodsworth's view of religious change was a little contradictory. On the one hand it seemed to sanction a peaceful kind of revolutionary change; on the other, he acceded to a much more gradual and syncretic pattern. (When, later, he came to think about political change he would leave a similar impression.)

In spite of his avowal of respect for 'the good in the old' in his lecture on new wine and new bottles, there can be no doubting his general disdain for tradition and established forms of social life. Two elements in his character conspired to produce this predominant disposition. Since he was a devotee of a progressive view of history, new ideas and institutions would always supersede the old and engage his loyalty – thus the new Christianity of Ivens necessarily displaced that of more traditional Methodists. But there was, as well, a restless rationalism about Woodsworth, the sort of outlook that animated the Rationalist Press Association, the Canadian Secular Union, and free thought in general in the nineteenth century. This part of him went beyond a simple relish for the new and rejected institutions altogether.[67] It reduced the meaning of Christianity to ahistorical and acultural axioms stripped of any conventional or inessential 'externals': 'Religion, in this broad sense, is simply the utmost reach of man – his highest thinking about the deepest things in life; his response to the wireless messages that come to him out of the infinite; his planting the flag of justice and brotherhood on a new and higher level of human attainment and purpose.'[68] Critics might plausibly claim that this was perhaps a bloodless and vapid form of religion, one that was too abstract and cerebral, certainly one that saw little merit in any religious 'community of character.'[69]

IV

In the same series of articles in 1913 in which he stated his abandonment of the Anglo-Canadian ideal, Woodsworth announced the obsolescence of the pastoral myth of a simple, benevolent, rural Canada:

Canada today is not the Canada of twenty years ago. Think back twenty years – Ontario, a small province, with a homogeneous agricultural population, living largely a self-contained and self-satisfied life; Quebec, a string of picturesque villages bordering the St. Lawrence, keeping happy holy-days half the year; the Eastern Provinces living quietly down by the sea; the West, a youthful pioneer going forth into unknown territory. Confederation had been effected, but national consciousness was only emerging ... We knew little of industrial disputes, and since most of us lived in the country, rural depletion was an unintelligible phrase. Within the two decades has come an inrush of over two million immigrants. Within the two decades our cities have grown at an enormous rate till now half of us are city-dwellers. Within this period we have emerged from our isolation and are rapidly being drawn into the great world currents.

Some of us shrink back from the deep waters and would gladly return to the simpler joys of earlier days. But that is a fatuous impulse. For good or ill we are launched upon the larger life. Its perils may be great, but its possibilities are boundless.[70]

Woodsworth went on to quote the last lines of Lowell's 'The Present Crisis': '[It is ours] / To steer boldly through the winter sea / Nor attempt the Future's portal with the Past's / blood-rusted key.' He used this article as the first chapter of his *Studies in Rural Citizenship*. There, instead of the last quotation, he returned once more to Whitman's lines about cutting the hawsers.[71]

Although Woodsworth had, apparently, rejected an Anglo-Canadian, nativist account of Canada's identity, this did not preclude him from thinking of the country as having a continuing historical connection with Britain. He saw no contradiction in talking of 'our forefathers [meeting] under the tree on the village green to decide on matters affecting the common interest,'[72] or in demanding, as he did in 1919, 'the full restoration of the "ancient rights of the British people" and other rights which through the centuries have been won by our fathers with much struggle and at great sacrifice.'[73]

The British inheritance was one of exemplary whiggish liberty, but, economically and technologically, it provided another possible model, that of the earliest industrializing nation. Woodsworth was painfully aware of the new industrial and urban forces set loose in his own young society. Apart from Gustavus Myers's *History of Canadian Wealth* (1914) – and Myers was an American – he had few indigenous intellectual sources to help him piece together an understanding of these new socio-economic processes. Inevitably he came to depend on British authors and examples, and, of course, American ones as well. Indeed, down to the First World War, Woodsworth's thinking about industrial society, if anything, owed slightly more to American progressives and social gospellers such as Walter Rauschenbusch, Richard T. Ely, Shailer Matthews, F.G. Peabody, Lincoln Steffens, Jacob Riis, Frederic Howe, and Robert Hunter. He was not unfamiliar with H.G. Wells, Beatrice and Sidney Webb, Norman Angell, John Ruskin, Thomas Carlyle, J.A. Hobson, J.C. Hammond, and Arnold Toynbee. But only as time passed, and essentially coeval with the First World War, did British intellectual and political influences come to predominate in his thought, culminating in his unabashed admiration for the British Labour Party in 1918–19.

For Woodsworth industrialization was at bottom a *technological* revolution.[74] The discovery of the steam engine, he claimed, had destroyed an agrarian economy of simple, free producers and independent craftsmen. Steam allowed extensive mechanization of production and dictated centralized organization in the factory system. Steam brought the railway and the lessening of distances; it introduced a growing measure of mechanization to agriculture. Workers were drawn from the farms and craft shops into the factories and industrial towns, there to become tenders of machines. Mechanization promoted a growing division of labour. The commercialization of agriculture and trade and their integration into larger national and international markets intensified economic competition. In all this the lot of workers was not a happy one. They endured long hours, in wretched conditions, for less than a living wage. (There is some evidence that Woodsworth thought that industrialism might actually have brought about a decline in the real standard of living of the labouring classes.)[75] Workers now frittered away their leisure hours among the idiocies and temptations of the tenement, picture-theatre, saloon, and street corner. Put simply, human labour was degraded by industrialization;[76] the proudly independent, creative, and varied life of craftsmen was ended as they were turned into the wage slaves of a monotonous, prison-like routine of production in ever-larger, anonymous firms. Mechanization and centralization of production, Woodsworth emphasized, heralded the era of amalgamation, the epoch of trusts, combines, and monopolies:

The power of organization has ... developed into the mightiest social force of modern times. The capitalist-employer class has carried organization far beyond the bounds of the individual factory, and now not only industry but business of all kinds – commerce in general – is being organized. On every hand we have great companies, extensive combines, consolidated trusts, giant mergers and all-powerful monopolies. An ever lessening number of men control and reap the profits of the leading industries, the great business houses, the railroad systems and the financial institutions ... The business men have made and are still making a fight for independence. The newer the country the more successfully this may be carried on. But in face of such tremendous resources as are possessed by the great organizations, capitulation is only a matter of time. The most successful men become a part of the machine. The others go under or maintain an existence in an essentially dependent relation.[77]

The young and women, too, were greatly affected by the new economic order. Child labour denied education to the young, while work in the factory and office coarsened the refined virtues of women and opened them to egregious temptations: 'With long hours and inferior social status it is little wonder that girls are glad to escape from housework to the more independent if worse-paid work in shops and factories. Here we find a life that is full of temptations, and only girls of fine instincts, high character and good training will escape a sad coarsening as the months go by. The home, even though it is where their parents live, has little to attract. There is little accommodation, no comforts, no privacy. The girls must go out for their pleasures. Home is, for all practical purposes, but the cheapest of boarding-houses.'[78]

So a major consequence of industrialism was the demise of the home and family. Under the new economic regime many of the functions of the home – education, charity, medical care, recreation – had been taken over by other, more specialized, and often public institutions. The shrinking of the functions of the family, combined with the increasing dispersal of both parents' energies in the work place, left the home a diminished, unsentimental place. This especially affected children:

In our city life we are facing conditions that are undermining the home. So little is this understood and yet so important are the consequences that I venture to give at length a most admirable treatment of the whole subject. This is taken from Hunter's work [*Poverty*]: 'In the scramble to re-adjust ourselves to the cities and to this new industrial life, built up as a result of steam and electricity, the child has been forgotten. To a very large extent he has been left to readjust himself, and the result is a series of really appalling problems. His father now leaves the home and goes to the factory; he may not watch his father at work or work with him – and it would not be good for him if he could – until he is himself old enough to become a good laborer. He is in the city instead of in the country. He has lost the playgrounds which nature lavishly furnished ... Bored by the homeless tenement, he finds himself on an asphalt pavement, in a crowded street, amid roars of excitement – in a playground alive with business with which he must not interfere.'[79]

This account of industrialization, culled from British and American sources and examples, was superimposed on Woodsworth's own, often experientially derived, view of Canadian history. To him nineteenth-century Canada was rural, local, pastoral, and egalitarian.[80] Class systems, which were all but caste-like in Europe, were here, as in all North America, much more open and fluid. Life was mainly lived on farms and in small towns, in roughly egalitarian communities; markets were local and communications limited; social relations were kindly, personal, and tolerant; an ethic of neighbourliness prevailed. What businesses there were were small and local; managerial authority was personal and unoppressive. The owner of what was usually an owner-managed enterprise had probably grown up on a farm; his origins were simple and uncomplicated and these influenced the friendly labour relations he brought to the work place. All in all, early Canada was devoid of large integrated economic institutions; socially, it was little more than an archipelago of independent, self-sufficient, homogeneous, law-abiding, and god-fearing communities, inhabiting social space that was 'pretty,' well ordered, and homely:

Those who have come to Canada in recent years, especially to Western Canada, often fail to understand the Canadian life of a generation ago, in which the men past middle life were nurtured. Agriculture was the predominant industry. There were few cities and these were small. Social problems were unknown. The virtues and vices were those of a simple individualistic type of society.

The labor problem was confined to the hired man and the hired girl, but as there was plenty of free land, the hired man soon took up land himself. As there was a scarcity of women, the hired girl soon found herself in a home of her own . . .

In the nearer background of [the businessman's] consciousness is the life of the small town in which he experienced his first business struggles. Here he married and set up his first home. Here his children had measles and croup and he knew what it was to be on friendly terms with all sorts of neighbors. In his business, he called most of his employees by their first names and knew more or less their personal affairs. There were few poor in the town, and they were generally shiftless or addicted to drink. If a man didn't make things go, it was more or less his own fault. Organized labor was unknown and Socialism was unheard of. A few constables represented the dignity of the Law and rounded up petty thieves and disorderly persons. The church stimulated men to overcome temptations to appetite, and to strive for a certain type of personal goodness.[81]

Woodsworth was not unaware of the drawbacks of early pioneer life – its drudgery, its lack of privacy, and its conservatism – but there is no mistaking the idyllic nature of his account.

The serpent that had invaded Eden was the machine and its organizational imperatives of centralization and amalgamation. Late nineteenth- and early twentieth-century Canada had been quickly transformed. The young Confederation had become integrated economically and thrown into an increasingly interdependent world economy. The exploitation of natural resources, the building of railways, the growth of manufacturing and banking had created, overnight it seemed, a powerful monopoly business class that had corrupted politics and controlled parliament through the political machines of both established parties.[82]

According to Woodsworth, the concentration of population in Canadian cities was proof not just of the coming of industrialism but also of the desuetude of agriculture. Increasingly the town was coming to dominate the country. As he surveyed the various agricultural regions, from Nova Scotia to British Columbia, what struck him was not their vibrancy but their disrepair: out-migration, abandoned farms, creeping suburbanization, land speculation, the loss of an old communitarian ethos, the substitution of Slavs, Chinese, and Hindus for native-born Canadians, the growth of tenant farming. Even in Manitoba, where, when Woodsworth wrote, agricultural development was less than fifty years old, the situation was one of decline from a primitive exuberance.

While the intellectual origins of Woodsworth's analysis of Canadian industrialization were British and American, his recognition of rapid economic development and decay on ever-changing economic frontiers indicated a laudable sensitivity to indigenous factors and to some degree anticipated the perspective of Harold Innis, especially his theory of 'cyclonics': '[In Manitoba] too are changes – Good railway connections, telephones in many homes, the pioneer stage passed. But the villages are stagnant and in many parts the land yielding less and less every year, and in some districts seeded down with noxious weeds. The old timers? Some gone still further West; some made their money and gone to the city to live and speculate in real estate. Tenants are careless and do not keep the land clear, nor do they take the place of the owners in the community. The schools are not so efficiently manned and it is a struggle now to raise the minister's salary.'[83]

Clearly Woodsworth did not overlook the losses wrought by change, but, as with other aspects of his account of modernization, historical necessity was the mother of celebration. Science, technology, mechanization, and centralized industrial planning, if properly utilized, could become godsends to humanity. For they could eradicate the drudgery of labour and, through their superlative efficiency and productivity, overcome the age-old problem of material scarcity. Part of Woodsworth clearly lamented the passing of a simple, rural life; another part, larger in its significance for his thought, reached out to the possibilities of a 'cooperative' future. The old order was gone, and with it, its ethic of individualism; the new age of organization and interdependence dictated a cooperative mode of society.

Yet he did make one exception and this was in regard to farmers. The emphasis of his theory of industrialism was on centralized management, largeness of scale, and technological efficiency. At bottom, Woodsworth welcomed the coming of the modern corporation. What was applicable to industrial manufacturing ought, logically, to have been relevant to agriculture. But on this point Woodsworth demurred. He rejected comparisons between the wage labourer in the modern industrial enterprise and the farm labourer in the employ of what might be called 'corporate farming':

A friend has recently been telling me of an interesting prairie farm. It consists of 64,000 acres and is owned by an English Syndicate. It is under the direction of a manager, who is a graduate of an Eastern agricultural college, and who draws almost as large a salary as the president of a bank. The farm is to be worked in sixty-four units of 1,000 acres each. Over each is placed a foreman, who is given an outfit of steam plows and other machinery to sweep over vast acres of land. Big farms have often failed, but this is being run scientifically – a practical man at the head with plenty of capital behind him.

But what of life in that community, even if the farm succeeds financially? Ever changing gangs of men boarded in the company's houses – camp-life rather than home-life. Suppose a good wage was paid, a good house provided, would you, my farmer friend, choose to establish a home for your family under such conditions? If you incur the foreman's displeasure your tenure of your home would be short. Then what about church and school and social life?

Will the industrial revolution overtake farming? A century ago the village weaver in England lived happily his simple independent life. But today his son is working in a highly specialized trade in a huge factory in the city, in the management and profits of which he has no voice or interest whatever. How will modern commercial organization affect the farmer?[84]

The question was largely rhetorical. While Woodsworth certainly wanted 'scientific,' 'progressive' farming, that is, farming sensitive to such matters as mechanization, crop rotation, and seed selection, and while he encouraged farmers to obtain the benefits of producer co-ops, he never abandoned his predilection for a simple producer society of small, freehold farmers. Woodsworth was deeply aware of the degra-dation of labour brought about by modern industrial processes. His solution in the case of Canadian farmers presupposed the retention of a large part of their traditional way of life. Not so the industrial workers, whom he made much more subject to the logic of monopoly. Increasingly, for them, work would be monotonous, repetitive, and uncreative, at least until and maybe even after the coming of the 'cooperative commonwealth.'

If one idea lay at the heart of Woodsworth's social doctrine it was that of 'cooperation.' Of course, the idea was also used extensively by others. Marx employed it in *Das Kapital*, where it mainly referred to the increasingly interdependent and social character of labour under capi-talism. One of Marx's earliest American disciples, Laurence Gronlund, wrote a book entitled *The Cooperative Commonwealth*. The idea also appeared in the works of Edward Bellamy, L.T. Hobhouse, and Robert Blatchford. In Canada, the cooperative movement was a growing intellectual and economic force before and after the First World War, led by the likes of E.A. Partridge, T.A. Crerar, George Keen, and

Alphonse Desjardins. One of Woodsworth's closest allies, William Irvine, would in 1929 publish *Co-operative Government*, and in 1933 the political movement that Woodsworth himself came to lead would choose the name the Co-operative Commonwealth Federation. A term so widely employed by such a disparate group of people bore a multitude of meanings. What did Woodsworth understand by it?

The particular ontology of society that underlay his main theory of cooperation asserted that, because of technological innovations associated with steam and electricity, industrialism engendered ever-greater economic specialization, centralization, interdependence, amalgamation, and integration.[85] Society had become an 'organism,' 'a spider-web,' a 'system'; it was an 'association' of parts rather than a 'heterogeneous aggregation' made up of 'isolated atoms' of 'unrelated phenomena,' with 'little coherency' or 'active unifying principle.' More than anything, the contemporary world was an holistic entity with an inherent unity and solidarity that transcended the parts that composed it:

It is only in recent years that we are beginning to learn that as the city is not a mere aggregation of independent individuals, but rather a certain type of social organism, so the physical city must be considered as a whole and the various parts must be subordinated to the whole, and that their highest welfare is dependent on that of the whole.[86]

[The English] are so consciously individualistic that we can't get it through our heads that society is a solid body of which we are only the molecules. There is our good old English expression that ought to help us to understand the idea of the French Communists – "We're all in the same boat." We must sink or swim together – that's solidarity.[87]

The machine has brought about an industrial revolution. We have passed from an age of individual production to an age of social production. But the machine has gotten into the hands of a few who control the operations of industry for their own advantage. The next step is for the people to gain control of the machine and operate it for the benefit of all. This development is inevitable.[88]

This conception of cooperation was fundamental to Woodsworth. From it he deduced his belief in public regulation, planning, and social ownership as well as his hope of the egalitarian distribution of wealth. In this primordial sense, cooperation was a technological and technocratic notion emphasizing the unimaginable efficiency and productivity of the contemporary industrial firm and the blessings of centralized procedures for making managerial decisions. We may call this sense of cooperation the 'technological' one.

A second sense, the 'relational,' saw cooperation as denoting the quality of human relations in a future utopia.[89] Here Woodsworth argued that a life lived unto oneself or one's group was ignoble and delimiting; instead, a life of love, care, and responsibility was what human beings were destined to achieve. Hence his predictable affinity for such socialist ideas as brotherhood, comradeship, association, and partnership. At the back of this was the assumption that participation in a concrete particular was inferior to identification with an abstract universal. Thus, as was explained earlier, just as in religious matters association with a historic denomination or sect was inferior to association with an ecumenical ideal, so aligning oneself with 'humanity' was preferable to a life immersed in the 'artificial' narrowness of race, group, region, and, indeed, as Woodsworth would argue, class.

A third sense, the 'voluntaristic,' referred to the various initiatives of farmers and workers in producers' associations and trade unions to exert some degree of control over their economic circumstances.[90] What this conception shared with the first was the rejection of competitive individualistic models of economic behaviour in favour of more 'collective' ones. In this case, however, the associated efforts of workers and farmers were voluntary, participatory, and democratic. In contrast, the 'technological' conception projected an image of industrial society that was *dirigiste*, hierarchical, and centralist. Early in Woodsworth's intellectual development, then, there were at the heart of his account of cooperation two distinct meanings, which taken together postulated contradictory patterns of economic organization.

Finally, there was the 'democratic' sense of cooperation, which emphasized social unity and integration as prerequisites of democracy.[91] This claim was integral to his early thinking on the national question not just in *Strangers within Our Gates* but later on as well. Sometimes he came close to expressing all four senses within one complete argument:

If the people of any neighborhood are not yet ready for co-operative business, could they not at least get together for discussion and comradeship. A report from one rural district states that the people meet together three times a year. The other three hundred and sixty-two days they grub along with no associated effort. Is such a life worth living or is it likely to lead to a life worth living?

Let people get together frequently and they will soon learn to want to be together. They will learn how to work together. Then they will discover the wonderful advantages of working together – then will develop that community spirit without which democracy is a ghastly failure.

In a recent conference on the open forum movement held in Buffalo, the ground was taken that the forum is essentially an instrument of democracy. 'The Forum is a method, not an institution, an agency whereby classes may be reconciled, differences minimized and the common denominator of all ethical impulse determined and applied to social formulae.'

Forums have been successfully conducted in our large Canadian cities; why not in our towns and rural districts? If anywhere men need to get together and try to get the other fellow's point of view it is in our mixed districts in the West. Democracy commits us to an intelligent, interested and co-operative electorate.[92]

Cooperative and organic theories of community do not logically require the existence of either sociological or normative unity. This is, for example, the argument of F.M. Barnard in his book on the eighteenth-century German philosopher, Johann Gottfried Herder, and in his and Richard Vernon's work on socialist pluralism.[93] In *Spheres of Justice: A Defense of Pluralism and Equality* (New York 1983), Michael Walzer also attempts to accommodate the claims of community and pluralism. Woodsworth derived from a different tradition of speculation. Raised on frontier liberalism, he would never cease to be a liberal of sorts. What his early account of cooperation did make evident, however, was the inordinate unliberal tilt in his thinking towards a definition of cooperation as unity, centralization, homogeneity and, if one is critical, conformity. And it was both a sociological and a normative unity that his theory presupposed. There had to be a rough identity of socio-economic characteristics on the part of Canadians as well as a shared moral purpose in order to realize the cooperative commonwealth. These goals required a public policy of assimilation towards immigrants and the creation of nation-wide and communal institutions for Canadians and newcomers. Woodsworth's early theory of cooperation made difficult, though admittedly not impossible, an account of community that included within it arguments for either group pluralism or competitive individualism.

V

In the late summer of 1918, after his resignation from the Methodist ministry, Woodsworth's life assumed a markedly political direction. His exploration of the question of change, first undertaken in the context of the church, was now transformed into a commitment to change through more conventionally political channels. The political party now became the focus of his practical and intellectual concerns.

In January 1918 the British Columbia Federation of Labor had finally decided to form 'a united working class political party.'[94] While it was to be broadly based and 'calculated to enlist the interest and activity of every advanced and progressive thinker,' the Federated Labor Party was not to be tepid or temporizing. Admittedly, its founding was criticized by such noted left-wing radicals as Joe Naylor and Ernest Winch; but, equally, its early leadership included such socialist luminaries and former members of the Socialist Party of Canada (SPC) as E.T. Kingsley, R. Parmeter Pettipiece, and J.W. Hawthornthwaite. In a speech in early March 1918, Pettipiece made clear that, although more broadly based than the SPC, the FLP was to be militantly anti-capitalist: 'All shades of opinion are represented from the social uplift element to the red-hot revolutionary. The policy of the party hinges upon the property question. The party stands for the collective ownership of the property which is collectively used, and is unalterably opposed to capitalist ownership and control of all such property.'[95]

But the barometer of radical opinion was swinging wildly in British Columbia. No sooner was the FLP in place than there developed an overwhelming support for industrial syndicalism and the One Big Union (OBU). This movement for industrial action also was led by members of the Socialist Party of Canada but, in this instance, they were drawn from those who had originally opposed the FLP: Ernest Winch, Victor Midgley, Jack Kavanagh, and Bill Pritchard. Throughout 1919 the tide ran decidedly with the industrial actionists so that the Vancouver Trades and Labor Council and the British Columbia Federation of Labor were quickly won over by them.[96]

Woodsworth moved into this cockpit of radical politics in the summer of 1918. He came from Gibson's Landing to Vancouver with a reputation, as one contemporary correspondent put it, for 'commitment, tolerance and brotherliness.'[97] As early as June, just after his resignation from the church, he began speaking on behalf of the FLP. He was befriended by Winch, a leader of the International Longshoreman's Auxiliary, and, for a while in 1918–19, he lived with him on Howe Street, while their respective families remained in Gibson's Landing and White Rock. Woodsworth wrote of his living 'in the house of the President of the Trades and Labor Council – a SPC man. So you see I'm pretty well soaked in radical surroundings.'[98] Dorothy Steeves, in her biography of Winch, records that: 'Young Harold Winch was often there and heard the sound of their voices, far into the night, as they hammered out socialist theories together.'[99] At work on the docks, active with the FLP from 1918 to 1921 and in discussions with the likes of Winch and other SPC'ers, Woodsworth was privy to a world of intensely exciting ideas and experiences. His reading, too, was hardly conventional; he read among other works, Engels's *The Origin of the Family*, and Ernest Untermann's *The World's Revolutions*. Untermann was the editor of the first American edition of *Das Kapital* and the translator of Karl Kautsky.

In his years with the FLP, then, Woodsworth participated in a culture of enthusiastic political speculation that had Marxism as one of its constituent elements. Out of this emerged two crucially important sets of articles in 1918–19. In them Woodsworth made as complete a statement in support of democratic socialism as he ever did. The first set appeared in the *BC Federationist* between June 1918 and February 1919; the second, a series of five articles with the overall title 'What Next?' in July–August 1919 in the *Western Labor News*. Between the two fell Woodsworth's involvement in the Winnipeg General Strike. When it is remembered that the Bolshevik Revolution was still in its uncompromised, prepossessing infancy and that the strikes in 1919 had demonstrated the unusual solidarity and militancy of Canadian workers, it is surprising perhaps that in both sets of articles Woodsworth would have defined his position to such a great extent in contradistinction to Marxism. At the bottom of his quarrel with Marxism was a disagreement over the nature of economic class.[100]

Ironically, Woodsworth's own philosophy of history showed many affinities with that of Marxism. Both were ostensibly progressive, materialist, and scientific, and emphasized that history was a process of change. Woodsworth's view, however, entailed a much more empirical and, therefore, protean and fluid account of social categories such as class. Since history, he reasoned, was in fact changeable, conceptual categories must always be regarded as tentative and provisional. Also, and perhaps here he was un-Marxist again, there was always with him a sensitivity to contingent and local variables.[101]

Canada, for him, was not a class system necessarily patterned after Europe's. It lacked a landed aristocracy; its agricultural development had been in the hands of a large class of freeholders; it did not have a long-established bourgeoisie and it was not yet a generation removed from frontier simplicity; and, until recently, there had been extensive individual mobility. Forged in a different world from Europe, Canada's distinctive class system had produced its own special kind of politics.

What he was denying was a binary division of class into bourgeoisie and proletariat. He was, of course, not denying the existence of classes as such. His thought was in fact riddled with class categories, indeed so many that he might be criticized for lacking a coherent account of the subject. Sometimes he used a Marxist and almost 'productivist' vocabulary: 'capitalist-employer class,' 'working class,' 'class war,' 'class ethics,' and 'wage slave.'[102] On other occasions his language insinuated populistic notions of a fundamental division between 'the privileged' and 'the people';[103] or again, at other times he used terms that cut across different class categories: 'farmers,' 'industrial workers,' 'returned soldiers,' and 'middle class progressives.'[104] His settled, preponderant view of class derived not from a productivist view of capitalism but from a distributivist view of monopoly capitalism.[105] Yet this settled notion was itself not without ambiguity since it was often intertwined with conceptions such as 'producers' and 'parasites,' and 'useful labour' and 'useless labour' that implied a more productivist view of class division.[106] In any event, both languages allowed Woodsworth to postulate a more broadly based class constituency for radical politics than was sanctioned by Marxism.

The essence of exploitation to Woodsworth was the lack of a living wage or a decent standard of living. By this measure not just industrial workers were exploited but farmers as well. Farmers may, technically, have owned capital and hired labour but, more importantly, they were the victims of adverse terms of trade under monopoly capitalism. Their economic circumstances were execrable:

[The farmers] run up against the capitalist system from a different angle. But fundamentally the interests of the farmer and the individual worker are one. They will come to recognize this most clearly as they find themselves fighting a common foe. The farmer, like the miner, the factory worker or the logger, is a producer. It is true that he is not a wage earner but, as the trek from country to city shows, he is not economically as well off as the wage earner. Nominally, he owns the tools of production; in reality, he is anything but independent.

The mortgage company often owns the land; the banks, the manufacturers and the railroads have the farmers at their mercy. The costs of production and the prices of his produce are fixed by forces over which he has no control. Under such conditions the old individualism is breaking down and the farmer is organizing industrially and politically.[107]

Woodsworth did not hold that every expression of farmer discontent was consistent with his own version of agrarian radicalism. In his mind, 'progressive' ideas were not the same as 'radical' ones, just as there was a profound divergence between policies based on many good ideas and those founded on 'fundamental principles.'[108] But, even so, he never held that, in principle, the class interests of workers and farmers were irreconcilable; nor were they at odds with those of small businessmen and professionals:

The little business group are almost as much the victims of the system as the industrial workers. Many men in this group are beginning to realize it. Many are being squeezed out. For others, conditions are becoming so intolerable that they are ready to desert. When a storekeeper can get only so much goods and at such a price and must sell only so much on a fixed margin, he is little better than a 'wage slave.' He is becoming suspicious of the system. He can't give much, but his vote will count. Perhaps as in Russia, try out his good faith! ... In the old land emphasis is laid on the broadening out of the party to include all who work by hand or by brain. Too long, so-called 'brain workers' have been separated from 'hand workers' to the disadvantage of both groups. Undoubtedly many 'brain workers' have assumed a superior and exclusive attitude and on the other side, 'hand workers' have sometimes maintained that they were the only producers. The old artificial distinctions are breaking down. The modern surgeon, for example, true to his name, is very decidedly a hand worker and needs a mechanic's skill, while on the other hand no one will deny that he is performing a useful function in the community ... The new party will be open to all who are performing useful work in the community. Fundamentally the social war is between the producers and the parasites.[109]

The above quotation expresses well the second-order language on class that Woodsworth sometimes used. This saw the fundamental antagonism in Canadian society as not so much between those exploited by monopolies and the monopolists, as between 'producers' and 'parasites': those performing 'useful' work and those doing 'useless' tasks. (There is, after all, a discernible distinction between the two definitions;

some 'producers' might in fact have better than a living wage, for example, doctors and teachers. That is, exploitation as material deprivation generates a slightly different definition of the underclass compared with one that includes those who simply perform 'useful' work.) In general Woodsworth concluded that farmers, workers, middle-class professionals, and small businessmen produced useful goods or performed valuable services and in actuality most of them were materially impoverished. The parasites either did not labour at all or they laboured at irrelevant tasks. Such were monopolists, financiers, land and stock market speculators, and many middlemen in the wholesale trades. As well, Woodsworth believed that there were prudential, political considerations to support a latitudinarian conception of the underclass.[110] He argued that Canada would for a long time be an agrarian society and any hope of electoral success was predicated on reaching beyond a relatively small working class. He expressed this view as early as 1912 in a speech to the Winnipeg Social Democratic Party, and he continued to hold it even after his experiences in Vancouver.

At other times he also employed a moral argument for an inclusive definition of class.[111] Unlike Marxists, Woodsworth did not regard class conflict as an engine of historical change. Certainly he held that the maldistribution of material and cultural amenities would spark the sort of moral outrage that would be an impetus to change, but for him the mode of change would not be conflictual, insurrectionary, and physical, but conciliatory, rational, and non-violent. This is where his notion of cooperation can be seen to be such a powerful force in his thought. Woodsworth disdained not only non-economic forms of sectionalism such as religion, race, and language, but also distinctions based on economic class. A basic pre-condition of a politics of cooperation was to bring people together, to transcend differences, to emphasize what was held in common. Socialist politics aimed to reconcile classes:

We dream of a socialistic state and yet sympathize with Mr. Brooks when he says that 'the Mecca of the Co-operative Commonwealth is not to be reached by setting class against class, but by bearing common burdens through toilsome stages along which all who wish well to their fellows can journey together.'[112]

We acknowledge that we are still divided into alien groups separated from one another by barriers of language, race and nationality; by barriers of class and creed and custom. May we overcome prejudice. May we seek to find common ground. May we recognize the beauty in other types than our own. As we claim that our own convictions should be respected, so may we respect the convictions of others. May we grow in moral stature till we join hands over the separating walls. May we enter into the joy of a common fellowship.[113]

Thus, when Woodsworth himself experienced deep class antagonism in the Winnipeg General Strike, his instinctive initial response was to seek common ground.[114] This did not prevent him from aligning himself with the strikers but, obviously, he felt that a long-term solution did not lie in advancing the concerns of just one side, even that of the workers.

Also, compared with contemporary Marxists, Woodsworth evinced a more qualified materialism in regard to class consciousness.[115] While Woodsworth subscribed to a theory of the relativity of human thought and ideas, he allowed room for the notion of the autonomy of human reason. He did not hold that human beings were captives of their class status or historical conditions; men and women were capable of reflecting on their predicament and choosing the rational course of the common good. (Woodsworth probably believed that, since he had extricated himself from the professional middle class, his own life was an illustration of this principle.)[116] For him politics was an engagement of intelligence, an enterprise of education and persuasion. As he put it in 1918, the revolution, when it came, would emanate not from material circumstances that allowed the workers no other course of action but from the already achieved transformation of the 'minds and consciences of the people.' He was an idealist not just because he believed that ideas preceded action but also because he regarded the obtaining of a revolutionary consciousness as tantamount to the act of revolution itself, so that the actual winning of power became a relatively incidental inevitability. The political constituency of a labour party, in his mind, was as wide as the appeal of reason itself: hence his disagreement with the Marxist practice of damning certain classes as inevitably reactionary and uncooperative. Farmers could see reason, so also could small businessmen and professionals, if they were not insulted. No doubt, monopoly businessmen were quite incorrigible, yet even they could be persuaded at least not to resist inevitable change. A recurring theme in Woodsworth's speeches and writings of 1918 and 1919 was the crucial role he believed powerful businessmen could play in determining whether change would be peaceful or violent.[117] If they threw themselves in the way of progress, they would ensure – given their control over the politicians, the courts, and the military – that change would be pursued unconstitutionally. It lay within their power to determine whether the revolution would be 'moderate' or not.

There were other differences between Woodsworth and Marxism. Woodsworth was a convinced pacifist in both domestic and international politics. To him the morality of political action, and therefore the legitimacy of change, derived from its peaceful, consensual nature. Moreover, *pace* Marxism, he clearly believed that the making of a revolutionary transformation was neither easily nor quickly obtained. Woodsworth could be giddily utopian in expressing the coming of the new society, but he could be coldly realistic in assessing the difficulties in actually building it:

It is comparatively easy to say, 'we must have a social revolution.' Under certain circumstances it is possible for the people suddenly to grasp the reins of power. But like marriage that is not really the end of the story, but only its beginning. Everything has still to be worked out.

The message of Lenine [sic] to the Soviet last April is full of suggestions for those who look forward to a violent cataclysm as the end of their troubles. Lenine urges that production is as necessary under the Soviet government, as under the Czar's government, and that the people must learn to work more efficiently. He urges the need of introducing the Taylor system of business efficiency. Labor in America has depreciated the introduction of this system as tending to a speeding up of industry that would be detrimental to the workers. Yet the Bolsheviki leaders advocate it! Further, Lenine justifies the employment of highly paid bourgeois specialists on the ground that the workers have not as yet men in their own ranks who are trained to conduct modern business enterprises. Lenine frankly states that the government has taken over more industries than it is able to manage, and that it is necessary to call a halt in order to consolidate the ground already under control ... It reflects no discredit on the Bolsheviki that so soon they are learning to adopt a constructive policy. But decidedly it is a warning to us that we cannot hope at one fell swoop to reconstruct our economic system.[118]

The above was written in January 1919, not two years after the October revolution. It was a curiously early criticism of the Russian revolution and it put him out of step with most of his left-wing comrades, Marxists and non-Marxists alike, for whom 1917 was still a beacon of socialist promise, unity, and celebration. To Woodsworth the manner of Lenin's triumph owed everything to peculiar Russian circumstances and so offered little example to Canada. The dictatorship of the proletariat and the use of force were, perhaps, appropriate as the means whereby Czarism and sundry other autocracies had been and would be terminated; and in Russia a 'benevolent working class dictatorship' was certainly preferable to a 'callous bureaucratic dictatorship,' but it was not the 'co-operative commonwealth.'[119] Also, he had qualms about the centralizing of power that violent revolution seemed to bring about. As the BC *Federationist* reported: '[Woodsworth] confessed he was somewhat of an anarchist – that is, that though state control might be an intermediate stage, the end was self-determination – that each man was able to express his own life in his own way. So with physical force – what was won by physical force must be held by physical force.'[120]

There were two other significant elements in his disagreement with Marxism. In keeping with his idealist approach, Woodsworth espoused a voluntarist notion of political action; that is, he rejected the fatalism of Marxists who held that there was little point in organizing and hurrying along the revolution.[121] And, finally, disagreement prevailed over what were called at that time 'palliatives.' Woodsworth, although a utopian, could be remarkably sensitive to the vagaries and absurdities of history. Change never quite occurred in expected or hoped-for ways; it often took unique, local forms; it would not necessarily obtain, all at once, a total transformation of society. Sometimes change would produce only limited advances; or indeed it might fall to a particular generation not to make any improvements at all but to consolidate whatever incremental progress had already been made. There was no universal archetype of change; socialist politics must be adaptable and multiform. Woodsworth espoused a politics of what might be called 'principled opportunism':

We believe in opportunism and compromise in securing practical reforms, but never when they involve the abandonment of the hope of attaining the ultimate goal, or the sacrifice of vital principles. Without losing sight of our ultimate object, we believe in taking advantage of every opportunity to better our conditions. In this way we attain a stronger position from which to carry on the fight.[122]

In our sense – and, in our sense only – we are opportunists. We refuse to compromise our principles but we regard every foot of ground taken as a

distinct gain, and sometimes we would even pause to 'consolidate' our position before advancing to another attack.

Popular education, shorter hours, prohibition of intoxicating liquors, prohibition of child labour – these and similar 'reforms' are advocated not as
'palliatives,' but as various means by which we may increase our fighting
efficiency.[123]

Needless to say, to many Marxists such reforms were indeed 'palliatives,' since they drew the sting of the revolutionary discontent of the
workers. Woodsworth did not agree; limited reforms could be won
without compromising or postponing the final goal. (As we shall see,
he never quite explained satisfactorily how this juxtaposition of ends
and means was to be obtained.) To Woodsworth, Marxists, in rejecting
'palliatives,' were morally obtuse and contradictory:

Public ownership even under the present system may reduce my light bills
from ten to three cents per kilowat hour; trades unionism may dam back the
tendency for wages to drop to the level of subsistence; co-operative stores may
eliminate one toll gate on the profiteers' wad, yet some doctrinaire marxians
will stoutly maintain that none of these things are of any advantage whatever
to me. He will so claim even while he works for them and votes for them.
Surely he is not very different from the Christian 'Scientist' who gets the
dentist to extract an aching tooth, or the 'orthodox' christian who advocates a
Jewish pogrom.

As again some 'scientific' orthodox 'Marxians' will unblushingly declare that
men are actuated only by meal-ticket motives at the very time that they are
sacrificing everything for the movement.

Comrades, the scientific spirit never ignores facts whether these relate to
economic conditions or human nature. If our theories do not square with the
facts so much worse for the theories. Probably they only need a re-statement or
a further understanding. Down with dogmatism![124]

If, then, Marxism and Bolshevism were deficient, how should the
Left in British Columbia proceed? Ironically, given his early preference
for an indigenous, Canadian socialism, Woodsworth's prescribed
model for the FLP was the British Labour Party (BLP). Writing in January
1919 he declared the latter's report on post-war reconstruction, known
later as 'Labour and the New Social Order,' 'the most adequate presentation of the aims of Labor which has ever been put forth by a
responsible political party.'[125] To Woodsworth the BLP was broadly

based and inclusive, in regard to both class and ideology. It had chosen to unite all workers by hand and by brain, and its program, if anything, rejected dense theory in the name of a general socialist plan of action against the established order. Finally, the BLP was exemplary because it pursued its aims democratically and constitutionally.

Kenneth McNaught interprets Woodsworth's predilection for the British Labour Party as confirmation of his commitment, primarily, to gradualism and, indeed, to all the other liberal qualities of social democracy.[126] Woodsworth's thinking in 1918–19, he asserts, displayed pragmatism, was 'averse to easy answers,' and expressed a 'sceptical individualism ... a common-sense approach ... [and] a moderate political stand'; that is Woodsworth was already a model revisionist, a liberal-socialist. Certainly there is no disputing Woodsworth's decided anti-Marxism, and McNaught's judgment that there were important liberal properties in his thought is undoubtedly correct. But McNaught's general characterization is tendentious and fails to catch the subtleties of Woodsworth's mental world at that time. Woodsworth, in fact, eschewed identifying himself as a revisionist. As for McNaught's claim that Woodsworth was a gradualist, it is even more misleading. A careful reading of the sources will reveal that, in espousing the 'British way,' Woodsworth was certainly being anti-Marxist but he was also consciously turning away from the sort of gradualism and reformism that McNaught imputes to him. To Woodsworth there was a third way, a 'bloodless,' democratic revolution:

How is the vision of Labor to be realized? Some say by gradual – very gradual – reform. But Labor has become impatient of delay and suspicious either of the sincerity or the clear-headedness of those who advocate such a policy. Some think that the better day can be ushered in only by a bloody revolution. But it would seem that what is won by force must be held by force and a state maintained by force is not the co-operative commonwealth of which we dream.

When the people are ready for it revolution is inevitable – rather it is an already accomplished fact. Education is the getting people ready. A part of this education is organization. A social era involves social action. The extent to which we have advanced towards Socialism is indicated by the degree to which we have developed effective organizations. Such organizations are in themselves the government and would automatically replace the individuals and institutions that now function as 'the State.'[127]

At the end of the war Woodsworth was deeply convinced that history was at a turning-point. The years 1918–19 were a watershed; there was no going back to the pre-war world. His inveterate utopianism, fed by apocalyptic imagery, led him to this conclusion, as did the fundamental changes to public policy brought on by the war effort and the political upheavals of the time, especially the Russian and German revolutions. The language he employed to denote the impending transformation was radical in the extreme.[128] What was imminent was 'a new social order,' 'a complete turnover of the present economic and social system.' There was a need for 'reconstructing society':

[Established leaders] don't seem to be able to get it into their heads that in their sense of the terms there 'ain't goin' to be no' reconstruction – that the workers have received a revelation of a new heaven and a new earth for the first heaven and the first earth are passed away. So the workers generally prefer the term revolution to the term reconstruction. Only on the basis of a new social and economic order are they willing to plan reconstruction.[129]

Some of the reddest of the 'Reds' have condemned the [report on reconstruction] as 'sloppy – a programme of reform rather than a revolutionary appeal.' Undoubtedly, the form is not such as will appeal to doctrinaire Socialists and the methods advocated are peaceful and constitutional. But the document is anything but sloppy, and the programme most thorough-going ... All this involves no mere 'reforms,' but rather a complete economic and social revolution.[130]

A revolution, then, was imperative and it was to be consummated democratically. But this did not mean that its attainment would be extended over many generations. Woodsworth was not using the notion of revolution casually. In his earlier years he occasionally described relatively small marks of social progress as 'revolutionary' or as examples of 'socialization.'[131] However, by 1918–19 he was clear that 'revolution' meant a wholesale, structural transformation of existing society and, if not the immediate, at least the rapid dispossessing of the ruling classes' power and wealth. At this point in his intellectual development Woodsworth may be faulted for naivety but not for sceptical gradualism.

It was to the British Labour Party that Woodsworth turned in support of the possibility of democratic revolution. Unlike the Russians, who had been 'impulsive' and 'hot-headed' in their pursuit of change, the English displayed a mien of atheoretical practicality and patience. But by no means did this make their political methods less revolutionary:

Most socialist manifestos analyze the existing system and then proceed to prophesy the revolution that will usher in the new social order. The Labor Party's report says very little about theories, but English-like, at once gets down to business and asks two questions: First, what do we want? Second, how are we to get it?

What do we want? Again, English-like, instead of demanding the whole loaf and then gratefully accepting a slice, the report modestly asks for a slice, and then proceeds to eat the whole loaf. We want education, leisure, recreation not for a few privileged folk, but for all the people ... We want the democratic control of industry ... All this involves no mere 'reforms', but rather a complete economic and social revolution. This becomes clearer when we ask the second question: 'How are we to get what we want?'

Good hours, good wages, leisure, education, opportunities for all, socialization of industries, surplus revenues – how are we to secure all these? The Labor Party does not suggest confiscation but in the long run it very effectively confiscates private capital.[132]

The Labour Party's scheme of socialization involved not the outright, immediate dispossession of the landowners and capitalists, but rather proceeded more slowly with an income tax policy with high marginal rates combined with a deep-cutting inheritance tax. The net effect would, in Woodsworth's view, be confiscatory as well, but on the fair-weather side of democracy and constitutionality. After exemptions had been put in place for those of modest incomes, an income tax would begin at miniscule rates but rise steeply so that for the wealthy there would be a marginal rate of nineteen shillings in the pound. What remained of the wealth of the privileged classes would be captured at death. An inheritance tax would be premised on the principle of 'naked a man comes into the world and naked he leaves it.' It was to be all so bloodless and efficient; socialism by legal and constitutional means, within a generation: 'A few respectable funerals and private capitalism will be a thing of the past ... Done for good.'[133] By his own intellectual lights he should have been less confident, for in other contexts at this time he made it clear that the ruling class of businessmen, politicians, military, and church exerted a tight control over the state system of even parliamentary democracies. Yet his

optimism was incorrigible. Not only could wealth be confiscated democratically and constitutionally but the building of the new society could
proceed without disruption; there could be revolution without tears or
inconvenience. How to undertake transformative change had been a
concern of Woodsworth since his days in the church. Then, it will be
remembered, he had raised the dilemma of putting new wine in old
bottles. In 1918–19, he concluded that society did not need to choose; it
could enjoy and consume the old at the same time as the latest vintage
was being bottled:

Sometimes in the reconstruction of a large hotel or store, it is necessary to
continue to do business on the premises. The new building is designed
without reference to the old; broad, deep foundations are laid; the walls rise
steadily skyward; great arches are constructed, beautiful rooms are finished
now in this part of the building and again in that. All the time in spite of
building activities and scaffolding, the old business goes steadily on. The old
roof is not removed till the new roof is completed. Something after this fashion
the Labor Party seeks to reconstruct society. The new must not be limited by
the old, but there must be no unnecessary dislocation of trade, no suffering for
the people while the transition from the old to the new is being made.[134]

For Woodsworth all of this foregoing analysis of the proper goals
and strategy of the FLP could not but be exploratory and preliminary.
Woodsworth was feeling his way. Apart from the Canadian Labor
Party (CLP), with which he had had little contact, there was no indigenous model of the sort of national party he envisaged. (While Woodsworth was, at this time, a champion of the FLP, his political coordinates
were, clearly, national.) Otherwise, there were only the examples of
several local, provincial labourist parties, especially in Manitoba. None
of them had established much permanence and towards them he had
in any event preserved an attitude of benevolent independence. What
he *was* certain of was that there was a ferment of discontent in Canada
among workers and farmers, especially in the west, and among middle-
class professionals. To galvanize this unrest, some inclusive party was
necessary. The FLP, he believed, represented the local, initial response
of British Columbia. But there were still many unanswered and ill-
defined questions in his mind.

It therefore was not a little fortuitous that a reconstituted British
Labour Party was at hand at the very same time as Woodsworth made
his unprecedented commitment to left-wing party politics. Partly he

embraced the BLP because of anglophilic admiration; maybe he implicitly recognized that the British example might be especially convincing to a people still imbued with strong imperialist sentiments. There was also, perhaps, the aesthetic appeal that grew out of the intellectual coherence of the BLP's draft program, the work mainly of Sidney Webb.[135] Finally, and not least, there was the obvious fact that, in the important respect of it being an open, broad party seeking revolutionary change constitutionally, the BLP with its new constitution and program in 1918 corresponded to his own deeply held beliefs. Woodsworth could not know of the complex manoeuvres among Arthur Henderson, the BLP leader, the parliamentary caucus, the trade unions, and the Independent Labour Party that had preceded this historic self-definition.[136] From his distant perspective he knew two things: that the BLP could be successfully imitated by the FLP, and that what would be imitated, intellectually speaking, would be 'socialism.'

No sooner had the FLP been given life than it seemed about to expire because of the turning of much of the Left in British Columbia towards industrial action and the idea of the general strike. Woodsworth's position here was unmysterious. He did not deny the utility of industrial action of whatever kind, including the general, sympathetic strike, as long as it was undertaken in conjunction with a commitment to parliamentary politics.[137] By itself, he argued, industrial syndicalism was deficient since its overly economic focus left untouched such institutions of the state as the courts, army, and parliament. He regarded the idea of the one big union as nothing more exceptional than industrial workers deducing for themselves, as business already had, the integrative implications of growing industrial and organizational amalgamation and centralization. What cannot be found in Woodsworth was any inclination to abandon politics altogether in favour of an economic strategy.

In February 1919, in the last of the *BC Federationist* articles, Woodsworth took stock of six months of intense political activity and speculation.[138] He admitted that there were many matters still to be clarified. Labour's voice was still indistinct and muted. Wartime censorship, the banning of the national Social Democratic Party, the breaking up of meetings, and the arrest of leaders had taken their toll. Also, labour was still divided, the result of differences over war aims and policy and disagreements between a 'conservative' east and a 'radical' west. Yet a new unity was emerging. In British Columbia, he believed, there was a growing 'movement,' albeit one expressing itself in such different organizations as the FLP, the SPC, and trade unions. For its part the FLP believed in industrial *and* political action, and, although it lacked a 'detailed programme,' it was animated by a deep resolve to overthrow capitalism:

As a member of this party, and for purposes of discussion, may I venture to interpret the attitude of the party towards the problems that face Labor at the present time. The party is in no sense responsible for the views here presented:
1. The party accepts the draft programme of the British Labor Party as expressing in general the viewpoint and aims of this party.
2. The party looks forward to the formation of a truly Canadian Labor Party broad enough to include or to work in closest co-operation with organizations of farmers and returned soldiers.
3. The ultimate object of the party is the collective ownership and democratic operation of the means of wealth production. This involves a complete revolution in our whole economic and social structure.
4. Such a revolution may, we believe, be brought about by the peaceable methods of education, organization and the securing by the workers of the control of the ministry of government.
5. In the attainment of its objective the party realizes that many obstacles must be successfully overcome and ever changing problems dealt with. The programme must of necessity vary to meet the needs of new situations as they arise. A party in the minority cannot effectively advocate far-reaching measures that are possible when the party is returned with a majority.
6. The promotion of an immediately practicable programme is not in any sense a compromise of principle or a relinquishment of ultimate aims, but rather an advance as far forward as, under the circumstances, seems possible.[139]

In passing, it should be noted that, without denying his anti-Marxism, Woodsworth still found room within the movement for the SPC. Such broadmindedness was not always reciprocated. One N. Booth, a member of the SPC in Prince Rupert, referred to Woodsworth's theories in May 1919 as 'consummate twaddle,' confirmation perhaps that local Marxists were recognizing early on his leading role on behalf of labourism.[140]

In popular history Woodsworth has become the one figure indelibly identified with the Winnipeg General Strike. Such was his apparent importance, it might almost be believed that he instigated the strike, prolonged its life and, in the aftermath, was the primary victim of the judicial prosecution that took place. In fact, Woodsworth did not take part in the strike's planning and he arrived on the scene after the strike was already three weeks underway. He did speak on the workers' behalf and he distinguished himself by filling the breach as an editor of the *Strike Bulletin* after William Ivens was arrested. Yet others bore much more the brunt of the state's judicial reaction. The non-British-born who were arrested have largely been overlooked by history. Of the Canadian and British-born who were arrested and charged, Woodsworth endured the least suffering and inconvenience. He might even have welcomed his martyrdom a little.[141] He spent five nights in jail but the charge against him of seditious libel was less serious than the charges laid against the other strikers, except Dixon's, and, in the end, the Crown stayed proceedings.

On 9 June, the day after he reached Winnipeg, Woodsworth spoke to the Labor Church.[142] He boasted of his United Empire Loyalist background, no doubt in large measure to squelch the view that the strike was an alien conspiracy, and commended the strikers for their non-violence. On 12 June he published an open letter in the *Strike Bulletin* to his 'old Winnipeg friends.' Recounting his long experience with the Winnipeg Trades and Labor Council, on the docks, and with the FLP in Vancouver, Woodsworth claimed to be at one with the workers. Yet he also claimed to know the minds of the business and professional classes: 'they are not all the hard-hearted hypocrites pictured by perfervid orators':

Further, this strike is not, in the least, in the ordinary acceptance of the word 'revolutionary.' It is true that as the French Revolution stirred Europe, so the overthrow of the old bureaucratic Tzarist regime has caught the imagination of the working classes of the world ... It is true that many Socialists in the working classes despair of radical economic changes being brought about by parliamentary action. But even these, who are in the small minority, recognize the absurdity of using physical force in Canada ... The overwhelming majority of labor people say that they are British, not Russians, and are quite content to do things in the British way. But remember, the British way is much more radical than most Canadian employers realize!

In reality this strike has nothing to do with Revolution. It is an attempt to meet a very pressing and immediate need. The organized workers like every-one else are faced with the high cost of living. Most of them are not economists. Like most people they imagine that if they can get higher wages they can buy more food. They are out for higher wages.[143]

Finally, Woodsworth argued that, faced with miserable conditions, workers had no recourse but to strike. Apportioning blame was pointless; what was necessary was to uncover the causes of human poverty in order to overcome them. He ended with a clarion call to reasonable men on all sides to come together: 'We sit stupidly by; attempt to negotiate on technical points and the strike goes on. The city is being ruined; untold hardships lie ahead; there is imminent danger of bloodshed, and nothing is done. The crisis calls for extraordinary measures. Troops and more troops will not settle the question. Constructive radical action must come sometime. Why not now? Let me assure my friends that the strikers are as kindly and as reasonable people as they are. If only the public could understand the real position, we might have peace.'[144]

Even after the events of 'Bloody Saturday' ten days later Woodsworth continued to pursue this last theme in an article entitled 'Is There a way Out?'[145] Without denying his solidarity with the strikers, Woodsworth argued that irreconcilable conflict must breed disaster. The two sides were like 'two unkind goats meet[ing] on a narrow bridge and each insist[ing] on fighting it out.' Whoever won, the public interest would be harmed. Admittedly, in setting the terms of his conciliatory approach, Woodsworth did so more than a little to the advantage of the workers; but, equally, as we shall see, he committed himself to policies that he had recently rejected as unacceptable. Thus 'cooperation' for him could entail, in practice, a posture of compromise and contradiction.

There were three parts to what he believed 'reasonable' far-seeing employers and political leaders must embrace. First, an acceptance by the state of a duty to find a job for everyone, at a living wage; secondly, the appointment of an economic commission with extraordinary powers 'to suggest and to enforce radical and far-reaching policies, powers, if found necessary to actually keep the business of the country going.' Both proposals, he believed, grew logically out of the actual practices of governments in Britain and Canada during the war. He turned to the British for his final suggestion: industrial democracy in the form of joint worker-employer committees, which became known as Whitley councils. Woodsworth's language on this point was enlightening. The 'British way' now stood not for efficient, democratic revolution but for expediency and muddling through: 'Behind the whole question of collective bargaining and the sympathetic strike lies the question of the democratic control of industry. The British Government is attempting to solve this most important problem by creating new machinery in the form of industrial councils. These are not solutions proposed by the workers, but apparently they have been successful in forming a sort of *modus vivendi*. That, after all, is the British way. Adopt some temporary expedient by which we can keep things going and then, someway, a policy gradually shapes itself.'[146] Not six months earlier he had resoundingly rejected the Whitley council concept: 'The industrial council could not be carried out under the conditions which prevail in Canada. Indeed the Whitley report has little to offer that attracts the Canadian worker.'[147]

In the General Strike, Woodsworth attempted to ride two horses: sympathy for the strikers and a cooperative attitude towards business. In the end the final repressive measures of the authorities made impossible his search for bi-partisan ground. It would not, however, be the end of his penchant for accommodation and reconciliation.

In his five 'What Next?' articles in the *Western Labor News* in July–August 1919 Woodsworth attempted to absorb the implications of that monumental Winnipeg spring. Given the likely unsettling effect of the strike, perhaps most remarkable was the large measure of continuity that existed with his earlier pieces in the *Federationist*.[148] In the first two *Labor News* articles, the example of the British Labour Party was again proffered and he reiterated the need to transform the present state of society by peaceful methods rather than by bloody revolution. Industrial democracy was once more recommended and he encouraged the use of 'both political and industrial power and any other legitimate power at our disposal.' Where there was a significant advance over the earlier articles was in his specifying, for the first time, a list of 'immediate demands.' The measures proposed were the repeal of repressive wartime laws and regulations; economic opportunities for demobilized soldiers; provisions by the state of work for all, with a living wage and equal pay for equal work irrespective of sex or nationality; imposition of a capital levy to pay for the war debt; and, finally, schemes to encourage agriculture.[149]

The remaining three articles were given over to a listing of the long-range goals of the non-Marxist Left: extensive 'socialization'; universal, public services such as medical, hospital care, and education; social insurance covering unemployment, accident, sickness, and old age; and far-reaching political changes. Some elements in this congeries of utopian prescriptions, though not exactly new, had only now risen to such programmatic significance on Woodsworth's political horizon. Before the 'What Next?' series, he had not specified in such detail his commitment to public ownership. All but personal goods and chattels, the land of small farmers, and the assets of small businessmen were to be socialized; transport and communication companies, mines and natural resources, banks and insurance companies, and manufacturing and commercial institutions were to be brought under public ownership. Perhaps because of this degree of socialism, he implied a much greater recognition than before of the need for an extensive public-planning establishment. New as well were several of the arguments he used to justify social ownership. Hitherto he had mainly used the justificatory principle that, since monopolies were such coordinated and interdependent entities, that is, were essentially 'social' organizations, they should be publicly owned. In these articles Woodsworth employed additional arguments: that some services were essential; that credit was a public utility; and that natural resources belonged to the people.

Moreover, the 'What Next?' articles contained a strong commitment to women's rights. The Woodsworth of *My Neighbor*, with his desire to protect women from the 'temptations' of the workplace, saloon, and picture-theatre and, to preserve their proper role in the home, had disappeared by 1919. Earlier, in a speech in March 1919 on 'Women's Relation to Social Change,' he had embarked on a profoundly original analysis. The slavery of women, he dramatically announced, was soon to end – thanks to the machine. The *BC Federationist* reported Woodsworth's remarks as follows:

The introduction of machinery, which had socialized industry, had so far been the means of exploiting both men and women; it would however, in [Woodsworth's] view, prove ultimately to be the means of emancipation. Even now, the housewife was relieved of a great deal of her work by help from the outside; on the other hand, her daughter was now going out into the world to do work that was formerly done inside the home. The laundry, the soap-works, the cook-shop, the textile factory and the department-store were all illustrations of this change; the school, the public library, and even the picture-show were further examples ... Woman's work in the home was going away from her, and she consequently had to get out, too, and follow it. 'Forever and forever the old home-life is gone,' declared [Woodsworth]. They could not bring the old times back; the most they could do was to keep the best that old home-life had contained.[150]

Woodsworth continued: traditionally, women had either been pampered and worshipped within marriage or exploited by industry without. Women wanted neither, but wished to be the equal 'companions' of men. According to the *BC Federationist*:

[Woodsworth] scorned the view that the excuse of sexual functions constituted the be-all and end-all of women's existence. She would come to be recognized as a 'pal', and there would be many sides to her nature that would be developed. On the other hand, he looked for a recognition of the naturalness and sacredness of the sexual relationship in the new social order; even now, children were being instructed on such subjects as 'where the baby comes from ...' ... Celibacy, he declared, as a feature of 'holiness', was 'the most abominable doctrine ever taught.' Were their own mothers less holy, less pure, and less good than those who had been kept shut up in convents and the like? There was 'nothing more beautiful or tender than the normal relationships that may exist between men and women.' [Woodsworth] in conclusion strongly condemned the position taken by law and custom with regard to birth control. In the new social order he believed the prospective mother would be allowed to say whether she wished her child to be brought into the world or not.[51]

So in 'What Next?,' it fell naturally to him to recommend that women should receive equal pay for equal work; that, as he awkwardly put it, 'the financial burden of race preservation,' the raising of children, should be borne by the state in the form of equal wages for homemakers; and, finally, that all women should have the vote.

The 'What Next?' articles enumerated a list of political reforms. Again, with few exceptions these had circulated in his thought before, but only now did he bring them together in a coherent statement. Starting from what he believed was the indisputable premise that Parliament was not representative of the people, first, because certain groups were dis- or un-enfranchised and, secondly, because economic interests financed and therefore controlled both established political parties, Woodsworth recommended a mixture of universal adult suffrage, proportional representation, and the initiative and recall. An intriguing addition to the list was political syndicalism. He referred to the possibility of an occupational basis of election to some mysterious 'administrative body.' It is unclear whether he meant the cabinet, the bureaucracy, or central-planning agencies. What *was* unambiguous was his view that one of the houses in a bicameral system might be elected by occupation.

In a highly industrialized society the old geographical system does not seem to meet the case. For instance six machinists work side by side in the same workshop. They live in six different wards surrounded by shopkeepers, lawyers, doctors, etc. At election times they vote for six different candidates, none of whom they know personally. Men are more closely united 'on the job' than they are by residing in the same district. Why should not the machinists or those engaged in the iron industry have their representation?

In times of special need this form of representation is used. Representation of the Canadian Manufacturers' Association, of the Canadian Council of Agriculture and of the Trades and Labor Congress are called in for consultation. If we retain two chambers one chamber might be elected along the old geographical lines. [152]

Woodsworth concluded with a call for Canada's complete constitutional sovereignty and for greater international cooperation through free trade and the adjudication of international disputes under the auspices of a 'democratic league of peoples,' by which he made clear he did not mean the League of Nations as then constituted. The latter themes especially occupied him later in his political life.

VI

By 1921 Woodsworth seemed to have travelled a great distance from 1909 and *Strangers within Our Gates*. The Methodist Church was far behind him and his thought was unabashedly secular and rationalist. Indeed more sense can be made of him in 1921 if he is seen as a free-thinking deist and humanist rather than a social gospeller, even a radical one. The nativist solecisms of his early years had been moderated, although they would never disappear, and his socialism was more thorough and radical. Also, he had abandoned much of the liberal individualism of his youth. Yet continuities were aplenty. Christian thought-forms and images still leapt automatically to his mind, so that disentangling the theological and rationalist origins of his world view is perhaps next to impossible. Other elements also remained: a progressive, optimistic view of history, a high regard for science and social planning, and a belief in evolutionary, parliamentary change. Especially striking was his continued belief in social unity, although in 1909 his conception was of unity on behalf of the Anglo-Canadian nation and individualist values while in 1921 it was on behalf of the cause of cooperation. In both cases he gave short shrift to the value of intermediate, local, or partial communities, always focusing attention on an all-encompassing, inclusive Canadian national state as the primary political community.

In 1921 Woodsworth was on the threshold of an auspicious political career. How prepared was he for the novel tests of the 1920s and 1930s? The answer is that he went forth with many matters unresolved and untidily defined. There were several glaring contradictions in his world view. His settled judgments were clear: the importance of parliamentary politics; the unsuitability of violence and yet the need for transformative change; a distributivist notion of class. But overlying these were several paradoxes: the use of revolutionary language here but eschewing it there; holding that change must make a complete break with the past but later suggesting a more syncretic, continuous pattern; and preaching the imminence of a new heaven and new earth, but then drawing back to press caution upon those who would fatuously assume that history's vagaries and contingencies could produce immediate, predictable, and gratifying outcomes. Woodsworth combined an indulgently idealistic rhetoric with a cold-blooded and sometimes faint-hearted prudence of action. He was a philosophical extremist with the tentativeness of a cautious political operative.

There were other contradictions and ambiguities. Because of his respect for the ironies of history, Woodsworth espoused a politics of principled opportunism. He desired non-violent revolutionary change that would be combined with a sensitivity to exigent circumstances. In his view there was a vast array of historical possibilities that socialists might have to confront. Socialists should do what they could; they should have a conception of long-range goals but also a clear idea of immediate and attainable demands. But how were all these strategic calculations to be made without compromising essential principles? Woodsworth himself was only too aware of the problem, as he was as well of the particular possibility that a politics of limited demands could have the perverse effect not of incrementally realizing the cooperative commonwealth but of reinforcing the legitimacy of the established society through a policy on the latter's part of strategic concessions.[153] Even in a minority situation in Parliament the possibilities were numerous: coalition government, obstruction, radical abstentionism, uncompromising opposition, or negotiation and compromise. On all these issues Woodsworth was silent or unenlightening. He was unambiguous in his anti-Marxism but not overly clear-headed in laying down strategic guidelines for a parliamentary road to socialism.

Curiously, Woodsworth had in fact contemplated the intellectual possibility of contradiction. Discussing antinomies and the idea of contrary laws within one more general law, he concluded that 'pushing things to their logical conclusion you usually come bang up against a practical absurdity.'[154] Woodsworth's early thought was riddled with antinomies. A criticism of him might be that, in being too fearful of absurdity, he did not push hard enough to resolve what were perhaps only chimerical contradictions. In not making the effort he entered on a course of socialist politics with a personal political calculus that was often little more than an attitude of 'on the one hand ... and on the other.'

Woodsworth's eldest son, Charles, once revealed that his father never could quite bring himself to believe reports that businessmen at their hunting lodges engaged in hard drinking and womanizing.[155] As innocent, perhaps, were aspects of his espousal of the 'British way' in the years immediately after the First World War. Woodsworth consciously placed himself between the Scylla and Charybdis of ineffectual gradualism and violent revolution, an intermediate position that held out the possibility of peaceful, constitutional revolution. The British way of deeply biting income and inheritance taxes would, he thought, not be as rapid as Bolshevism but it would be as thorough in its confiscatory effects. Woodsworth could know little of the difficulties actual socialist governments would confront in pursuing radical policies. Even so, someone more worldly wise than he might have anticipated some of the likely obstacles in the way of a 'democratic' policy of avowed and categorical confiscation. The social gospel, it has been sometimes said, lacked a doctrine of sin. Woodsworth certainly lacked a doctrine of the immanence of evil, at least in regard to the imaginable behaviour of powerful economic classes facing their own approaching extinction.

Yet, while he showed naivety towards businessmen, he was extremely suspicious of Marxism. True, he was not wholly uncooperative towards Marxists, at least at this time. But even in the dawn of triumphant Bolshevism he showed signs of deep disquiet. To make his case against the dogmatism of Marxism Woodsworth availed himself of the arguments for scepticism inherent in the positivist tradition. Science, he claimed, did not establish eternal truths but rather a sense of the variability and multiplicity of existence. This must lead to a disposition of openness, uncertainty, and tolerance. Woodsworth turned such a doctrine mainly against Marxist class theory. However, his own account of class was just as arbitrarily derived and thus as uncertain and provisional as the Marxists'. Indeed a corrosive scepticism was not applied to his own early world view. When one remembers the range of claims that he confidently asserted – the progressive nature of history, the propinquity of revolutionary change, the coalescence of class interest of workers, farmers, and small businessmen, the etiology of criminality and mental illness, the origins of industrialism, the demise of the family – it is clear that his 'undogmatic scepticism' masked a supreme self-confidence about what he himself believed.

3

Politics, Parliament, and Revolution, 1922–1940

These are the darkest years:
When old forms of thought,
The old customs,
The old systems,
Are beaten at last to dust,
Soil for the world to be!

Anna Louise Strong
(Reprinted in J.S. Woodsworth, *Hours That Stand Apart*, 1929)

As I write, my train is rushing forward through the night carrying me homeward. The universe too is driving onward – we may well believe it is toward some goal and inspired by some increasing purpose. But as I rest back in my seat in the car, I must confess that I am not bothering about the road-bed or the train dispatchers or even possible accidents. I am being carried forward – that is enough. So in his study of phenomena or in his dealing with practical affairs, the modern man is not worrying much about first causes or final causes. He is absorbed in the consideration of the process itself. His faith is shown in his reliance upon the force which seems to be driving the world onward and upward.

J.S. Woodsworth, 'My Religion,' 1926

I

The image of life as a train journey was particularly apposite to Woodsworth. On his election to the House of Commons in December

1921, he gathered up his wife and children from British Columbia and settled them in Ottawa. Later, in 1925, he set up domestic headquarters in Winnipeg, first at 67 Chestnut Street and then at 60 Maryland. Each year he would journey to Ottawa for the new session of the House which usually began in January and lasted until June or July. On weekends he would make speaking trips to places in eastern Canada. During the recess he travelled the length of Canada on his railroad pass, speaking as often as two hundred times a year to all sorts of groups. The frail man with the vandyke beard, oddly shaped ears, and well-worn, conservatively tailored suit must have been an incongruous sight, sitting in the tourist section with a suitcase and golf-bag. In the latter were the charts and paraphernalia that illustrated his lectures on the spider's web of connections which, he thought, constituted the structure of economic and political power in Canada.[1]

The tireless traveller spent endless hours alone. Only an extraordinary faith could have sustained him. He convinced himself that he was making history. Sometimes he implied that the journey was all that mattered; motion, process, and becoming were everything – the destination was inconsequential. This was, of course, not completely how he saw it. There *was* an end or goal and it was summed up in the idea of cooperation; socialism was an inevitable tendency within Canadian society. The conviction of being borne along by the very 'forces' of history and progress[2] no doubt sustained him during long, dark nights. Yet his practical realism was in equal proportion to his metaphysical optimism. He had few illusions about the difficulties confronting the Canadian Left in the early 1920s:

A number of factors contribute to render very difficult the formation and expression of new ideas and policies in Canada. There is a lack of the sense of national responsibility. We have not outgrown either our colonial status or the colonial psychology ... Economically and socially we live under the shadow of our great southern neighbour. Our young life is drained off to the American cities; our intellectual leaders are constantly tempted toward larger fields.

The heterogeneous character of our population prevents cultural unity. Exclude the French and the Jewish and other non-British groups and judged by the standards of Toronto, Montreal is about the size of Hamilton. In the West, there are large unassimilated blocks of Europeans who live in Canada in the flesh but spiritually live still in the old world. Ultimately these various cultures may blend into something new and higher. At present, they are almost mutually exclusive.

The problem is further complicated by our vast distances, geographical barriers, and provincial institutions ... Canada has attained constitutional unity before she has developed a national ideal.[3]

Cultural and geographic obstacles to progressive politics were exacerbated by other impediments. Trade unionism was weak and divided; and labour parties were, with minor exceptions, ill-organized and electorally ineffective. Only among the farmers were there signs of political vitality. To Woodsworth the future was unclear as he journeyed to Ottawa in early 1922. He could not know that his political cause would eventually be electorally unsuccessful and that parliamentary socialism would, in his lifetime, always be a decidedly minority phenomenon. The forces of electoral history were 'kind' to him only in one instance – when he and A.A. Heaps held the balance of power for a few months in 1926. Otherwise his twenty years in Parliament were a period of Liberal hegemony under Mackenzie King, with a Conservative interregnum between 1930 and 1935 under R.B. Bennett.

Throughout his public life Woodsworth was resolute in his opposition to both established national parties. But, at least until 1934, if he had to choose he said he preferred the Liberals.[4] On the evidence of *Industry and Humanity* and the Liberal platform, he believed that King was a free trader and reformer. He also recognized that the electoral base of the Liberal Party was one that any successful national party of the Left would itself have to appropriate. In contrast, the Conservatives were the party of protectionism and social reaction.[5] As long as Arthur Meighen was their leader Woodsworth maintained a special animus towards them as the party of Section 98 and the political repression of the Winnipeg General Strike.[6] His judgment of Bennett was, at least before 1934, no more charitable. In 1932, at the height of the Depression, Woodsworth portrayed Bennett as a demented ship's captain destined to destroy himself and his ship. It was as damning a critique of a Canadian prime minister as the Commons ever heard: 'The season was becoming late, ice floes were gradually pressing in, and there were only one or two avenues of escape left. The crew became almost mutinous, and even the officers ... were getting dubious and urging that he should turn south while it was still possible to do so. Then one night at a late hour, the ship's doctor ... unexpectedly

... came upon the captain performing some mystic rites. All of a sudden the doctor realized that the captain was mad, that here they were in these far northern waters with every avenue of escape rapidly closing up and the ship commanded by a captain utterly irresponsible as a navigator.'[7]

Woodsworth quickly recognized that Mackenzie King was also a conservative of sorts, ever beholden to the protectionist and reactionary interests in his caucus from Quebec and Ontario.[8] He also came to see him as a prevaricator and procrastinator, a man of unceasing bombast and guile, who sought an opening to the Left on the hustings but who, once in power, used *laissez-faire* doctrine and the strict letter of the BNA Act to prevent reform.[9] After Bennett had apparently embraced public planning and economic intervention in 1934, Woodsworth's opinion of the Conservative Party changed markedly.[10] The philosophy of that party, he now claimed, had all along been committed to the directive state and was far better positioned than free-market individualism to capture the inevitable contemporary trend towards cooperation. Unreconstructed Canadian liberalism, as embodied in the Liberal Party, risked extinction and could well go the way of British Gladstonian liberalism.[11] Liberalism had fought mighty historic battles for political freedom but had failed to recognize that by itself political liberty in an era of economic monopolies was irrelevant. None the less, it was the Liberals who were returned to office in 1935. In 1936 Woodsworth described the Liberal Party's philosophy as follows: 'Do nothing. Wait. Appoint a committee. Do something later.'[12]

The federal election of 1921 broke the two-party mould of post-Confederation politics. Woodsworth and Irvine were part of this auspicious moment but more so was the large Progressive caucus. Woodsworth knew Canadian prairie society intimately and he always sought to include farmers within the base of appeal of a national left-wing party. But even as early as 1921 he was not altogether at one with the Progressives. Of course he favoured free trade but, unlike the 'Manitoban' strain of progressivism, he did not regard a low-tariff policy as a panacea for the country's ills. The root of the economic problem was industrial concentration; and free trade, he believed, did little to change that reality.[13] Also, by the 1920s, Woodsworth was beginning to show the effects of his reading of Hobson's under-consumption theories. Through him he came to see the economic problem as not so much the diminished internal size of over-protected national markets but rather the unequal distribution of income and effective demand between classes.

Accordingly, he did not believe that Progressive initiatives designed to refashion the Liberal Party along reformist, low-tariff lines would adequately satisfy the aspirations of contemporary radicalism. Woodsworth was a committed socialist, irrevocably disenchanted by the 'two old parties.' Indeed the very existence of parties left him unimpressed. The curse of contemporary parliamentary government, he believed even before his election in 1921, was the dearth of independent judgment exercised by elected members. Woodsworth's own parliamentary experience only confirmed this view, and so he remained to the end an undying foe of 'partyism.' The ideological realignment of the party system, another imperative of Manitoban progressivism, was not enough. Predictably, Woodsworth sided with the Albertans and other radical anti-partyist Progressives: the likes of Robert Gardiner, E.J. Garland, H.E. Spencer, and Agnes Macphail. Out of their mutual intellectual attraction the 'Ginger Group' was born. Throughout the 1920s Woodsworth nurtured this loose 'caucus' of 'cooperating independents.' The constitutional crisis of 1926 suspended relations for a while but by 1928 they were united enough to begin the train of events that led to Calgary in 1932.

The upsurge of radicalism among farmers in the early 1920s was not equalled among industrial workers.[14] Trade-union membership declined in the first half of the decade, militancy was low, and there remained deep divisions between the Trades and Labor Congress (TLC), the remnant of the OBU, the supporters of labourism and, after 1921, the Workers Party of Canada, the forerunner of the Communist Party of Canada (CPC). Independent labour parties, with the possible exception of Manitoba's, were ineffectual. The experiment in national labourism that was the Canadian Labor Party was in political limbo and by mid-decade had been taken over by the Communists. Woodsworth's analysis of the political situation in Vancouver in 1927 was, with slight changes, applicable right across the country:

Ten years has made a great change in the Labor world. The loggers' union, once a strong militant organization has gone by the board ... The longshoremen's union has been smashed and replaced by submissive company's organizations. The fine Labor Temple years ago became the property of the School Board and the Council is now much reduced ...

The Socialist Party of Canada is no more ... Some of the old members are in the I.L.P. [Independent Labor Party], some in the Communist Party which seems to have inherited a good deal of the dogmatism and intolerance of the old school ... The Communist group, small in number but active in various organizations, controls the policy of the Canadian Labor Party and seems likely to wreck the organization. In spite of one's desire for 'a united front' one cannot but ask in the words of the old proverb: 'Can two walk together except they be agreed?' Our divisions in Winnipeg are bad enough but the C.L.P. [Canadian Labor Party] federation scheme doesn't seem to have helped matters. The old Federated Labor Party which nearly perished has been revived as the Independent Labor Party. It is on an individual membership basis and is affiliated with the C.L.P. There has been expressed a strong desire for affiliation with the I.L.P. in Winnipeg. A similar suggestion has come from Calgary. In Ontario, after the formation of the C.L.P., the I.L.P. was allowed to go to pieces but an effort is now being made to reorganize it. Thus it would seem that a federation of Provincial I.L.P.'s may sometime become possible.[15]

Woodsworth believed that the most advanced centre of labour party activity and one crucial to the development of a national party was in Winnipeg. There, within two years of its founding in December 1920, the ILP had established a significant political presence at all three levels of government. Woodsworth had high hopes for his home province approaching the federal election of 1925.[16] The ILP ran five candidates, all in the city. In the country it deferred to the Liberals and Progressives. In the north, the ILP's branch in The Pas was uncertain how to proceed: 'It was felt that we should support the progressive member, as a labor member was not running. It was proposed ... that Sec. write Bro. Woodsworth at Winnipeg. If Mr. Bird the Progressive M.P. of Nelson had been any help to the Labor Members in the house and that upon his answer shall depend the amount of support we should tender him in this upcoming election.'[17] 'Brother' Woodsworth must have responded favourably because the executive decided to support Bird.

The year 1925 saw Heaps and Woodsworth elected from Winnipeg, the only labour members in the new House. There was cause for local pride, but nationally it meant little. Before the election of September 1926, Woodsworth was not altogether sanguine. He recognized his political weakness; and perhaps because of it, he rebuffed Mackenzie King's offer of an electoral understanding. As historian Blair Neatby has written: 'King wanted "to deal in a generous way with Labour" by offering Liberal support for a Labour candidate in one constituency in exchange for Labour support for a Liberal in another ... King had already corresponded with Woodsworth on the subject of cooperation. Woodsworth, however, while admitting that he preferred Liberals to Conservatives, had a strong preference for Labour members and would not intervene.'[18] Nevertheless, the Liberals did not run candidates in either Woodsworth's or Heaps's seats and the ILP did not field candidates in either St Boniface, or in Winnipeg South or South Centre. In the last two constituencies 'Labour votes,' said the *Weekly News*, 'spontaneously went Liberal and were probably the deciding factor.'[19] There is in this *prima facie* evidence of an implicit electoral pact between the ILP and the Liberals, at least in Manitoba.

The painfully unsuccessful results of 1925 and 1926 underlined again the immobility of the Canadian electorate. But there were small breaks in the clouds. In 1926 Woodsworth and Heaps had participated in the founding of a new independent labour party in British Columbia.[20] In late 1927 a new ILP was formed in Ontario. And throughout the late 1920s Woodsworth was successful in encouraging the exodus of democratic socialists from the CLP.[21] The final death of the latter, by 1928, cleared the ground and made possible the founding of the Western Labor Political Conference (WLPC) in November 1929, an early antecedent of Calgary in 1932. (It was at the founding meeting of the WLPC that Woodsworth clearly embraced the conception of a future national party of the Left as, of necessity, a federation.)[22] Still, progress was slow. The 1930 election was as unsuccessful as previous ones and brought from Woodsworth a touch of disillusionment and self-pity:

Perhaps we too may be feeling rather disappointed over the last election. We had thought that we had already demonstrated the power which an Independent group could exercize in the House and we felt very sure that our policies were in harmony with the real needs of the majority of the common people of this country. However it seemed that in the heat of an election the old party slogans were too strong. People wanted a change and voted for the party which promised the most, almost regardless as to what those promises might involve. Now it would appear that as tax payers they must foot the bills, and as consumers must contribute to the relief of the harassed manufacturing industries.

Yesterday I had a telegram from the Labor people of one of our Eastern cities. 'Urge introduction of unemployment insurance this session.' Of course I shall be glad to do this, but one cannot but reflect half bitterly, that the majority of the Labor people in that city voted in favor of a party not pledged to unemployment insurance and refused to elect its own representative to plead for this policy in the House ...

We say these things, not in bitterness, but rather because we believe that clear thinking at this time is absolutely essential. Political institutions may not be able to get very far in the way of social and economic change, but surely they may be used to advantage.

The country has again committed itself to party government and to a party of high tariffs. Those of us who believe in neither can do little more than continue to point out the inevitable effects, and to state our alternate policy.[23]

For the non-Marxist Left between the wars, the founding of the Co-operative Commonwealth Federation (CCF) stood out as a beacon of hope in an otherwise tenebrous political landscape. The CCF met all the basic criteria of Woodsworth's model of a Canadian socialist party: it rejected Marxism (for the most part), was broadly based and national in scope (at least, it aspired to be), sought simultaneously to pursue immediate demands and long-range goals, and was committed to a pattern of non-violent, parliamentary action. Without Woodsworth's contacts with a large cross-section of Canada's farmers, workers, and intellectuals, a national party might have been impossible. Many crucial initiatives affecting the founding and early character of the CCF were his doing and devising: the exploitation of divisions within the Progressives in 1924 and after;[24] the abandonment of plebiscitary notions of politics;[25] the approach to King in January 1926 leading to the introduction of the old age pension; the nurturing of the Ginger Group; the suggestion to found a Fabian-like research group, the eventual League for Social Reconstruction;[26] the conception of the CCF as a loose federation of parties and groups; the writing of the statement of principles that became the Regina Manifesto;[27] the decision to set up CCF clubs;[28] the expulsion of united front supporters from the Ontario CCF in 1934.[29]

There were early provincial successes in British Columbia and Saskatchewan, where in 1934 the party became the official oppositions. The national election of 1935 was the grand test. Perhaps the election came too soon after the CCF's inception. It lacked money and organization, was confronted by an unhelpful press, and was haunted by the incubus of being viewed as Communist in ideology or in sympathy. In early 1935 Woodsworth believed that it was impossible for the CCF to win a majority in the next House; the best that could be expected was to hold the balance of power.[30] Writing in May, he showed himself more than a little annoyed at the unfulfillable rising expectations of some supporters:

I do not think that I ever made the statement that the most the CCF could expect, as a result of the forthcoming election, would be to hold the balance of power. I have stated ... that I do not think we could hope to be the government. I have even taken the opportunity of showing that if we were only a minority group we could still exercise a very decided influence ... I suppose that the next report will be that I expect in the next Parliament we shall have only two labor men elected! ...

I confess that I am a bit tired of the mentality of our people who get discouraged unless they can delude themselves into the belief that we are going to be the government. There are more of this class of people in Ontario than anywhere else, and possibly, if they cannot see more clearly or have not more courage, they might as well turn back at this stage than later on. You will argue with me that we are fighting for a principle, and that we should fight for this principle even if we should go down to defeat.[31]

The young David Lewis received a letter in August 1935 in the same realistic vein:

I had not realized how destitute the CCF was at that time. Mr. Woodsworth informed me that there was no central campaign fund and that a candidate 'must either finance himself or, like invading armies of old, live on the people it conquers.'

His letter was full of thoughts characteristic of the missionary. 'We are,' he said, 'in the position where a man must show his qualities of leadership by leading, by drumming up a group and gradually securing support.' Mr. Woodsworth could not suggest a safe seat for me in the coming election and did not know of any position into which I could step ...

He added a passage which illumined his personal approach to the difficulties which confronted the movement. 'I'm afraid,' he wrote, 'this is all very indefinite but for me life has been rather indefinite and yet things have worked and so I suppose one gets into the habit of relying upon hidden opportunities ahead – as in a fog each step opens up the step ahead.'[32]

The CCF fielded candidates in less than half the seats. It was in Quebec, Atlantic Canada, and rural Ontario that it found greatest difficulty recruiting candidates. It received some 391,000 votes, 8.8 per cent of the votes cast and elected 7 members. This was an advance of sorts but from another perspective the CCF had failed. The Depression had brought forth other minority political movements – Social Credit and the Reconstruction Party – and had increased the popularity of the Communists. In short, the electorate had turned away from the two main parties; close to a quarter of those voting supported third parties or independents. The CCF was the most popular of these protest groups, but the electoral map of Canada would have looked very different after 1935 if it had been able to monopolize this mood of disenchantment. To boot, all the United Farmers of Alberta (UFA) Members of Parliament, now running as CCF'ers, went down to defeat at the hands of Social Credit candidates. The loss of Spencer, Garland, G.G. Coote, D.M. Kennedy, and Alfred Speakman was incalculable. Woodsworth would lead the CCF one more time in a general election. But by 1940 he was in ill health and his leadership of the party overshadowed by his stand against Canada's participation in the Second World War. In 1940, as in 1935, the CCF would fail to make an electoral breakthrough.

II

In his attitude towards established institutions, Woodsworth could be sublimely inconsistent. He found some institutions unreformable or unusable and cast them aside. Through others he attempted the difficult task of achieving political change. Towards the church he, finally, adopted the former view; towards Parliament, at least much of the time, he took the latter position. His opinion of Parliament was crucial because, in contrast to Marxists and syndicalists, he regarded political democracy as an imperative means to the creation of a new society. Yet as a political radical, Woodsworth knew that Parliament, too, was in need of fundamental change. Such was its central role in his scheme of democratic socialism that compromise or failure in its reform or reconstruction would render the wider goal of the transformation of society unattainable.

To Woodsworth the independent power and sovereignty of Parliament was one of Canada's contemporary collective myths. In earlier times, he claimed, the doctrine of responsible government captured quite accurately the actual relationship of elected government to the larger society. (Somehow he overlooked the Family Compact). But this had changed. The sinister *deus ex machina* was, of course, economic monopolies.[33] Until, roughly, the last ten years of the nineteenth century, Canada was a simple society of freeholders and small businessmen; markets were local and economic relations mainly personal and familial. The coming of monopolies had brought the expansion and integration of markets and the concentration of economic power. Canada's new financial and industrial oligarchy possessed unparalleled economic power and dominated Parliament and the political élite. Through economic mergers and interlocking directorships the power of monopolies had become ever more centralized and hierarchic. They controlled press and church and had insinuated their influence into education, the home, the courts, the military, and the police. Especially in the case of company towns they treated workers like economic slaves. Ideological and organizational integration had fused the economic and political sectors, making the new business class the true rulers of the country. Normally the established political parties did not, in any event, disagree with their economic masters; were they to do so they were easily brought to heel by the witholding of campaign donations or other such pressures:

Gradually throughout the country the realization is growing that we are not in reality a democracy. Anyone who listened to the reading of the long lists of interlocking directorates given by the hon. member of Macleod (Mr. Coote) and the hon. member for Wetaskiwin (Mr. Irvine) must realize that the small group of men who control our banks ... also control correlated financial institutions. They also control the main industrial and commercial concerns of the country. A great many of these selfsame men are on our leading educational institutions, our universities; they control our press and so on. So that a situation has developed in which a comparatively small clique of people practically control the industrial, commercial and educational life of the country. Further than that, in my judgment ... these same men to a very large degree control the policies of this house.[34]

Controlling the parliament is our financial oligarchy. In Japan the military have never fully been brought under the control of parliament; in Canada even the Central Bank legislation has not successfully challenged the sovereignty of finance. As Mr. Grattan O'Leary pointed out some years ago, it is behind green baize doors in the counting houses in Montreal and Toronto that the destinies of Canada are determined ... Long study, at close range of the operations of parliament, has convinced me that the financiers pull the strings. A prime minister may protest that he is free, but then a man is not likely to become prime minister unless he is willing to travel more or less in the 'right' direction.[35]

Political parties in Canada were simply instruments for winning and holding political power. Considerations of electoral success made them non-ideological, leader-dominated hierarchies.[36] In Parliament the two old parties were indistinguishable philosophically. To hold power in this system required that each party exhibit an iron-handed group discipline. Individual Liberal and Conservative members thus became uncritical supporters of the leader's policy. The House of Commons had become an arena of sham contests and contrived distinctions, a charade played out for political power:

> After the election, then, the party [discipline] is in the saddle and the Prime Minister is virtually a Dictator ... Cabinet responsibility is largely cabinet subserviency and the caucus a convenient method of issuing an advance copy of cabinet decisions and permitting the blowing off of steam in private ...
> The party fight in parliament is not primarily over this or that measure but rather one for power. So long as one party has the monopoly of power, of 'the sweets and emoluments of office,' so long will that party attempt to retain power and the rival party seek to dislodge it from office. The particular measures are more or less the counters in the game; the whole elaborate machinery of the debates a costly stage performance designed to influence public opinion.[37]

There were two levels of meaning in Woodsworth's critique of parliamentary government. Each level corresponded to and indeed grew out of what were the two principal parts of his political persona, namely the reformer and the reconstructionist or democratic revolutionary. A difference of philosophical temper underlay each of them. Woodsworth, the reformer, viewed the impotence of Parliament as the accidental result of contingent, historical circumstances.[38] That is, he did not postulate any *necessary* relationship of dominance by the economy over the state, by capitalism over parliament. In an earlier era, the existence of capitalism did not, *ipso facto*, threaten Parliament's sovereignty. Rather it was the unprecedented and unique mutation of capitalism under monopolistic conditions that had led to the subordination of parliamentary institutions. This account led logically to the idea that, in spite of having been so completely compromised, Parliament could with a transformed membership be used to pave the way towards a new society, albeit gradually.

The other level of meaning was less confident of the efficacy of small measures of reform of Parliament or of other things, and was doubtful of political and parliamentary methods of change.[39] Embedded in this part of Woodsworth's thought was the perspective of economic determinism. Different techno-economic modes of organization brought forth not just varying images of, for example, God and society, but also different political regimes. Parliamentary government, like Protestantism, was the product of a commercial, business-dominated economy. Or, as he put it, fusing at least two types of economy, 'so-called democratic institutions are, after all, feudal-bourgeois institutions.'[40] His claim was that the economy necessarily dominated and determined politics; and so monopoly capitalism's dominance of parliament was the particular instance of this constant relationship. The inferiority of Parliament was structural and necessary:

It is a curious thing but as one studies the development of social institutions one cannot but note that the form persists long after life has fled. For example, at the beginning of our sessions we have what is known as the king's speech, or, in Canada, the governor general's speech ... We keep up the old form but we all know that there has been a shifting of power away from the king or his representative to the prime minister and his cabinet who are theoretically responsible to the house.

I submit that there has been another shifting of power. In recent years there has grown up behind the political power, a financial and economic power. Today the financial power is much stronger than the political ... It is quite true that parliament must still register legislation, that parliament must still formally confer privileges, but we are becoming more automatic registers of these things. Theoretically the banks would have no power unless they came to this house to obtain that power but we all know perfectly well that in practice they simply come here and demand it. We give it to them and legalize what is actually already in effect ... We in this house go through the forms of granting power already held ... [41]

Although the nominal representatives of the people are supposed to form the government of this country, in practice the real government is a financial oligarchy functioning through the forms of democracy. In this connection I recall a statement made in 1923 by Mr. Harold J. Laski: 'The modern state is the protective armament of a property system which emphasizes inequality throughout society. Its claim to sovereignty is – once it is realized that political power is the handmaid of economic power – in effect, a claim to maintain these inequalities.'[42]

In this view the inherent structural imperatives of monopoly capitalism would transform Parliament into something else. Economic consolidation centralized economic power; it made economic organization more 'collective' and 'cooperative.' In time these economic tendencies would throw off the lifeless forms of private ownership of the economy and the monopolies' control of the parliamentary state. It would be economic forces that would initiate the establishment of new, authentic democratic forms. That is, the emphasis was upon democracy arising not from out of the existing parliamentary state and being imposed on the surrounding economy and society but rather as welling up from the point of production itself through unions, cooperatives, and wheat pools. It was this emphasis upon economic democracy that contributed to Woodsworth's interest in the occupational and vocational emphases of group or cooperative government.

Group-government theory was part of the intense interest in syndicalist ideas in the industrial world before and after the First World War. In Canada the theory had its largest following among agrarian radicals. Its most complete exponent was, of course, Woodsworth's colleague in the House after 1921, William Irvine, the author of *The Farmers in Politics* (1920) and *Co-operative Government* (1929). In its application to politics, group-government theory was a sustained critique of 'partyism': the tendency, that is, of modern parliamentary parties to become hierarchical, leader-oriented, highly disciplined formations that denied creativity and independence to their individual caucus members. Group-government theory also focused on the state-cum-party domination of civil society and the incapacity of ordinary citizens to initiate change and participate in lawmaking. Hence it favoured the plebiscitary principle of the initiative and recall, proportional representation, and free votes. A parliamentary system governed by such principles would have displayed much more open and unpredictable patterns of voting.

The theory would have generated other important consequences. In its extreme rejection of partyism, it challenged the very premises of traditional cabinet government. Normally the cabinet is an executive drawn from the governing party or parties. Cabinet members are appointed by the prime minister and once in office are required to maintain collective solidarity. Under group or cooperative government, cabinet would be a committee of the Commons, representation in which would be proportionate to the party's number of elected members. The 'groups' could be political parties; the more radical and economic version of group-government theory designated occupational groups or classes as the basic units. The theory, then, was a complex, many-sided idea. With the exception of the principle of the initiative and recall,[43] Woodsworth advocated all of its many parts throughout his long parliamentary career.

As with other aspects of his world view, Woodsworth recognized that circumstances did not easily allow the immediate application of a good deal of group-government doctrine. Yet in one definite way it did influence his actual political behaviour. Fundamentally he behaved in the House of Commons not as a party man but as a 'co-operating independent.'[44] He complained constantly that unlike at Westminster there were no cross benches at Ottawa and that the House's procedures were too rigidly based on a two-party system. But he made clear that cooperative independence did not entail political quietism or isolation; it entailed rising above party and group precisely in order to make alliances with others. In fact, it could involve compromise.

Independence, we take it means co-operation, that is working together or, if you will, taking part in the game but – co-operation on our own terms, playing our own game not someone else's game.

If I 'work together' with some one on his own terms I am something less than free. The Labor Party must not place itself 'under the yoke' to any other organization. Of course in practice, I cannot have things all my own way. Nor in parliament can one group drive its policies through regardless of all others. Here is where Morley's idea of compromise comes in. A compromise not necessarily of principles but a compromise in order to give effect to principles as far as possible under existing circumstances. A builder can build only with the material that is available.

Take for example the old age pension bill in the last session. Neither party alone would have introduced it. Most of the Quebec Liberals were at the first not at all favorable. We secured the co-operation of the Progressives. The Liberals could not carry on without the aid of the Progressives and Labor. The Saskatchewan Liberals were favorable. How could the Liberal caucus go against the Bill?

But as to the terms. Had we pressed for too much we might not have secured the help of either Progressives or Saskatchewan Liberals. Certainly the bill would not have passed the House. The measure was far from our ideal but we accepted it as the best at present attainable.[45]

A constant perplexity of Woodsworth's thought, we will notice later, is that he never satisfactorily explained the dividing line between compromises that were affirmative of principle and those that were not. In sanctioning the pursuit of agreement, consensus, and accommodation, the theory of group cooperativism justified some unusual outcomes. Consider, for example, his support during the Depression for a parliamentary committee of national emergency. The context was the throne speech debate of 1931. Woodsworth argued that the sub-amendment moved by the cooperating independents was, to begin with, somewhat of a compromise between the labour and farmer groups. Had labour presented its own separate amendment it would have emphasized that 'emergency conditions' could be met only by 'extraordinary measures' such as public ownership. Instead labour and the farmers had agreed on two policies: government underwriting of farm credit, and expanded public-works projects and relief for city workers. These, said Woodsworth, would be their contribution to a general suspension of party politics and an all-party committee of enquiry. 'I do not think that the problems which face the farmers and the industrial workers of the cities to-day should be made a football for the party game that is played out in this house ... I would join with the other hon. members of the house in urging that at this session of parliament one of the best things for us to do would be to appoint a strong committee in which there would be representatives, as on all committees, from the different parties of the house. It should be a committee on which the best men in the house would be placed, and such a committee should seriously consider the whole economic situation.'[46]

To accommodate the claims of cooperation in this instance, Woodsworth moved from socialism to a policy of immediate relief which would in turn be only one of several contributions to a debate and a compromise policy on the economic emergency. In effect, cooperative independence could mean the lowest common denominator of an all-party consensus in support of measures that, Woodsworth admitted, would at best only marginally mitigate the economic catastrophe of the Depression. A doctrine that in its abstract purity stood as a compelling negation and defiance of the political arrangements of a degenerate parliamentary system might become, in its limited, actual application, an instrument of political conciliation at a historic moment of extreme popular suffering and class polarization. The best construction that can be placed on Woodsworth's view is that he believed that any compromise undertaken with the active participation of the Left and/or himself must thereby advance the cause of justice.

There were other ironies. The priority of independence that derived from the idea of cooperative government militated against caucus and party discipline and would make unlikely a definitive transition to socialism. Democratic socialist parties operating under traditional parliamentary and party systems have had available to them procedures that approximate to what might be called 'democratic Leninism': that is, parties elected with perhaps as little as a mere plurality of votes have through aggressive leadership and disciplined caucus behaviour been able sometimes to bull their way ahead and implement radical measures. In general Woodsworth gave little attention to the question of the transition to socialism. Certainly he knew of Frank Underhill's and the British Socialist League's warning in the early 1930s that any incoming and self-regarding socialist government must assume emergency powers to proceed by Orders in Council and rapidly dispatch parliamentary business. Also, soon after the founding of the CCF, Woodsworth received several impassioned letters from Underhill beseeching him to make the CCF a much more disciplined, integrated, and leader-dominated party. Woodsworth denied that the attaining of socialism required any major interference with Parliament's traditional liberties and privileges.[47] Towards Underhill's other suggestions his response was, for the most part, to reject them.[48] Thus Woodsworth's theory of the party and the democratic group-state envisaged decision-making as an endless, floating party-coalition with constant negotiation and compromise, an admirable vision but hardly likely to achieve the daring transition to a new society.

Moreover, group-government notions stood in awkward contrast with another of Woodsworth's characteristic beliefs: that politics was the rational, disinterested transcending of particular 'class' views. This idea was at the back of his inclusive conception of a national party appealing equally to worker, farmer, middle-class professional, and small businessman. Tending in an opposite, fissiparous direction was group government's emphasis upon the group. Only like could represent like, so that group government would lead to the breaking down of the community into its constitutent economic and political parts.

The theory emphasized that people were actuated by a subjective-minded interest rather than an objective reason. Whereas in Woodsworth's conception of the inclusive party the unifying appeal took place prior to the election and was then carried into Parliament, in other words a sense of community preceded popular decision-making, in the case of group government election-time saw the dissolution of society into its constituent components to be recombined later through endless compromise and negotiation. In the first place community derived from an original, rational account of the public good; in the latter it emerged out of the eventual conciliation of sectional wills.

Woodsworth's article 'Political Democracy,' published in 1935, is important on at least two counts. It was written in his later years and so allows us to assess how much his thinking had changed, if at all. And it was one of the few occasions in a busy public life when he provided a systematic account of a given subject. He began by observing that he wrote in a time of 'widespread discounting of our parliamentary institutions.' He, too, found fault with much in the Canadian Parliament but, all in all, he declared himself a believer in its procedures, at least insofar as they were reformed. Its failings, Woodsworth asserted, were mainly the result of the promiscuous pressures exerted by economic interests and lobbyists. Other problems were the hyper-disciplined nature of the political parties, the excessive authority of the prime minister, and, more indirectly, the political immaturity of the Canadian electorate. Reforms to correct the situation might include the abolition of the Senate or its recomposition as a house of the provinces in a loosely bound Confederation,[49] free votes, proportional representation, the streamlining of procedures, a study of the role of public commissions and their relationship to Parliament, and, finally, the amendment of the BNA Act. Much the most radical of his prescriptions was a scheme of vocational representation.

In sum, there was a dizzying complexity to Woodsworth's view of parties, groups, and the parliamentary state. He could be so practical, believing in Parliament even to the extent of being prepared to suspend partisan advantage altogether to make it work. Yet he could also be completely dismissive of traditional parliamentary practices, as in his scheme of political syndicalism. But when all is said and done, Woodsworth at bottom was an old-fashioned nineteenth-century reformer of Parliament, a sort of Jeremy Bentham or a John Stuart Mill. In spite of its defects, in spite of the intensity of the economic powers ranged against it, a fairly traditional parliamentary system with the support of a transfigured electorate could undertake the transformation of society. That was the parting message of 'Political Democracy':

I have dwelt on the obstacles to progress presented by our parliamentary system. They are not insuperable. I must not fail to point out that the system has also its advantages. Parliament is a high-powered broadcasting station. I know of no more effective agency for propaganda ... Even a small minority group can force discussion. Through their speeches and votes members of the old parties must declare themselves. Backed by favourable sentiment outside, the minority can force the pace of the majority. On occasion even the party-system may be turned to advantage. In 1925 when the two parties were almost evenly balanced, the Independents were able to secure considerable advanced legislation ...

A government pledged to socialism might not have plainsailing, but with an intelligent and determined electorate would surely win through. When we refer to democracy we think perhaps too much in terms of elections and parliamentary proceedings. We should think rather in terms of a socially conscious and politically trained body of citizens. A heavy task lies ahead but not an impossible one. The driving-force and intelligence which in a few brief years built up on this continent a remarkable system of production, if it were really applied to our economic and social problems, would in an even shorter period transform society.[50]

III

Woodsworth's political career was moulded not just by historical circumstance and intellectual belief. There were as well the more prosaic constraints of the rules of the House of Commons, rules that had come down from pre-Confederation practice and British precedent.[51] If anything, after 1867 they were less subject to change than at Westminster. Such rules as did exist were hardly oppressive of the rights of opposition members even after the introduction of a closure rule in 1913. Later changes in 1927 introduced a forty-minute limit on speeches for most backbenchers and opposition members and an 11 p.m. adjournment, but also allowed third parties for the first time to move sub-amendments to motions to go into Committee of Ways and Means and Supply. Probably the most obtrusive rule in Woodsworth's time was the one that required members who were in their seats in the chamber and who were not paired to register a vote in a division. There was no allowance for abstention as an explicit act of non-compliance.

This rule was challenged in the 1930s and fell somewhat out of acceptance thereafter.

The Canadian Parliament had no tradition of obstruction by third parties, such as was established in Britain by the Parnellites in the 1880s.[52] Here opposition parties had engaged in mild forms of obstruction which had, for example, led to the new rule on closure in 1913. But even after the changes of 1913 and 1927 it is arguable that there existed ample opportunities for quick-witted members to block and obstruct the business of the House. Even if the Parnellite option of 'creative abstention' was denied him or indeed deemed unacceptable, Woodsworth could have employed imaginative and unusual parliamentary tactics. He did so only on one occasion, between April 1928 and April 1930, and that, incredibly, was on the relatively marginal issue of divorce reform.

Elements of Woodsworth's theory of political cooperation militated against an unconventional use of the rules of the Commons. He was persuaded that a member's primary obligation was to facilitate an exchange of independent views in order to establish common agreement. He accepted the right of an elected government to govern and have its authority respected.[53] Obstructionism offended this principle, as did all the other sins that competitive partisan politics were heir to. It was as if, for all its faults, Parliament was for him the grand inquest of the nation wherein fair, reasonable, respectful, and broadminded persons pursued the common good.

Other factors also inclined him to a traditional use of the Houses's rules. While other Members of Parliament, most notably Conservatives, saw him as consummately doctrinaire, in his own eyes Woodsworth was pragmatic, sceptical, and undogmatic. Of course, he was also a self-confessed idealist. But, sometimes, he claimed to be uncertain of the connection between ideals and practice. 'General principles' were difficult of application to 'concrete situations.'[54] 'Metaphysical and theological distinctions' were constantly in problematical juxtaposition with 'practicality and common sense.' Knowledge was open-ended and incomplete, and dependent on experience and action.[55] Knowing what to do was not always easy:

Under the circumstances it seems as if the only course is to attempt the very delicate and perhaps doubtful experiment of co-operation with the group which under the pressure of circumstances is willing to co-operate.

Just now we are being told that we ought to have a strong government. The two-party system is built up on the idea that it is not safe to trust one group of men but that there must be a strong opposition to hold the government in check. A strong government, such as the Conservatives now desire, would be a protectionist government, and apparently one that could flout the will of the great masses of the common people. The weaker is perhaps more amendable [sic] to public opinion.

The course which lies ahead even during the present session is by no means clear. It is easy to lay down general principles. Every group and every section of every group may easily quote these general principles in justification of its action but it is not easy to apply general principles to concrete situations. All we can say is that the Members of the Independent Groups are endeavoring to do their utmost to steer their way through a very difficult channel. If their craft strikes a rock the fault may not lie in their lack of skill so much as in the very nature of our present parliamentary institutions.[56]

The above was written in the admittedly difficult circumstances of the minority Liberal government in 1926. But two years later with a majority Liberal government, Woodsworth still exhibited a tentative, sceptical attitude towards the complexities of parliamentary choice. He was sometimes perplexed, to the point of numbing immobility:

The first stage of the session is over! The Address was adopted without division. Perhaps someone may ask why the Independents do not move an amendment? This is the situation which faces your representatives. We are not at all satisfied with the Speech, but suppose if by any chance the Amendment carried, then the Government would go out. This, of course, is outside the possibilities, but should we make a motion if we are not prepared to stand by the possible results? Is that not merely playing politics? On the other hand, in the event of the Amendment not carrying, what amendment could all the Independents unite upon? Supposing also lower tariffs were included, was this the time to introduce this question, or should we wait until the Budget had been brought down? Again, could an Amendment be provided that would win the support of the Progressive-Liberals? Would it be good tactics to emphasize the smallness of the numbers of the Independents? – or would it be good tactics to take every opportunity to drive the old parties to vote together? Such are some of the considerations that face us in connection with almost every party vote.[57]

A more fundamental philosophical disposition lay at the back of his sense of the opacity of political choice, and that was his belief that history demonstrated few general or universal laws. As an empiricist of sorts Woodsworth was capable of claiming that there existed indubitable relations of social causation; for example, his examinations of the origins of mental illness and the economic causes of war made precisely this point. Yet more often he seemed impressed by the variability and particularity of place and time:

This tendency toward broad classifications, or classifications based on foreign conditions, is especially dangerous when it is set forth as a guide to our own policy ... Undoubtedly [Canada's] development has been closely parallel to that of the United States, and one might infer that the future of the two countries will be along somewhat similar lines, yet one cannot travel in Canada and in the United States without noting very considerable differences. Our British connections have undoubtedly exercised a very great influence, and solid French-Canadian, Catholic, Quebec has been and will continue to be, one of the determining factors in our political life.

But does it help us very much in deciding our policy to say that we in Canada must follow either the lead of Communist Russia or Fascist Germany? It may be true, in a general sort of a way, that human nature is the same the world over. But it is also true to say that there are very great variations. An Englishman differs widely from an Italian; a white man from an oriental, or from a negro. They react very differently to the same stimuli and, in practice, the stimuli are usually quite different. Why insist that under the same circumstances – to say nothing of different circumstances – they must all act in the same way? So, too it may be said that economic laws are the same the world over, but history has proven that economic laws have worked out very differently in different countries.[58]

Consequently Canadian socialists would have to work out their own salvation in their own halting way. There were no universal blueprints or fool-proof patterns of the relation of theory to action. On some occasions Woodsworth even entertained close to an unthinkable view of the matter: that perhaps ideas themselves were irrelevant to politics. Especially after the 1930 election he sometimes evinced a deep cynicism regarding history and politics. In December he had taken a vacation through the Caribbean and the Panama Canal: 'As we passed San Salvador – the first landing place of Columbus – another of my illusions went by the board. I had always thought of Columbus as the man of iron determination, the pioneer, always facing and overcoming apparently insuperable obstacles. But now "I hae ma doots." Probably

Columbus got into these trade winds and was literally blown along to the New World. In this warm humid enervating atmosphere, he was probably too lazy to do anything but let things drift along day after day. Then he ran into San Salvador and found himself a world hero. Yet *he* had simply followed the line of least resistance.'[59]

Two months later, in an essay on 'Politics and Politicians,' Woodsworth dwelt on the ideas of F.S. Oliver, the contemporary English author of *The Endless Adventure*, a study of politics in the age of Walpole: 'Many of the generalizations may seem, to those outside, rather cynical if not Machiavellian, yet anyone who has lived on the inside must recognize in them a large measure of truth.'[60] He quoted Oliver at length, to the effect that ideals in politics produced misery and cruelty, that no politician had ever been able to govern according to the precepts of the Sermon on the Mount, and that without the use of sham and dissimulation politicians never succeeded. He did not express complete agreement with Oliver's views but that he gave space to them indicated more than a little sympathy. He had suggested a similar perspective five years earlier:

General principles may sometimes be advanced for public consumption but general principles do not determine policies. Policies are determined under political and economic pressure. Indeed the more one sees of life, the more one comes to doubt the value of these general principles, because after all, decisions must be made in concrete cases, where usually very high-sounding phrases may be used by either side. But it would seem as if a Government should have some definite objective and should not be blown hither and thither by every wind and when no wind blows should remain dormant. Outsiders frequently imagine that the Government sits up nights planning for the good of the country. As a matter of fact it would seem as if the Government has few ideas of its own, but waits until some outsider presents an idea with sufficient backing before it will even consider it.[61]

If all of these arguments militated against radical tactics in Parliament, how *did* he behave? Conventionally, of course, but not uncritically. To begin, Woodsworth was assiduous, perhaps to a fault, in his attendance in the Commons. Between 1922 and 1939 there were 379 recorded votes after Commons debates. Through absence or abstention he failed to vote on only 61 occasions. Possibly because of a relaxing of the rule on compulsory voting after 1930, Woodsworth abstained somewhat more. In the 1930–5 Parliament, he did not vote

28 per cent of the time, although this figure dropped to 10 per cent between 1936 and 1939. When he did vote his general tendency was to vote against government measures. Only 29 per cent of his votes were cast with the majority and only on one occasion in four (24 per cent) did he side with the government party. That is, on recorded votes, when he was present and voting, he was in the opposition 71 per cent of the time. This left a small but significant minority of cases when he sided with a clear majority of the Conservative or Liberal government caucuses.[62]

There were two exceptions to this pattern of opposition. The first was the 1926 Parliament, where early on he resolved to support the Liberal government and indeed did so on 25 occasions in 27 recorded divisions. The second was his abrupt change of policy towards the Bennett government in May 1934 and his support thereafter of such Conservative measures as unemployment insurance, the Bank of Canada, and natural products marketing legislation. Inevitably, in adopting a general posture of opposition, Woodsworth found himself in alliance with third or fourth party blocs. For 66 per cent of the time between 1922 and 1935, when he voted, he was in alliance with the independent Progressive bloc and the UFA contingent. From 1936 to 1939, although he voted against a small number of the more esoteric monetary resolutions of the Social Credit members, he sided with them 67 per cent of the time. Thus, while he was of an oppositionist tendency in his actual parliamentary behaviour, he was a *loyal* member of the opposition. He neither obstructed nor attempted to subvert Parliament's normal procedures. Only when he agitated for a new divorce court in Ontario did he ruffle the feathers of his fellow parliamentarians. Otherwise he used his rights and privileges to argue his case, present his amendments, assess the merits of each motion, and vote accordingly.

Amidst this pattern of conventional, albeit oppositionist, parliamentary practice, what was the ultimate end in view? Was there a unifying vision infusing these many separate acts? To answer this question, a delineation of a number of basic premises of Woodsworth's political outlook is in order. First, in spite of his scepticism and moments of near disillusionment, Woodsworth remained, in principle and enthusiasm, an idealist to the end. The reconstructionist or democratic revolutionary cast of his political thought in 1919 was not something he abandoned when he entered Parliament. Nor did he quietly set it aside in the more economically tranquil times of the 1920s, only to bring it forth once the Depression began. The emphasis on the need for a new society, on the necessity of going beyond mere 'tinkering' with the existing arrangements, was an integral part of his message to the very end. Secondly, he was not an 'impossibilist.' Even though circumstances were not always propitious, parliamentary socialists were never justified in a course of inaction; rather they should do the best they could. Thirdly, such a strategy of combining high principle with pragmatic action, or, as he put it in 1938, of associating 'spiritual idealism' with 'political realism,' would entail compromise. But compromise, he thought, need not be destructive of principle but could become an opportunity for its creative fulfilment. In his predilection for a politics of orderliness, evolution, practicality, syncretism, and compromise, Woodsworth could sound positively Burkean, although of course always with a dash of idealism. The occasion here was the death of George V in 1936:

The king embodies, as it were, in himself the great British Tradition. Those who have come under the spell of Westminster Abbey will know what I mean. From the figures of shadowy legend down through a long line of kings, some good, some bad; through victories and defeats; through constitutional changes, by incorporating ideals and institutions of other lands and civilizations, and again by sharply distinguishing our own type from others, this tradition has been built up. Not in disparagement of any other nation or culture, ... we are proud to call ourselves British ...

Further, the British king as a constitutional monarch represents the adaptation of old forms and institutions to new needs and new functions. 'Compromise' in the sense of the sacrifice of principles is a despicable thing, but compromise as the discovery of a working arrangement through which various points of view are reconciled and some advance made in the difficult art of learning to live together – such compromise is essential to successful democratic government. Herein, perhaps lies the peculiar genius of the British people. Without too violent a break with the past, the national life has again and again been revolutionized. In various countries monarchies have given place to dictatorships. In England, political democracy has broadened down from precedent to precedent. When I affirm that it must broaden still more I believe that I am in line with the best British tradition ...[63]

Five models of political change can be discerned in Woodsworth's thought and practice. Although analytically distinct, in actuality they often overlapped and fused, not to say contradicted each other. The first is what might be called the 'lesser-of-two-evils strategy.'[64] In some part, it was consideration of this moral criterion that induced him to prefer the Liberals to the Conservatives in 1926. A more interesting theoretical instance was the identical statement that he expressed on two separate occasions in 1935 and in 1936: 'In the actual world of affairs ... one must accept the half loaf and even support procedures which though repugnant to his principles, represent a real advance in public welfare and public morality.' He gave the example of capital punishment. Although he opposed the death penalty, sometimes the only choice offered to him concerned the relative 'humaneness' of methods of executing people. In that case he would choose the less evil one. Woodsworth characterized this position as 'ameliorative' and having to do with the winning of 'crumbs' or 'slices' of improvement.[65]

The second model is what I will call the 'if not x, then y' strategy.[66] This held that, if the ideal policy could not be attained, an alternative, lesser course of action was called for. It lay behind such claims as the following: if the Senate is not to be abolished, at least the government should appoint competent people to it; and, in the absence of free trade, subsidies to the hemp industry were justified.

The remaining three models move us on to the more usual terrain of the theories of change associated with the parliamentary Left: ameliorativism, gradualism, and reconstruction. In his political lifetime Woodsworth confronted a wide variety of issues and advocated a host of policies. At the most radical and extreme were policies of extensive public ownership of economic monopolies and, politically, the proposals of cooperative government and vocational representation. At the least extreme were policies such as old age pensions, the eight-hour day, unemployment insurance, taxes on unimproved land values, public works projects, and so on. Within this spectrum of ideas three further paradigms of change co-existed. The first, 'emergency ameliorativism,'[67] laid emphasis upon the necessity of immediate, concrete, limited measures to bring aid and comfort to people who were in evident and pressing danger. The tone of such appeals was urgent and utilitarian: 'immediately practicable,' 'very urgent measures,' 'humanitarian' acts, 'alleviation,' 'temporary help,' 'a tentative measure,' 'a palliative,' 'an emergency programme.' Such measures, Woodsworth conceded, were in no way subversive of the capitalist system.[68]

The second of this second set of models was the well-known one of gradualism, reformism, or *étapisme*.[69] Its ethical justification derived

from the proposition that the gradual, careful, and sometimes spasmodic accumulation of particular instances of social improvement
would over time produce a wholly new society. The attaining of this
utopia would be the happy outcome of the methodical endeavours of
persistent legislators: 'Every time we develop the cooperative principle
in industry we go one step towards bringing about a cooperative
commonwealth; every time we allow public ownership to replace
private ownership and to be operated under democratic auspices, we
take another step ... every time we allow more authority and control to
be given to employees, we come one step nearer a cooperative commonwealth. Every time we take wealth away from the wealthy and
thus make a more equitable distribution, we are bringing about a more
stable state of affairs and are taking a step towards the cooperative
commonwealth.'[70] Or, Woodsworth suggested, the good society might
be the benevolent consequence of history's inherent purposes, of
which even traditional parties were the unwitting or begrudging mid-
wives: 'Curiously enough, the CCF is these days more or less supporting
Conservative policies. This is not because the policies are Conservative,
but because the Conservatives have been forced by the general trend of
public opinion to adopt what have hitherto been called "socialist
proposals" ... Of course both Liberals and Conservatives would deny
their conversion to Socialism, and they would be quite sincere in so
doing. But the situation seems to be this; that the conditions are
inevitably driving towards Socialism.'[71]

The political crisis of 1926 illustrated especially well the extent of
Woodsworth's commitment to gradualism. On 7 January, when Parliament had opened, he sent letters to both King and Meighen enquiring
where they stood on the unemployment issue and an old-age-pension
program. The next day, in his first speech in the new House, Woodsworth talked spaciously of the need for group cooperation, and while
he voted against Meighen's amendment that the government's continuance in office was a violation of British practice, he drew back from
making a categorical commitment to the Liberals. Woodsworth and
Heaps met the Cabinet on 26 January to discuss their old-age-pension
scheme. Grace MacInnis claims that in late January King also entertained the two of them to dinner at Laurier House and offered the
Labour portfolio to each of them in turn. Both refused. King's positive
reply to the letter of 7 January was sent on 28 January and next day
Woodsworth threw his support unreservedly to the Liberals. King's
proposals, he said, 'commanded' his support; with the old-age-

pension proposal he expressed himself 'very, very glad indeed.'[72] So when the Customs Department crisis suddenly came to a head early in February, Woodsworth was on the horns of a dilemma. While he was clearly embarrassed in the face of Conservative heckling, and although he made a frank admission of the 'vulnerability' of his position, he stuck with the Liberal government through thick and thin, all to ensure the carrying of the old-age-pension measure. Though he participated in its drafting, Woodsworth would later claim that the bill was deficient: principally he wanted a wholly federal scheme; he felt the age limit was too high; the pension should pay a larger amount; and there should be portability from province to province.[73] But he supported it because it was all that was possible at the time and it brought society closer to socialism.

Finally, Woodsworth expounded a radical model of political change, one that went far beyond the other four in its disenchantment with traditional policies and political methods. This, the 'reconstructionist' one, sought the wholesale, immediate transformation of society.[74]

At times Woodsworth was doubtful of the possibility and effectiveness of emergency measures and gradual reforms. When of this outlook he regarded capitalism as trapped in a state of uncorrectable crisis, its inherent dynamics making it structurally incapable of undertaking the sorts of action necessary even to ensure its own survival. Thus, for example, in the conditions of the Depression it had become impossible to finance an unemployment-insurance program. Workers were too poor and businesses too unprofitable to sustain a contributory program; nor could the state finance it, even if it had wanted to, since it was under irresistible pressure to deflate public expenditures. In short, what should be done couldn't be done. Surprisingly, perhaps, when explaining this conception of political change, Woodsworth sometimes employed a frankly Marxist language of the 'internal' and 'inherent contradictions' of the economic system: 'It would seem likely that the socialization of our industry and finance may come, not through pre-concerted intelligent action, but rather by force of economic pressure. Perhaps Karl Marx was right when he suggested that in each system there were internal contradictions and that each held the seeds of its own decay. ... We have reached the point when such contradictions are evident. The very steps the government ought to take to save the situation they cannot take and meet their obligations. The very steps the business community ought to take in the way of putting into the hands of the people increased purchasing power they cannot take because of the huge capital indebtedness which has been piled up.'[75] So reform was unlikely. A more transformative strategy was needed:

Only last Saturday we had a meeting of the council of our Cooperative Commonwealth Federation, and I was very glad to have that council draw up a statement of our position in view of the Prime Minister's so-called reform legislation ... [The statement declares:] 'In the opinion of the National Council of the Cooperative Commonwealth Federation the program of the federal government is entirely inadequate to meet the situation.

'Reform or reconstruction; that is the issue.

'That capitalism has broken down even the old parties now agree. Debt, unemployment, insecurity, the hopeless position of youth, are signs of an economic system in decay. Their persistence and the failure of reform measures in all countries confirm the repeated declarations of the Cooperative Commonwealth Federation in respect to the economic problem.

'The old parties tell us that the system can be patched up by "reforms." But, if reforms have not solved the problem in other countries how can the same reform solve it in Canada?

'The Cooperative Commonwealth Federation believes that capitalism can be neither reformed nor restored. Profit for the few and prosperity for the masses are incompatible. The only permanent solution of our problems is to get rid of capitalism and replace it by a new social order, the cooperative commonwealth.'[76]

What is to be made of these five conceptions of change? One obvious point has to do with their relative incoherence and inconsistency. Consider the following pairs of propositions (the words are mine; the ideas Woodsworth's):

• In the name of simple humaneness, capitalist governments must introduce ameliorativist and reformist programs such as old age pensions and unemployment insurance.

Capitalism is structured in such a way that it cannot introduce such programs.

• Limited statist measures have the effect of stabilizing the system of capitalism. Measures such as the creation of the Bank of Canada, if introduced without an accompanying change of economic ownership, will increase the power of the dominant class.

Any statist measures must in the end be supported because they can be imagined as an integral part of a future socialist political economy.

• Ameliorativist and gradualist policies are not far-reaching enough to deal with an economy in crisis.

Policies such as old age pensions and unemployment insurance, although ameliorativist and gradualist in nature, can be seen as the first steps in a strategy that is avowedly reconstructionist.

All of the above were, of course, recurring themes in Woodsworth's program for political change. Perhaps the most dramatic and glaring instances of his contradictoriness was his stand on the idea of a central bank:

Recently Mr. W.C. Clark ... has been appointed deputy Minister of Finance. This appointment, perhaps, is rather significant as Mr. Clark has been an exponent of the principle of a central bank. Those of us who have advocated a central bank ought to be much encouraged. But, after all, in view of the situation which I have just outlined, what is the use of a central bank or any other institution, however good. It is not enough to have government control. We must have control of government. Government control under existing circumstances may mean simply putting even greater powers into the hands of the big business men who now dominate the situation. A sharp knife, however good in the hands of a surgeon, is very dangerous in the hands of an assassin. A central bank is probably the next step in capitalistic control. It would probably be necessary under a socialist regime. We would welcome its establishment, but at the same time point out that before it can be of any great advantage to the masses of the people, the masses must have their own representatives in control.[77]

The above was written in 1932. The two following statements were made at different times in 1934:

For years we have had in this country a financial dictatorship but it has been somewhat concealed. By this legislation, instead of challenging that dictatorship, we are in reality legalizing and stabilizing it. The Finance minister warns us against any possible delay in giving people the benefits of a central bank. I would say that the people have waited for some years for a central bank, and I think they can afford to wait a little longer rather than that we should saddle this country with what I regard as a private tyranny.[78]

This measure marks an advance on anything we have had in the past. It is by no means one hundred per cent perfect, it leaves much to be desired, and it does not safeguard the interests of the public ... nevertheless it does seem to be a piece of necessary machinery, and as such, an advance over the old arrangements we had under the Bank Act and the Finance Act ... Under a more advanced government it may be used in the interests of the people ... In the meantime ... we stand definitely and emphatically for public ownership and control of the central bank. That taken for granted, I am inclined to think that this measure marks an advance beyond anything we have had in the past, and for that reason, on third reading, I shall vote in favour of the measure.[79]

The rhetoric of extreme criticism is incongruent with the eventual pragmatic decision to support the policy.

Sometimes the contradictions were internal to a single speech or statement; other times they reflected a change of view over time. An instance of the latter was Woodsworth's belief in the eventual triumph of pacifism in international relations. Recall the 'lesser evil' paradigm. Compared to the alternatives of international anarchy, Woodsworth argued in the mid–1930s, the use of force was justified. By 1939 his rejection of this view was uncompromising and absolute. Immoral means could never be sanctioned. Among many commentators it was this act of moral defiance that established Woodsworth as a man of unexcelled ethical principle. Yet for a long time before he had expounded the 'lesser evil' alternative. Such was the inconstancy of the connection of principle and practice in his world view, not just on the issue of war and peace but everything else as well, that it could not have been necessarily predicted that he would have adopted a pacifist stance in 1939. Predictability is a hallmark of a good leader. Woodsworth may not have been always predictable.

In less intellectual and more personal ways Woodsworth could display a stubbornness and contrariness that made his leadership more ambiguous again. Jock Brown, who was the CCF candidate in Marquette, Manitoba, in the 1935 election, recalled a visit by Woodsworth to speak on his behalf.[80] The farmers who had turned up were sitting at the back of the hall. Woodsworth petulently refused for a long time to speak until they came to the front. In the end Woodsworth gave in. On other occasions the outcome was not as accommodative. It seems that to advise him against a certain course of action was almost to induce him to pursue that very action. In June 1937, G.H. Williams, the CCF leader in Saskatchewan, wrote to Woodsworth advising him to 'refrain from discussing the question of cooperation with other groups and also the question of complete neutrality, in his proposed series of meetings in Saskatchewan.'[81] Woodsworth's response was direct and perfunctory: 'Your extraordinary letter of June 11 has just reached me ... There is no other course for us than to ask you to cancel the ... schedule of meetings at which you have asked me to speak. I regret this very much indeed and regret even more the inevitable split which will come in Saskatchewan if you persist in your present policy.'[82]

King Gordon has recounted a similar story about the time he was a CCF candidate in the by-election in June 1936 in Victoria:

Mr. Woodsworth and M. J. Coldwell had been invited to take part in the final rally in the Victoria armoury. Mr. Coldwell tells the story of a conversation he had with Mr. Woodsworth on the way across on the ferry. Coldwell said: 'You know, J.S., Gordon has a good chance to win. Now, there is one issue that has not been raised in this campaign and I don't think it needs to be raised. We all know how you feel about British Columbia's discrimination against Asians and we are all with you. But probably you don't need to raise the matter at this final meeting.' According to Coldwell, Woodsworth had not intended to speak on the question, but when he was reminded the moral issue loomed large. At a dramatic point in his speech before the great crowd in the armoury, he stretched out his arm and waving his finger as it were in the face of the British Columbia authorities he said: 'And there is another thing: the treatment of our Japanese and Chinese and Indian fellow citizens ...' Coldwell reports that at this moment I turned to him and whispered: 'Doesn't he look like the prophet Amos?'

We lost – by 90 votes. I don't know whether Woodsworth's intervention had anything to do with it and I don't care. Woodsworth was greater than a politician – and he was one of the best parliamentarians of his day. It was his moral leadership which accounted for his commanding presence in Canadian life. And no election justified a compromise.[83]

King Gordon clearly accepted the conventional wisdom of Woodsworth as the heroic politician of stern and unbending principle. But this characterization simply does not make sufficient sense of the totality of his life. He was, in fact, committed to compromise as long as it was undestructive of principle. But the location of the dividing line between valid and invalid compromise was never clearly specified. It often changed and moved around. Only Woodsworth, it seemed, knew where it was. On the Oriental question on the West Coast, for example, Woodsworth was hardly an unqualified and uncompromised supporter of Asian immigration and Oriental rights. Nevertheless, in the 1936 Victoria by-election the prejudices of others had to be sternly chastised, and in the process the CCF may have lost the chance of electing a member to the Commons. Like George Eliot's fictional hero Felix Holt, 'he was addicted at once to rebellion and to conformity, and only an intimate personal knowledge could enable any one to predict where his conformity would begin. The limit was not defined by theory, but was drawn in an irregular zigzag.'[84]

IV

If the spectre of revolution haunted the established classes in the years between the world wars, its ubiquitous shadow also fell across Woodsworth's political path. To many, he was a dangerous subversive. Was he not, after all, one of the leaders of the Winnipeg General Strike? Did he not talk of revolution? Conservatives, especially, criticized him unrelentingly for his apparent sympathies with Canadian Communism and Russian Bolshevism. Although he disputed such claims, Woodsworth never could quite set himself free of this millstone. In large part he was unfairly judged; in other respects he brought the judgment on himself. A considered and consistent political pragmatism might have saved him some unnecessary embarrassment and heart-break.

Devotees of parliamentary socialism may take pride in Woodsworth's early criticism of the Russian revolution. He was percipient in seeing the trend towards political authoritarianism and the use of Marxism as a mask for rapid industrialization. Similarly, partly because of his suspicion of Bolshevism, he never acceded to an historical interpretation of the Winnipeg General Strike as a revolutionary event but instead saw it as something consistent with the evolution of a constitutionalist radicalism.[85] Fundamentally, he claimed, the strike had been over wages and collective-bargaining rights. Trade unionists in western Canada were, he admitted, more radical than their eastern brethren and to explore the possibility of more integrative, industry-wide unions they had met in Calgary in early 1919. However, they were, he said, all TLC men, albeit impressed by the idea of one big union. But the organization of this name had not existed when the strike had broken out and the pursuit of one big union had not been a goal of the strikers. The mood of the times, he argued, had been one of rising expectations because of war's end and certainly the Russian revolution was viewed as a sign of the coming new order. But the strike was not in conscious imitation of the revolution. No weapons were found on the strikers; their behaviour was perfectly peaceable; and, all in all, they had no political ambitions whatever. Were if not for the misguided and arbitrary intervention of the federal government, Woodsworth concluded, the strike would have been agreeably settled by the municipal and provincial governments.

Thus Woodsworth did not extol the strike as a harbinger of rising class consciousness and maturing labour solidarity. Yet he did sometimes diverge from a strict interpretation of the strike as the idealistic but conventional act of labour constitutionalists, as, for example, when he argued that the workers' organization of a 'soviet' was an understandable reaction to the activities of the Winnipeg Board of Trade, which, in defiance of democracy, had maintained an all-dominating 'soviet' from the beginning of the city's existence.[86] As well, Woodsworth never quite came to terms with the evident contradiction between an economic strategy of direct action and a respect for parliamentary processes. He clearly preferred the political course of legislative action, but he never rejected the tactic of the mass strike.

That said, although he never backed away from a defence of the strikers, particularly in the face of Conservative criticism, and although he consistently sought the repeal of the measures brought in by Meighen to repress the strike, Woodsworth's ultimate desire was to put the strike behind him, to have it somehow forgotten. It was as if he wished it had not happened. Consequently, in recounting its history he seemed to go out of his way to diminish his own participation in it; his involvement, he said, was belated and brought about only by the excesses of the federal government's intervention.

As indicated earlier, Woodsworth had arrived in Winnipeg on 8 June, while the strike was in its third week. Immediately he had busied himself on behalf of the workers. He addressed their meetings and wrote articles for their paper. Writing in 1922, Woodsworth placed his involvement somewhat later: 'When our British liberties were being torn to shreds, and the editor of the Workers' paper had been arrested, I found myself drawn into the scrap.'[87] Six year later, while discussing amendments to the Immigration Act, he stated: 'I myself have been accused of having been in the strike. I had nothing to do with it until it was half over. When I arrived in Winnipeg it was the third week of the strike and I did not take any very active interest in things until this legislation was passed and the leaders of the strike were summarily arrested with the idea that they were to be deported. Then I took the attitude which I take now, that this was outrageous legislation and that these arrests were absolutely unjustifiable.'[88] In 1933 he placed the beginning of his involvement at the time of the arrest of the strike leaders: 'I had nothing whatever to do with the calling or the conduct of the strike, but when the editor of the labour paper was arrested I took charge of it and carried on for about a week, when I was arrested, charged with sedition, and the paper suppressed ... I knew nothing of the details of the conduct of that strike until after I had acted as editor for a few days, when I was admitted to the committee.'[89]

There is some ambiguity in this. The amendments to the Immigration Act permitting the deportation of British-born immigrants without jury trial occurred two days before Woodsworth reached the city. The report of the Commons' committee to toughen the definition of sedition in the criminal code was accepted by the House two days after he arrived; and the arrest of the strike leaders took place seven days after that. A generous reading of Woodsworth's recollections can perhaps reconcile these several claims. Maybe he was arguing that his very decision to come to Winnipeg had been caused by the changes to the Immigration Act, although this does not make sense of all of the above statements. In any event, there is no denying the tone of personal distancing and even insouciance that they exhibit; as evident was Woodsworth's tendency to explain his involvement as growing not out of the economic issues of the strike but out of Ottawa's political and judicial intervention, a less contentious set of issues, perhaps.

It was only later that Woodsworth came to see his association with the Winnipeg General Strike as an albatross around his neck. Immediately after the strike he had undertaken several speaking tours on behalf of the strikers and their arrested leaders. Woodsworth's own case never came to trial. In 1920 he resumed political work in British Columbia and after that worked for the Labor Church in Winnipeg. In June 1921 he returned to Winnipeg and in September was an FLP delegate at an exploratory meeting for a revived Canadian Labor Party.[90] Woodsworth's travels meant that he did not take part in what was the most important political event for the non-Marxist Left in Manitoba in the immediate aftermath of the strike: the founding of the Independent Labor Party of Manitoba in December 1920. The latter was mainly the result of the initiatives of Fred Dixon and S.J. Farmer.

After the strike, trade unionists in Winnipeg had split into two groups: the conservative TLC people around Bill Hoop, R.A. Rigg, and James Winning, and the OBU led by R.B. Russell. Parliamentary labourists such as Dixon and Farmer saw no need to offend either group.

Such broadmindedness was hardly likely to survive the charges made by Hoop in August 1920 that the strike had been an OBU conspiracy to found a soviet system, the very argument used by the authorities. When later in 1920 Hoop was nominated by the Dominion Labor Party to contest a seat on city council, Dixon and Farmer resigned from the DLP and in December founded the Independent Labor Party. Thus, when the exploratory meeting of the CLP was held the following September, Dixon and Farmer brought along some bitter memories. Historians have repeated the contention that the ILP rejected the CLP because the latter favoured group affiliation while the former wanted membership by individuals.[91] This was certainly a concern but not the determining factor. Fundamentally the ILP refused to join the CLP because it would have had to share membership in a party with the reactionary leadership of the Winnipeg TLC and DLP. Farmer put it well: 'So far as the ILP is concerned the whole matter of affiliation hinges ... upon the possibility of lining up with other labour bodies, some of which are content at times to be represented by individuals with very shady records in the labour movement.'[92] Woodsworth suggested a similar explanation in an article in the *Canadian Forum* in 1922:

Several years ago there was organized in Winnipeg the Manitoba section of the Dominion Labour Party, which latter never existed even on paper. In the municipal elections of 1920 the bitter antagonism between the members of the American Federation of Labour and the One Big Union led to a split in this organization. It was claimed that the Trades and Labour Council officials tried to dominate the political organization. The Independent Labour Party was formed by those who held that under existing conditions the political end of the movement must be entirely free, and the membership open equally to Internationals or One Big Union men ...

At the last Trades and Labour Congress held in Winnipeg there was formed the Canadian Labour Party. Each province was left to work out its own form of organization. In Winnipeg an attempt was made to secure, through this new body, at least co-operation between the Dominion Labour Party and the Independent Labour Party. The partisan feeling, however, was too strong and the effort failed.[93]

This historical digression is important because when Woodsworth finally returned to Winnipeg in late 1921 and joined the ILP he was aligning himself with many of the already established priorities and directions of that organization. This meant, most obviously, that he would not support the project of a new, national labour party: 'Bro. Woodsworth and several members from the North End Board were present ... and it was devoted almost wholly to the discussion of Dominion-wide organization, and after going carefully into all phases of the question, it was decided that the time was not opportune for a venture of this kind.'[94] Woodsworth needed little convincing. His general perception of the Left in the early and mid-1920s was that it was disorganized and fragmented beyond immediate redemption. If he did harbour any private hopes for the CLP they were completely destroyed once it was taken over by the Communist Party between 1925 and 1928.

In this way the Manitoba ILP moulded Woodsworth's relations with the Communists. The Manitoba section of the CPC or, as it was called until 1924, the Workers Party of Canada, may not have been as important as its Ontario part but it did have strong leadership and in the far North End of Winnipeg it could count on a large number of eastern European immigrants to support its ideological mixture of Marxism and nationalism. Areas of north Winnipeg were referred to by the ILP as 'the Communist districts.' In the early 1920s relations between the CPC and the ILP were formal but not uncooperative. Things seemed to have come completely unstuck in 1925. In September the ILP accused the CPC of running against the ILP in Winnipeg North under the camouflage of the CLP.[95] The next year the ILP was not amused when Kolisnyk, a Communist, was elected to Winnipeg city council. The *Weekly News*, the voice of the ILP, in an editorial on the Communists' proposal of a 'united front,' gave some sense of the intensity of the ILP's disdain for Communist tactics:

Elsewhere in this issue appears a translation of a news item sent from Winnipeg, presumably by one of the local Communists to a New York Communist journal ... But it is not its untruthfulness, not its boastfulness, that makes this report of interest to the workers of Winnipeg. It is its brazen admission of treachery. While claiming the result of this election as a victory for the communist policy of the 'united front', the article also claims it is a victory over the Independent Labor Party! It says that Kolisnyk ran on the ticket of the Independent Labor Party (which is not true), and also that he ran as an opponent of the labor party candidate! There were six candidates in the field in addition to the Communist, and there were three seats to be filled, with only two ILP candidates nominated, but the only opponent mentioned by the report is the ILP nominee ... In its zeal for a united front to fight capitalism, the Communist party forgets all about the common enemy, and concentrates all its energies on attempts to sabotage any and every working-class organization which does not swallow the whole impossibilist doctrine. A united front, they cry – but it must be on their platform, or else, in the interests of harmony and concerted action, they will stab you in the back.[96]

Woodsworth's position on all this was little different from that of the ILP, although he was more guarded in expressing it. As early as 1918–19 he had rejected Marxism mainly because of its espousal of violent revolution and its rejection of parliamentary and ameliorativist change. In general he disliked what he felt was the dogmatic, doctrinaire temper of Marxism. In his earliest comment on the newly founded Workers' Party of Canada in 1922 he expressed concern over its possible tendency to 'dominate' the rest of the Left.[97] Later he was more vocal in his criticism of the Communists. In October 1927 he rejected any cooperation: 'Can two walk together except they be agreed?'[98] Always, however, his criticism was civil and at the level of high theory. He did not engage in *ad hominem* arguments.

Such courtesy was not always returned. Canadian Marxists had always recognized Woodsworth's individual importance to the parliamentary Left. With the CPC's abandonment of a united-front strategy in 1929 and with the intensification of competition over who would lead the working-class movement in the 1930s, the criticism directed by the CPC towards Woodsworth became uncompromisingly personal and bitter. He was regarded as the quintessential bourgeois ideologue and social fascist, deceiver of the working class, and dupe of the capitalist. From a safe historical distance the tone of this rhetoric is almost humorous in its straining after ever more acidulous forms of abuse. Woodsworth once wrote:

The official organ of the communist party of Canada, The Worker, which is to be found in the reading room, where I occasionally read it, on March 21, 1931, published the following:
'The treacherous labour parties of Woodsworth, Heaps and Company.'
And again:
'In Winnipeg, as elsewhere, the I.L.P. fakers are the righthand men of the fascist police administration.'
On March 7, this same organ of the communist party published this statement:

'The Abramoviches, the MacDonalds, the Blums and the Crespians of Europe have their counterparts in Canada in the persons of the Woodsworths, the Heapses, the Moores and the Moshers.'

Referring to a speech which I had given before a service club in Brantford the paper contains the following item:

'The labour-hating bourgeoisie of the Kiwanis Club had the pleasure of listening to a social fascist address them at one of their blowouts.'

Referring to myself I find the following:

'This slimy pacifist bleated out a lot of vague (but dangerous) banalities of a general character but when he got down to cases he soon showed his hand ... He is either a fool or a liar ... the faker.'[99]

Especially galling was the false accusation by A.E. Smith, a Communist leader, that Woodsworth had aided and abetted the authorities in the bringing of a charge of sedition against him in January 1934.[100]

In fact, if there was an instance of a highly principled but ultimately politically injudicious and thankless support of an unpopular minority it was Woodsworth's defence of the political rights of the Communists in the face of Section 98, the Immigration Act, and later the Quebec government's infamous Padlock law.[101] To Woodsworth the issue was clear. The state in a society espousing British standards of rights and freedoms could neither legitimately punish ideas and beliefs, nor summarily deport the non-Canadian-born without due process of trial by jury. It is not certain that Woodsworth was clear in his own mind what the precise limits of the rights of the state should be in the matter of sedition. Evidently, he believed that existing legislation was too vague in its definition of what constituted force, did not preserve a presumption of innocence, gave the state an excessive power of seizure, and prescribed penalties that were too severe. Woodsworth was also concerned about the police's discretionary use of the provisions on sedition, especially in Toronto, where public meetings had been forbidden unless English was used. After that there was some vagueness in his position. He seemed to hold that there were four possible definitions of sedition: membership in a political party that advocated force; a personal belief in force; the overt advocacy of force; and the actual use of force. The last two, Woodsworth seemed to say, could properly be proscribed by the state. This is a significantly different position from, say, Frank Scott's defence of the principle of freedom of expression as requiring a scrupulous distinction between a belief in or advocacy of violence on the one hand and its practice on the other.[102]

According to Scott, only the latter was truly seditious. Moreover, in his opposition to the Immigration Act Woodsworth never disputed the government's right to deport immigrants on a variety of grounds: criminal behaviour, mental defectiveness, moral turpitude, and, indeed, seditious actions.[103] Deportation, however, should be undertaken only after due process by jury trial. The subtleties of Woodsworth's position on these two issues made him not nearly as radical as his reputation would aver, but this was largely lost on contemporary critics who only heard him undertaking a blanket defence of Communists and Communism.

Woodsworth himself was adamant that the civil rights of Communists had nothing to do with approving either of Marxism or of the behaviour of Canadian Communists:

Although they denounce us; although the leader of the communist party has gone into the constituency of the hon. member for North Winnipeg (Mr. Heaps) and has put the whole organization of the communist party behind an effort to defeat him – despite all that I say that the place to defeat communism in a democratic country is at the ballot box ... and not by arresting people who do not agree with our political opinions ...[104]

I am pleading for their rights, not because I love communism or because I am cooperating with communism, but because I have at heart the old teaching of our childhood days, namely that the British citizen has certain inalienable rights, and I believe that those rights should be preserved. It is quite true that Trotsky, one of the great Russian leaders, was exiled, and that probably logically debars the communists in this country from protesting against any curtailment of speech here. But it does not debar me from protesting against curtailment of speech, for I believe that freedom of speech has always been the proud boast of Great Britain.[105]

As the 1930s wore on Woodsworth became more and more resentful of the bitterness of Communist criticisms and the constant about-turns in the Communist Party's policies. His suspicion of an inherent urge to dominance in all Communist overtures of cooperation towards the non-Marxist Left became stronger.[106] The election results in Ontario in 1937 especially convinced him of the electoral liability of too close an association with the Communists. If care was not taken the CCF might be destroyed: 'I think it should be clear now that the Communist Party vote and the Communist Party influence was against the CCF everywhere, regardless of protestation to the contrary ... There is nothing to be gained from a United Front ... Let us make no mistake – the CP is out to destroy the CCF ... The whole history of the Communist Party is a clear demonstration of the fact that what it seeks to accomplish is control of the working class movement ... We must drive home unceasingly the point that wherever the CP gets control every other party will be destroyed. Socialist parties as well as capitalist parties.'[107] With the appropriate internal resolve the CCF could hold the Communists at arm's length. But mustering that will was the problem. There was always a large minority of CCFers who sympathized with revolutionary causes and who, in pursuit of the unity of the Left, supported united-front organizations such as the Canadian Labor Defence League, the League Against War and Fascism, and the Committee to Aid Spanish Democracy. Unity was envisaged by some as involving electoral pacts and understandings; other saw it as including political fusion. Woodsworth was unalterably opposed to any of these forms of cooperation. In March 1934 he and the CCF's National Council suspended the Provincial Council of the Ontario CCF in order to discipline the labour section of the party, which was in favour of a collaborative strategy. Woodsworth's relations with Canadian Communists belied his customary proclivity for compromise and cooperation, even with political opponents:

As I see it, the Communists have been incurable romanticists. They delight in what we used to call 'Play acting.' The Russian scene has dominated their thinking. Their policies in Canada have been determined by developments in Europe. Recently the growth of Fascism has led Russia to co-operate with democratic France. Hence Canadian Communists are instructed to co-operate with the C.C.F., but will not deny that they believe revolutionary changes must come by force and by the setting up of a dictatorship. If they did not so believe, why should they not join the C.C.F.?

Their plan confessedly is to transform the C.C.F. into a loose labor-farmer federation with which they can affiliate. The Communist Party is to be a compact, well disciplined party that can dominate the federation. This is their so-called united front ...

The C.C.F. has already succeeded to a remarkable degree in building a united front of labor and farmers and small business men, intellectuals and church people ...

As one who has sat in parliament for 15 years, I recognize the desirability of co-operation, almost the inevitability of co-operation – in furthering particular measures. When the Communists show themselves willing to 'play the game,' larger measures of co-operation may well be worked out. But let it not be forgotten that in the past united front tactics have led to confusion and left behind a long trail of bitterness, disruption and disaster. Unity among ourselves is the first consideration.[108]

Yet at the same time as Woodsworth was waging battle with the Canadian Communists, he was becoming more and more enamoured of the Soviet Union.[109] And there was an even greater irony. While his principles may have required him to defend the political rights of Canadian Communists even if this made him unpopular, they did not necessitate an encomium of the Soviet Union. But such was what he eventually expressed, thereby confirming his reputation in the minds of impressionable political critics as a Bolshevik and secret revolutionary.

Woodsworth was not unusual either as a moral philosopher or political activist in expressing a historicism towards the past and a voluntarism towards the present. History's revolutions, he believed, were integral to the progress of civilization. However, this did not mean that their methods were to be imitated in the present. As societies faced their future, the determining consideration should be freely devised standards of right conduct. So Woodsworth's bifurcated ethical system justified violent revolution in the past but evolutionary and peaceful methods in the here-and-now.[110] Other elements of his thought allowed him to put himself at a distance from the Soviet experiment. Proper historical understanding for him must take account of the unique and particular circumstances of such events as the Russian revolution. The Bolshevik revolutionaries had succeeded neither through superior tactics nor greater political initiative; the old order had simply collapsed under the weight of its own incompetence, autocracy, and war-weariness.[111] Indeed the persistence of national cultural traditions meant that the new Soviet regime partook of many of the unfortunate characteristics of the old: political authoritarianism and the secret police. Obviously, therefore, what was culturally specific to Russia could be of little relevance to Canada.

Woodsworth had a perfect pretext to say little or nothing about the Soviet Union. If he had wanted foreign models to imitate and extol – and his method did not require them – he could, reasonably, have confined himself to more culturally and politically cognate countries such as Britain, Sweden, Australia, and New Zealand, where there had been early successes in parliamentary socialism.[112] But Woodsworth could not leave things alone. A scrupulous separation of himself and his party from the CPC, at least in most things, was not complemented by an equal distancing of himself from the Soviet Union. He took great pains to establish that there was no love lost between himself and Canadian Communists; he did not take the same care with the Soviet Union.

A certain minimal respect for the interests of the Soviet Union may not have been politically adventurous. After 1918 the new revolutionary state had been isolated and beleaguered. As much for considerations of *realpolitik* as high principle, Woodsworth was perhaps justified in arguing for an end of the embargo on trade with Russia and later its inclusion in the League of Nations.[113] He also pressed for an end to the more sensational accusations against the regime, that, for example, it exploited political prisoners and paid workers slave wages, and that Lenin had been personally responsible for killing a woman in a cave. In May 1928, however, Woodsworth went further and announced a positive sympathy with the Soviet Union. Referring to 'the general popular conception that the Labour movement is seriously affected with sympathy for Russia,' he said: 'We are sympathetic with Russia; I do not deny it. I regard the experiment in Russia as one of the greatest that has been made in any part of the world, or in any age in history. We can look back to-day with something like a dispassionate view to the achievements of the French revolution, and I believe the time is coming when we will look back to the Russian revolution of ten years ago as marking one of the greatest epochs in the history of the world. I am not suggesting that we in Canada should proceed along Russian lines – that is another question.'[114] For the moment, Woodsworth was content with a position of distant admiration for a historical experiment, which Canada nevertheless should not imitate. (Why an avowedly practical politician, preaching to a hostile, sceptical audience, was justified in expressing abstract wonderment, he never explained.) He continued his speech by employing what was for him a typical rhetorical device: quoting the approving conclusions of reputedly neutral, independent observers. In his many speeches and writings on the Soviet Union he appealed to a number of such authorities: Sidney Webb, Stuart Chase, Sherwood Eddy, Norman Angell, Sir Frederick Banting, Anna Louise Strong, and Maurice Hindus. On this occasion in May 1928, he quoted Colonel Mackie, a former Conservative Member of Parliament from Pembroke, Ontario. Mackie had claimed that western leaders had systematically misrepresented what was going on in the Soviet Union; from his own travels he had found the situation very encouraging; people in Moscow and Leningrad were well dressed, contented, and prosperous; and great strides were being made in education. Turning to affairs of state, Woodsworth quoted from Mackie's complimentary account of the Soviet political leadership. Read today it reveals an almost indecent measure of bad judgment, perhaps the inevitable consequence of attempts to have the heart pre-emptively rule the head in matters of complicated and contentious political significance: '"I have been greatly impressed with the absolute sincerity of the men at the top of Russian affairs. Stalin is the great man of Russia to-day," said Col. Mackie. "He is a quiet, reserved man, but he is very able, and the people trust him. Trotsky's power is on the wane. One thing that has impressed me greatly in Russia is that the leaders there are willing to admit their mistakes and to change their plans if they find they will not work."'[115] Woodsworth's defence of the Soviet Union was not without reservation. The tone of his speeches was never as optimistic as those of such complete fellow-travellers as the Webbs, Hindus, and Strong.[116] Still, such criticisms as he did advance – that the economy was inefficient and wasteful, that the regime used autocratic methods, that farm collectivization may not have been wholly successful – were invariably qualified and mitigated by comparison with an equally bad or worse situation in Canada or the West:

The political situation is still dominated by the Communist Party which maintains a rigid discipline over its membership. However, it was pointed out that in using machine methods at election times, the Communists were simply doing what the capitalists were doing in this country. We talk glibly about the people in Canada being in control, but any one who has been in close touch with the political situation must admit that the policies of this country are not determined by the needs of the industrial workers and farmers and small middlemen who form such a large proportion of our population.[117]

[Hours and wages in Russia] compare favourably with the hours and wages that prevail in Cape Breton ... I have seen photographs of the housing conditions in the mining districts of Russia that put to shame the housing conditions in Cape Breton.[118]

The charges with regard to the mining of coal have not been proven. It is stated that political prisoners are exploited. What about political prisoners in Italy? It is stated that the standard of living in Soviet Russia is low. I will admit that, but it is higher than that under the Czarist regime and higher than the standard of living in China or in India.[119]

I am not one of those who would lightly dismiss communist ideas; certainly the communists have hit upon something that is producing results. I am quite willing to admit that it may be that an autocratic system of this kind is possible only with a people having the Russian temperament. It may be that a democracy would not lend itself to the successful carrying through of a communist program. I would take exception however to what was said here yesterday, that we are a free people and can do as we please. We have very little freedom in this country, and while I do not like the dictatorship they have in Russia, and do not hesitate to say so, neither do I like the dictatorship we have in this country of ours, a financial dictatorship which operates under the guise of democracy.[120]

Woodsworth had his own chance to examine the Russian experiment. In August 1931 he was seconded to work for the League of Nation's Secretariat. His expenses were paid from Canada to Geneva and back. After the league's annual session was over he journeyed to Vienna and then to the Soviet Union, returning through Berlin. Woodsworth kept a brief diary of his and Lucy's trip.[121] They crossed the border at Orscha and proceeded by train through Minsk to Leningrad. There they visited the traditional sights: the Hermitage Museum, the Winter Palace, and a number of churches. In Moscow they toured art galleries, factories, schools, and a people's court; and met with the former Soviet trade commissioner to Ottawa as well as with Strong, Hindus, and a number of British, American, and Canadian journalists.[122] The overall atmosphere conveyed by the diary was of endless delays and inefficiencies and of the claustrophobic press of humanity in railway cars and streets. That the Woodsworths arrived at all in Leningrad seems to have been a minor miracle of Soviet railway logistics. Only there did they finally meet up with their Intourist guide. Their travels, confined as they were to the two main cities, left them with little exposure to the countryside.

On his return Woodsworth published two articles in the *Toronto Star Weekly*.[123] He reported honestly on the inefficiency, the overcrowding, and the shortage of materials and labour in the economy, as well as on government autocracy and red tape. Yet the predominant impression he gained was of activity, energy, construction – a people on the move: 'It is easy to criticize Michael Angelo's statues. Many minor parts are crudely executed or entirely in the rough. Should we centre our attention on obvious defects, or is not criticism silenced by the overpowering impression of a great idea emerging from a rough block of marble?'[124] Offsetting Soviet achievements was the ubiquitous and intrusive presence of the state, but Woodsworth implied that this was a natural and perhaps understandable continuation of Russian cultural habits: 'An eminent English historian has advanced the thesis that in each country, though names and parties and personalities may change, institutions continue much the same. In other words, they remain true to the fundamental national type. The developments in Russia lend some colour to this theory. The dictatorship of the czars has been replaced by that of the Communistic party. The traditions of the secret police have been carried on by the O.G.P.U. Central authority is everywhere in evidence. Reliance seems to be placed on edicts, and then popular slogans.'[125] Particularly in Leningrad Woodsworth had confronted the question of the treatment of the church by the new regime. He recognized that the cult of personality attending Lenin had obvious religious overtones.

The overall fate of the old Orthodox Church, however, met with his approval. His own early astringent, Protestant, anti-sacerdotal views merged nicely with his later scientific rationalism:

The church, once so strong, has not been extirpated. The Bolshevists have been content to cut its main roots and leave it to die. Its revenues have been largely cut off and its educational work has been forbidden. Only formal services are permitted. The death of the church may prove no great loss. As I visited these Russian churches I was reminded of a phrase used many years ago by Principal Fairbairn, 'Baptized Paganism.' This mummery, this appeal to superstition, this lack of ethical training, this yielding to the baser elements in human nature, this subservience to the Powers That Be – what claim has such an institution on our sympathy? ... In Leningrad one magnificent church, St Isaacs, has been turned into an anti-religious museum. Curiously enough, many of the evils against which there is the strongest protest are those against which in western Europe, the Reformers struggled in the Sixteenth century. The eyes of the people are being opened to the large amount spent on candles and on securing spiritual benefits. Frauds connected with the relics of saints are exposed. A curious exhibit is that of the mummified bodies of some of the pre-historic peoples of northern Siberia whose remains are shown to be as well preserved as those of the miracle-working saints. By pictures and various devices and slogans the church is represented as standing in with the nobles and with the wealthy classes, as blessing war, as uttering no protest against capitalistic cruelty, as amassing wealth at the expense of a people kept in superstition. We were reminded that during the Civil War, the counter-revolutionaries, accompanied by the clergy, carried a banner with the inscription, 'In God We Trust.' Is it to be wondered at that their defeat spelled disaster to the Baal with whom they stood identified?[126]

In Moscow the Woodsworths had greater opportunities to view industrial and social developments. They visited a textile factory. The equipment was inferior and its organization inefficient, but Woodsworth was impressed by the joint management provided by workers, managers, and the party. In the streets the workers were clean and well dressed though they were often unsmiling. High culture was available to the workers; they went to the opera, for example, dressed in ordinary clothes and, like true proletarians, left not in a carriage but on foot. Woodsworth was especially impressed by the revolutionary techniques of jurisprudence and criminology. In the new people's courts justice was meted out by ordinary citizens who had been elected judges for a short time. At trials lawyers were rarely present and legal precedent only infrequently followed; each case was decided on its own merits, with an eye to the reform of the accused: 'Surely this is judgement by one's peers.' Schools for delinquent boys and the new system of prisons also impressed him. In the prisons the majority of the guards were elected by the prisoners, and discipline was maintained by a committee of prisoners: 'All this sounds like a fairy tale, I know, but the thing was actually working.' After describing the availability of easy-going divorce procedures, Woodsworth concluded on a note of cautious optimism: 'The revolution in Russia is not only political. It is in reality the building of a new social order with a new standard of morality, new notices and new ideals. But what of the future? The forces at work in the present are too vast and too complicated and too little understood to be comprehended. Why waste time in speculation?'[127]

Certainly, for his part, there was no conscious attempt to recommend such policies to Canadian decision-makers, although it is difficult to believe that Woodsworth in his private moments did not think that Russian initiatives in prison reform and industrial co-management were inappropriate to Canadian society. He came closest to prescribing Russian methods for Canada in his discussion of the success of the

Soviet Union's economic plans, especially the Five Year Plan that had begun in 1928.[128] Russia, he observed, had begun the Bolshevik experiment in 1920 from scratch; progress had been slow and sometimes irregular, but in the course of ten years, without the benefits of foreign credits, the country had built up a remarkable industrial infrastructure while also raising the standard of living of its people. The efficiency to be derived from public planning would of necessity force other nations to introduce it too. On his return to Canada Woodsworth told the Commons:

I talked to a large number of American technicians, who had no interest whatever in communism ... One of them who was on the train with me as we came out ... said, 'I have been all over this country in the last three or four months making a survey. If things were done as efficiently here as they are in America I could have done my work in as many weeks. No doubt there is a great deal of inefficiency and waste, but these Russians do not often make the same mistake twice. They are learning, and I think they are going to make good. If they do there is going to be a hard time ahead for us in America.' He was from the western United States and, after having made a survey, that was his opinion. Whether or not we agree with communism it is absolutely stupid for us to adopt that policy which traditionally belongs to the ostrich, that of burying its head in the sand. We cannot refuse to see what is going on. If for no other reason than to compete with communism I think it would be a good thing if the members of this house, and representatives of western Europe generally, looked well into what is going on.[129]

In the late 1930s, however, disillusion set in. The venomousness of Canadian Communist attacks on him, a growing recognition that the CCF was in mortal combat with the CPC for dominance of left-wing politics and the trade unions, the slow revelation of the true face of Stalinism, the astounding turnabout in Soviet foreign policy in 1939, and perhaps plain, personal exhaustion, all contributed to his final change of heart. His nemesis from Winnipeg, Jake Penner, a Communist and city councillor, had been arrested in 1940 under the wartime emergency regulations. Mrs Rose Penner wrote to Woodsworth seeking his help to obtain the release of her husband. In one fell swoop Woodsworth threw over a political lifetime of defence of the 'inalienable' rights of Communists, an admiration of the Soviet Union, and a profound conviction that emergency circumstances never justified emergency powers:

Dear Mrs. Penner,

I have not sufficiently recovered to be able to deal with any public questions as yet. May I point out nevertheless that with the legislation now on the statute books, it would seem that the authorities are within their legal rights in taking the action they have.

For me war almost inevitably means that those civil liberties which we took for granted in peacetime became precarious if not lost. Underlying the action of the authorities is the whole conception of communism, its objects and methods and further, the question as to whether a man can give his allegiance to the Soviet State and still retain any real loyalty towards a state organized under what is known as a democracy. Of course I note that you use the phrase 'democracy' but I cannot see that dictatorship of the proletariat, whatever its supposed advantages may be, bears any close resemblance to the ideals underlying what is generally accepted as 'democracy.'

You speak of the 'secret service agents.' I regret that we are apparently increasing the use of methods of this character but perhaps I might point out that it is generally believed that such agents are commonly used in the Soviet Union and that many of the practices of getting rid of political enemies without full and open trial are there prevalent. I do not propose to discuss these questions but would point out that Canadian citizens naturally wish to protect themselves against the growth of a movement under foreign direction.

If certain organizations have been declared illegal it is not altogether illogical that representatives of these organizations should be prevented from holding office or exercising public influence.

Personally I have always heard Mr. Penner well spoken of and can well understand how in these difficult times, it becomes increasingly hard for a man to retain his own political beliefs when they differ fundamentally from those of the majority and at the same time, carry on along ordinary lines which he has perhaps almost uncritically followed. As the crisis becomes more acute many concealed contradictions manifest themselves. It becomes clear that one cannot have it both ways.

I still have a profound believe [sic] in civil liberties and in democratic principles. My fear is that war imperils both.[130]

V

Woodsworth believed that the Left in Canada would pursue its own unique political trajectory. Its course would be unlike the revolutionary pattern of the Russians and instead similar to that of the Swedes or the British. But if that was to be the likely *mode of change*, what about the prospects of *success*? The Left in Canada would pursue socialism constitutionally but might it not do so unsuccessfully? Perhaps the fate of the Left here would be closer to the dismal failure of socialism in the United States than to its encouraging development in western Europe? Woodsworth did not know all the answers as he embarked on his parliamentary odyssey in 1921. He perceived the need for a national, non-Marxist, socialist party that would be inclusive, constitutionalist, and practical but also revolutionary in social and economic intent. In retrospect it might be said that history was neither kind nor helpful to him. Canada, in terms of the success enjoyed by socialism, was more like the United States than Europe. Still it may be asked: did Woodsworth through his decisions and actions make the best of the admittedly bad hand history had dealt to him?

In the 1920s the Canadian Left was divided, disorganized, and demoralized. Where labour parties existed, and often they did not exist at all, they were usually weak. After the First World War the Canadian Labor Party might have functioned as the basis for a successful, national party of the Left except that, in the minds of Woodsworth and other leaders of the influential Manitoba Independent Labor Party, the CLP was fatally compromised by its early associations with conservative unionists in the DLP and the TLC, not to mention its eventual domination by the Communist Party. Only by 1932 did circumstances allow the formation of a new national democratic party of labour, farmers, and middle-class progressives. As a national party leader the crucial test for Woodsworth was the federal election of 1935. The results proved that the new CCF was badly organized, underfunded, and vulnerable to charges of being close to the Communists. By 1940 Woodsworth was outside the mainstream of Canadian politics and, in any event, in a condition of terminal ill health.

This in sum was the unencouraging environment Woodsworth had to confront. Even so, there were successes. In spite of his symbiotic relationship with the Liberals, he handed on to M.J. Coldwell, his successor, a political party that was politically independent. Earlier, in the 1920s, he had also prevented the radical farmers from being absorbed by the Liberal Party. And though this begs many questions, it can be said that Woodsworth 'saved' the Canadian working class from the embrace of the Communist Party. Finally, if he was politically powerless for much of the 1920s and 1930s, he was not devoid of that more intangible quality, namely political influence. He was deeply involved in the growing contemporary leftward movement of social thought in Canada, especially on matters to do with the welfare state. Indeed he did much to establish the threat from the Left that was so great an influence on the behaviour of succeeding Liberal governments, most obviously in 1926 but increasingly after 1943.

There were personal achievements, then, but what of the personal failures? And how far did these limit the potential success of the Left in the inter-war years and thereafter? Clearly his lack of intellectual clarity and coherence has to be remarked upon. His complicated personality fused an incorrigible passion for ideas with a conception of political action of almost mundane practicality. In the gap between the two, no doubt many a supporter fell through, in confusion. Woodsworth never gave a consistent account of the relationship of theory to practice, especially in the matter of how to make change. If, as he believed, principle must be open to compromise in order to bring about a practical effect, and if action should never be undertaken at the expense of fundamental principle, where lay the dividing line between acceptable and unacceptable compromise? Woodsworth never clarified this distinction. In its absence we are left to wonder whether indeed such a distinction really existed in his own mind, or whether he was the only arbiter of it.

Nor were the elements of pragmatism and principle always carefully and effectively mixed in his political practice. Here his position on Communism and the Soviet Union is instructive. Woodsworth's defence of the rights of Canadian Communists was noble and heroic although probably politically naive, as he himself belatedly recognized in his letter to Mrs Penner in 1940. It may well be that, to preserve its moral fervour, radicalism must embrace a quixotic idealism now and then. Let us grant that the defence of the Canadian Communists was Woodsworth's particular indulgence of this necessity. But what of his defence and admiration of the Soviet Union, not to mention his visit there in 1931? These added little if anything to the integrity of the message to his fellow Canadians, invited the inevitable and electorally damaging charge of being a fellow-traveller, and seemingly contradicted all that he so strenuously had said about the evils of the home-grown Marxists in the Canadian Communist Party.

There was also the perplexing contrast between the vast variety of the ideas he entertained and articulated, and the often decidedly narrow focus of his actions. Recall his position on cooperative government. At the level not of private musings but public debate, he espoused almost the full panoply of political syndicalism. Yet his own behaviour in Parliament was remarkably conventional. Only on the divorce issue did he test the patience of the House and the limits of its rules. He never really pursued adventurous or imaginative strategies. If one's political behaviour is to be so conventional, perhaps politicians, even radical ones, have an obligation to curtail their publicizing of luxuriant and fanciful ideas. Sometimes, it seemed, Woodsworth enjoyed not only the sound of his own voice but, especially, the sound of his own ideas. While his passion for ideas seemed to flow from a joyous enthusiasm for intellect itself, it also derived from the ruthless self-criticism of the would-be Christian saint. To Woodsworth, to say nothing was to refuse to take a stand and thus to admit to sin. Thus thought and action came together. The common denominator of his life and thought was a refusal ever to say or do nothing. The necessity of action led to a praxis of compromise; the equal compulsion always to state a position led him to articulate a belief system of uncommon variety and spaciousness. Bringing the two together was never easily accomplished. Somehow he managed to combine an excess of political pragmatism with a superfluity of political rhetoric.

The worldly desire to have a practical effect bequeathed to the Canadian Left what was probably the most ambiguous of his legacies: the political entente with Mackenzie King in 1926 to establish an old-age-pension program. Woodsworth had been in Parliament only four years when he concluded this agreement, and the founding of the CCF was still six years away. The entente quickly entered the mythology of the non-Marxist Left in Canada as the definitive proof of the effectiveness of even a small caucus of labour Members of Parliament. To this day it is held up as a glorious example of Woodsworth's triumphs. And it *was* a triumph of sorts, even if it was very dependent on the unusual circumstances of a Commons in which the labour members held the balance of power. But it can still be asked whether the entente of 1926 froze much too quickly the still fluid pattern of centre-left politics in this country in the inter-war years and beyond. As a model of change it began the tradition of symbiosis mainly with official liberalism and established the ideal of political action for the Left in Parliament as the immediate influencing of the government. It fostered the idea of the Left as a splinter or interest group seeking to influence usually the Liberals, thereby limiting it to the role of marginal participants and petitioners in the government process, the conscience of Parliament – Liberals in a hurry. Something of immediate advantage was gained but perhaps at long-term cost. Old age pensions arrived but the labour members' identification with the Liberals (or the Conservatives after Woodsworth's support of Bennett's New Deal legislation), made difficult an unambiguous appeal to voters at subsequent elections to support them rather than the governing party that had, after all, brought forward the legislation in question. Besides, now that the Liberals had finally proven that they were capable of reform, in the minds of some it was better not to split the reformist vote and let the usually reactionary Conservatives gain power. The 1926 election set in motion a minority-party syndrome which made it difficult for the Left to attain what was, no doubt, its primary aim, namely winning control of government. Never popular enough to aspire to power, it could always gain support for a promise to keep the government honest and progressive. This was essentially Woodsworth's position in the elections of 1926, 1930, 1935, and 1940. The pattern continued long after his death in 1942.

4

Economics, Cooperation, and Socialism, 1922–1940

The efficiency of the capitalist system
Is rightly admired by important people.
Our huge steel mills
Operating at 25 per cent of capacity
Are the last word in organization.
The new grain elevators
Stored with superfluous wheat
Can unload a grain-boat in two hours.
Marvellous card-sorting machines
Make it easy to keep track of the unemployed.
There isn't one unnecessary employee
In these textile plants
That require a 75 per cent protection.
And when our closed shoe factories re-open
They will produce more footwear than we can possibly buy.
So don't let's start experimenting with socialism
Which everyone knows will mean inefficiency and waste.

F.R. Scott

I

Canada's economic performance in the inter-war years, as with most economies at the time, fell into two markedly discordant parts: the 1920s were generally buoyant and the 1930s scandalously depressed. In Canada, as elsewhere, economic expansion had resumed in 1895 and had continued until the eve of the First World War. In these years the burgeoning vitality of the prairie wheat economy had confounded even the greatest sceptic: immigrants had poured in, wheat prices had been high, two new national railway systems had been built and, with the increased use of machinery, farm productivity had leapt ahead. Whatever trends were in place before 1914 were stimulated anew in wartime. Government borrowing to finance large expenditures attained unprecedented proportions and gave additional stimulus to the economy. Growth faltered in the immediate post-war period but reasserted itself after 1923. Canada's Gross National Product expanded substantially between 1926 and 1929, and between 1925 and 1928 unemployment was cut in half. The country ran consecutive positive trade balances throughout the 1920s and profits were high; wages failed to keep pace but, in general, they did not decline; prices in the decade were amazingly stable, and, with the exception of 1922-6, when there was extensive worker unrest at the British Empire Steel Corporation, relations between labour and capital were uneventful, which is to say, perhaps, that labour's influence was weak. Much changed after 1929 with the onset of the Great Depression. Prices dropped, confidence in the stock market evaporated, demand contracted, and labour agitation was eventually reborn; almost every indicator plummeted to unimaginable levels of economic dislocation and mass indigence. The year 1933 was the nadir of the Depression. Thereafter matters slowly improved until war's outbreak in 1939.[1]

Canada, in 1920, was more recognizably 'modern' in its economic structure than it had been just twenty years earlier. In the intervening period the west had been settled and a national economy rounded out. Industrial companies and extractive enterprises such as pulp and paper, mining, and refining assumed a larger place in the nation's economic life. Canada became more and more urbanized; industrial ownership became more concentrated; and extensive American direct investment with its organizational corollary, the branch plant, made major inroads.

To radicals slightly older than Woodsworth, the *bête noire* of an early expansionist capitalism was Max Aitken, later Lord Beaverbrook, with his financial manoeuverings in areas such as trust companies, steel, and cement.[2] To Woodsworth in the 1920s the unacceptable face of monopoly capitalism was epitomized in Sir Herbert Holt, who, he pointed out in 1928, held 135 directorships and controlling interests in such companies as Montreal Light and Power, United Securities, Dominion Bridge, Dominion Textile, Famous Players, Canadian Pacific

Railway, Ogilvie Mills, Sun Life Insurance, Besco, and the Royal Bank.[3] Canada's industrial magnates not only had diverse interests; they increasingly controlled large, concentrated enterprises. The merger movement had peaked in 1908–11; but there was another round of intense merger activity between 1924 and 1928.[4] 'In 1890, about 63 per cent of manufacturing value added was produced by 2,879 plants. By 1922, about 66 per cent of manufacturing value added was produced by only 936 plants.'[5] These trusts and combines introduced the new systems of scientific management. The most innovative industries, such as high-technology manufacturing, smelting, and pulp and paper, were the most frequent practitioners of the new management theories; typically they were also the ones most subject to foreign ownership.[6]

Concentration and centralization were particularly evident in another sector: banking. From before Confederation, banks had been commercially oriented and conservative.[7] With the support of the administration in London and later the federal government, the banks had resisted the American example of free, unit banking, and by the turn of the century they had begun to extend their branches to the west. In the beginning, they were numerous;[8] in 1874 there were fifty-one chartered banks. Thereafter their number declined. By 1920 there were eighteen and in 1930 eleven, four of which were comparatively large. Under the Dominion Bank Notes Act (1870) and the Bank Act (1871) the banks were permitted to issue bank notes in the higher currency amounts and were required to hold half their reserves in government notes.[9] As a result, a limited measure of government control of the money supply was possible. But since Canada was on the gold standard the regulating of the money supply was mainly on an international basis. In 1914 Canada went off the gold standard and did not return to it until 1926, only to go off it again in 1931. Under the Finance Act (1914) the Minister of Finance could issue government notes to the banks 'on the promise of acceptable security. The banks could use such ... to expand their note issues and so to be multiplied by deposit creation to a larger change in the money supply.'[10] By such expedients the federal government inched towards assuming a larger control of money, a trend that culminated in the establishment of the Bank of Canada in 1935.

The inter-war years brought home to some that, in addition to mergers and monopolies, foreign ownership was a new, disturbing feature of the Canadian economic system. One of the earliest articles on the subject was 'The Penetration of American Capital in Canada' by J. Marjorie van der Hoek in the *Canadian Forum* in August 1926. She observed that the British had invested sparingly in the nineteenth century but had increased their activities substantially after 1900 with investments in the two new trans-continental railways. After 1900 the Americans, too, increased their investments sharply though, as she put it, theirs were 'speculative and industrial.' During the First World War American investment overtook the British and it zoomed ahead throughout the 1920s. Already by 1920, van der Hoek concluded, United States interests had control over copper and smelting, drugs and chemicals, autos, steel mills, and electrical firms.

The distinctive instrument of American investment was the branch plant, a subsidiary of the parent firm in the United States. The branch plant allowed American firms established in Canada to escape the 1879 tariff and to acquire Canadian status under imperial preference arrangements in the export of goods to the United Kingdom. Branch plants imported many finished goods to reassemble; as well, they introduced new technologies and management strategies in this emerging progressive world of science, efficiency, and multi-nationalism. Gordon Laxer states there were as many as 450 American subsidiaries in Canada in 1914;[11] van der Hoek put the number at 700 by 1922; Woodsworth said there were 1,500 in 1931;[12] Marr and Paterson claim that between 1914 and 1936 'the stock of United States direct investment alone expanded at a rate of about 6 per cent, compounded annually' and that in 1926 'non-residents directed about 17 per cent of the book value of all Canadian industry.'[13] In 1930 foreign investment stood at an inter-war peak of $7.6 billion, 61 per cent of which was American in origin.[14]

The Canadian federal state emerged from the First World War in a financial straitjacket. As with the financing of the infrastructure of the young Dominion, the conduct of the war had been undertaken on credit. In 1915 the federal government had an accumulated direct and indirect debt of close to $1 billion; by 1920 it stood at almost $3 billion and it rose in the 1920s.[15] The Depression made debt matters worse again. A more adventurous government might have retired some of its debts by greater use of income and business taxes or a capital levy, or perhaps even a partial repudiation of its bonded indebtedness. Cautious governments instead maintained the *status quo*. They continued, willy nilly, to rely on the established revenue source of indirect taxes, particularly customs import duties.[16] Throughout the 1920s and 1930s the latter constituted never less than 65 per cent of federal revenues and often a good deal more. (In 1925 they accounted for 83 per cent.)

If indirect taxes were dependable sources of revenue, they were hardly 'growth' taxes. Cautious Liberal governments under Mackenzie King came to the inevitable policy conclusion: if the national debt stood at such heights and if new tax sources were unusable while traditional ones were already over-exploited, expenditures had to be either contained or cut back. There was little fiscal room for new legislative measures or spending programs. (Bennett held to a similar view, though he was willing to raise tariffs somewhat.) The expenditures of the federal government stood at $529 million in 1920, dropped to $356 million in 1925, and rose to $442 million in 1930; in 1935 the federal government allocated expenditures of $533 million.[17] Thus there was little growth of government spending in these years and what change did occur was frequently in a downward direction. Expenditures continued to be spent in the traditional areas: debt payments, veterans pensions, defence, and the post office. On average in the inter-war period these areas consumed about one half of government's expenditures. As Woodsworth tartly pointed out on several occasions, in comparison the federal government spent less than 1 per cent on health, science, and labour.

II

When Woodsworth entered Parliament he was already a convinced socialist. He believed he was borne upwards on a rising tide of economic collectivization, that is, monopolies and the factory system. This auspicious transformation had been brought about because of the mechanization of the workplace. Woodsworth's socialism served him well in his time in the Commons and had the advantage, as well, of clearly distinguishing him from the Conservatives and Liberals. It was not, however, the only important part of his economic thinking. He derived his socialism from two other intellectual sources: J.A. Hobson's under-consumption doctrine and Irving Fisher's and Frank William Taussig's quantity theory of money.

Woodsworth drew much of his account of the rise of industrial society from British history. He also attempted to make some sense of the particularity of Canada's economic experience so that what emerged at his hands was a curious melding and separating of the economic histories of the two countries, typical indeed of Woodsworth's general relationship with his native country and the 'motherland.'[18] Compared to Britain, Canada, he believed, lacked an aristocracy and its class system was much more fluid and undeveloped. Early manufacture here, as in Britain, had been undertaken by independent craftsmen and operators of cottage industries. The early Canadian political economy had been greatly shaped by its being a freeholder society with free land always available on some distant though accessible frontier. For much of the nineteenth century a national market for agricultural products had not existed; everything was local; society was roughly equal, social and geographical mobility was high, and, he implied, early political institutions provided a satisfactory measure of responsible government. Many of these arguments had already been set out in his writings and speeches before 1920.

Woodsworth knew that this was not all that early Canada had been. He was aware that from a very early time economic development had been significantly influenced by a directive state.[19] As long ago as 1670 there had been the grant to the Hudson's Bay Company; later, charters to other fur companies, the providing of the clergy reserves, and, after Confederation, the subsidies to the Canadian Pacific Railway, the 1879 tariff, further subsidies and loan guarantees to the Canadian Northern and Grand Trunk Pacific; and, in the late 1920s, the notorious contemporary example of state capitalist development, the Beauharnois Corporation's development of power sites on the St Lawrence. Woodsworth did not use the term 'state capitalism' to describe the Canadian state's relationship to the economy but it would not have been inapposite; he did not explicitly claim that the state had in essence created an indigenous capitalist class *ex nihilo* but his reasoning led to that conclusion.

For Woodsworth, in Canada, a sturdy, yeoman class of independent commodity producers and craftsmen had developed side by side with a growingly powerful class of state-sponsored businessmen. The latter were clearly destined to win the upper hand not just because of the continued favour of government but because they were more advantageously situated to exploit the astounding powers of technological innovation and monopolies. To take advantage of the benefits of mechanization required extensive capitalization, largeness of scale, and centralization of management direction, all of which were summed up for Woodsworth in the notion of cooperation.[20] Mechanization made inevitable the superseding of the classical free marketplace. Here, as elsewhere, a *laissez-faire* system had been a sort of brief, idyllic dream, an unsustainable interlude before the onset of large-scale production.

With mechanization had come a transformation of class relations. Independence had vanished and workers had become wage-employees. Proud craftsmen and producers had lost control over the production process; economic and geographic mobility was destroyed; the concentration of power in the hands of a few owners had reduced wage-earners to economic dependence and political impotence; in the modern firm the division of labour had been accentuated and work had become less fulfilling. Much of this account of class has affinities to Marxism. This is seen in Woodsworth's claims about the rise of wage labour or, as he sometimes called it, 'wage slavery.'[21] Yet, more fundamentally, we must recognize the unmetaphysical, eclectic nature of his many references to class. To Woodsworth most farmers were still independent producers and not yet wage slaves; nevertheless, they were part of the 'exploited.'[22] Insofar as he ever attempted a definition, he located the defining characteristic of capitalism in its oligarchic structure: it was, simply, an economic system controlled by the few.[23] He really said little, if anything, about a labour theory of value and indeed seemed to deny its validity when he claimed that with the emergence of large, mechanized firms there was no determinate relationship between what someone laboured to produce and what he received by way of economic compensation.[24] Woodsworth was also convinced that Canada was still in a developing stage and not easily fitted into 'mature,' European-derived models of class polarization; he believed that there were many intersecting and cross-cutting divisions in modern societies: consumers, professionals, educationists on salary, the middle class, farmers, the rentier class of middle men engaged in 'parasitic' activity, small shopkeepers, as well as capitalists and workers.[25] But out of this miasma of different definitions of class one evident theme emerged, namely a materialist, distributivist one: what ailed the vast majority of people was their lack of a living wage, a decent standard of living.[26] In other words Woodsworth was a rough-and-ready, materialist egalitarian. He was sufficiently unspeculative, in contrast, say, to George Bernard Shaw, that he avoided prescribing a levelling account of equality. He simply said that Canadians should receive 'enough,' enough of the means of material survival, and left it at that. Satisfying such a principle was to be the first charge on the resources of a socialist society. Clearer again to Woodsworth was the fact that the deficiencies of monopoly capitalism that socialism would overcome were its material ones. The exploited, and the list included independent farmers as much as dependent workers, were so not so much because they lacked creative jobs or a sense of control over the production process but, at bottom, because they were *poor*.

Woodsworth, as we have seen, was a son of the pioneer frontier; his family's traditions, intellectually speaking, were those of Manchester liberalism; and he was a Protestant by birth and disposition. Altogether he was, he knew, a cussed individualist. Unsurprisingly, the rise of factories and monopolies with their size, power, and economic reach deeply disturbed him. Indeed the extreme anxiety he felt over their coming leaves the reader to wonder how it could ever have been that he would have found advantage in them at all:

As long as a man, with his own hands and a few tools, could provide for his own needs, he might have been said to be a free man. If he did not produce, it was his own fault; if he did not make his living, it was his own fault. But when the big factory was set up and in order to carry on his work of weaving he had to leave his hand loom and to go to the factory then he ceased to have that freedom which once he possessed; he became simply a wage worker. He had no control over his tools of production; he had no voice in the management; he had nothing to say with regard to the disposal of his product. The owner of the factory claimed to own the product because he owned the machinery, and thus the hitherto free workman of Great Britain was reduced to being simply a hired man, a wage earner, or as he himself sometimes bitterly puts it, a wage slave. There is a good deal of truth in that expression; for whoever controls a man's livelihood really controls his life. I could make this position of the industrial worker understandable by our farmer friends if I could picture a great syndicate coming into the West and buying up several thousand square miles of territory and proceeding to organize it under scientific management. The individual farmer would become simply a tenant, a hired man. Possibly he would be reduced to the position of being forever a hired man and his children forever hired men. That is the position of the industrial world. In this connection I should like to submit that perhaps the farmer is not so very far from reaching that position.[27]

I confess that I feel a great deal of sympathy for the small business men who are being gradually crowded to the wall ...

In my judgment the business man today is very much in the position in which the industrial worker was at the time of the industrial revolution. We have the organization of industry which is something like a concentration of effort within the walls of a factory. In many ways a large departmental store is like a factory and many of the smaller business men have had to desert their small businesses to work as departmental heads in such concerns as Eaton's. Instead of making their own profits, running their own businesses, they are simply hired men in the large departmental stores. Looking at things in the large way, it would seem as if this concentration in a comparatively few hands was an almost inevitable development and that the change that is taking place in our merchandising is very closely parallel to the change that took place in industrial life at an earlier period.[28]

Of course, there was another side to Woodsworth's account of monopolies and industrialism and that was his view of their sumptuous, unimaginable productiveness. To Woodsworth efficiency was a function not of competitive markets and innovative, adaptable enterprise but of rational, scientific, and deliberate planning brought to bear on a mechanized, extended process of production. This emphasis on the importance of management is part of what Friedrich Hayek calls the logic of rationalist constructivism.[29] The machine joined to a directive human intelligence were keys that would unlock the riddle of existence: material scarcity. Woodsworth may not have worshipped unreservedly at the altar of efficiency but he did come close to so doing:

Take for example one phase of this situation, the wonderful productivity of the machine to-day. Roger Babson, the well-known statistician, in a recent article in the Cambridge Tribune, stated that since 1914 such progress has been made that to-day thirty men can produce as many motor cars as one hundred men could produce fourteen years ago; forty men can produce as many rubber tires as one hundred men could produce fourteen years ago; in the iron and steel industry forty men can produce what one hundred men produced fourteen years ago; and in metals other than iron and steel sixty men can produce as much as one hundred men could produce fourteen years ago. In varying degrees this is the experience in industry generally.[30]

I remember several years ago reading an interesting little book by King C. Gillette, a practical business man who was accustomed to sizing up industries from the standpoint of the efficiency engineer. He looked over the industrial field and asked whether we were at all efficient? He said, among other things: The engineers estimate that the loss to industries, through lack of efficiency, is as follows: Men's clothing industry, 63.78 per cent; building industry, 53 per cent; printing industry, 57.61 per cent; boot and shoe industry, 40.03 per cent; metal industry, 28.06 per cent; textile industry, 49.20 per cent.

This, he points out, must average something like 50 per cent, a loss which he thinks is chargeable to lack of co-ordination. In the author's opinion, an individual under the system of co-ordination which he is advocating could produce enough in five years to maintain him for a lifetime of seventy years, no matter how extravagant he might be. This comes ... from a practical business man who, after looking over the arrangements of our industrial system as it operates to-day, suggests that there are great gaps to be filled in and duplications to be cut out, and that co-ordination is absolutely necessary if we are to produce and distribute economically and avoid the waste which is now taking place.[31]

The theme of efficiency provided a crucial part of Woodsworth's moral justification of monopolies. Socialism was not about equalizing poverty but equalizing plenty, or at least sufficiency. His socialism was not primarily an aesthetic or a communitarian doctrine but, in the end, a materialistic one. Sober-minded socialists grasped how indispensable were science and technology as means to equality's attainment. Another important theme was Woodsworth's inveterate historical determinism: monopolies were part of humanity's destiny; one wished them away with as much prospect of success as wishing away the existence of the machine itself. They were inseparable. Thus the task of socialist leaders was to convince workers of the desirable and, in any case, ultimately inevitable implications of the industrialism that lay before them:

When the factory system came into existence and the individual workman gave up his little home workshop and went into the factory, we entered upon a new period in the development of industry, the period of combinations – and we cannot avoid the consequences. In those early days of the new age when the machine threatened to take the very bread out of the mouths of their children the workers in desperation threatened to break the machine. They thought that this was the only way of attaining their end. They learned in later days that what they should have done was to have gained possession of the machine. Now there are those who, fearful of the combinations of the elaborate organization which has been set up on the basis of the physical machine, would try to break up the combinations, break up the elaborate organization. We take the ground that such a policy would be as fatal as the machine-smashing policy of one hundred and fifty years ago. It is impossible for us effectively to break up these combines. The only possible thing for us to do if we want really effective action is to take hold of them and carry them one step further until we have such a complete combine that the public through its various organizations co-operative, municipal, provincial and federal, will be able to use it for its own purposes.[32]

The retail men are becoming alarmed. Bitter competitors as they have been, they are now attempting to unite against the big fellow. Unless they are prepared to substitute genuine co-operation, the task is hopeless. Business efficiency demands an organization that the small men cannot provide ... Will some financial Colossus bestride the world? We cannot tell. But we would point out that the old-time independence and initiative are passing almost as quickly as the horse has been replaced by the motor.

Big business is here! No more use trying to 'smash the Trusts' than it was for the workers to smash the millionaires. Instead of being dominated by organization, the common people – industrial workers, farmers, business men – must dominate organization and use it for the common welfare.[33]

This coalescence of the actual and the desirable that lies at the back of progressive accounts of history was also evident in Woodsworth's prognostications about the changing role of women. Women's work was different, he said, because work in general had changed. Labour activities traditionally undertaken in the home – weaving, spinning, cooking, laundry, teaching, health-care – were now increasingly performed in larger specialized institutions. Women now should leave the home, in large part because they had to: 'We are – women as well as men – living in a new and rapidly changing world. There is an inexorable law of nature – "Change or die!" This is as true in the social as in the physical realm. It is at our peril that we fail to adapt ourselves to new conditions. In a wistful fashion we sometimes long for the good old days when we were young and "mother" – the old fashioned "mother" filled our lives. But if we should attempt to train our daughters to be like "mother," their lives would be dismal failures. "Mother's" world is not their world!'[34]

The same evolutionary tone of 'adapt or die' informed another short article on women. In this piece, entitled 'Hail to the Typewriter! Emancipators of Women', and published in 1926, Woodsworth added an optimistic moral tone: that modern technology and industry had brought an important measure of freedom to women:

A few days ago, I had occasion to visit a large typewriter establishment and was shown the first machine made in America – a curious contraption, yet the ancestor of a progeny that in a little better than half a century has revolutionized the business world.

My guide must have been a successful salesman: he had imagination and enthusiasm. 'Woman owes more to the typewriter than to any other agency.' Well the idea is suggestive.

There are tens of thousands of neatly-dressed girls, more or less efficient, taken out from housework, drilled in business methods, made to feel independent, given at least some training in co-operation. What will be the social effect?

Well, compare our daughters and grand-mothers. – Advance or retrogression? Certainly difference!

For good or evil, women are taking their place beside men more as comrades than as dependents. The world outside is less sheltered than the home circle. But it is a bigger world and women are forced to develop hitherto unused powers.

In business and political affairs, man's superiority is not so clearly conceded as it was a few years ago. But on the whole, women are still following the old trails. One of these days, they will strike out along new lines. Why not? And then what?[35]

Whatever sense can be made of the mild triumphalism of much of Woodsworth's view of the emergence of modern technology and monopolies, there can be little doubt of the risky strategy he was putting before the Canadian people. He was arguing that monopolies and combinations had created a ruling class of unprecedented economic power which currently used that power to consolidate further the technological productivity of modern industrial organization as well as to appropriate its phenomenal wealth. Politically, also, Canadians were worse off than they had been in the nineteenth century, in the happier, less complicated days of responsible government. Yet the people were to seize democratically a frail and compromised Parliament and use it in the pursuit of socialism, substituting a public-spirited and humane élite of governors and planning commissioners in the place of a self-serving 'tyranny' of business magnates and their political cat's-paws. If the people succeeded, all would be well. If they didn't, Woodsworth's listeners might well have concluded that it would have been better not to have pursued industrialism and monopolies in the first place.

Harnessing, then, the productiveness of large-scale industry for public and egalitarian distribution was the crucial overall task of socialism. Its attainment would be a matter of democratic debate and parliamentary action. Woodsworth offered numerous and cogent arguments on socialism's behalf.

Monopolies were not just sanctioned by history, which to an inveterate historical determinist and progressive such as Woodsworth was compelling reason in itself, but their very organizational structure made nonsense of traditional arguments founded on individual, private property rights.[36] The nature of monopolies was that they operated, internally, as collective, interdependent, cooperative bodies; they were 'organic' in ways that firms operating in a competitive marketplace were not. A crucial premise here was that monopolies, through their overwhelming use of mechanical processes, vitiated any possible intellectual attempt to calculate a relationship between individual effort and individual output. Allocating rewards and entitlement within such a complex, interdependent chain of actions was impossible. Consequently, the wealth produced by such organizations could be said to be public, corporate, or collective. To Woodsworth, 'cooperation' was a principle that clarified not just the process of production but that of distribution too. What was created together must be distributed on a similarly indiscriminate, egalitarian basis.

The special historical circumstances of the development of Canadian capitalism complemented these claims. Woodsworth came close to asserting that the Canadian business class had shown no initiative whatever in its varied ventures, except, that is, an initiative in cornering state privileges and largesse. The story of Canadian business was, to him, one of state munificence towards selected entrepreneurs: the Hudson's Bay Company, the CPR, and, recently, the Beauharnois Corporation.[37] Since 1879 industry had been further coddled by tariffs so that every tariff-protected firm could be regarded as a public company of sorts; the same was true of banks with their government charters. The skill of Canadian entrepreneurs lay mainly in graft and corruption:

I suggest that that principle of private property has been unwarrantedly extended. We create an artificial body which we call a corporation, and then, without imposing upon it any responsibilities we give it all the privileges of a private person; without its having any soul, we endow it with immortality. I do not think we can allow an assumption of that kind to continue. It may very well be that my home is private property, that other things which I use and enjoy are private property, but the original idea of private property should never have been extended to the machinery by which modern production is carried on. It does not belong there at all and ought never to have been extended to such a degree – that will have to be altered. Who can contend for a moment that the Bank of Montreal or the Canadian Pacific Railway are private property in any real sense? They have been given certain charters and certain privileges which they enjoy just so long as they are considered to minister to the welfare of the country. Many believe that our banks are inviolable, but I would remind the country at large that our banks exist because of charters which really terminate this year. Those charters need not be reissued if parliament so desires; they are given at the will of parliament for a ten year period only, and the sooner the banks recognize that they are dependent upon the people the better for all concerned.

The Prime Minister R.B. Bennett in his Toronto speech said: 'Are you prepared to give up those things which have been earned by honest toil?' Does anyone mean to say that the great fortunes in Canada have been build up by what could be termed 'honest toil'? Has the Prime Minister's own fortune been gained by honest toil?[38]

Such conclusions left little room for possessive individualist claims. Woodsworth had other arguments: natural resources were peculiarly a public patrimony and their development fell naturally under public ownership; essential services or utilities were in essence public activities; credit and money were by nature 'fiduciary,' dependent for their effectiveness upon community confidence and trust, and a sort of 'utility,' providing the life-blood of the economy so that such a crucial function could not be left to private control; land values were communally created and ought to be socially appropriated; and, finally, monopolies brought such a concentration of economic and political power that the very survival of democratic values required public ownership and control.[39] It is an exhaustive list of reasons for public ownership; together they crowded out any moral possibility of private enterprise. As Woodsworth put it: 'Only under a regime of public ownership and operation will the full benefits accruing from centralization of control and mass production be passed to the consuming public.'[40]

The notion of centralization was crucial to Woodsworth's thinking on industrialism and socialism. He held that the integrity of economic decisions and actions derived from the pre-conceived rationality and intentionality of a finite body of decision-makers. The wider and larger the context of their decision-making, the more rational, in principle, it would be. A national scale of decision-making was better than a local one, and an international scale better again. Until institutions of internationalism developed and schemes of planned international exchange were undertaken, national planning was about as far as contemporary government could go. Woodsworth said little about the finer details of how a national planning commission would operate, but the general structure he envisaged is clear.[41] Public-spirited, humane planners would receive overall policy directions from a parliament of socialists and, thus legitimized, they would through explicit direction and coercive sanction plan to maximize production and ensure the fairest distribution. It was an avowedly hierarchical, centralist, technocratic, and unitary system that was imagined. It would be fair and equitable but efficient as well. Woodsworth did prescribe actual solutions for two contemporary, ailing industries: railways and coal-mining.[42] In both cases the planning he proposed entailed extensive direction, large-scale rationalization, amalgamation, and consolidation, and there was to be a redeployment of redundant labour. To Woodsworth monopolies *and* central planning were integral to a contemporary account of socialism. Just as monopolies were inevitable, so too was planning. Nations, such as Russia, that conducted extensive national planning were destined to become the economic powers of the twentieth century; if Canada failed to deduce similar conclusions it would be left behind. Planning was occurring everywhere. Canada had much to learn not just from Russia and Britain but even from such unlikely examples as Italy and Germany:

We are being driven by irresistible economic forces to the regulation of trade ...

In Russia there is perhaps the most complete regulation of industry that exists anywhere in the world to-day, but I might also mention another country, namely, Italy, where there is a dictatorship under which there is a great regulation of industry ... I might mention the recent occurrences in Germany. Hon. members who are following European politics know that at the recent elections, the rise not merely of the Socialist groups but of the so-called Fascist groups indicates that the general public is very much dissatisfied with existing governmental machinery and methods and is feeling its way towards something else. In Great Britain, if we may come to the country that we know best, I think the very existence at the present time of a Labour-Socialist government is an indication that the older policies of the Conservative party and the Liberal party were not meeting the needs of that great industrial country ... The fact is that the world is groping its way out of the industrial, financial and commercial anarchy which we have been experiencing towards a more satisfactory system.[43]

III

Fathoming Woodsworth's view of markets is not a straightforward matter because he was often of two minds about them and frequently his terminology was unclear and unhelpful. He used the terms competition, free trade, and *laissez-faire* interchangeably. That, at least, was clear though not altogether enlightening. Ambiguities arose when he applied these similar-meaning terms to very different economic regimes and arrangements.

A classical *laissez-faire* system, that is, an open, market economy with many buyers and sellers and supervised by a minimal government, was, Woodsworth asserted, largely an historical anachronism, mainly confined to Britain in the early days of its industrial revolution.[44] Insofar as it allowed a truly competitive economy, he suggested that it was not altogether unacceptable. But in other contexts Woodsworth told a different story. To him what was undesigned and unplanned was without order and rationale; it was 'anarchic' as he put it in the early 1930s,[45] or, as he had stated in 1923, a sign of 'incomplete development ... unorganized ... a transitory stage.'[46] Also, free, competitive markets were inefficient and wasteful because they sanctioned too many suppliers of a good or service.[47] He had other, more purely ethical objections: truly competitive markets were driven by the ruthless, restless compulsion of selfish, acquisitive, profit-oriented individuals.

In any event, the pros and cons of a competitive free economy were, according to Woodsworth, largely academic because the British *laissez-faire* system was by the late nineteenth century part of history, overwhelmed by the rise of the machine and monopolies. Moreover, British industrial superiority assisted by the imperialist policies of its government was by the turn of the century being challenged by other nations. Industrialism, presumably spearheaded by more protectionist, *dirigiste* policies, had been established in France, Germany, United States, Japan, and now in China. The logic of monopoly capitalism was to seek control of foreign markets and investment frontiers, and protection in the exploitation of them from the home government. Imperialism was monopoly capitalism's agnate. (Again, we see Hobson's influence on Woodsworth.) Not only was the trend of business towards concentration and combines but the increasingly pyramidal income structure of monopoly capitalist societies, combined with their phenomenal technical productivity, led, first, to foreign expansion and then, eventually, to a crisis of over-production. The upshot was an international order of sectionalism, protectionism, imperialism, and finally war:

As long as there were external markets a country like England, which was the first in the race, might dispose of her surplus goods. The system developed and the markets kept expanding, so the opportunities for disposing of the surplus product increased with the development of the system. The few people who owned the machine were able to pay back in wages to their employees only a part of what was produced; the balance was retained by them and put back into the industry ... We have now reached the stage where there seems to be a surplus of capital – that is, a surplus that awaits investment in the machinery of production. We have reached the stage where the great mass of the people do not seem to be in a position to buy back what has been produced. So our machine is very largely stalled at the present time ... The unregulated competition in which private individuals and great corporations have been engaged is in itself probably the prime cause of modern war. When we cannot get rid of our goods at home we have to ship them to foreign markets, and so there has been a race all over the world for foreign markets and for the sources of raw material. I think that the struggle between nations for economic advantage has undoubtedly been one of the major causes of modern warfare.[48]

This protective craze is but a symptom of the post-war recrudescence of nationalism. We find on every side a certain reaction. After the war we hoped that we would have a little more of the international or world idea and that that would find expression in our national policies. However, all over Europe we find nationalism on the increase and thousands of miles of tariff walls are being built to-day in Europe. The same applies to this continent ... I am sure that we never will have world peace as long as we continue to fight our tariff wars. It has been shown again and again in the past that tariff wars have led to physical wars. I urge that the world can never be split up into self-contained national units, and the effort to bring about that condition is fraught with danger.[49]

In the first of these two quotes Woodsworth continued to apply much of the nomenclature and terminology of a classical market economy – competition, profit, and individualism – to the altered context of a monopoly economy. Sometimes he made clear that the old concepts, if understood aright, were still applicable even in a world that had changed: 'Individual competition is giving place to competition of groups. We have to-day mergers, combines, trusts and international cartels, and individual competition is no longer practicable. No, we must have still further organization. The trouble to-day is that conflict is taking place between these great mergers, these great combines and these great international industries; we are faced with a warfare between the nations in the economic sphere. It is high time that we arrive at some sort of international understanding. Only thus can we solve our problems.'[50]

Other times he implied that there was a total disjunction between the language of the old anachronistic *laissez-faire* and the present condition of the economic world. Those who insisted on confusing the two were guilty of self-delusion. The Liberal Party's parliamentary leadership was an example of this:

I would say that the Liberals, by this bill [the Marketing Act of 1934], are placed in a very bad predicament. The leader of the opposition, quite honestly I think, still clings to the old laissez faire school of thought ... We are faced with a situation in which we have a large measure of monopoly, either private or public. I cannot think that we are going back to the old, individualistic way of doing things, and I do not think it is possible either to control these big trusts or to break them up in such a way as to overcome the terrific power they exert at the present time. Under these circumstances some of us believe that the only possible way is to have governmental monopoly or centralized government control over these monopolies which, if effective, would be pretty much the same as actual ownership. As I see the situation it is because we are living in an age of highly organized industry and yet have governments that are attempting to carry out policies that belong to an earlier age that we find ourselves in our present difficulties. If we went back one hundred or even fifty years I think a laissez faire policy would be good and that a free trade policy would be good, but unfortunately the stage of society has passed. Under these circumstances I would say to my Liberal friends that the only way to carry out the fundamental principles of Liberalism in this day is to secure some sort of planning which will be under democratic control.[51]

It is futile to talk about competition in the old sense or about free trade in the old sense. At best it is free competition only between big industries and free trade only between huge corporations. Superimposed upon that we must remember that we have arrangements existing with regard to prices, tariffs, gentlemen's agreements, and what not. Free trade under those circumstances becomes an almost meaningless term.[52]

So what was Woodsworth saying in all this? It was, I submit, that there had been a regime of competition/profit/individualism long ago, under a *laissez-faire* system, and there was now another form of competition/profit/individualism that applied under monopolies. (The ambiguities arise of course because modern industry was no longer owned and controlled by individuals, and operated in a market place that was by no means classically competitive.) Let us at least determine the crucial difference between the two for Woodsworth. His claim was that *laissez-faire* had been left behind and in its place there prevailed a sort of dog-eat-dog world of competition between groups – associations, unions, trusts, combines, and so on – which sought sectional, that is, 'individual,' profit either through control of the market, special deals with the state, or imperialist bounties. These present economic arrangements would best be overcome not by a reintroduction of the market in its classical form but by a political economy of public planning and controls in a socialist commonwealth. Private markets of whatever kind were to be replaced.

But what did this entail for free trade, that intellectual bulwark of prairie radicalism before and after the First World War? If classical *laissez-faire* was dead, had not free trade between nations also died with it? A cursory reading of Woodsworth may seem to lead to this conclusion. For did he not say repeatedly that Canadian liberalism's traditional emphasis upon the need for international free trade and an end to protectionism was irrelevant?[53] In fact, a careful sifting of Woodsworth's views will reveal that, oddly, there was inside him a Manchester liberal straining to get out.

Throughout the inter-war period, Woodsworth, with the help of Hobson, was emphatic about the economic causes of war and the universal trend towards imperialism. The consequence was a world divided into economic blocs competing between themselves, either peacefully in the form of protectionism or violently in the form of war. Yet in contradiction to this was his conviction that there was a trend towards international community and integration. To be sure, monopolies, in their transforming of themselves into what now is called multinational enterprises, were part of this trend. But the forces of community took other, more agreeable forms: international cultural and scientific exchanges, communication, and travel: 'There is a growing sense of world community.'[54] It was, then, clearly the best of times and the worst of times; humanity's fate hung in the balance until it was decided whether imperialism would be defeated and, if so, what kind of internationalism would prevail: the sectional 'internationalism' of the multinational firm or the communal internationalism of, say, the Red Cross. But, obviously, from the perspective of an emerging, interdependent world economic order, free trade between firms operating across national boundaries could not be terribly unacceptable. Even if these firms were large, in the context of an open world-wide economy they surely provided some of the advantages of an acceptable competitive market system: low prices, comparative advantage, and the expansion of trade and wealth. Clearly Woodsworth was no protectionist.[55] Nevertheless, his espousal of international free trade, though genuine, was often awkward, convoluted, and hesitant. He seemed to sleep-walk into support of it.

If Canadian Liberals, before and after Wilfrid Laurier, prided themselves on any particular intellectual distinctiveness, it was their belief in free trade, in contrast to the perfidious protectionism of the Tories. Laurier's long term in government from 1896 to 1911 muddied this party difference because he came to accept much of the tariff arrangements of the Macdonald years, something radical historians such as Frank Underhill delighted to point out in the 1920s and 1930s. This was Woodsworth's view too; the two major parties were identical in their resolve to serve the interests of the business class, especially in the matter of protective tariffs. Yet, between the wars, Liberals, on their better days, still clung to the notion of the rightness of free trade and certainly it was an issue that Mackenzie King exploited in the 1920s to secure the support of western Liberals and Progressives. Perhaps Woodsworth overstated his position, thus leaving the false impression that he did not support free trade at all. Of course, his claim was that the old dichotomy of free trade and protectionism should no longer be viewed as the central issue of national politics, that free trade was no longer in itself a panacea, and that the simple expansion of Canada's trade was not necessarily the means to solving all its economic difficulties. He was arguing that there were other, more crucial problems to resolve, such as the crisis of privately controlled monopolies and that of under-consumption/over-production. His central claim, then, was that liberalism was not enough; socialism was an advance over it. But that he was a definite socialist is not to say that he was not liberally minded and did not support free trade.

It is certain that, in the day-to-day politics of Parliament, Woodsworth was an implacable foe of the protectionism of the Conservative Party. Tariffs were one of the primary privileges granted the business class by the Canadian state. The words of what follows are mainly those of Thorstein Veblen but Woodsworth's quoting them does give some sense of the extent of his dislike of protection and its tendency both to diminish the amount of goods in circulation and to increase their price:

'The great standing illustration of sabotage administered by the government is the protective tariff, of course. It protects certain special interests by obstructing competition from beyond the frontier. This is the main use of a national boundary. The effect of the tariff is to keep the supply of goods down and thereby keep the price up, and so to bring reasonably satisfactory dividends to those special interests which deal in the protected articles of trade, at the cost of the underlying community. A protective tariff is a typical conspiracy in restraint of trade. It brings a relatively small, though absolutely large, run of free income to the special interests which benefit by it, at a relatively and absolutely, large cost to the underlying community, and so it gives rise to a body of vested rights and intangible assets belonging to these special interests.'

I suggest that the economic developments of recent years are rendering the older political divisions obsolete. These great industrial, commercial and financial concerns reach across our international boundaries and we can no longer carry on the affairs of any one country as if we were or could be self-contained in our business activities. Let me put it this way: Capital is international: why therefore should we attempt to make industry and commerce national?[56]

Woodsworth knew of the conventional apologetics of supporters of tariffs and showed sympathy towards none of them. He rejected a tariff to raise revenue; indirect taxes were unfair since they bore disproportionately heavily on people of poor or average means.[57] Nor did he believe that protected industries particularly benefitted Canadian workers; such enterprises, he said, typically paid their employees below-average wages; indeed the direct and indirect subsidies by consumers and taxpayers to protect industrialists were so great that the state could pension off their work-force and still have money to spare.[58] It is the sort of cavalier claim that a radical free trader such as E.A. Porritt might have uttered. As well, Woodsworth was not impressed by

arguments in favour of protecting recently established, 'infant' industries or designing so-called 'scientific' tariffs that would take account of
the different circumstances of individual industries:

We in Canada have heard much about infant industries for a great many years,
and we know how long these infant industries persist in remaining infants ...
This principle of reasonable competition based on relative cost of economical
and efficient production is wholly illusory. [Sir Arthur Salter] says: 'A so-called
scientific tariff usually means one which is based on the principle of compen-
sating for differences in costs of production. This either represents a mere
fallacy, or it is a policy destructive of international trade in anything except the
few things that cannot be produced at home at any cost however exorbitant –
such as rubber in England or America. For why does any one ever buy
anything from abroad if it is not because he gets a given article at a lower price
– or a better article at a given price? Abolish this advantage and why should
any one buy from abroad at all?'

   'Indeed, if we believe in international trade the only mitigating circumstance
about what are usually called "scientific tariffs" is that they never are in fact
scientifically framed and applied, for if they were trade would disappear. But if
this is not their principle, what is? Let us face frankly the fact that the operative
principle underlying the flexible, varied and changing system is usually just
this, and nothing more; that those interests which are so organized as to
exercise the strongest political pressure get protection, or the highest rates of
protection, at the expense of the rest of the community.'[59]

   In this 1932 speech Woodsworth went on to quote Salter's diatribe
against the spoils system of the modern protectionist state and how
this vitiated its proper role as a neutral, independent umpire. He also
quoted his conclusion that 'the complexity of the essential tasks of
govenment under modern conditions strains to the utmost the limited
resources of man's regulative wisdom, competence, and public honesty.' Such libertarian, anti-collectivist sentiments no doubt helped
Woodsworth make his point. But Salter's claims were equally damning
of Woodsworth's own view of the potentiality of government as a
planner and owner of economic enterprise. In any event, Woodsworth
was profoundly anti-protectionist. In 1929, even in the face of rising
protectionism from the Americans, he advised against retaliatory
tariffs.[60] And, at the height of the Depression, with the bottom having
fallen out of the price of wheat, he advocated wheat-trading with the

Russians, even though further imports would exacerbate an already glutted Canadian market.[61]

And so in a back-handed sort of way, Woodsworth put together a case for free trade that, however obliquely, made use of typical market ideas to do with efficiency through competition, trade, comparative advantage, and the price mechanism. In the abstract, of course, his preferred ideal was a system of international-planning agreements and planned commodity exchanges, which together would overcome the impersonal dynamics of the world trading system.[62] But in its absence and as a second choice, Woodsworth recommended the main prescription of Manchester liberalism. There were, however, two rubs, which he tried to overcome and reconcile with his economic internationalism.

Even though a believer in an open, international economy, Woodsworth recognized a particularly troublesome problem: wage rates and costs of production in Canada were noticeably higher than those in such latecomer industrial countries as Japan and China. Canadian industry under free trade, therefore, faced the unsatisfying prospect of pricing itself out of the market. Here Woodsworth's recommendation was ingenious though, one suspects, not altogether practicable: the international community should agree to certain world-wide, minimum standards of economic behaviour: wage-rates, standards of employment, length of the workday, and so forth, the sort of provisions that had been embodied in the founding principles of the International Labour Organization. Nations refusing to cooperate would be subject to a boycott of their goods. To Woodsworth this was not protectionism because it protected not a specific industry but a world-wide class of workers:

All goods should be produced under standards of living that measure up to a certain level. For that reason we in the labour movement are interested in the maintenance of the standards in Europe. We are interested in raising the standards in the Orient. If we are to have goods imported from Germany or other parts of Europe where their standards have been forced down since the war we will inevitably have our standards here forced down, and in some way we should be protected from goods of that character. If we are to have huge quantities of goods shipped in from the Orient where their standards have never been as high as our standards, we will meet with difficulties; we will be ousted in this country. It is no solution simply to say, 'exclude the orientals'; we need to go further and see that the standards in the Orient are raised ...

Undoubtedly we should extend and strengthen the conventions of the Washington conference following the principles laid down by the Versailles treaty, and should insist that we should not have dumped on us goods that came to us from countries which maintain a low standard of living, and refuse to ratify those conventions ... Sooner or later we shall have to face the fact that the world is a unit and that no part can retain a low standard without its adversely affecting the other parts.[63]

In a similar vein Woodsworth opposed the immigration of workers who would over-supply the labour market and depress wages, or who would through their low expectation of adequate remuneration have the same negative effect.

The other perplexity was the incidence of foreign investment in Canada.[64] There can be no doubt as to Woodsworth's general opposition, especially, to American investment: he disliked American branch plants, particularly their exploitation of British preferential trade arrangements; American investment was a 'penetration,' 'a conquest'; it 'mortgaged' the future and represented the 'evil consequences of the get-rich-quick policy that characterized some of our businessmen today'; dividend payments and bond interest to the United States were the payment of a 'tribute'; foreign investment in natural resources represented the 'forfeiture' of our 'natural inheritance'; unless Canadians were careful Americans would control all our natural resources; Canada had to run constant trade balances in order to pay for the patriation to the United States of interest and dividends: 'If it were proposed that the border line between us and the United States should be moved a few degrees further north there would be a tremendous hubbub in this country, but the same patriots who would raise an army in such a case not only look with equanimity upon the Americanization of this country, but further, they are glad to welcome any amount of this foreign capital for any purpose so long as they secure a certain proportion of the loot. The United States, I say, is extending long arms to the north, and since the world war it has dictated the financial policy of Europe until, as a recent writer has put it, Germany is in danger of becoming an American colony. We have the Americans to-day sitting in Paris and dictating European policy. What is to be Canada's attitude to this increasingly powerful neighbour of ours?'[65]

What, indeed, was to be done? Here again Woodsworth expressed himself imprecisely, as if the problem of riding two different horses led to double vision. Consider, for example, the curious logic of his speech in the budget debate in 1927.[66] He claimed that the world was more and more 'a co-operative community ... interlocked ... and ... interrelated.' Instances of this process were British and American capital invested here and Canada's trade with the far-flung corners of the world: 'we would be turning the clock back if we were to revert to the idea of self-contained communities with other communities as commercial rivals profiting at our expense. Rather I think we are advancing to the stage where the benefit of one is the benefit of all, and where world trade flows freely there is mutual benefit.' Here again was Woodsworth's familiar encomium upon international cooperation except that on this occasion he used the unimpeded flow of capital and goods to illustrate the new world order. Yet Woodsworth was also deeply disturbed by and clearly opposed to American investment. American-owned companies would have been subject to his general strictures regarding the undesirability of private ownership of monopolies.[67] More immediately he proposed a surtax on the patriation of American interest and dividends and a similar surcharge on Canadian investments abroad.[68] Nevertheless, he seemed uncomfortable with this position, perhaps embarrassed by what might be viewed as a policy of financial protectionism. The confusion was evident when he suggested that he did not personally advocate investment controls but that his hypothetical advocacy of them was to expose the hypocrisy of Canadian businessmen whose protectionism was well known but who at the same time made money off foreign investment or who were only too happy to invest abroad:

May I point out that if I were a protectionist I would suggest: Why not develop our Canadian natural resources by keeping our capital at home? I would suggest: Why not a super tax on this capital which is invested abroad? I think I should be quite consistent in urging that we develop our natural resources in Canada where more capital is necessary. If our financiers think they can make greater returns by investing in Mexico, or in South America, or in Cuba, I suppose that is their business; but if we really are in earnest about developing our own natural resources why cannot we take some means of keeping Canadian money at home?[69]

Let me make this suggestion – it may seem rather fantastic, although I do not think it is inconsistent: We do not want foreign goods, why should we want foreign capital? Why not exploit our own natural resources and take advantage of our own business opportunities? We urge foreign capital to come here, and that often means the importation of foreign goods. In any case we are putting ourselves in a tributary position to a foreign nation. Why not carry out consistently this proposed policy. If we are going to attempt to be self-contained along one line, why not be self-contained in our financial affairs as well as in our industrial affairs?[70]

There is one good thing in the budget [1931], for which I should like to give the government credit, and that is that they are putting on a 2 per cent tax on returns of all investments made by non-residents of this country. They confess that the tax is higher in most other countries, and that the tax here is actually confined to those non-residents in other countries. There is no danger of driving capital out of this country. Let me give the total investments of outside capital in Canada: Great Britain, $2,197,000,000; United States, $3,470,000,000; rest of the world $237,000,000. Why could we not tax these investments even more heavily? I proposed that last year. I do not know whether the government listened to what I said, but I am glad that they are making a beginning along the lines I suggested. I made another proposal, and that is that we should put a supertax on Canadian capital invested abroad. I am told that one reason why we should be so careful not to tax too heavily the very large incomes is that otherwise capital might migrate from this country. There is a great deal easier and far more effective way of keeping it here, and that is to put a supertax on all of it that goes abroad. If the government is really in earnest about having business retained in Canada, let them keep Canadian capital in Canada. I am not putting this forward as my own position, because I think that policy along these lines is all nonsense, but I say that if the government is in earnest about its policy, that is what should be done.[71]

To expose 'bogus nationalists' and the 'hypocrisy' of the protectionists was no doubt well and good but it did not help him clarify his own position on investment controls. His imprecision was perhaps understandable since he was in this case an internationalist who saw advantages in the preservation of a national capital market. His general support of national, government planning entailed a similar conclusion.

IV

In the budget debate of 1924, Woodsworth announced his intellectual debt to J.A. Hobson:

In his book on the Economics of Unemployment [Hobson] says that the fundamental trouble to-day is that we have had altogether too much saving of a kind. Owing to the unequal distribution of the world's wealth, a comparatively small number of people have been able to retain as their own the greater part of what has been produced. In this respect Mr. Hobson is simply carrying out the thesis which was proposed by Mr. Maynard Keynes several years ago. This accumulated wealth, which could not be consumed by the people who owned it, had to be invested; it had to be put into fixed capital, and so there came to be an undue proportion of the annual production invested in fixed capital. That was all very well as long as the earning was confined to Great Britain, or confined to a few of the European countries, but as the development of the machine went forward and the organization of capital became more complete we had production on a large scale in almost every country of the world, including the great oriental countries. And so we have the anomaly to-day of goods being produced in enormous quantities, quantities that are too great for the purchasing power of the people and in some way or another, he points out, we shall have to have a more equitable distribution, or if not that at least in some way we must ensure that a large proportion of the annual output finds its way to the great mass of the people either in the form of services or wages. Now, this is an economic theory that, perhaps, is novel to a great many who have not studied the question, and yet one that is being endorsed by a growing number of economists.[72]

Indeed the newer lines of thinking had not percolated through to Canada from Europe and the United States. Not until the 1930s and later did schools of Keynesian, nationalist, and socialist economics come to exist. In the meantime the Canadian establishment in economics was dominated by classical economists for whom socialism was anathema and the free market and the gold standard revealed truths. Even the economists who wrote in the early 1920s for the relatively *avant-garde Canadian Forum*, G.E. Jackson, H. Michell, and B.K. Sandwell, conformed to this pattern. Woodsworth himself noted the absence of homegrown, academic contributions at the hearings on the banking system of the Commons' Committee on Banking and Commerce in 1923.[73] Professor William Swanson of the University of Saskatchewan and Adam Shortt, chairman of the Board of Historical Publications, were the only Canadian academics to appear and neither was especially unconventional in his economic views.[74] The radically minded instead turned abroad; some, such as the Labour MP William Irvine, looked to Major C.H. Douglas, the English social-credit theorist; Woodsworth, himself, found intellectual succour in Hobson and to some extent Keynes, and the American monetary theorists Irving Fisher and Frank William Taussig.

There was little in common between Hobson on the one hand and Fisher and Taussig on the other. Woodsworth took selectively from each of them and was especially skilled in knitting together their different views. To Woodsworth the central economic problem of the age was one of distribution rather than production.[75] The economic system already in place in Europe and North America and newer industrial countries such as Japan and China was more than adequate to meet the material needs of everyone. The tragedy was that disposable income and purchasing power were so unequally distributed that those with the greatest need were unable to buy. The problem was one of under-consumption or, to use Hobson's succinct phrase, poverty in the midst of plenty. It followed that there was an imperative role for government as a stimulator, sustainer, and manager of demand, a notion that Keynes was to bring to its theoretical apogee in the 1930s. In the meantime, thanks to Hobson and to a lesser degree Keynes,[76] the crucial parts of this theory were already in place in Woodsworth's mind. Government must redistribute income and spend money on public works, all to ensure that demand kept pace with the potential productivity of industry.

If Hobson helped him understand the issue of distribution, Fisher and Taussig made Woodsworth sensitive to potential financial obstacles to optimal production.[77] Under their influence he concluded that the rise and fall of the money and credit supply were crucial in determining the rate and cycle of economic growth. Not only was Woodsworth offended that this crucial lever of financial policy-making was in private hands but more damning again was the fact that these private hands were so few in number. For the banks, also, had been subject to the same trend towards monopoly. Woodsworth believed that the banks, especially the four largest – the Bank of Montreal, the Bank of Nova Scotia, the Imperial Bank of Commerce, and the Royal Bank – stood at the very apex of the economic pyramid in Canada.[78] Their power was manifold. Through the issue of credit and currency they controlled the life-blood of the economy; the analogy that Woodsworth himself used was that they provided the water that irrigated dry land; they could make it verdant or keep it parched. Also, the banks had attained new influence through closer relations with industry. They had helped fuel the takeover binges of the 1910s and 1920s; they were no longer just financiers of commerce and issuers of currency but investors in large industrial enterprises; through interlocking directorates they held controlling interests in many companies. As Woodsworth observed in 1928, fifteen Canadians controlled corporations with $4.3 billion of assets while the assets of the four largest banks were over $2.5 billion. The banks were so powerful that they held the political élite in their grip not least because it was invariably in debt to them either for political expenses or as holders of government bonds.

The influence of Fisher and Taussig on Woodsworth was an intriguing one. Both were noted American economic theoreticians and neither was of an especially left-wing outlook, though Fisher was interested in public issues and was a Rooseveltian Democrat in the 1930s. Both were part of the neo-classical tradition. Fisher (1867–1947) taught almost completely at Yale and made a major contribution to the mathematizing of economics and the development of general equilibrium theory. Taussig (1859–1940) was at Harvard; his expertise was mainly in wages and international trade. How Woodsworth came to be influenced by them is not clear. Probably as part of his voluminous reading, in the late 1910s or early 1920s he came across one or another of the general or specialized textbooks they had written before the First World War. Taussig's *Principles of Economics* had appeared in 1911; Fisher's *Introduction to Economic Science* in 1910 and his *The Purchasing Power of Money* and *Elementary Principles of Economics* in 1911. Fisher made a presentation to the Banking and Commerce Committee in Ottawa in 1923.

What Woodsworth principally took from them was the quantity theory of money. This held that the value or price of money was in inverse proportion to the amount that was in circulation; the more was in supply the cheaper it was; the less it was in supply, the more expensive it was. Woodsworth observed that banks had a profit motive; they therefore supplied money at a price and in a quantity that maximized their returns. Sometimes expansion of the money supply was in their interests; sometimes the opposite. In Canada the banks had helped expand the money supply in the First World War but their contraction of it in 1920–2 had helped produce the recession of these years and, of course, they were to do the same with even more devastating results in the early 1930s. To Woodsworth the obvious conclusion to draw was that government should manage the money supply in the general interest. Since the overriding crisis of the economy was one of under-consumption, credit and money should be expanded consistent with the potential productivity of industry. If undertaken with intelligence this policy would produce an expansion of real, aggregate wealth without price inflation. Woodsworth rejected the charge that he was an exponent of 'easy money';[79] he insisted that he saw no necessity for inflation as a general feature of economic life. (He conceded, however, that in specific circumstances an inflationary policy might be advisable.)[80] Woodsworth, of course, doubted that a monetary policy consistent with the public interest would result from a privately controlled banking system. Hence he insisted with special vehemence that banks must be publicly owned and controlled.

The influence of Fisher in particular on Woodsworth was salutary in two other important ways. Fisher especially had explored the distributive relationship between the money supply and its price.[81] Those who controlled the money supply, he argued, could directly determine the share of national income that went to different sectors, most obviously creditors and debtors. Woodsworth employed this insight to argue that it was a crucial matter of practical social justice to confront Canada's post-war public debt. Canada, he observed, had fought the First World War by raising money not through taxes but through borrowing. Thus the ultimate irony of the war was that the common man had given his life and effort while the wealthy had stayed at home and loaned their money to the government. Now that peace had come, indirect taxes that fell disproportionately on the survivors of those common men had been raised in order to retire debt obligations to the wealthy. To Woodsworth it was not enough that the public debt was owed mainly to Canadians. For it was only *some* Canadians that held the bonds. As well, a deflationary policy would actually increase the value of these securities, which was of course what happened in the early 1920s and 1930s. Woodsworth's conclusion was that the structure of inter-war Canadian public finance generally had a negative redistributive effect: the rich got richer at the expense of the poor. To remedy these matters he proposed a number of measures. He dallied with the idea of a wholesale government repudiation of its debts but eventually thought better of it.[82] Instead he proposed, at various times, a levy on capital holdings, and a reduction of interest on government bonds and a partial reduction in their face value. Particularly in the early 1930s he recommended an extensive reduction in the value of money, not just to help stimulate an economic recovery but also to reduce the real value of the public debt. This latter policy, he said, would only return bond values to the actual level they had had at the time of issue during the war.

Fisher had one other evident influence on Woodsworth, although in this Reginald McKenna, chancellor of the exchequer in Britain in 1915–16 and, after 1919, chairman of the Midland Bank, was very much a helpmate.[83] It concerned the banks' capacity through the issuing of credit and the honouring of cheques to create deposit substitutes for money and thus increase the money supply.[84] Woodsworth estimated that as much as 90 per cent of the banks' business derived from this arrangement.

Early on Woodsworth had rejected the gold standard. He knew that Canada had 'gone off gold' in 1914 and that economic activity had not come to a halt. It seemed to him absurd that the securing of economic activity should be made to depend on a mainly useless metal, the supply of which was itself subject to capricious market circumstances. He was also convinced that the banks' loans were not in any way covered by the amount of paper currency, specie, or securities that they held. Woodsworth emphasized, therefore, the sense in which modern banking was an especially fiduciary activity in which trust and confidence played determining roles. This was seen in the banks' powers to augment the money supply by increasing deposits through lending money drawable by cheques. Clearly such a large power should be subject to public economic priorities. The logic led him impeccably, he believed, to the need for a publicly owned, central bank.

Woodsworth was not the only person who was critical of the behaviour of Canadian banks at this time. In the period of agricultural expansion before 1914 prairie farmers had become increasingly suspicious of the banks and had begun the search for credit institutions that would be more open, competitive, and local. In part the Progressive revolt embodied this outlook as did the emergence of Douglasite arguments in the mouths of Irvine and Albertan Progressive MPs in the 1920s. Woodsworth, for his part, always distinguished himself from single-issue monetary reformers, as some Progressives were and as Social Credit devotees certainly became after 1935.[85] He frequently complained that he never quite understood all the mysteries of the Albertan view of money matters and held that monetary reform was not by itself a solution. Nor did he believe that the issuing of money, social dividends, scrip or whatever would solve any fundamental economic problem. On the other hand, there were obvious continuities between him and Albertan monetary reformers: both believed fundamentally that bankers were up to no good and both espoused an essentially under-consumptionist view of economics. Between them there could be some measure of cooperation.

One of the earliest parliamentary demonstration of Woodsworth's interest in monetary policy was his resolution in March 1925 that 'the privilege of issuing currency and controlling credit should be withdrawn from private corporations': 'Thus we face the larger question as to whether or not parliament is to be sovereign, as to whether or not the people are to be sovereign, or whether we have not had our liberties filched from us without most of us having been aware of what has taken place. Many advocate the breaking of monopoly. My thought is not that we should attempt to break this monopoly that we have to-day, this money monopoly, but rather that in some way the people themselves should assume the direction or control of the monopoly, and use it not in the interests of a few but administer it in the interests of the whole of the people of Canada.'[86]

The next year Woodsworth called for 'the establishment of a national system of banking' and proposed a central bank board and, more immediately, a government monopoly of the issuance of currency, encouragement of post-office and provincial-savings banks and, finally, greater allowance for what he called 'co-operative credit,' an arrangement whereby producers' groups could get loans and advances on the collateral of their produce rather than having to resort to the banks. He moved a similar motion two years later, in February 1928. In all these manoeuvres Woodsworth never hid his belief in the desirability of a publicly owned and controlled, national banking system, but he also strained after the 'practical' and the 'immediately' attainable. In the 1928 debate he called for an evolutionary change that would incorporate the proposals of 1926 and, also, include 'an enlargement of the functions of the present treasury board ... to work out a central bank board which would be responsible for the issue of currency and would become a bank of re-discount.'[87] This, he emphasized, would still leave private banks in business.

In his more practical proposals for banking in the 1920s and early 1930s, as with many other matters, Woodsworth was leaning against an open door. As early as 1932 two reform-minded Liberals, C.A. Curtis of Queen's University and Norman Rogers of the University of British Columbia, tried to move Mackenzie King in the direction of a more publicly managed monetary system. Other reform Liberals such as Vincent Massey held similar views.[88] R.B. Bennett was a convert to the idea of a central bank perhaps as early as 1931, and in July 1933 he appointed the Royal Commission on Banking and Currency, chaired by Lord Macmillan, a British jurist.[89] The commission reported with indecent haste just fifty days after its inception and recommended the hybrid arrangement that became the Bank of Canada in 1935: a privately owned bank with monopoly control over the issuing of currency and greater control over the money supply.

The bill to incorporate the Bank of Canada introduced in the Commons in March 1934 was quite within the terms of the evolutionary, practical sentiments Woodsworth had nurtured in the previous fifteen years. But the legislation drew from him an extremely vitriolic criticism:

'Are we in danger of Fascism in Canada?' is a question sometimes asked among the workers. Thinking in terms of brown shirts, parades and salutes I would say no, but when I come to a measure of this kind I am rather doubtful. In the days of the Romans we are told it was their practice to erect two upright spears, then place one transversely upon them and force their conquered enemies to pass under the spears, sub jugum – under the yoke – and usually a heavy tribute was exacted from the conquered enemies. It would seem to me that in the bill now before us we are arranging for the people of Canada to pass under the yoke, and if the bill is passed they must expect to pay a heavy tribute in the years to come.[90]

What most disturbed him were the provisions to allow private shareholders to own the bank and, secondly, the government's declaration that the board of directors of the bank would be independent of the government of the day:

There are also decided objections to, and inevitable dangers in a privately-owned institution. Undoubtedly class interests would prevail; only fairly well to do people could own stock; and, as was pointed out last night by the hon. member for Bow River (Mr. Garland), this means, as in ordinary companies, that the control would not be widespread but would rather be concentrated in a few hands, ultimately in the hands probably of one person ...

That is about what would happen in the case of a national bank if it were organized on the basis proposed in this bill ... Whilst we talk about the danger of political influence, we must remember that if we have no political influence we are thereby giving up the very essence, the very foundation of democracy. It may very well be that sometimes democracy may make mistakes in its decisions, but that is the only way in which higher levels can be attained. We believe the ultimate control of policy should rest with government, but detailed administration should be left to the appointed board; that governments should have the right to appoint and dismiss members of the board; that there should be a minister of state responsible for answering in parliament for the affairs of the board, but that parliamentary discussions of financial matters should be confined to questions of policy and not matters of detail.[91]

As noted earlier, Woodsworth voted on third reading in favour of the legislation, describing it as an improvement over the *status quo*.[92] Later, in 1936 and 1938, the Liberal administration provided for government control of the board and capital stock of the bank. Thus Woodsworth *étapisme* was not without effect. Canada, too, would have a central bank under public ownership and control though, of course, the chartered banks remained powerful and under private ownership.

V

As we have seen, Woodsworth was at once both a reformer and a democratic revolutionary or reconstructionist at least as early as the immediate, post-First World War period. Just as there was constancy in his resolve to pursue a thorough socialism, so there was a continuity in his desire to be 'practical' and to advocate 'immediately' useful and, as he oddly put it once, 'sensible' measures.[93]

Speaking on financial matters as a practical politician in the 1920s and 1930s, Woodsworth called for an end to the state's dependence on indirect taxes and instead proposed a tax on land values, inheritance taxes, a capital levy, and increased income taxes on the wealthy. While he clearly believed in a confiscatory level of taxation for the rich he did not specify the precise level at which such a tax would apply. In 1935 he stated only somewhat clearly that the amount at which this 100 per cent tax would begin might be anywhere between $10,000 and $50,000.[94] For farmers he recommended such immediate measures as cheaper credit, higher prices for their produce, and lower freight rates and tariffs. In non-fiscal matters Woodsworth reiterated the need for unemployment insurance, old age pensions, a minimum wage, the eight-hour day, and medicare. Especially at the height of the Depression he insisted on public-works projects. With his advancing knowledge of Hobsonian under-consumption theory and Keynesian counter-cyclical policies, such projects not only would put people to work but might, if employed judiciously, stimulate the economy:

I am not denouncing bitterly the present administration, I think they are largely in line with other administrations, but I do want to point out that the leading economists of the world are telling them that they are on the wrong line, that instead of adopting a policy of rigid economy they should expand industry in some way and thus give more purchasing power to the people ...

If we could go through with the St. Lawrence waterway it would be a good thing because such an undertaking would release a considerable amount of money for construction work. However, there are other public works which could be undertaken at this time. I was very much struck with the suggestion of the hon. member of Macleod (Mr. Coote) when he urged the adoption of a housing scheme. Many skilled mechanics in our city are receiving relief and under the contemplated legislation they will continue to receive relief for months or years to come. These mechanics might as well be building houses for houses are very much needed in most of our communities. The building of houses would stimulate trade activity all along the line. Such an undertaking should be commenced not only in the interests of the workman and in the interests of the country, but because of purely economic reasons. It would start the wheels of industry going again. I again quote Mr. Keynes:

'The voices which – in such a conjuncture – tell us that the path of escape is found in strict economy and in refraining, wherever possible, from utilizing the world's potential production are the voices of fools and madmen.'[95]

Where there was evident change in Woodsworth's perspective on economic matters during the Depression, it lay not in a tendency to be less practical but in the emphasis he gave to centralized planning, as in his various comments on the advantages of the Soviet Union's economic system. As well, there appeared in the Depression years a noticeable emphasis on the 'contradictions' of the economic system.[96] This came from a belief – one that showed Woodsworth at his most historically fatalistic – that the disastrous times had produced such narrow thresholds of manœuvreability that the economic system could not satisfy its dominant, structural purposes *and* undertake the changes that cried out to be made. The Depression, he asserted, was a worldwide phenomenon of such unmitigated, economic dislocation that governing political parties were powerless to effect any change or improvement. Economic extremities, he said, revealed the inherent structural relations of capitalism: it was a hierarchical arrangement in which the dominant interests of owners and monopolists must first be satisfied so that, in a time of exigent scarcity, satisfying their interests excluded altogether the possibility of meeting the needs of ordinary people. Increasingly of this outlook in the early 1930s, Woodsworth more and more speculated on the historical finitude of capitalism and how it would soon be overcome by the cooperative commonwealth.

The present economic system, he explained, was at a breaking point; an explosion was imminent. The political and economic stewards of capitalism, even with the best will in the world, could not make the marginal concessions that would ease the pressure and save the system: business could not pay dividends and decent wages, *and* underwrite an unemployment-insurance scheme; government could not pay its debts *and* finance public-welfare measures. Yet, paradoxically, Woodsworth continued in the 1930s to proffer immediate measures such as unemployment insurance, minimum wages, and the like. Here, once again, was the antinomy within Woodsworth's conception of change: gradual change was and was not possible; reformist measures would and would not stabilize existing society; reforms were steps on the long road to socialism but had the perverse effect of consolidating the hegemony of monopoly capital. Although the Depression moved Woodsworth more and more to doubt the durability of capitalism and to dispute the ability of its leaders to ensure its legitimacy by implementing reforms and concessions, this did not stop him offering and proposing his own reformist program. Intellectually he saw things with the distant eye of a revolutionary, but he always behaved with the stoical immediacy of a gradualist and a reformer.

There is no disputing, then, the radical character of Woodsworth's theoretical speculations on economic matters throughout the inter-war years. He moulded the three parts of his economic doctrine – monopolies, under-consumption, and the quantity theory of money – into a case for statist socialism. The most inclusive concept of this position and a synonym for his socialism was cooperation, which principally denoted centralization, mass production, largeness of scale, collective ownership, and hierarchical decision-making, albeit all at the behest of an egalitarian scheme of distribution. This is what we earlier called the 'technological' sense of cooperation. We concluded then that Woodsworth had three other conceptions of that term: the relational, the democratic, and the voluntaristic.

In the 1920s and 1930s the relational and the democratic types were not overly present in his thought. Woodsworth in these years talked little of the intrinsic merits of cooperation as brotherhood and sociality; instead his reasoning tended to be based on instrumentalist and utilitarian considerations of rational self-interest; that is, men and women cooperated not because in the absence of cooperation they ceased to be human but because cooperation was a more expedient and successful method of attaining what they desired: a decent, secure livelihood. Nor did he have much to say at this time about cooperation as social unity, the precondition of an inter-subjective democratic community. Nevertheless, whenever elements of an earlier nativism and cultural conformity persisted, they presupposed this pre-1918 conception of 'democratic' cooperation.

What was significantly present in his thought during his time in Parliament, however, was his belief in the voluntaristic conception of cooperation.[97] With this the basic idea was not that of central direction from on high of a mass of citizens but of workers and producers spontaneously banding together to pursue common purposes and directing their leaders to common ends. Woodsworth often protested that he knew well of the evils of a 'bureaucratic' or 'state' socialism that was overly directive, custodial, and hierarchic. He avowed that he wanted a socialism that was democratic and participatory.[98] And so his aim was, apparently, to create a society in which both major senses of cooperation, the technological and the voluntaristic, would be combined. But how would this be done: in harmonious counterpoint or in domination of one over the other?

Woodsworth's economic theory presupposed a large state sector: all industries approaching a monopoly condition were to be publicly owned. With his strong sense of historical inevitability as well as his capacious definition of what constituted a monopoly, there would be very few businesses that would not eventually be publicly owned. (The one exception was agriculture.) The state sector was to be supervised by a central-planning commission that would receive a mandate from Parliament. The overall direction of public policy would come from the people and its details from the planners. (Just as Woodsworth had little idea of how to attain successfully a parliamentary transition to socialism amidst the hurly-burly of competitive party politics, not to mention political and economic sabotage now and then, he was also innocent of the difficulty of keeping analytically and practically separate the directions and details of public policy. Is not the power of modern bureaucrats mainly derived from their ability to determine general policy by being masters of the details?) In principle, however, there was a degree of pluralism in Woodsworth's account of the politics and economics of the planning state; there would be planners, bureaucrats, politicians, the media, and the public, even if private business was largely no more. Trade unions, agricultural producers, consumers and, presumably, sundry interest groups – the bearers and guardians of the principle of voluntary cooperation – would embody this pluralism.

The grand exception in Woodsworth's economic theory was his attitude towards the farmers.[99] To everyone else he overwhelmingly applied the logic of monopolies: the larger the scale of enterprise the more efficient and beneficial the economic outcome. If industrial workers were to be wage labourers, why not farmers? Before the First World War Woodsworth had known of the trend towards corporate farming and the conversion of the farmer from an independent producer to a salaried worker, and he saw no reason to encourage farmers in a similar direction. For him, farmers were victims of monopolies present in the infrastructure of the agricultural industry – grain companies, banks and mortgage companies, implement dealers, the railways, and so on – and in a socialist society these would be subject to public ownership: 'In connection with the farms, the individual farmer owns his own tools. To that extent he is free. I should say with regard to the farmers' problems that we have advocated public control of marketing operations, and public ownership of abattoirs, stockyards, elevators and things of that kind because we believe that in this direction the farmer is exploited. But we are not advocating public ownership of farm lands, and we do not think it necessary to do so. If the time should come when in western Canada, for example, the mortgage companies take over large tracts of land and operate them as great company farms, it might very well be that we should then consider it was time for the state to intervene and take over farm lands.'[100]

In an inhospitable future, the state might buy up bankrupt farms and rent them at a nominal rate to the previous owners, as the Saskatchewan CCF in the 1930s proposed with its so-called use-lease policy,[101] but, otherwise, farmers were to be encouraged to remain as independent, self-supporting producers, seemingly defying the economic logic of their times. Where collective action by them was required, they should band together in voluntary cooperatives such as the Wheat Pool, or government could ensure a 100 per cent compulsory producers' marketing cooperative as envisaged in the Natural Products Marketing Act of 1934, another part of Bennett's 'New Deal.' Woodsworth justified this measure on a frankly utilitarian basis. Farmers, like anyone else who pursued cooperative ventures, did so, he said, for two principal reasons: they wished to acquire a measure of power and freedom in an unbalanced, exploitative market-place; and, secondly, they sought a more expedient method than individual action to ensure a decent level of income: 'In [British Columbia] there are fruit growers who desire to make a living, who have invested their capital in properties and who through a number of years have planted trees and put work on them. Now they find they have a crop to market, but they also find that the market is so arranged that they cannot possibly sell their individual crops without having some sort of cooperative scheme. They have tried voluntary cooperation, but because of certain individuals who are anti-social in their outlook they have been prevented from carrying out their scheme of cooperation. Is it strange that they should come to parliament requesting that it be made possible for the majority to obtain their will? The fact is that the majority of citizens out there feel that they cannot carry on without some sort of coercive measures.'[102]

Yet, whether through a voluntary form of cooperation or a state-sanctioned one, farmers' co-ops and the farming economy in general would represent a sector of partial independence, outside of though not exempt from the strictures of the planning or state sector. But were all of these elements of a voluntaristic sphere – trade unions, co-ops and farmers – enough to counterbalance the power of the state-regulated and -owned planning sector and thus produce a genuine measure of economic pluralism? Just as Woodsworth found a place for a market-based version of international free trade in an economic system that emphasized central direction and coercive allocations, so he espoused a sphere of voluntarism for workers in trade unions and farmers in co-ops. But just as free trade was of a secondary order, in his scheme of things, the same was true of this espousal of voluntarism. The state sector was too large; it incorporated too many industrial activities; it allowed too little place to private ownership. The basic sense of cooperation that prevailed for Woodsworth was the technological one: cooperation as hierarchy and central control. In the end his conception of socialist community was only loosely and marginally committed to pluralism and voluntarism. Instead, if pursued, it would have raised up the daunting prospect of a society of theoretically economic equals submissive to a political and technocratic class of exceptional power and authority. In the end, Woodsworth's economic account of socialism has to be seen as having little to do with William Morris, John Ruskin, and Peter Kropotkin and everything to do with Auguste Comte, Edward Bellamy, and Sidney Webb.

5

Canada, Its Peoples, and the World:
Identity and Security, 1918–1939

When I saw him last, carving the longshore mist
With an ascetic profile, he was standing
Watching the troopship leave, he did not speak
But from his eyes there peered a furtive footsore envy
Of those who sailed away to make an opposed landing
So calm because so young, so lethal because so meek.

Where he is now I could not say; he will,
The odds are, always be non-combatant
Being too violent in soul to kill
Anyone but himself, yet in his mind
A crowd of odd components mutter and press
For compromise with fact, longing to be combined
Into a working whole but cannot jostle through
The permanent bottleneck of his highmindedness.

Louis MacNeice

I

Woodsworth often claimed that wars never resolved conflict, and that
one war only made another one inevitable. Whatever can be made of
these judgments when applied to the general course of human history,
the particular years between 1914 and 1939 revealed them to be remarkably apposite. The First World War seemed to solve little more
than who would be the victors and who the vanquished. In the other

matters that the victors tried to resolve, they only stoked the fires of the next conflagration.

The allies of the Triple Entente held Germany and Austro-Hungary responsible for the war. Austro-Hungary was dismembered, and Germany was punished in a variety of ways: by the loss of territory and colonies, the requirement to pay reparations, the destruction of its armaments, and the demilitarization of part of its territory. To be sure, the post-war settlement was not without its idealism and out of Versailles emerged Woodrow Wilson's grand conception of the League of Nations. In fitful and finally faltering steps the nations experimented with internationalism and collective security. Yet for all that, in the 1920s, France, Germany's immediate western neighbour and constant rival, continually felt insecure and pressed for additional pacts and alliances. The effects of Versailles together with French belligerence contributed to the endemic economic and political instability of the Weimar years and, in time, German resentment and grievance lubricated the rise to power of Hitler and the Nazi Party. Germany was not alone in the lurch towards dictatorship and territorial expansion. Japan, which had become the major power in the Pacific after 1918, periodically tested the strength of its neighbours, especially China. In 1931 it invaded Manchuria. Japan's example was contagious; in 1935 Italy attacked Ethiopia. Historians would look back on these two invasions, especially the latter, as an augury of the end of the League of Nations and the beginning of the slippery slope down which the nations careered to war in 1939.

In these matters Canada would be, mainly, a distant non-participant. Confederation in 1867 had brought independence in domestic matters but scarcely in foreign affairs. For a long time the British Foreign and Colonial Offices would shape Canada's external relations. Macdonald and Laurier asserted a careful and gradual independence of the British while never challenging the imperial connection outright. It was largely the First World War that provided the opportunity for a more rigorous assertion of Canadian sovereignty in foreign policy-making. Canada's contribution of men and material was, for its size, of gargantuan proportions and, after its successful participation in the Imperial War Cabinet, Prime Minister Robert Borden claimed separate representation at the peace conference and in the post-war settlement. The paradox was, however, that by 1920 Canada had established an independent, international status before it had established any foreign policy, let alone the machinery to implement it. At war's end and in the early 1920s only a handful of Canadian politicians and civil servants knew about or were interested in foreign policy. It was Loring Christie, Borden's wartime adviser, who began to equip government with a policy-making capacity in international relations. He was succeeded by O.D. Skelton, who in 1925 became under-secretary of state for external affairs, a position he held until his death in 1941. Skelton was the grey eminence of Canadian foreign policy-making in the inter-war years. That one man could exercise such phenomenal influence is perhaps proof of the degree to which Canadian external affairs at that time were conducted in an undemocratic and secretive way. There were, of course, other interested and involved citizens, such as John Dafoe, editor of the *Manitoba Free Press*, and John S. Ewart, an Ottawa lawyer and constitutional expert, and thousands of Canadians would in time join the League of Nations Society after its founding in 1921. But the circle of the influential was tightly drawn. Only a dozen or so had any significant say in the inter-war years: Mackenzie King, R.B. Bennett and Ernest Lapointe, King's Quebec lieutenant; Skelton and one or two others in the Department of External Affairs; a few individual parliamentarians, such as Henri Bourassa and Senators Raoul Dandurand and George Foster; Walter Riddell, for a long time Canada's Advisory Officer at the League of Nations, and Ewart and Dafoe. International affairs were rarely debated in Parliament. There was no standing committee of the House of Commons given over completely to international relations; the Committee on Industrial and International Relations was only established in 1924 and met infrequently. Often the estimates of External Affairs were presented at the end of the session. By dint of his persistence and dogged debate Woodsworth managed to break into this exclusive hermetic circle. His effect was such that he may be said to have pioneered in Canada almost single-handed the notion that world affairs warranted an informed, public debate.

Membership in the League of Nations had given Canada a new independent and international status. To what purpose would it dedicate this new identity? The league and the imperial connection pulled it into the wider world; geographic isolation and the proximity of an increasingly powerful United States pulled it inward to North America. In the event, in the inter-war period, Canada would settle for isolation, while keeping open the possibility of allying with Britain should circumstances require it. Few if any bridges would be built but what bridges did exist would not be completely burned. Towards Britain, without ever delivering the final insult of rejection, Canada came to adopt an attitude of increasing independence in imperial and constitutional affairs. Towards continental Europe and other international areas, it was also uninvolved and non-committal. As for the United States, Canada desired not to offend. And at the League of Nations, apart from First Delegate C.H. Cahan's eccentric and unilateral position on Manchuria in 1932 and Bennett's surprising support of sanctions in the last year of his government, Canada was proud to be a member but was hardly an active participant. In the end, of course, the imperial connection registered a belated victory. In September 1939, Canada made its own declaration of war and, alone of the nations in the western hemisphere, chose to come to the aid of the British in what many Canadian opinion-makers thought was a British and a European conflict.

Woodsworth would constantly complain about the extravagance of Canada's expenditures on defence. (He considered any expenditure on defence to be extravagant.) But by realistic standards the country's spending on defence in the 1920s and early 1930 was small.[1] In the 1920s expenditures were, annually, between 13 and 21 million dollars, figures that represented, roughly, 4 per cent of total federal expenditures. In the early 1930s spending on defence dropped below 3 per cent, only to begin to climb in 1936 as Canada, with other nations, began to rearm. The size of the armed forces ranged from four to five thousand in the 1920s and between five and seven thousand between 1930 and 1938. In 1939 Canada had only nine thousand men under arms. Its air force was small while its naval capacity was in the inter-war years of legendary insignificance and barely existed at all even if it did grow somewhat in the late 1930s.[2]

II

One event in Woodsworth's life is especially riveted in the Canadian imagination: his lonely independence, some would say defiance, of his party and political community in his opposition to Canada's declaration of war in September 1939. This particular event more than any other helped establish the many interpretations of him as a saint and prophet, a man of principle even unto political death. There can be no gainsaying Woodsworth's courage in 1939; nor can the primacy of pacifism in his life and thought be denied. Still, there were several balancing and offsetting ideas in his international theory between the wars. While pacifism was, in the end, the most fundamental of these, his position in September 1939 was not overwhelmingly entailed or theoretically required by the full texture of his thinking in this period. In fact, in addition to pacifism and isolationism, Woodsworth's world view contained other, competing themes of realism, collective security, and the possibly moral use of power. A curious observer of Woodsworth's politics might have concluded in, say, 1935 that in the event of an eventual war against fascism Woodsworth would not necessarily have chosen personal non-violence and national non-involvement.

Historically, pacifism in Canada derived from sects and churches that were decidedly outside the mainstream of religious life: the Mennonites, Hutterites, Doukhobors, and Quakers. However, before 1914 there was beginning to develop a strain of pacifism that Thomas Socknat calls 'integrational' and 'liberal'; 'integrational' because it derived from within the conventional churches and sought to be part of the wider society, and 'liberal' because it joined together a concern for individual non-violence with the project of changing society and the international order. The pre-war Methodist Church was the principal exponent of this new pacifism and Winnipeg its most important centre.[3] Partly this was due to the presence in the city of James Shaver and Lucy Woodsworth, but there were other influential leaders: F.J. Dixon, after 1914 a member of the Manitoba legislature and an intrepid opponent of registration and conscription in the First World War; William Ivens, a Methodist minister and later one of the leaders of the General Strike in 1919; and the journalists A. Vernon Thomas and his sister-in-law, Francis Marion Beynon. All were close to the Woodsworths. Grace MacInnis recalls meeting Peter Verigin, the Doukhobor leader, in their Winnipeg home;[4] in 1907 the Woodsworths billeted Doukhobors at their North End mission;[5] and after his dismissal from the Bureau of Social Research in 1917 Woodsworth actually contemplated joining a Doukhobor community.[6] Thanks to Socknat's compendious account of Canadian pacifism the Woodsworths can be seen more and more as important leaders of pacifist opinion within liberal Protestantism and secular radicalism between 1910 and 1939, and in Lucy's case for a while afterwards. Lucy Woodsworth helped found the Vancouver chapter of the Women's International League for Peace and Freedom (WIL) in 1921. She attended the world conference of the WIL in Washington in 1925 and chaired the national conference in Winnipeg in 1937. James was a frequent speaker at WIL conferences and at those of the Fellowship of the Reconciliation (FOR) after its founding in 1930. The Woodsworths were part of a sort of family compact of pacifists in the inter-war years. Anna Sissons (née Normart), Charlie Sissons's eventual wife after the early disappointment of his unrequited love for Lucy, was leader of the Toronto WIL in the early 1930s and Mildred Fahrni, a noted Gandhian and leader of the FOR, was a close friend of Woodsworth and one of the two speakers at the memorial service for him in Vancouver in March 1942.

Woodsworth's own pacifism pre-dated the First World War. During his year in Britain at the turn of the century the Boer War had begun to undermine his comfortable assumptions about Britain's benevolent role in the world. In one of his early sermons, while at Grace Church in 1903–4, he talked of the evils of nationalism and militarism, and of how war was opposed to Christian teaching. Throughout his life Woodsworth claimed that his conversion to pacifism had taken place in 1906.[7] Returning from a holiday in Palestine and Egypt he had met, he said, an English civil engineer who told him of how imperialism's vicious system actually worked: 'The typical procedure was something like this: a white trader would open up business with a native tribe; some quarrel ensued; the blacks killed a white man; of course the blacks must be punished and taught their place; there was an attack on a native village; other villages rallied to repel the whites; an expeditionary force became necessary; this involved the establishment of a protectorate to maintain law and order and to teach the natives to govern themselves; it was only another step to colonial status. So grew the British Empire and other Empires.'[8] When he reached London he visited the Army and Navy Museum in Whitehall and observed the tattered, blood-stained flags and uniforms of British soldiers and 'the wretched rags torn from the corpses of natives from almost every part of the world.' He left the museum, he said, sick of heart: 'So this is Empire?' However, for the moment, Woodsworth said little about international matters. He opposed Canada's naval policy in 1910[9] and supported Laurier's Reciprocity Treaty with the United States in 1911.[10] In December of the same year he reviewed favourably Norman Angell's highly influential work, The Great Illusion: 'The author shows that human nature is not unchanging; that the war-like nations do not inherit the earth; that warfare does not make for the survival of the fittest.'[11] It was the First World War, however, that brought Woodsworth to a more public expression of his pacifism. Appalled by the loss of life and the use of the church for recruiting purposes, he submitted an anti-war article to the Manitoba Free Press at Christmas-time in 1914. 'Out

of the Night, the Angels' Song' was rejected but was eventually published in the labour newspaper the *Voice*. It was a statement of the
absolute immorality of physical force and drew upon the example and
teaching of Jesus for its moral authority: 'To overcome militarism by
physical force seems like attempting to cast out Beelzebub by the power
of Beelzebub ... To secure his own victory, Jesus refused to call out even
the legions of angels that awaited his bidding. He, true to his teaching,
could save his life only by losing it. Is the disciple above his Lord?'[12]

After 1918 Woodsworth's account of the origins of war would depend very much on Hobson's theory of imperialism. But in 1914, he
rested his case on the simple, general premise of the bellicose consequences of the undemocratic structure of the state and the competitive
organization of industry:

The War is the inevitable outcome of the existing social organization with its
undemocratic forms of government and competitive system of industry. For
me, it is ignorance, or a closed mind, or camouflage, or hypocrisy, to solemnly
assert that a murder in Serbia or the invasion of Belgium or the glaring
injustices and horrible outrages are the cause of the war.

Nor, through the war, do I see any way out of our difficulties. The devil of
militarism cannot be driven out by the power of militarism without the
successful nations themselves becoming militarized. Permanent peace can
come only through the development of good-will. There is no redemptive
power in physical force.

This brings me to the Christian point of view. For me, the teachings and
spirit of Jesus are absolutely irreconcilable with the advocacy of war. Christianity may be an impossible idealism, but so long as I hold it, ever so unworthily, I
must refuse, as far as maybe, to participate in or to influence others to
participate in war. When the policy of the State – whether the policy of the
State be nominally Christian or not – conflicts with my conception of right and
wrong, then I must obey God rather than man.[13]

There is a categorical, uncompromising quality to the above, underlin-
ing the extent to which Woodsworth believed that war was always
wrong and that in the choice between duty to the state and one's
individual conscience the claims of the latter were inviolate. This is an
anticipation of his position in September 1939, except that in the
intervening twenty years or so Woodsworth took on a good deal of
other intellectual baggage on the question of war and peace.

Another dimension of his pacifism had to do with the extent to which he believed non-violence could be a scheme of change and political action. Woodsworth combined a belief in non-violence with an active concern to overcome social injustice. His commitment to pacifism led naturally to his notion of the moral priority of legal, constitutional methods of change and of conventional behaviour in parliament. But pacifism in this era was influenced by another strain of thought which, while it held to the absolute importance of non-violence, prescribed a model of action that was morally and politically 'aggressive.' This was the example of Gandhi and his notion of 'satyagraha.' In the inter-war years Woodsworth was certainly familiar with Gandhi's ideas. In 1930 he expressed his admiration of him but stated that he could not endorse many of his methods.[14] The context was probably Gandhi's recent campaign of mass civil disobedience against the salt tax. (Woodsworth also took a critical view of the tactics of the radical Doukhobors, the Sons of Freedom, even calling them 'fanatics.')[15] The clue to understanding Woodsworth's perspective here is to recognize that, for him, the act of witnessing to the truth of pacifism did not so much carry individuals into an alliance with others as lift them into a sort of ethereal space of individual protest and self-sacrifice outside history. This witnessing would likely be without immediate effect but, in the great cosmic scheme of things, it would one day be vindicated. What he called the 'moral force' of pacifist dissent was less a summons to collective action than a lonely plaintive protest of the soul in the face of the inevitable, immediate triumph of evil. In Woodsworth's version of theodicy, evil would be overcome but only because truth and love must inevitably triumph. That, said Woodsworth in 'Out of Night, the Angels' Song,' was the Christian's faith: 'In the midst of the perpetual warfare of an early age came a dream of the time when men should beat their swords into plowshares and learn war no more. That dream has appeared to men in all ages. It has so gripped men's imagination and conscience that the most warlike have died ignominiously rather than shed one drop of human blood. Witness the wild Indians, who, converted through the efforts of the Moravians, were massacred in 1782 by white men beyond the Ohio, or the fierce Don Cossacks who helped to form the Doukhobor community, and in 1895 burned their arms, and then quietly submitted to inhuman torture.'[16]

'Out of the Night, the Angels' Song' made use of Lowell's poem 'The Present Crisis':

> Though the cause of Evil prosper, yet 'tis Truth alone is strong,
> And albeit she wanders outcast now, I see around her throng
> Troops of beautiful bright angels to enshield her from all wrong:
> Truth forever on the scaffold – wrong forever on the throne;
> Yet that scaffold sways the Future, and behind the dim unknown
> Standeth God within the shadow, keeping watch above His own.

This, too, captures the character of Woodsworth's pacifism: immediate historical pessimism, intense religious anxiety, the timeless witnessing to truth, the lonely, innocent, childlike and sacrificial path of the pure-in-heart, and the consoling, final belief in the ultimate triumph of good.

Woodsworth returned to the same themes and idioms in his speeches on the eve of the Second World War:

Mussolini is correct. Since prehistoric times it has been, 'Woe to the weak.' We as a race began down in the slime, yet in some way or another we have risen to the stage we call civilization, and this in spite of the brutes that our ancestors were. The race has risen because there were a few men of each generation who caught a gleam of something greater ahead. There are such things in my judgment as truth and justice and love ... And in my better moments I have the courage to believe that truth will prevail even though there is falsehood on every side ...[7]

To-day I do not belong to any church organization. I am afraid that my creed is pretty vague. But ... I still believe in some of the principles underlying the teachings of Jesus and the other great world teachers throughout the centuries. For me at least, and for a growing number of men and women in the churches ... war is an absolute negation of anything christian. The Prime Minister, as a great many do, trotted out the 'mad-dog' idea; said that in the last analysis there must be a resort to force. It requires a great deal of courage to trust in 'moral force'. But there was a time when people thought that there were other and higher types of force than brute force ... [Recently] I was staying at a little resort near the international boundary south of Vancouver. Near Blaine there is a peace arch between the two countries. The children gathered their pennies and planted a rose garden and they held a fine ceremony in which they interchanged national flags and sang songs and that kind of thing ... I have sometimes thought, if civilization goes down in Europe, as it might go down, that in America there may at least be the seeds left from which we can try to start a new civilization along better lines ... I do not care whether you think me an impossible idealist or a dangerous crank, I am going to take my place beside the children and those young people, because it is only as we adopt new policies that this world will be at all a livable place for our children who follow us.[18]

But Woodsworth's road to 1939 was not a straightforwardly pacifist one. There were many twists along the way. Woodsworth never wrote a book on world affairs as he had earlier with immigration and the city. Instead he produced a stream of speeches and articles from which a general description of his views has to be constructed. But the most reflective and complete of any of his statements was the speech he gave in the Commons in April 1935 in response to Henri Bourassa's neutralist motion on the European crisis:

In matters of peace and war I must confess that I find myself torn by various conflicting convictions and considerations ...

First, I believe that military force is stupid; that it settles nothing and that it creates serious trouble. This conviction may be the result of Christian idealism but it is confirmed by a study of psychology and a reading of history.

Second, I believe that among the many causes of war the economic are the most fundamental, especially in modern times. Capitalism, social injustice, imperialistic expansion and war are inseparable. In my judgment war will not end until we destroy capitalism, with its social injustice, and imperialism.

Third, as a born individualist and an inheritor of pioneer traditions I have an instinctive desire to keep myself and my country out of the troubles of other people. In this I think I am a fairly typical Canadian.

Fourth, as a student of our complex industrial and social structure I realize that no individual can live to himself, or that no nation can live to itself. Self-sufficiency, independence, sovereignty and isolationism belong to the past. It is here perhaps that I begin to differ with the hon. member for Labelle (Henri Bourassa). I would emphasize that the mere declaration of neutrality is not sufficient. As I tried to point out the other evening, military defence does not seem to me to be an adequate defence. However, I do not think that mere disarmament will settle our problems.

Fifth, in practice political power with its military force is still largely in the hands of the predatory classes, hence national and international policies are dominated by anything but idealistic motives.

Sixth, as an individualist I refuse to participate or to assist in war, yet I am a citizen of a country which still relies upon force and as a public representative I must vote on alternative military policies.[19]

He continued with what was for him the quintessential statement of the importance of combining a politics of principle and conviction with one based on amelioration, incrementalism, practicality, and immediacy:

In the actual world of affairs, one must try to hold to his own convictions and keep the ultimate objective in view, yet advocate measures that are recognized as merely ameliorative. One must accept the half loaf and even support procedures which though repugnant to his principles, represent a real advance in public welfare and public morality. For example, I am opposed to capital punishment, but rather than have a woman's head torn from her shoulders, as was done a few days ago at a hanging in Montreal, I would vote for the electric chair, the lethal chamber, or perhaps even the axe. In a decently organized society we would not need a police force, but in our present semi-barbarous civilization I prefer a police force to bandits and vigilantes. So in international relations, until war is actually and wholeheartedly repudiated as an instrument of national policy, an international police force under proper control, if that is possible, might be preferable to anarchy. This statement more or less outlines the background from which I view the external policies of Canada.[20]

III

Often human beings choose to deduce apparently indubitable, universal conclusions from the unique circumstances of their times. Woodsworth's view of international relations was profoundly shaped by the First World War. His resignation from the Methodist ministry, in June 1918, was precipitated by the hyper-patriotic and militaristic tone of the church's wartime leadership. Woodsworth was deeply affected by the horrors of the war, its unending violence and innumerable deaths. Even before it had ended he was voicing the view that the war had been a tragic blunder that served no ostensible moral or political purpose. It confirmed his pacifist conviction that wars settled nothing.

The peace settlement only compounded the absurdity of the war in Woodsworth's estimation.[21] Woodsworth was capable of coming to his own critical conclusions about the Treaty of Versailles but he was also deeply indebted to the revisionist historiography of the early 1920s, particularly the work of John Maynard Keynes, E.D. Morel, H.N. Brailsford, J.A. Hobson, G.P. Gooch, and J.S. Ewart as well as the memoirs of generals and politicians such as Lloyd George, Earl Grey, Lord Fisher, and Lord French. Drawing on these writers, Woodsworth advanced the proposition that the treaty was fundamentally flawed in holding Germany mainly responsible for the war. Germany had only behaved in the time-honoured manner of great powers and empires. It was, therefore, morally inappropriate to punish Germany, just as it was, practically speaking, counter-productive. Reparations destroyed the international division of labour and prevented the recovery of world trade. The eventual effect of Versailles, he thought, would be to force Germany into a politics of revanchism and extremism. Other parts of the settlement disturbed him. In its redrawing of the political boundaries of central Europe many ethnic and national minorities had been left behind as national irredenta, and no doubt they would pray and prepare for the day of their liberation. Of the new state of Poland he said that it was 'more or less an arbitrary creation,'[22] including as it did unassimilated minorities of Ukrainians and Germans. He felt the same way about Czechoslovakia.[23] Consequently a recurring theme in Woodsworth's prescriptions for the post-war world was the need to revise the peace treaties.

Four fundamental theoretical perspectives informed Woodsworth's account of international relations in the inter-war period: pacifism, isolationism, internationalism, and economic imperialism. In the pre-1914 era he was certainly aware of the evils of imperialism but only in the early 1920s did he settle on the particular version that so moulded his thinking for the rest of his life: Hobson's notion of economic imperialism.[24] Woodsworth did not read Hobson's classic work, *Imperialism* (1902), until about 1920, but having done so there was no containing his enthusiasm for its ideas. He avidly consumed Hobson's other books, including *The Evolution of Modern Capitalism* and *The Economics of Unemployment*. The heart of Hobson's theory, as noted, was his notion of under-consumption. As modern capitalism developed, its stupendous exploitation of technology brought on a series of crises. Machine production displaced workers yet labour productivity increased exponentially. The poverty of the unemployed and the low wages paid to workers prevented them from consuming the bounteous fruits of an ever more productive economy. The owning classes could gorge themselves on additional consumption, but since there was a limit to the useful or indeed the useless material consumption even they could appropriate, there occurred a crisis of over-production. Imperialism in its modern form, then, was the policy of the state in alliance with the owning classes to establish protectorates over foreign raw materials and new markets with a view to guaranteeing the

continued profitability of the business ventures of the national capitalist class. Expansionist, national, capitalist classes, with their respective
governments in support, often collided with each other. Woodsworth
knew that there were many causes of war – the vanity and stupidity of
leaders, racial and religious prejudice, the collective egotism known as
nationalism, standing armies – but the economic factor was the primary one: 'I think the cause of modern wars might be classed largely as
psychological and economic. Many nations have developed a sort of
megalomania, or, a magnified sense of their own importance ... We
learn to think and speak contemptuously of our rivals or of those
whom we call "lesser breeds without the law."' He went on:

As long as we apply opprobrious terms and have this manner of looking at
things, we are undoubtedly laying up trouble for ourselves in the future. But I
submit that the economic causes of war are more fundamental. Since machine
production has been adopted there has been a search for markets and for
sources of raw materials. This was followed by an effort to secure fields of
investment, which generally meant markets for capital goods. Markets and
investment and trade routes had to be protected. The flag followed trade. Thus
we see the development of that imperialism which is one of the characteristics
of the last fifty years. Modern wars in a very large measure have been
occasioned either by the extension of territory or by the defence of empire.[25]

Woodsworth, of course, exaggerated the extent to which the economic factor was primary. His own pacifism instructed him in the
equal importance of armaments themselves as the cause of war. His
claim was staggeringly simple: not only was the use or threat of force
absolutely immoral but, more concretely, the very existence of arms
guaranteed that they would be used.[26] One wonders whether Woodsworth may have been saying something much more complex and
subtle, but has simplified it for effect. Perhaps he was impugning the
efficiency of the traditional balance-of-power system as a means of
keeping peace? Indeed he was doing that too.[27] But, in fact, his claim
was as straightforward as it appeared. The existence of the means of
violence will produce their use. It is the sort of argument made today in
support of legislation to control the ownership of guns by ordinary
citizens: if people own guns, they will commit murders:

To-day we are living in peace alongside the great American republic to the
south of us – a wonderful example of how nations can live in peace. I venture,

however, to say that if cannon were placed on the international border along the forty-ninth parallel we should have trouble. We are at peace because of the very lack of border patrols.[28]

I do not know that I would go quite so far as has the hon. leader of the opposition. I am inclined to stress the economic causes of war. I think they are the fundamental causes, and so long as there are economic maladjustments in the world, so long as there is fierce competition between individuals, between groups, between nations and between empires, then so long shall we have war. But undoubtedly another cause which lies side by side with the economic cause is the fact that we are prepared for war, and when there is economic friction the tendency is for us to plunge into war before the people have had time to bring themselves under control.

MR. BENNETT: There would be no war if there was nothing to go to war with.

MR. WOODSWORTH: As the hon. leader of the opposition has said, if there were no instruments of war we could not very well conduct a war.[29]

Another of the fundamental premises of Woodsworth's international theory was isolationism. As a young man he had experienced the blessedness of pioneer independence, the *sine qua non* of North American isolationism, but from his family and his schools he had also learned of the glories of the British Empire. He went to Britain in 1899 in part to explore his cultural roots and discovered that he was more distinctively Canadian than he had thought. Indeed, in no area of his intellectual life did Woodsworth change as much as he did in his attitude to the 'motherland.' He went from being a profound believer in the British Empire and all its 'glories' to holding that Canada should become totally free of British political and constitutional connections. Britain should continue to be an object of the cultural and sentimental attachments of Canadians but in all other matters it should be seen for the imperialist power that it was. Instead Canada should nurture its connections with the United States. It should come to terms with being a North American nation.[30] Set apart from Europe for a long time, composed of peoples often in flight from old-world militarism and aristocracy, Canada should leave Britain alone to operate in its own essentially European and imperial orbits. Canadians should appreciate the extent to which they had been the plaything of British interests. The Canadian Pacific Railway had been built to meet imperial defence requirements[31] and the flower of Canadian manhood had been sacrificed in Flanders to help Britain maintain its European and imperialist hegemony over Germany. Isolationism would protect Canada from many heartaches:

I should like our representatives in going overseas to carry with them some of the ideals that are common among the ordinary people of this country. We are longing for peace and for economic justice. We are a people whose forefathers came to this country prepared to work hard in the hope that they might be able to found homes for themselves and their children. We are a people who in the pioneer days knew a great deal of neighbourliness. We are not anxious to interfere with other people's affairs; we are anxious to live and let live.[32]

One can hardly go to the province of Quebec, or read even cursorily the French-Canadian press, without realizing that there is a very strong sentiment there against being dragged into another war. I would respectfully suggest to the French-Canadian members of this house that if that is so, their responsibility is to say so here and now. I would suggest that when increased expenditures are proposed they ought to join with some of the rest of us and ask the reason for these increased expenditures. Are they merely for our own defence or are they being made in order that we may one day participate in a European war?

I think of the situation in the west. I do not think the west is any less loyal than any other part of this country. But over fifty per cent of the people there are not of Anglo-Saxon origin. They are interested in the welfare of Canada; they are much less interested in the adventures which may be entered upon by Great Britain in various parts of the world. Many of them came here to escape the burden of militarism, and hence perhaps are able to see things a little more clearly than those who are almost blinded by a certain emotional attachment to the motherland.[33]

Antinomy may have been the basic structure of Woodsworth's mind. Isolation was desirable, especially in wartime, but it was not a solution for all seasons. Woodsworth knew there could not be a retreat from the world, either on moral or technological grounds. The overwhelming moral imperatives of the age, indeed they were allied to the very tendencies of human evolution, were brotherhood and cooperation; as well, the complementary tendencies of technology were those of interdependence and integration.[34] On every hand, he claimed, international exchange and solidarity were flourishing, in the arts, science, trade, finance, and labour unions, even in the means of travel not to mention – with the development of the airplane – the means of destruction. Only politics lagged behind, becalmed in the backwaters of nationalism and nationalism's spurious internationalism, imperialism. Theoretically, at least, but more and more in reality, the only ultimate hope of the species was a world state or, to use his beloved phrase from Tennyson, 'the Parliament of man, the Federation of the world':

In the old days peace was simply an armed truce, and the only way we could think of maintaining peace was by defensive alliances. But to-day all that is changed. We have already developed economic inter-dependence. There is a growing sense of the world's solidarity. In the scientific world we have stepped over international boundaries. Any great medical achievement in one country is rapidly carried to other countries, and we rejoice in it. Culture is becoming international; literary, artistic and religious movements sweep rapidly over international boundaries. But there is a development that has not been so clearly understood, and that is that class and group conflicts are also worldwide in character. To-day the great industrialists and financiers have their interests in different parts of the world, and hardly recognize international boundaries. The great financiers are international in their outlook. In fact, labour man as I am, I would say it is not impossible that the development of international finance may one of these days prove to be the very surest way of effecting some sort of world solidarity.[35]

It is all very well to say that we should get out of the British Empire, if anyone does say so, or that we should get out of the League of Nations, as somebody has suggested. But we cannot get out of the world, and to-day the world is one vast neighbourhood. We can no longer maintain the policies of isolation which were possible for the United States and Canada until a comparatively few years ago ...

In the old days we might very well have said, 'Well, if China and Japan want to go to war let them go to it; we will stay safely on this side of the Pacific.' That would be quite an impossible thing for us to-day. Surely we have not forgotten that it was a murder away in Serbia that was the match that brought about the conflagration which spread to all parts of the world. We can no longer remain isolated; whether we like it or not we are in contact with the other nations of the world, even those in the most remote parts, and in my judgment we must build up some sort of world arrangement, some collective system, or we can look forward only to chaos and disaster in the years to come.[36]

It followed that Canada's foreign policy should support, as much as possible, the only present attempt at international organization: the League of Nations. As we shall see, however, Woodsworth's support of the league was not always constant and unwavering.

Apart from the league, two other imposing forms dominated Woodsworth's thinking in the 1920s and 1930s. These were, as already intimated, Canada's relations with Britain and those with the United States. In effect the consequence of Woodsworth's recommendations on these issues would have been to destroy the imperial connection and replace it with a state of affairs in which Canada would be militarily and economically dominated by the United States. In a strange, inadvertent, and convoluted way he promoted the Americanization of Canada.

Woodsworth did not see the United States as a fundamentally different historical project from that of British North America; the United States was neither culturally alien nor politically or militarily threatening.[37] The continuities and uniformities between the two countries were more important. They shared the same language and the same 'social ideals' and political institutions; racially, Canadians were of the same 'kith and kin,' and the United States was that 'great and friendly country to the south of us.' Culturally, especially, there was nothing to fear: 'We must recognize that just south of the line there is a great population of over 100,000,000 people, people speaking the same language that we do, people who have a much longer history than the English speaking peoples of Canada, people who have had time to develop a very considerable literature, people who have a certain class that is more or less free to do writing, people who have the same old English backgrounds, and to a large extent the same British institutions that we have in Canada, people who to a considerable degree have the same social ideals that we have and, I would say, people with whom, whether we like this or not, the future of Canada at least socially is inevitably bound up.'[38]

On economic matters, however, Woodsworth was less certain. From an early date he had recognized the rise to world importance of the United States as a financial and economic power, not just in the Far East and Latin America but in Canada too.[39] 'In recent years,' he said in 1929, 'we have had two events at least of vast importance – the world war, which has reconstructed what we used to know as "modern Europe," and released forces the effect of which cannot as yet be determined, and secondly, the rise of what might be termed the American United States Empire. Throughout a little more than a century the United States was united and consolidated and extended, and then during the past forty years it has become a great modern empire, changing the centre of gravity of the entire political world.'[40]

No doubt Canada, too, was an American colony. But this sad predicament, about which presumably something should be done, did not lead him to assert the importance of greater Canadian military and political independence vis-à-vis the United States. That would have jeopardized his pacifism and confounded his conception of a sort of fortress North America. These were higher priorities.

What Woodsworth did recommend was that Canada undertake complete, unilateral disarmament.[41] The defence and militia forces should be disbanded and cadet-training ended; departments of peace and international fellowships should be established; Canada should remove itself altogether from the ugly business of manufacturing arms; especially it should ban the export of nickel – over which it exercised a virtual world-wide monopoly of production – destined for use in arms manufacture. Such injunctions, once implemented, would have left Canada without military defences. This was of course Woodsworth's conscious intent. It is here that his conception of a 'benign' United States was so useful. Militarily, he said, Canada had nothing to fear from its southern neighbour.[42] Also, Canada's isolated position in the world provided it with a heaven-sent opportunity to pursue disarmament without any dangerous consequences.[43] Canada, then, would disarm, unilaterally if need be; he never implied, certainly never stated explicitly, that the United States was likely to disarm – empires rarely do; but that was useful, too, since as he argued in the late 1930s, it would allow a disarmed Canada to shelter under the American military umbrella.[44] For the everlasting truth of American foreign policy, proclaimed in the Monroe Doctrine, was that the United States rejected external interference in the western hemisphere. Mostly Woodsworth doubted that the rest of the world had any military interest in Canada anyway because of the great distances involved. But, should Germany or Japan, say, threaten Canada – and this was not inconceivable in the era of the airplane – Canada could count on American protection. There was an advantage, then, in the United States *not* being disarmed:

Let us consider realistically the defence of Canada. If we start with the assumption that Canada's first obligation is to her own citizens, our problem is: How can we save our next generation from annihilation? I submit, as I did on the defence estimates, that with our present military equipment or any which this country can support, Canada unassisted cannot defend herself against all comers. Fortunately she does not need to do so. The United States will not attack us, and under her Monroe doctrine the United States would protect us, not because of her interest in our welfare, but because of her interest in her own affairs. At the moment, then, I have a good deal of sympathy with the isolationist position, though I quite agree that it cannot ultimately save us. We are a part not only of North America but of the world.[45]

What should be Canada's policy from a purely Canadian standpoint? Canada as a nation is not in any immediate danger. The United States is our only powerful neighbor. The United States will not make any military attack – in fact, those who rely on military force may rest assured that the United States would resist outside aggression. Some may feel that we should not be under obligations of this kind. On the other hand, why should we not take advantage of our advantageous position? If I live in an area of fire-proof buildings why should I not be happy in enjoying immunity from fire hazards?[46]

Of course Woodsworth was not altogether uncritical of the United States: the Americans deported people for political reasons and they still had much to learn from the British about political freedom.[47] Mainly his criticisms had to do with the dangers of American imperialism. Yet the dangers were, it seems, never large enough to cause him to worry about Canada being militarily dependent upon the Americans. As a matter of fact Woodsworth used the inevitable, immovable reality of American economic domination as one more argument in support of his proposal for disarmament and isolationism. He claimed that, with its economic investments in Canada, the United States had already obtained all that it wanted:

Surely Canada is in a peculiarly favourable position; I do not think this can be stressed too strongly. We are side by side with this great nation to the south, a nation which speaks the same language and which has very largely the same British traditions. Her interests are similar to ours at least to a very large extent. Millions of native-born Canadians or their descendants now reside in that country. If the Americans wanted to invade us I fancy that they have a better way of accomplishing that purpose, that is by means of the economic penetration which is going on. If the United States ever conquers Canada it will be in that way rather than by the use of physical force. We need then have no fear of an invading army from the south. Why do we need to maintain ours?[48]

Is the United States likely to attack us? I fancy United States financial interests have a great part of what is worth having in Canada, anyway, and they have secured it, not by means of military tactics but by way of financial penetration … The United States does not want to attack us; there is no doubt of that.[49]

To Woodsworth it followed logically that the highest priority of Canadian foreign policy should be the resolve not to offend the United States.[50] He recommended other things too: the Rush-Bagot and Root Treaties should be renewed; and Canada should build upon the example of the International Joint Commission by concluding an arbitration treaty with the Americans for the peaceful resolution of all North American conflicts.[51]

Woodsworth's insistence that Canada should give no offence to the Americans had significant implications for Canada's traditional relations with the British Empire and showed him as having moved a long way from the confident imperialism of his youth. Equally clear is the fact that this particular concatenation of policy positions in the interwar years revealed him as swimming not just in personally unfamiliar waters but waters with tricky logical currents and eddies as well. Puzzling questions spring to mind. Why, if the United States was so wantonly imperialistic, should Canada render itself defenceless against it? Why should American economic penetration and putative domination be acquiesced in as a means of justifying Canadian disarmament? How could a country with pretensions to a proud independence – Woodsworth did after all hold out this hope for Canada – submit not just to imperialism but to the virtual determination of its external policies by another power? In posing these questions we are perceiving something of the welter of ideas and the ethical asymmetry – of vice justifying virtue, of cruel necessity justifying the highest ideals – that swirled around in Woodsworth's mind. We are brought to recognize the rhetorical and political limits to which he would go to achieve his pacifism and isolationism.

To repeat, in any clash between claims on its loyalty by the United States and Britain, Canada should, Woodsworth argued, align itself with the former. It should remain aloof from such potential points of friction as the Anglo-Japanese alliance and the Anglo-American naval rivalry.[52] And it must avoid international agreements and treaties such as Lausanne (1924) and Locarno (1925) that would join it with Britain or other powers in opposition to American concerns and interests.[53] Above all, entanglements with Britain had to be avoided.

It must be emphasized that Woodsworth's position on Anglo-American relations, like his account of Canadian relations with the United States, was not without its ambiguities. Britain was still for him the 'motherland'; the 'spiritual' unity of the British Empire was something still worth preserving;[54] Canada owed Britain an 'enormous debt' for its language, literature, political institutions, and traditions;[55] even towards the end of his life he confessed to feeling 'spiritually more at home in England than in Canada.'[56] Moreover, on one occasion at least, he claimed that American imperialism constituted a greater threat to Canada than the British variety and that the British connection was important as a way of resisting American imperialism.[57] But, in spite of these considerations, in the end he held that Britain was a greater danger to Canadian interests since it drew Canada into illegitimate foreign, capitalist adventures.[58] In a similar vein, another of Woodsworth's great fears was that Canada's membership in the empire gave her obligations without influence. In this regard he asserted that Canada should press not just for the sort of constitutional independence of Britain that would allow it to make its own foreign policy but also for the power to make its own declarations of war. Dallying with these ideas, Woodsworth sometimes implied that he was, with these conditions met, a firm believer in a unified commonwealth of free and equal nations. But such notions were mainly window-dressing for him. If he believed in the new idea of a British commonwealth, he did so only in an anodyne sense. Fundamentally he desired complete independence for the Dominion of Canada not as a means of allowing it to make a voluntary commitment to imperial affairs but as a prelude to withdrawal from imperial entanglements altogether:

From my standpoint the relationship of the autonomous nations to the empire is by no means clear; and the mere fact that we belong to this commonwealth of self-governing nations should not lead us to assume obligations with regard to the policies of the empire. I suppose that technically if Great Britain is at war Canada is at war, at least unless there is some further declaration than we have yet had. I wish we could have such a declaration. Canada cannot consent to come to the assistance of the empire in some war brought about by policies in which she has no voice; and on the other hand, as we develop our independent policies, we cannot expect support from Great Britain – we must expect to be on our own. Actually we took pretty much this position in our signing independently the Versailles treaty. Although all the implications of that position have not been manifest, I think they are implicit in our signing of the treaty.[59]

Let me point out that our connection with Great Britain might easily lead us into troubles that we as Canadians otherwise might escape. Great Britain has a far-flung empire; trouble might break out in India, in Hong-kong, in the islands of the sea, in the nearer east, in Egypt or in any one of a hundred places where Great Britain has interests. Under those circumstances what is to be our attitude as a Canadian people? Are we prepared to do our share in the defence of the empire, and to come to its defence as we did in 1914?[60]

With regard to the empire, it does seem to me we must recognize that the empire as we have known it was built largely on conquest ... If I can do anything to prevent it, our Canadian boys shall not shed their blood in any more imperialistic schemes – all under the guise of patriotism.

We must claim our right to be neutral.[61]

Canada, Woodsworth felt, should avoid imperial entanglements completely as long as Britain's foreign policy was under the control of its traditional, imperialist-minded, capitalist class and its political instruments, Stanley Baldwin and Neville Chamberlain. He knew there was another Britain, that of Ramsay MacDonald, the Labour Party, and the common people. He believed that Labour's foreign policy would likely be more liberal and internationalist, more conciliatory towards the cause of Indian independence, and more willing to convert the empire to a consensual, cooperative commonwealth. But by the mid-1920s he also knew from actual experience that not even a Labour government would automatically recognize Canadian interests. It had been MacDonald that had pressed in 1924 for the adoption of the Geneva Protocol at the League of Nations, which Woodsworth had advised against Canada's supporting.[62] Ultimately it did not depend on who was in power in Britain. Canada should go it alone.

Pacifism, isolationism, internationalism, amity towards the United States, and distance from Britain, these summarize the central tenets of Woodsworth's view of international affairs between the wars. How successful did he believe he was in gaining acceptance of these ideas in Ottawa?

It should be recognized that, unlike his views on economic and social policy, many of Woodsworth's foreign policy assumptions were shared by the key members of the Canadian policy community at the time. Of course, Mackenzie King, prime minister for most of these years, seemed mainly to choose ambiguity. But what can be discerned of his foreign policy views often put him close to Woodsworth: independence within and of the empire, the attainment of full Dominion status, and warm relations with the United States. Also, Skelton's isolationism had many affinities with Woodsworth's. As for the Conservatives, they were more in favour of the British connection, imperial preference, and protectionism than Woodsworth ever could countenance, but Bennett did in 1934–5 make a more categorical commitment to economic sanctions and collective security than Woodsworth probably ever expected of a Conservative prime minister. While Woodsworth himself changed his mind on sanctions, advocating them at first but rejecting them later, he generally supported the League of Nations and in this he had much in common with thousands of other Canadians. The Canadian League of Nations Society enjoyed a large membership in the late 1920s and early 1930s. After refusing to join initially Woodsworth became a member and in the 1930s served on the Society's executive council. There were other personal connections. Woodsworth was greatly influenced not just by socialist intellectuals – for example, Escott Reid, Frank Scott, Frank Underhill, and Eugene Forsey – but by such liberals as John Dafoe, Brooke Claxton, Norman Rogers, and N.W. Rowell. Perhaps the greatest Canadian influence upon him in international matters was John S. Ewart, who lived in Ottawa until his death in 1930. Woodsworth periodically visited his home. Ewart similarly influenced Mackenzie King and probably has a greater claim to the title of creator of Canadian foreign policy in the inter-war years than even Skelton.[63]

Woodsworth's criticism of the elected policy-makers emphasized the process as much as the substance.[64] In his opinion international relations were simply not discussed enough in Parliament and, when they were, the discussions failed to produce a clarity of purpose on the government's part. King, he felt, especially worshipped at the temple of the cult of ambiguity,[65] and Bennett had been no better.[66]

When King's and Bennett's foreign-policy goals *were* clear, Woodsworth invariably disagreed with them. King, he believed, was in the 1920s too slow to extricate Canada from British influences, although he did support his position in the Chanak crisis of 1922. King was also too unassertive in pursuing Dominion status and in drawing out the implications of the Statute of Westminster. Of course neither King nor Bennett were sufficiently pacifist, isolationist, or internationalist for his taste. And, at the end of the 1930s, Woodsworth contended that King was too quick to ally Canada with the British, thus leading to rearmament after 1936 and the declaration of war in September 1939.

IV

As an idealistic internationalist, Woodsworth found much to celebrate in the League of Nations. His enthusiasm for the league was stronger at some times than at others, but he never wished to abandon it; for him, a League of Nations in one form or another was crucial to the keeping of the peace.

For all of the 1920s, however, Woodsworth was cool towards the league.[67] He claimed that, instead of being as inclusive as possible, it had started out on the wrong foot with the absence of the United States, Germany, and Russia. He also worried that it had become a tool of the great powers. The latter held permanent positions on the league council and increasingly exercised a stranglehold over international financial matters, especially the renegotiation of Germany's debt payments through arrangements such as the Dawes Plan. Woodsworth was especially concerned about the legal obligations Canada had assumed in becoming a party to the Treaty of Versailles and the league covenant. The treaty, he believed, was unfair and yet Canada, particularly through articles 10 and 16 of the covenant and their requirement of collective action to defend and protect the existing territorial integrity of the nations, was obliged to maintain the political *status quo*. In his mind, the post-war settlement and the subsequent attempts to improve it – the league's Geneva Protocol, for example – might place Canada in an untenable position *vis-à-vis* the United States. Specifically, Canada might be required to apply economic sanctions, which the Americans opposed. Maintaining friendly relations with the United States was, for Woodsworth, second in importance only to the necessity of avoiding war.

On the other hand, even in the 1920s, Woodsworth recognized that the league did perform or at least had the potential to perform a number of laudable functions.[68] It could become the vehicle for general arbitration procedures. He called on Canada to submit itself to the optional clause of the Statute of the Permanent Court of International Justice and to support the General Act for the Pacific Settlement of International Disputes. The league could be the forum for the negotiation of a covenant of the seas. And it could become the agency for establishing international standards for an eight-hour workday and a minimum wage, thus preventing the undercutting of living standards in the industrial countries of the West through the dumping of cheap goods from low-wage economies.

In April 1930 Woodsworth announced a change of heart regarding his generally conditional support of the league.[69] There must always exist, he said, some kind of international organization. The league fitted the bill exactly and already it was becoming something of a world parliament. But there were troubled times ahead. In September 1931

Japan invaded China and set up a client state in Manchuria. The league's response was slow and ineffectual, mainly taking the form of the creation of the Lytton commission of enquiry. Woodsworth believed that the league should have declared Japan the clear aggressor and fully applied economic sanctions against it. His position after 1931 – in contrast to his position in earlier years – was that Canada should embrace its obligations under the league covenant:

I think there could have been certain economic sanctions taken that would not have involved war. But we did not propose to take those sanctions, we did not even make any strong protest in the matter. There is my point. I am not saying whether Canada acting alone could have taken any economic sanction, but I think we might very well have joined with other nations in taking such sanction, and in that case I do not think a general war would have been precipitated. But I would point out that through our inactivity we are laying the foundation for a war in the future.[70]

As a member of the league [Canada] has undertaken some very serious responsibilities. I do not think most hon. gentlemen have stopped to think what really is involved in our membership in the league ... It may be said that we are not going to take these covenants very seriously ... if we had done so, Japan would not have gotten away with things as she did. That Treaty of Versailles, which at the time was supposed to give promise of an era of peace, surely ought to mean something to us. If it means nothing whatever, I suppose the only thing for us to do is to get out of the league, but at the present moment we are members of the league and as such are bound in honour, as well, I take it, as by what might be considered international law, to live up to our obligations.[71]

For Woodsworth the advantage of economic sanctions, universally and effectively applied, was that they would obviate war rather than precipitate it. If they brought war, they could not be justified. He admitted that one could never know for sure whether, in any given predicament, economic sanctions would in fact prevent war but probable deductions could be made. What, however, about military sanctions? They, too, were part of the league covenant and part of the potential duties of the member states. As a pacifist Woodsworth held that force of any kind, actual or threatened, was categorically wrong. But what about the force employed by a collective-security agency or international police, or the militia of a world-wide super-state, perhaps called the League of Nations?

In dealing with Woodsworth's position on this knotty question, it is important to keep several things in mind. First, as a pacifist, he held that the state, in its traditional national form as a sovereign authority instituted to keep the peace through the threat or use of force, was *a priori* illegitimate. All force was wrong. Secondly, in his several disquisitions in the mid-1930s on collective security he invariably drew an analogy between the domestic state and its use of force to control recalcitrant and rebellious individuals and groups, and an international system in which a universal agency of some kind imposed order on belligerent nations and governments. And, thirdly, again specifically in the context of a discussion of the league and the morality of force, Woodsworth confessed to being under conflicting moral constraints when resolving this kind of dilemma. He was a pacifist and an idealist, – and here was another antimony – but he was also a realist. Often he was confronted by the need to choose between the lesser of two evils; he might also be required to choose a course of action which, while not perfect, would make small improvements to the state of the world. Another consideration was his responsibility as a Member of Parliament to represent the wishes of his constituents rather than his own beliefs:

As an individual I refuse to participate or to assist in war, yet I am a citizen of a country that still relies upon force, and as a public representative I must vote on alternative military policies ...[72]

Often one has to choose between two alternatives. If there were an alternative between spending $150,000 for cadets and $300,000 for cadets I would vote for the $150,000, not because I believe in cadets but because I believe it is the lesser of two evils. I can conceive that under certain circumstances some sort of world international police force might be better than our present rival standing armies. It is not that I want to depend upon force, used even by an international police force ... I confess that I have very little confidence in physical force as a means of settling disputes. Within the bounds of the nation we have set up courts and most of us obey fairly well the decisions of the judges in those courts. I think we will not be on a safe basis until we come to some such arrangement in our international affairs, set up our courts and all agree to abide loyally by their decisions. That would be civilization. I do not know whether we can attain that position at one jump, but in the meantime I believe in working as rapidly as possible in that direction.[73]

It is fair to conclude that Woodsworth was not always a systematic pacifist and that, logically, he would not have been beyond the ambit of his own declared moral principles were he to have advocated military sanctions as part of a league-sponsored international police force. The fact is, however, that in none of the actual crises of the inter-war years did he propose either the use of force by individual nation states or military sanctions by the League of Nations, although in the minds of some of his colleagues there was confusion about his position on the latter issue. Certainly his commitment to economic sanctions was spasmodic and fitful. He supported them strongly after 1931 but he would eventually have doubts.

In early 1935 Woodsworth still held unambiguously to the policy of applying economic sanctions against aggressor nations, as long as these would not cause war. Yet, on the eve of Italy's invasion of Ethiopia in October 1935, he had second thoughts. Ironically, his ambivalence occurred at the very moment when Britain and France and many other nations were most willing to support a league-sponsored strategy of economic sanctions, including an embargo on oil. At a meeting of the League of Nations Society's National Council on 8 November 1935 Woodsworth sided with Escott Reid, who had introduced a motion stating that Canada should refuse to apply sanctions against Italy and should withdraw from the league unless it was exempted from articles 10 and 16 of the covenant. Woodsworth moved an amendment: that sanctions could be supported only if they were accompanied by a determined effort to discover and resolve the causes of war.[74] Three weeks later, on 30 November, the National Council of the CCF met to consider the gathering crisis. William Irvine moved that the CCF should support economic and military sanctions by the league, but his resolution was ruled out of order on the grounds that it conflicted with the party's position – established at its last national convention in 1934 – that sanctions should be rejected until the league was thoroughly re-organized. According to the council minutes, Woodsworth 'sketched the history of the League to show that for a long time it had been dominated by France, and her satellites and more recently by Great Britain. He contended that the original conditions of Canada's adherence to the covenant had been disregarded. The nations had not disarmed as they had promised to do. Any support to the imposition of sanctions should be accompanied by a demand for disarmament. He pointed out that our dilemma arose out of contradictions of the capitalist system. He expressed himself as being in favour of sanctions conditionally upon the carrying out of the disarmament proposals of the covenant.'[75]

Woodsworth could never be accused of being uncritical of the league; the extent of his disappointment with the organization provided him with an infinity of possible arguments against it. It seems that, at the high-water mark of his support for economic sanctions between 1932 and early 1935, he muted his criticism in order to use this weak vessel for immediate apparent good.

One of his most radical claims against the league in the mid- and late-1930s was that not only had the great powers treated it as a plaything but that none of the nations had been willing to abandon national sovereignty in favour of making the league a world state.[76] (For a gradualist Woodsworth could be exceptionally impatient with the slowness of change.) Another prominent criticism he advanced at this time emphasized the complete lack of moral order in the international system and thus the impossibility of morally supportable action by the league through its leading members. He condemned Japan over Manchuria and Italy over Ethiopia but, by his stringent logic, neither had behaved any worse than the other major powers in the last hundred years.[77] Germany was only as bad as Britain, and Japan as bad as France. (The 1930s, perhaps more than most times, was a period when subtle judgments were required; the broad brush strokes of his criticism prevented him from making them.) Woodsworth was coming perilously close to saying that, given the dire lack of international morality, the league was completely illegitimate. He was aware indeed that such was precisely the message many of his listeners were hearing.[78] This was, of course, not his position; the league was not to be abolished but was to be reconstructed. But, realistically, how quickly could the league be restructured to meet Woodsworth's internationalist ideal of a world state composed of compliant, disarmed nations, given the continuing international crisis of the time? And, in any case, could this end not be achieved in steps? Such was the rigour of his criticisms that it was well-nigh impossible for the league to meet any of his conditions of acceptability. Altogether, Woodsworth was risking the abandonment of his customary willingness to work with flawed instruments to bring about marginal improvements.

In March 1936 Woodsworth had an opportunity to clarify his position. T.C. Douglas, the newly elected CCF member from Saskatchewan, had moved an early resolution in the new Parliament on the international crisis. His motion called for Canada to prohibit the export of war materials and asserted that the application of sanctions was futile and dangerous unless accompanied by a move towards disarmament and the revision of the post-war treaties; until the latter occurred Canada should refuse to participate in foreign wars. Douglas was never a pacifist and represented a 'muscular' school of thought on international relations in the CCF. In his memoirs twenty years later, he indicated that Woodsworth's speech in the debate saw him make a public commitment to both economic *and* military sanctions:

I had quite a battle in our camp before I got support, because in this resolution I stressed for the first time in the House of Commons that we ought to have an international police force, and have not only economic sanctions, but if necessary, military sanctions. Some of our own people were pacifists, and were a little reluctant to support the idea of military sanctions, although they could agree to economic sanctions. I took the position then that you couldn't set up an international body and ask them to make the international pirate behave if all they could wave in his face was an empty gun. Nations would ultimately have to give an international police force the power and authority to deal with an international bandit. This is important because it was the first time that Mr. Woodsworth, after a great deal of argument, finally moved to that position and was prepared to support it. Remember he was a pacifist, against all force and all use of force. But he was prepared to concede that force could be used to maintain international law and order. This was a big advance for us.[79]

Douglas's memory is probably faulty; he is perhaps talking about another debate in 1936. But his comment does attest to the strength of the disagreement within the CCF at this time between the pacifists and those who wanted stronger action by the league.

What, in fact, did Woodsworth say in the March debate? He stated that he was unalterably opposed to war 'as an instrument of national policy [and] ... as a recognized means for settlement of international disputes.' He quoted approvingly from CCF resolutions which held that the league was a tool of 'the great capitalist powers' and that, until it was restructured, Canada should refuse to give it 'military assistance.' He then cited a statement by George Lansbury which implied that all war was wrong, even a league-initiated one: 'The longer I live the more convinced I become that war settles nothing, that war is the greatest disaster that could come upon any nation ... I have a good deal of respect for Mr. George Lansbury who, speaking of his resignation as leader of the Labour party in Great Britain, made this statement: "It is impossible for me to believe anything good can come out of mass murder, whether this is carried out by order of a league of nations or by a single nation. Evil cannot be swept out of our lives by evil; the spirit of war cannot be destroyed by more war." I want to adopt that statement as my own, so there may be no doubt in the mind of any hon. member as to where I stand.' In regard to Canada's role in the world, Woodsworth claimed that isolationism, while attractive, would not do because the world was increasingly a 'neighbourhood.' So Canada should support the league 'in so far as it is an association of nations seeking to promote peace.' The problem was that the league at present was dangerously flawed as an instrument for peacekeeping. He repeated his traditional litany of complaints against the league, ending with a denunciation of it as a potential tool of imperialist domination: 'There is a very great danger that the League may be made a kind of smoke screen behind which imperialist aims and ambitions may be carried forward.' He next turned to the issue of sanctions and, apparently, reassumed a position of support for economic sanctions:

I think we may distinguish between economic sanctions and military sanctions. I know there is a danger that economic sanctions may provoke an enemy in a desperate position to reprisals, perhaps even to the declaration of war. In the case of Italy I cannot but think that a declaration of that kind on our proposal to extend sanctions was a good deal of a bluff. However, there is that possibility. As the hon. member for Weyburn (Mr. Douglas) suggested in moving the resolution, however, there is also the danger that unless we do exercise economic sanctions we may very easily provoke war. There is danger in every direction, but if we were only sincere and thorough-going in our exercise of sanctions it seems to me we would not have to face war ...

But if sanctions are to be applied, they must be made effective, and all nations must be willing to do their share. I am glad to think that at last we have come to the point of recognizing the desirability of not allowing war materials to pass into the hands of the aggressor. I think it is two years since I brought in a resolution in regard to nickel, urging that we express our willingness to cooperate with the League of Nations in seeing that no nickel found its way into war materials.

What he gave with one hand – support of universal and effective sanctions – he took back with the other: 'The purpose of the resolution is to point out that sanctions in themselves are not enough ...' First, the nations should honour their obligations under the league covenant: disarmament and the revision of the treaties:

Thus we are forced to recognize the danger of sanctions unaccompanied by other actions. Sanctions in themselves might simply maintain the status quo, which might prevent a just solution of existing problems ...

In summing up my position I believe I could do no better than quote the observations of Mr. Escott Reid in a statement before the National Council of the League of Nations Society in November:

'An effective collective system means not only the restraint of the aggressor but also disarmament, international instead of imperial control of colonies, and effective machinery to deal with treaty revision and the problems of markets, migration and raw materials. The crisis which presents itself to-day gives us an opportunity to build the foundations and perhaps some of the framework of such a system. If we seize that opportunity we shall greatly diminish the prospects of war. If we fail to seize it, war will not be far off.'

I know it is very difficult for most of us to come to anything like a satisfactory conclusion in connection with the Italo-Ethiopian tangle. I should like to express my personal sympathies for Ethiopia. I cannot see how possibly we could too strongly condemn Italy's action. At the same time I am conscious that other nations have sinned in much the same way as has Italy ...

Undoubtedly the British empire has been built up by methods not greatly dissimilar from those now being used by Italy and Japan. I think of India, of Egypt from 1882 to 1895, of the Venezuela boundary dispute of 1895–6, of Persia in 1896, of South Africa in 1895 and through to 1902 ...[80]

Woodsworth repeated this line of reasoning in a speech in the Commons in June 1936 in which he welcomed Mackenzie King's announcement of Canada's withdrawal of sanctions against Italy.[81] The league had failed, he said, but the ideal of the league should not be forsaken; a restructured league was the world's only hope. Isolationism was not good enough; the nations should disarm and cede their sovereignty to a world-state; all of the great powers were responsible for the horrid condition of the world; economic imperialism lay at the bottom of everything. Again he referred to the position he had taken at the League of Nations Society's meeting in November 1935: 'Without seeking to alter conditions, some of which I have described, I believe that sanctions might become worse than useless.'[82] Yet in this same speech Woodsworth admitted to a concern for realism and immediate practicality. He was, he said, a citizen of a country that still relied on force; as a member of parliament he often had to vote on alternative military proposals; he had to juggle a belief in final principles with a concern to attain ameliorative measures or the lesser evil. Ideal societies, he argued, would have no need of police forces but we must deal with the actual: an international police force under proper control would be preferable to world anarchy.[83]

Is this not a statement of support for the league as an international policeman? Perhaps its unstated assumption is the prior existence of the league as a super-state. Woodsworth said in a speech of January 1937:

I urge that Canada should work for a league in which each nation would be willing to surrender its sovereignty and its individual armaments; that is, in very simple terms, the right to do as it pleases and, in the last resort, the power to enforce its own decision. That is what we do in our community life. We surrender to the courts what were once regarded as individual rights. There has been a general tendency to decry any attempt to erect the league to the position of being a superstate. I am convinced that it is only that kind of league which is going to prove worth while. Mr. Eden, according to the papers, is now advocating what is termed a tame league. Let me suggest that collective security should be more than a phrase. If we are to have collective security insured by armaments, then those armaments must be collective armaments. If we are to have collective security by other and more peaceful means, then there must be collective agreements. To those people who charge that we are giving up the league, I should like to put the question: Are you prepared to work for a league that will have teeth in it, a league that will be effective, a league to which the nations will give such allegiance that in the last analysis they will be willing to give up what the lawyers hitherto have termed our national sovereignty, and our national armaments?[84]

But, if the above makes clear Woodsworth's opinion that only a reconstructed league could constitute the basis of a world state, it does so only by raising again the question of the degree to which he was a consistent pacifist. World states, one presumes, will threaten violence against those who refuse to keep the peace and, in enforcing peace, like the policeman within national states, they will periodically avail themselves of the help of the militia and army. Further, world states might lack sufficient legitimacy and, like domestic states, collapse into civil war. Is duly constituted government to give up without a fight?

Woodsworth never ceased to believe in the ideal of a League of Nations that was true to all of the elements of the covenant and thus true to its purpose as a proto-world state. It was a position he articulated as late as August 1941, six months before his death. Yet, at the same time, he set his ideals for the league at such a stratospheric level that they became unrealizable standards for the international order of the time. When he did explicitly use the language of practicality and supported a role for the league as a policeman, the clarity of his message was distorted by the undulations of his thinking on sanctions, collective security, the unreconstructed league, and the immorality of force. Here, it seems, was, – to use Louis MacNeice's phrase – 'the permanent bottleneck of his high-mindedness.' Woodsworth suggested that an international police force was the pragmatic hope of the world in the absence of a democratic and socialist League of Nations. In fact, for him, the actual pragmatic alternative to utopian internationalism was not an international police force but isolationism. That was his stand in September 1939; it was also his stand on the Spanish Civil War.

In February 1936 a Popular Front government of anarchists, socialists, and communists was elected in Spain. The fledgling republic was only five years removed from military dictatorship and had not yet gained widespread acceptance. Yet, by most reasonable standards, the Popular Front was democratically elected and duly constituted. In July 1936 the civil war began with General Franco's invasion of the mainland from Morocco. In the mythology of the international Left, the Civil War was a conflict between light and darkness. Moral support for the republic poured in from around the world and thousands of young socialists and Communists went as volunteers. The Soviet Union gave military aid to the government side, while Italy, Germany, and Portugal assisted the rebels.

Woodsworth's sympathies naturally lay with the young republican government. He had talked in the mid-1930s of the moral advantages of established government as opposed to 'bandits and vigilantes.' One did not need to be too far to the Left to hold that Franco was at the head of a column of just such unpleasant people. The Spanish government defended itself but was severely limited by the decisions of the French, British, and Canadian governments to place an embargo on the shipment of war materials to Spain. There was clearly a dilemma in all this for Woodsworth. He was a socialist but also a pacifist. He surely did not expect the Spanish government to lay down its arms. Indeed was it not the obligation of established government to keep the peace? But to resist aggression required the use of force and this was immoral, was it not?

Some Canadians took a more aggressive approach to support of the Spanish government. The Committee for Spanish Medical Aid was set up, to be followed in early 1937 by the Committee to Aid Spanish Democracy. Volunteers came forward; they would become the famed

Mackenzie-Papineau Battalion.[85] Many of the supporters were Communists but a large number of them were CCF members and, in some cases, colleagues of Woodsworth. In Montreal Frank Scott worked with Norman Bethune in the medical committee and was directly involved in October 1936 in finding a hall for speeches by representatives of the Spanish republic.[86] In Winnipeg local branches of these same organizations held frequent meetings and some ILP-CCF members took part. Conspicuously absent from all these activities was Woodsworth. On only one occasion did he assume a public role in the debate on the war, and the statement he made at that time set out a position of complete Canadian neutrality and isolation.

The occasion was his speech in the Commons on the Foreign Enlistment Bill in March 1937. Probably to accommodate clerical and conservative opinion in Quebec, Ernest Lapointe had introduced legislation that forbade any Canadian to enlist in or recruit on behalf of any foreign army of a government at war with a friendly nation. Woodsworth objected to some of the bill's terms, particularly its unstated implication that whereas Canadians were forbidden to serve in the army of a foreign *government*, they were still allowed to enlist in the service of a foreign rebel *army*. His fear was that the government might be showing favour to Franco's cause so as to appease its Quebec supporters. He was also critical of the bill's failure to prevent the export of war materials. Many of his objections were in fact accepted by the government, which also in time banned the export of arms and war materials to Spain. In general Woodsworth supported the legislation. If anything he wanted matters to be as watertight as possible; he wanted 'thorough-going neutrality.'[87]

After this Woodsworth could offer the Spanish republic little more than moral support. He, apparently, wanted the disengagement of the great powers from the conflict and, even after it had become apparent that Germany and Italy were increasingly supplying arms and personnel to the rebels, he did not show support for the possible intervention either of the league or of the French or the British on behalf of the Spanish government. In February 1938 he cabled his best wishes to the Spanish Cortes, now located in Barcelona: 'May struggle of Spanish people soon end in victory and democracy triumph.'[88] This was not enough to help and by early 1939 the government was defeated and Franco's regime was recognized by France and Britain. In February Woodsworth called on the Canadian government to impress upon the British government and the other members of the League of Nations the need to secure from Franco guarantees to protect the defeated government forces and refugees.[89] Thus in Spain moral support proved ineffective. In the same month Woodsworth wrote a long, reflective letter on the Spanish conflict that showed just how isolationist his feelings were in the late 1930s:

I, myself, could never get enthusiastic over Canadians going as soldiers to Spain. And it would seem to me that perhaps it was not wise for our people to put themselves so definitely behind all the various organizations that are professedly assisting the people of Spain. These organizations were chiefly dominated by Communist groups, and hence, the result was that we more or less played into the hands of the Communists.

In saying this, I am not suggesting that the republic in Spain was not in the right. My sympathies have all been with the government and not with Franco. It was the entrance of the Germans and the Italians that bedevilled the whole situation. But whether under these circumstances we helped the situation very much by sending in a few hundred volunteers, I really do not know.

All this is preliminary to my urging that primarily our work in the C.C.F. is not Russia or Spain or China, but here in Canada. Our contribution to a better state of affairs in the world is by cleaning up the mess within our doors. I fancy, if we lay stress on educational and organizational work at home, we shall get much further.[90]

If, then, it came to the use of force either by a duly constituted, foreign government or by the league through collective-security procedures, Woodsworth declined participation, both for himself and his country. The 1930s were unkind times and, as all the more civilized alternatives to war were unsuccessful, a pacifist such as Woodsworth could do little more than recommend that his country not become involved. But in coming to this final position over Spain in 1937 and Poland in 1939, Woodsworth left behind a trail of moral and political contortions. Consider, for example, the inconsistencies, ethical solecisms, and perhaps outright self-deception of his short article 'The Threat of War' in September 1938, written just after the loss of the Sudetenland by Czechoslovakia and the confirmation of the same in the Munich agreement:

It is highly necessary to examine slogans and catchwords, especially those offered in the names of 'peace' and 'democracy' and 'freedom' and 'self-determination'. Frequently they conceal policies that are bound to lead in the opposite direction.

So with official and class names. The interests of Mr. Chamberlain or Herr Hitler may not be identical with those of the men, women and children of Great Britain or Germany and certainly not with those of the world at large.

Remember that these same people permitted the conquest of Manchuria and Ethiopia and the insurrection in Spain. Why this flaming idealism for a state composed of apparently incompatible races set up twenty years ago?

Must we not concede that the larger empires fear the growing power of Germany? If we get rid of this re-incarnated 'Beast of Berlin' would we get rid of the dangers inherent in Imperialism? Did the last war settle anything? Does the threatened war offer any great hope?

Have we not in our sane moments declared that war is an inevitable outcome of our present system of capitalism with its glaring inequalities and injustices. Are we now to scrap our Socialist beliefs? And for what?[91]

Here are some intemperate judgments. To be sure, the great powers *had* 'flouted' the League of Nations but Woodsworth's own position on the league was not always helpful. In the 1920s he had rejected the league as a means of collective security; he had supported economic sanctions only after Manchuria had been invaded and then rejected their application against Italy in 1935; after that he had held to such exalted standards for the league that it was impossible for it to play a constructive role. When he said that the 'great nations' had 'permitted the conquest of ... Manchuria and Ethiopia and the insurrection in Spain,' by extension the same verdict should have been made concerning Woodsworth's own small contribution to the debate. He had not supported league action against Italy and, in Spain, he sat on the sidelines like Britain and France, and resisted any Canadian participation. And if Spain might fall because Germany and Italy were assisting the rebels, how did Woodsworth propose to deal with that contingency? Through the league? Or through involvement by the other great powers? Clearly not. We should also notice the extent of his moral disenchantment if not outright cynicism in his claim that all imperialisms were somehow equal in the context of the international order of the late 1930s. Was the 'Beast of Berlin' no worse than the 'beasts' of Paris and London? Did they all equally threaten the territorial integrity of Czechoslovakia and Poland? And was it valid to claim that every war was the result of capitalism?

By 1939 Woodsworth had weighed all the alternatives and found them wanting. In September of that year, all that was left him was neutrality and isolation, a repairing to fastness North America: 'I have sometimes thought, if civilization goes down in Europe, as it may go down, that in America there may at least be the seeds left from which we can try to start a new civilization along better lines.'[92]

V

Once peace came in 1918 immigration had quickly resumed.[93] It would never be of the proportions of the pre-1914 period but large numbers of newcomers continued to arrive in Canada. Between 1920 and 1930, on average, 137,000 immigrants landed each year. With the Depression the numbers dropped off precipitously; from 1931 to 1939 immigration averaged just over 16,000 a year. Between the wars most immigrants continued to come from Europe and the United States. Chinese and Japanese immigrants represented an insignificant proportion, before 1923 a few thousand in any given year. After the exclusion of Chinese immigrants in 1923, immigrants from the Orient become an invisible part of the total. Oddly this did not quell racist antipathy towards Oriental immigrants, especially in British Columbia.[94]

In May 1923 Woodsworth spoke on the bill to exclude Chinese immigration. He expressed a sympathetic view of their plight, although he would in the end support the legislation as being necessary in light of contemporary Canadian attitudes. To confute those who argued a prejudiced position he said: 'All students of ethnology will recognize that after all there are a great many more things in common between the different races than things which separate us, and the apparent divergencies are not so great as sometimes we imagine. The stranger has always been regarded as more or less an enemy, and we are naturally content to look down upon those who are not of our kind.'[95] Twelve years later, in an article in which he speculated on whether political trends in Europe might be universal or not, there is the following statement: 'It may be true, in a general sort of way, that human nature is the same the world over. But it is also true to say that there are very great variations. An Englishman differs from an Italian; a white man from an oriental or from a negro. They react very differently to the same stimuli and, in practice, the stimuli are usually quite different. Why insist that under the same circumstances – to say nothing of different circumstances – they must all act in the same way?'[96] These statements are reproduced here not to establish that Woodsworth was a contradictory thinker – even if he sometimes was – but to dramatize the poles between which his thinking about ethnic and immigration issues reverberated during his years in Parliament.

We encountered this polarity earlier in our consideration of Woodsworth's nativist views before 1914. Understandably, Woodsworth was preoccupied with other questions between 1914 and the early 1920s. When he again spoke extensively on the subject of immigration in 1923, he did so from a less emphatically nativist and Anglo-Saxon perspective. In the intervening years he had become less enchanted by the British and less wedded to the imperial connection; indeed by the early 1920s he spoke the language of a post-colonial Canadianism. He believed there was a new *Canadian* identity aborning. As much of his nativism fell away, he expressed with greater confidence and clarity the need to respect and preserve the diverse, multicultural character of Canada.[97] But he did this while also continuing to evince a profound concern for social integration and the assimilation of the alien.[98] He talked of 'uniting' immigrants into a new Canadian type; sooner or later he said, Canadians would have to deal with the problem of 'absorbing' the Doukhobors; he worried that the melting-pot was not working and that the country would become 'Balkanized'; there was a necessity to 'absorb,' 'weld,' and 'incorporate' immigrants into the Canadian way of life. Even at his most universalistic, Woodsworth never ceased to be preoccupied with elements of his earlier nativism.

In the 1920s and 1930s Woodsworth was opposed to immigration.[99] In principle, he favoured a much larger Canadian population; but, given what he believed were the parlous economic conditions of these years, Canada could not afford new immigrants. There were not enough jobs available to absorb an increased supply of workers.

For all his fascination with the new and the modern and his optimism regarding the purposes of social evolution, Woodsworth could also express a deep sensitivity towards ways of life and cultures that were marginal, overwhelmed, or derelict.[100] From his travels he knew old Quebec and the Maritimes, and his years on the prairies had made him aware that economic progress *and* decay could succeed each other with startling speed. He also knew that the margins of prairie settlement contained not proud, inventive, successful freeholders but farmers and their families who were more often poor, vanquished, illiterate, and in debt. Accordingly, in weighing the advantages of further immigration, he was especially concerned with the demise of prairie agriculture:

high taxes, low incomes, unused lands held for speculative purposes, the inability of farmers to attract and keep farm labourers, the exploitation of the labour of farm wives and children, the dearth of local schools and medical services, and the alarming rate of mental illness. In these circumstances, he claimed, it was pointless to bring in more immigrants. Even British agricultural immigrants should be discouraged; they could never be paid enough and they soon drifted to the cities. Without an aggressive federal policy to tax unused lands or to expropriate them, and to provide free land, cheap railroad rates, and low-interest loans, agricultural immigration would be counterproductive. Other considerations justified limiting immigration. He feared that Canada had become a dumping ground for the weak, incompetent, diseased, and immoral of the Old World. And its cities, not to mention its jails and asylums, were full of Europe's rejects.

Woodsworth still flirted with the notion that mental illness and criminality were racially linked. But, taken as a whole, his remarks cannot be construed as a eugenic theory of mental and moral deviance. If Ukrainians showed up in disproportionately large numbers in the jails of western Canada, a preponderance of British women showed up in the statistics of unmarried mothers.[101] His earlier eugenic theories, then, were receding somewhat, although he did, for example, still hold that 'sexual perversion' (in this case buggery) would be cured by a surgical operation of some kind[102] and that the sterilization of some criminals and the insane should be made compulsory.[103] Again, though of declining virulence and frequency, his nativist belief that there was a hierarchy of 'races' and cultures was still evident: 'I have no doubt we would all like to get northern Europeans ... They are hardy settlers and would do well in Canada. But unfortunately, for the past twenty-five years the stream of immigration has come to North American shores not so much from northern Europe as from southeastern Europe ... A good many of the people coming to us from southeastern Europe belong to the trading classes. Hebrews, Greeks, and people of that character are coming in considerable numbers, but they are not the agriculturists about which a good many people tell us; they almost invariably go to the cities.'[104]

Woodsworth was also concerned that Canada was losing many native-born citizens, mainly to the United States, who were essentially being replaced by foreigners, 'a substitution ... of the city-bred people of Great Britain and the peasant people of southeastern Europe for the native-born, sturdy Canadian.'[105] In his important speech on immigration in 1923, the specific form in which the problem was posed was that of replacing 'long-established' Mennonites with newer Poles: 'Take another group, also a peculiar people, the Mennonites ... They were among our very best settlers. I am not sure that we can gain a great deal by allowing tens of thousands of Mennonites who have been here for forty years to go to another country and then bring in fresh streams of Poles from another country. It may be quite true that Mennonites are a brand of Protestant while Poles are a brand of Roman Catholic. In other words, we have a change of religious belief, but we have the same European peasant to deal with; and that is a difficulty that we face throughout western Canada.'[106] In all this Woodsworth sometimes gave the impression of being a cold-eyed judge of the relative assets of the immigrant groups, rather like an ambitious farmer shrewdly contemplating the improved quality of his herd should he add a certain strain of breeding stock. Simultaneously, at the other end of his moral spectrum of views on immigration, he was becoming increasingly sensitive to the unspeakable conditions confronting many immigrants. Later in the 1920s, for example, he argued that responsibility for their plight should be placed on the host country rather than on the immigrants themselves. If eastern Europeans, especially in the west, lacked schools and medical and community facilities, that was because of the stinginess of the government; if they lived segregated lives, among their own ethnic kind, this was because English-speaking settlers had moved away, out of prejudice:

Do we ever consider what Canada looks like through the eyes of a foreigner? We have given them the very roughest and hardest side of Canadian life. Many of them have been here for years, yet they know nothing of the history, traditions, or cultural life of this country. Sometimes we find the results in the police court when boys or girls who have run wild are brought before the magistrate, and then we have the task of sending them to the reformatory or attempting to punish them. Perhaps we ought rather to adopt the attitude which is said to be that of the Chinese educationist, who, when somebody goes wrong, punishes the parents and guardians and not the children. The fact is that in a great many of these cases it is we who are to blame and not the foreigners who have come to our midst. It may be true that the foreigner comes here with a small percentage of assets in money, but I submit he brings with him cultural assets that are by no means negligible. We have people coming to us from all parts of the European continent who seem to be born with an innate love of music and with an ability to express themselves through music.

Foreigners who have all their lives been accustomed to the drama and dramatic representations come to our country, and we laugh and scoff at them, trying to get them to leave these things behind them.[107]

Such was Woodsworth's respect and admiration for the cultural traditions of immigrants that he was even led to doubt the virtue of any attempt to assimilate them:

We have not tried to understand them; we have despised them more or less. We have said to them: 'You ought to become Canadians; you ought to leave everything foreign behind.' We talk very lightly about assimilating our immigrants. I presume the meaning of that word 'assimilate' is 'to make like.' Do we want these immigrants to be made like us? I think I might say: God forbid! We in this country have not so far attained such a standard of beauty or goodness that we want all the people to be made in our own image. We forget sometimes that in the effort to make these people like us we drive out of them the very highest things which they bring to us.[108]

I confess sometimes I have a little bit of sympathy with the feeling that we should leave Europe behind and build up a new civilization on this North American continent. But I would point out that Britishers have not done that, and when the great war arose in Europe, tens of thousands of British born went back to their homes in order that they could, as they thought, defend the motherland. I would suggest that the man who forgets his fatherland and who is indifferent to the welfare of his own brothers and sisters will not make a very good Canadian citizen. We ought to bear that in mind. I have heard those who say: let these people remember they are Canadians; let them forget the old country. Surely in this country we value men who do not forget the old, but rather bring with them the very best of the old. You cannot divest yourself of the old associations and traditions and be worth anything. The Englishman remembers the country from which he came; the Scotchman remembers the country whence he came. We value them because of that. The same thing is true with regard to Ukrainians or peoples of other nationalities who have thrown in their lot with us.[109]

Just as Woodsworth's four years in British Columbia between 1917 and 1921 may have blunted some of the sharper edges of his views of the oriental question, it may have been his direct knowledge of the Ku Klux Klan's explicit and ugly racism in western Canada that brought him in the late 1920s to a sober realization of the dangers of ethnic and racial intolerance. He poured scorn on the Klan's preoccupation with white races, Nordic peoples, and Protestants: '"White" simply means that they are against not only orientals but against all foreigners. They are the Nordic class. I have never been able to determine who the Nordics are, but apparently they are ourselves, and all who are not ourselves are not Nordics. That is as far as I can get the term defined. And the fact that they are "Protestant" indicates that they are against Catholics. Then they are "Christian" which merely means that they are against the Jews, for I do not think that the term refers to the qualities they have so far exhibited.' As for the Klan's boast that it was 'law-abiding,' Woodsworth took that to mean that 'they are against the people who do not think as they think, and are prepared to take extreme measures to make others conform to their ideas.'[110] (Of course, Woodsworth blithely overlooked the fact that his book *Strangers within Our Gates* had talked extensively about the Norse and Teutonic peoples, the superiority of Protestants over Roman Catholics, and the cultural inferiority of blacks.) In another statement in 1928 rebutting the claims of home-grown Saskatchewan nativism and the Ku Klux Klan, he expressed a high regard for the homely, albeit sometimes awkwardly expressed, multiculturalism and neighbourliness of small-town prairie people:

Saskatchewan 'the melting pot.' Well, the fat is bubbling merrily; one is not so sure about the melting! There's Bishop Lloyd who seems to have been trained in a school that combined the teachings of Nietzsche with those of British-Israel; there's J.J. Malone, a second Father Chinaquay [Chiniquy] but who specializes in the flag and country stunt; there's the Ku Klux Klan – an American organization 'which maintains our British heritage of freedom' by denouncing all who do not adhere to their two-by-four ideas; there are groups of non-English immigrants who have been debauched by Roblin-like methods – these and many more swirl around in the melting pot sizzling and spluttering.

Yet the common-sense of the majority holds this 'fitful realm' in order. Only the other day at Gravelbourg I had a rather unique experience. The town and the surrounding district are predominantly French-Canadian. The Farmers Union had arranged a 'get-together banquet' at which I was the chief speaker. The banquet was held in the Knights of Columbus Hall; the catering was done by the ladies of the United Church; the Mayor, representatives of the local Board of Trade and the Wheat Pool, were at the head table. French and English all had a very happy evening together. But how lacking in tact were those who arranged to open the program by singing 'Wolfe the dauntless hero came,' and entwining 'thistle, rose and shamrock.' Why not, as in Quebec City, a joint monument to Wolfe and Montcalm. Or better still why not leave the dead past to bury its dead? If we insist on cultivating thistles out of gratitude to one sturdy specimen that forced a yell of pain from a bare-footed Scotch rebel and thus saved the garrison, why not also cultivate the graceful fleur-de-lis and perhaps even an occasional Iceland poppy or a Russian sunflower? In this country we are of many origins: the Canadianism of the future must be inclusive enough to arouse the enthusiasm of 100% of our citizens.[111]

The Canadian identity of the future would encourage the expression of a multitude of ethnic traditions. But what would unify and incorporate the parts, in short hold them together? Divining Woodsworth's position on this issue is not easy. In some of his speeches and writings he left the impression that the cultural traditions of the immigrants that were to be preserved were only the quaint, ornamental features of dance, music, and cuisine. In others he intimated that he was saying something more: language, ways of life, religion perhaps, although in his later years he did not think highly of official religion. What *is* clear is that, whatever his position, Woodsworth presupposed the existence of a multi-functional, efficient social-service state whose effect, willy nilly, perhaps intentionally, would have been to integrate minorities and immigrants into a mainly English-speaking, scientific, and secular culture, supervised by a centralized state. This is the implication of his recommending the extension of medical services to the rural hinterlands, the consolidation of school districts, the enforcement of school-attendance laws, and the teaching of English, hygiene, and the principles of scientific farming. Woodsworth's vision of Canada was not so much a patchwork of peoples sustaining a multitude of autonomous jurisdictions and ways of life but a national community with a strong central government and relatively weak provinces; a community that was mainly English-speaking, with historic bilingual rights of some limited sort extended to the French and some recognition of multiculturalism for those who spoke neither French nor English. There would be diversity but also unity:

The immigrants should be protected against exploitation, because they are particularly liable to this through their lack of knowledge of the English language. There should be provisions made for closer settlement than we have given them in the past. In some instance there should have been financial assistance and expert advice given, especially the latter, because many of the immigrants have had to learn at great cost to themselves what they might have been told had there been an arrangement such as we now have under the Soldier Settlement Board. There should be special opportunities provided to enable the younger people and adults to learn English. There should be instruction given in sanitation, and in farming methods, especially in dairying. This is being accomplished to a greater degree to-day than it was at that time. There should be encouragement in the native handicrafts, some of which are wonderfully beautiful and would be a great asset if they could be developed ... If we bring in people of other languages we must not wonder that they want to have the language rights of the minorities of Europe. If we bring in people of alien habits and customs, we must not expect them to live like puritan Englishmen. The tirades which we make against the foreigners, calling them bolsheviks, merely reveal our own ignorance. The immigrant brings with him his own mental, moral, social, religious and political backgrounds. His back-grounds are not those of either English Ontario or French Quebec. It is for us older Canadians to find common ground with the newcomer. Only in this way can we prevent what might become something of a Balkanization of this country. Only in this way can we build up a greater Canada which will not be an English Canada or a French Canada but a larger and more inclusive Canada in the building of which all these various people will contribute.[112]

What of non-white immigrants in Canada? How did Woodsworth conceive of their place? On the matter of blacks he said very little. There was, however one curious allusion to 'negros' in a 1930 speech on the new Conservative government's policy of imperial preference: 'I do not think I have any very strong colour prejudice, but I would just as soon buy fresh vegetables grown by white labour in California or Oregon as vegetables grown by the negros in the West Indies. I do not know whether the latter may be said to be our own kith and kin; I do not know that they are altogether under kindred institutions even though they may belong to the British Empire. It seems to me that in regard to matters such as this, there is great need of puncturing the sentimentalities in which we have indulged.'[113] He was a somewhat more frequent commentator on the subject of Canadian Indian, but like much of the Left in Canada at that time, he accorded them a very minor role in his prognostications about social justice.[114] Essentially he held that Indians, though they possessed a measure of self-government, were wards of the state. They must be encouraged to acquire agricul-tural and industrial skills and, as far as possible, should leave the reserves and integrate with white society. There was here no intrinsic respect for the 'primitive' and authentic culture of the native. The Indians' inferiority derived from their pre-industrial, even pre-agricultural, way of life. Once, when discussing the need for a better transportation policy for western Canada, Woodsworth said: 'Without transportation the west would still be in the control of the Indians; and if we do not give suitable transportation rates the west might as well revert to the Indians.'[115] He was also, perhaps unconsciously, insensitive to Indians in a comment he made when Tim Buck, the leader of the Communist Party, was shot at in his cell in Kingston penitentiary in 1934: 'I remember in our childhood days we used to read the tales of Fenimore Cooper, and we learned it was the practice of the Indians in the olden days to tie a captured enemy to a tree and to fire arrows at him, seeing who could come nearest his head without hitting him. It looks to me as if this practice has been translated into the more modern method of putting a man into a cell, caging him up and then firing at him.'[116]

The concerns of Canadian politicians over non-white immigration in these years were focused not on blacks but on orientals. By the time of the First World War, immigration had produced perceptibly large communities of Japanese and Chinese, particularly in British Columbia. White opinion was markedly exclusionist. This was partly the result of unmitigated racial prejudice, but for the white working class it was also caused by resentment of the tendency of Oriental workers to work for lower wages and without benefit of trade unions. Official opinion was equally intolerant. The British Columbia legislature disenfranchised Chinese in 1875 and Japanese in 1895. The federal government was less draconian, but in time it too bowed to public pressure. (Woodsworth must have known that British Columbia was more extreme than the federal government on this issue, which leads one to wonder why, in the 1920s, he advocated a greater role for the provinces in both defining citizenship and naturalization, and managing immigrants.[117]) In 1885 the federal government imposed a poll tax on Chinese immigrants, and the amount levied was increased in 1900 and 1904. Discrimination against the Japanese was less easily obtained, since Britain was a commercial and political ally of Japan for much of the period and Ottawa had to tread carefully.

In 1923 the federal government introduced a bill to exclude Chinese immigrants altogether. There were a few exceptions – diplomatic personnel, native-born children absent from Canada for educational reasons, and merchants and students – but the terms of the bill were sufficiently extreme to prevent the overseas wives of Chinese men already landed from joining them in Canada. Woodsworth was sympathetic to the Chinese cause. He pleaded that Chinese wives be allowed to enter and he encouraged Canadians to overcome their prejudices towards Orientals. The serious matter of cheap labour from abroad should be dealt with, he said, not by exclusion but by a minimum-wage policy in Canada and international wage standards supervised by the League of Nations. He described China as 'a very ancient and a very high type of civilization' whose only inferiority was that it lacked the industrial and technological capabilities of the West. These it was now acquiring and soon it would catch up: 'If we have anything superior in our civilization to give them, by all means let them come over and discover it, so that they may learn what has made our nation great and may take that knowledge back to their country with them. We must get away from the old idea that we would lose by their gain, that we are superior so long as we can keep knowledge and information and science to ourselves and keep these other people more or less in ignorance. I would say rather that we should welcome their students. Let us take them in and give them the very best we have to offer intellectually and morally.' Yet in spite of all this, he supported the legislation: 'No one who has lived where there is the conflict of two civilizations, of two different types of people, can be oblivious to the seriousness of the problems which arise. I am not making light of them. I confess that I am not at all sure that we are prepared at the present time to receive more orientals than we have. I know that at the present time at the coast conditions are far from satisfactory, and it may be necessary to have total exclusion for some time, until we are prepared to deal properly with the matter.'[118]

Woodsworth's position on the 1923 bill set out what became the dominant cast of his response to similar political and legislative initiatives on the question of Oriental immigration: he recognized that much white opinion was prejudiced and hoped that it would become more open-minded, but in the meantime he supported exclusion. Yet Chinese and Japanese, or Doukhobors, or whoever had become naturalized Canadians, he insisted, must enjoy the same rights as other Canadians.[119] Woodsworth was probably more liberal and far-sighted than any other Canadian politician at this time on immigration from the Far East. A speech he gave in 1934 showed him as being remarkably percipient about the role of Pacific nations in the emerging world order;[120] in the same year he visited several Far Eastern countries – Japan, Korea, and China – and his eldest son would write his dissertation on Canadian policy and the Orient.[121] But there were limits to his broadmindedness. Two influences pressed in on him. The first was his residual nativism. He did, after all, claim that there were problems in assimilating the Japanese, and on one occasion, in 1938, he admitted that he did not believe in intermarriage between Japanese and whites.[122] There was also his sense of political prudence. He knew full well that the Left, particularly in British Columbia, was exposed to the charge of being overly sympathetic to Orientals and this made difficult a political appeal to white workers.

To Woodsworth the greatest injustice had been the exclusion of naturalized Chinese and Japanese immigrants from the franchise, both in British Columbia and in federal elections. (They experienced other forms of discrimination: they could neither vote in municipal elections nor be employed on public works or in law or pharmacy; they were excluded from jury duty and prevented from obtaining fishing licences. Oddly, they *were* eligible for military service in times of conscription.) Woodsworth raised in the Commons the issue of the civil rights of naturalized Orientals as early as June 1923. He was emphatic that there should be national standards for voting rights; indeed, if need be, federal legislation should override provincial jurisdiction governing provincial elections.[123] Supporting the rights of unpopular immigrants in this way opened him to all sorts of attacks from white supremacists. One of them was Alan Webster Neill, a businessman and politician from Alberni, on Vancouver Island, who represented the constituency of Comox-Alberni for all of Woodsworth's time in Parliament. For Neill, an independent, even the 1923 legislation was not extreme enough.

Woodsworth had no illusions about Neill. In a private letter of 1926, Woodsworth wrote that Neill's 'antipathy to the Orientals amounts almost to an obsession.'[124] His remarks were occasioned by Neill's proposal to exclude orientals from the old age pension. Woodsworth verdict on this proposal was that 'it is unjust to a class of Canadian citizens (some of them born in Canada) and is moreover a gratuitous insult to the Governments of India, Japan, and China and out of harmony with the principles advocated by the League of Nations ... Mr Neill's assertion that if the exemption is not made the measure would not pass the British Columbia Legislature is, in my judgement, quite unwarranted ... I think I know the sentiment of the labor men as well as Mr. Neill. White men who last year refused to 'scab' on Chinese crews will not refuse to secure the advantages of Old Age Pensions because a few Orientals may be included.'[125]

After the CCF was founded, the accusations by Neill and others that the party was pro-Oriental had serious implications for its future on the west coast. The situation did not go unnoticed by the Liberals either. Woodsworth estimated that the charges of Neill and like-minded racists did great damage to the CCF's fortunes in the 1935 general election:

May I point out that in 1934 when we were discussing a bill to disfranchise the Doukhobors of British Columbia I pointed out incidentally that we had already gone too far in the way of regional disfranchisement and instanced the case of disfranchisement of the orientals in one province. My friend immediately jumped up and asked whether I would advocate the enfranchisement of orientals ... I said immediately, 'By all means, if otherwise qualified.' In our Cooperative Commonwealth Federation manifesto, although we have not dealt definitely with orientals we have stated that our organization stands for equal rights to citizenship irrespective of race, colour or religion. I could not go back on the terms of that platform. Then the hon. member for Comox-Alberni went back to his constituency and published in the local press an advertisement in which he quoted from Hansard, and stated that we of the Cooperative Commonwealth Federation stood for all sorts of things. Then the Liberal party took up the hue and cry and tried to make it one of the main issues in the last campaign.[126]

In the same speech Woodsworth went on to make a courageous defence of the civil rights of the Doukhobors, Japanese, and Chinese. But he was equally insistent that he not be falsely accused of positions he did not hold. The CCF, he asserted, did not want more Oriental migration: 'We are told that the Cooperative Commonwealth Federation wants to flood this country with orientals. This is not so. Under present conditions I am opposed even to immigration from the British Isles.'[127] He continued somewhat defensively, saying that language requirements prevented many Oriental immigrants from becoming naturalized. (This was contrary to his earlier position that language requirements were an unjustified condition of citizenship, and indeed of his later view that most Oriental immigrants spoke English.)[128] Yet he was adamant that those who were naturalized citizens must be guaranteed their rights: 'In [Stanley Park, Vancouver] there is a beautiful monument erected to the Japanese soldiers who fell at the front. A great many of them enlisted, and the ones who enlisted were given the franchise. Other Japanese, just as loyal, did not enlist and have not the franchise ... Further, the sons and daughters of the men who fell at the front are not given the rights of citizenship. We have a monument to those who fell; we give the franchise to those who came back, but we refuse the rights of citizenship to their sons and daughters. Is that how a grateful country treats those who have been willing to lay down their lives for their country?'[129]

Similar problems arose in the federal by-elections in Victoria in 1936 and 1937. As indicated earlier, King Gordon, the CCF candidate in the 1936 by-election, thought that Woodsworth's 'prophet-like' speech on the Oriental question contributed to his defeat. A year later, it was Woodsworth's view that misrepresentation of the CCF's policies had helped bring about another election loss: 'The Liberals ... sought to stir up fresh anti-oriental prejudices by pointing out that the CCF group was in favour of granting the franchise to Canadian-born or naturalized Orientals. In their presentation, however, they gave the impression that the CCF would enfranchise all Orientals; also were in favour of Oriental immigration, and refused to defend Canada against Oriental invasion.'[130]

Neill's fine hand returned in early 1938 when he introduced a private member's bill that would have applied to Japanese immigrants the same sorts of restrictions applied to the Chinese in 1923. His bill was defeated by a vote of 79 to 42. In the CCF caucus, Woodsworth and Angus MacInnis supported it, while Douglas and M.J. Coldwell did not vote. That same session, Neill moved an amendment to the Immigration Act which would have required immigrants to speak either French or English or some European language. Woodsworth's position was captious. He declared his opposition under present circumstances to further Japanese immigration: 'I do not like the idea of rigid exclusion, but knowing British Columbia as I do, and as I have known it some years, I realize that a feeling exists there at the present time that makes it unwise to allow any more Japanese to enter that province. We have to be realists in this matter; we have to recognize that there are a considerable number of Japanese already in the province who have not been assimilated. Under these conditions I do not think it would be in the public interests to admit more orientals to British Columbia.'[131] But he then reasoned that the proposed amendment was too indirect and devious. Its transparent purpose was to exclude the Japanese. And so he would oppose it. Only two months earlier he had supported a direct and undisguised attempt to exclude the Japanese. Moreover, at the same time as he was arguing for realism regarding the Japanese, Woodsworth was giving support to the efforts of his colleague A.A. Heaps to induce the government to admit Jewish refugees into the country.[132] *O diversitas, mater veritatis.*

VI

Between the wars Canada continued to evolve towards complete constitutional independence. This was not just a matter of obtaining an effective independence in foreign policy-making but, as well, completing both a symbolic and real sovereignty in its internal constitutional matters. Although he drew on the expert opinions of liberal nationalists such as Ewart, Skelton, and Dafoe, Woodsworth's advocacy of, to use an old-fashioned term, 'home rule' in all its aspects was the most radical position on the constitution articulated in Parliament at that time, with the exception of that of Henri Bourassa. Woodsworth's endlessly repeated criticisms of King and Bennett on this issue emphasized not that they were moving in the wrong direction but that they were not moving fast enough.

On the central question of the constitution – the division of powers – Woodsworth was a definite centralist but with a strong pragmatic streak. His proposals, once accepted, would have produced a type of what later constitutional theorists have called cooperative federalism. He claimed that his interest in the constitution had first been piqued by a desire to gain acceptance for a provision of an eight-hour day and a forty-eight-hour week in accordance with the code of the International Labour Organization, another product of the Versailles settlement.[133] Confronted by federal insistence that such measures would invade provincial jurisdictions, he embarked on his own exploration of the BNA Act. He developed a raft of legal and political arguments in support of federal jurisdictional primacy in such areas as social welfare, wages, economic development, energy, medicine, and education.[134] Under the existing constitution, he said, the federal Parliament possessed a treaty-making power; it had the power under Section 92.10 to declare works for the general advantage of Canada; and it enjoyed residuary and emergency powers under Section 91. There were other ways Ottawa could obviate provincial jurisdiction: through attaching conditions to the receipt of federal contracts and subsidies; and, somewhat imperiously perhaps, since it might have destroyed the federal system and private enterprise altogether if implemented, he claimed that federal jurisdiction obtained over any industry or enterprise that received benefits under the protective tariff. He described some other practical expedients: the federal government could raise monies and turn them over to the provinces for them to spend in areas of provincial jurisdiction, an early version of the concepts of unfettered federal-spending power, shared-cost programs, and federal transfer payments; and he also proposed that provinces might informally 'cede' areas of their jurisdiction to Ottawa.

Yet Woodsworth's basic message was that, while there were ways and expedients for a bold federal government to take the initiative in social and economic policy, the BNA Act was a wholly anachronistic document in the new environment of an industrial society and an increasingly interdependent economy. The integrative and cooperative effects of technology and modern economic organization necessitated a new division of powers and a greater jurisdictional role for the central government. His justification of such a role in technical education was typical of his views: 'Technically the provinces have jurisdiction over education but ... an altogether different situation exists today from that which existed in this country sixty years ago. At that time education consisted very largely in teaching the three R's to the children in the little local schoolhouses. No one will say that that situation any longer exists. We have passed from being a merely agricultural community to a community in which technical education becomes absolutely necessary to success .. We must recognize that the resources of the provinces have not increased as rapidly as the new responsibilities.'[135] He advanced other arguments in support of augmented federal powers: the national government possessed greater financial resources; there was a need to establish national, 'uniform' standards; and efficiency in planning could better be achieved in the larger, inclusive unit of the national state.

It is hard to believe that Woodsworth's proposals would have left much power in provincial hands. Evidently, for him, the federal government must have jurisdictional primacy for reasons of socialist as much as nationalist priorities. The national state would own industries that approximated to a monopoly condition while the standards of efficient planning and social equality supported federal jurisdiction in social security, energy, transportation, communications, banking and economic development, and medicine. In one speech he proposed that the Maritimes be amalgamated and the prairie provinces too.[136] Yet Woodsworth's constitutional prescriptions were grounded not just in systematic, rational principles but also in practical arrangements. They had a sort of mixed or improvised tenor. This had to be his view because he held that inter-connectedness and complexity were the very stuff of the modern world. Thus federal-provincial questions could not be allocated to 'water-tight' compartments. A consultative – in a word, 'cooperative' – approach was essential. His comments on how national policies for energy and health might be pursued captured well this practical side of his constitutional advice:

I do not for a moment mean that the Dominion government would administer the whole of the development of these water powers. The work is now being carried on in Ontario in a very satisfactory way and certain municipalities such as the city of Winnipeg are carrying on their own electrical power development very efficiently, but the whole field ought to be surveyed, and the possibilities fully developed.[137]

I do not ask that the whole of medical aid should be brought under a centralized agency, but I cannot see that there is any reason why the Dominion government could not have an active health department which would help to coordinate the work of the provinces and municipalities, which would under-take certain types of work common to all the provinces and, above all, which would give financial backing to the various schemes already under way.[138]

Any centralist interpretation of the constitution would certainly be resisted by supporters of provincial rights, many of whom, of course, resided at the centre of the Liberal national state of King and Lapointe. Predictably, Woodsworth took steady aim at those who viewed Con-federation as a compact of the provinces.[139] He first bruited his criti-cisms in March 1924 and he gave fullest expression to them in a magnificently informed and detailed speech in May 1931. His views, he generously conceded, derived from J.S. Ewart, John Dafoe, Norman Rogers, Frank Scott, R.K. Finlayson, Grant Dexter, Brooke Claxton, and Eugene Forsey, an amalgam of liberal and socialist nationalists. At the heart of his disquisition was a highly literal and positivist examina-tion of the historical origins of Confederation. The provinces, he claimed, could not have consented to the BNA Act in 1867 because they had not existed then; only three colonies had been involved and their consent, if that is what it can be called, was ambiguous. Had they in fact agreed to the Quebec and/or the London resolutions? Or to the BNA Act itself?:

Canada approved the Quebec resolutions but prorogued before the appointment of delegates to the London conference, and therefore could not approve the British North America Act before it was passed. New Brunswick authorized the appointment of delegates to the London conference but prorogued before the conference, and met again only after the British North America Act was passed. Nova Scotia authorized the appointment of delegates to the London conference and was the only one approving the reference after the British North America Act was passed. Prince Edward Island and British Columbia assented to the terms of union. There were no legislatures, of course, in Manitoba, Saskatchewan or Alberta until they were created by the Dominion parliament.

Woodsworth went on to delineate many instances in which the terms of 1867 had been amended by initiative of the federal cabinet or Parliament, that is, without consultation with the provinces, let alone consent: 'The basis of confederation has changed a great deal since 1867. Judicial decisions have fundamentally changed the balance of legislative power ... There have been other developments which I can only enumerate: development of Canada's diplomatic service; appointment of the Governor General on the sole advice of the Dominion cabinet; separate negotiation and signature of treaties; membership in the League of Nations and on its council. The provinces were not consulted in any of these changes – changes which were much more important than many of the little things about which we make so much fuss ...'[140]

Woodsworth was well aware that opposition to provincial-rights theory would land him in hot water in Quebec, where such theory was integral to the province's pursuit of cultural survival. In general, while Woodsworth's mature perspective on French Canada was intended to be sympathetic, it was often awkwardly expressed. More significantly, his difficulty was that Quebec and things French Canadian did not figure centrally in his overall scheme of politics and change. He therefore risked becoming irrelevant to the concerns of Quebeckers and French Canadians and out of step with their particularist aspirations. As with his views on race and immigration, his attitude to French Canada, to be at all accommodative, had to somehow rise above the egregious Anglo-Saxon and Protestant nationalism of his early years. But here again the grown man never quite left behind his youthful ways. In *Strangers within Our Gates* Canada was a country where Quebeckers and French Canadians were somehow invisible and irrelevant to the definition of its national identity. The book contained the bald assumption that eastern European immigrants, for example, undermined the 'homogeneity' of a basically Anglo-Saxon and Protestant nation. French-Canadian concerns about immigration – that it increasingly tipped the demographic balance in favour of the English – did not cross Woodsworth's mind. French-speaking immigrants were for him not unlike any other category of immigrants – Jews, Mennonites, or Ukrainians – and, as with them, the important questions had to do with the ease with which they could be integrated and assimilated. In this respect French immigrants, he claimed, were generally anodyne in their effects.[141] They did not settle in large, unassimilable colonies and they usually became thrifty and successful farmers. It was not their language but rather their religion that was the main stumbling block to social unity. Woodsworth noted the presence among them of the parish priest and how the latter's paternalism made them less apt 'to learn and act for themselves.'[142]

Later in *Strangers within Our Gates* Woodsworth turned to the contentious issue of whether the Methodist Church should continue its missionary work among French Canadians. He conceded that there was no consensus of opinion on this issue but went on to quote 'one of our correspondents' who evidently believed that it should. This person claimed that Roman Catholics could of course be saved in their own church because souls were saved in all religions, 'even among the heathens'; but that the Catholic Church suppressed the Word of God and was the sworn enemy of 'our liberties and our principles.' And if that was not enough to bring on a stampede of missionary recruits, the call to evangelization in French Canada must be heeded to prevent its people from falling into 'the abyss of free thought.'[143]

Woodsworth's articles in 1913 in the *Manitoba Free Press* also talked of the danger of too many Roman Catholics coming to Canada. In addition, they give us the clue to understanding how it was that an intelligent, perceptive mind could so generally overlook the central importance of French Canada in his early considerations on national identity. French Canadians, he conceded, were the exception to 'our British-Canadian ideal' of a 'homogeneous people with a common language and common "Mores,"' but they were 'segregated' in Quebec and somehow outside the mainstream of Canadian life.[144] The implication was that Quebec was a sort of stolid, culturally quaint backwater that would not participate in the new, dynamic world which was arising in the rest of Canada and in which Woodsworth was primarily interested. There was a danger that Quebec would become marginal to this thinking, particularly as western Canada came more and more to occupy his practical concerns.

It is not clear that this did happen but, in spite of extensive personal contact with Quebeckers and French Canadians, he never came close to aligning himself with the aspirations of French Canada's opinion leaders. Altogether we may say that, while Woodsworth sought support in Quebec as much as anywhere else, and while he was in his parliamentary years a good deal more sympathetic to the goals of French Canadians than he had been before, he never ceased to be a predominantly English-Canadian nationalist; that is, his nationalism emphasized the primacy of the English language, central federal authority, pan-Canadian cultural unity, and a secular civic culture.

Woodsworth travelled in Quebec in 1913 and 1915, but he does not seem to have travelled far outside Montreal. His *Studies in Rural Citizenship* (c. 1914) made mention of the ebb and flow of Quebec rural life under the influences of industrialism and creeping suburban growth. He lectured at McGill University in late 1915 and it was then that made the acquaintance of Henri Bourassa, leader of La Ligue nationaliste and editor of *Le Devoir*. Indeed Woodsworth contributed a number of columns to the latter at this time. Perhaps it was Bourassa's influence that brought him to a somewhat more broadminded position on the question of bilingual education.

As fate would have it, Charlie Sissons was also preoccupied with this issue then, his interest having been aroused by the conflicts over French schools in Ontario and non-English education in Manitoba in the early years of the First World War. Sissons's position was by no means close to Bourassa's idea of bilingual rights for English and French throughout the country, but it was a large step beyond unilingualism and it did see positive advantages in a multilingual curriculum. In 1917 Woodsworth wrote a non-committal introduction to Sissons's *Bi-lingual Schools in Canada*. In private, however, he gave evidence of being prepared, at least in theory, to go somewhat further than Sissons in the direction of bilingualism. Of course he never budged from the position that, outside Quebec, English must be the basic language of instruction, even for native French speakers. The difference between him and Sissons lay in the degree to which French or some other language might be taught within the overarching 'Englishness' of the school system. In 1916 Woodsworth did imply that Manitoba's legislation on the subject was going too far in making no concession to bilingualism.[145] Later the same year he entertained a more expansive perspective on the matter: 'Below the technically legal question there is the moral question. This, in my judgment, cannot be dismissed simply by saying that we are a federation and not a union. All we English speaking people take it for granted that this is an English speaking country. I am not at all sure but that the French presumption that it is a bi-lingual country is at least as much warranted. If that is in any way conceded, the whole thing resolves itself into a jurisdictional dispute as between the rights of the federal government and of the individual provinces.'[146] In this perhaps is a reference to the possible primacy of Ottawa in the provision of bilingual education. But questions of moral, legal, and historical right would have to be compromised by other considerations, especially those emerging out of changes brought on by developments in western Canada: 'As a matter of historical right or from the standpoint of political expediency, probably the French language occupies an exceptional place, but considering the welfare of the people or from the pedagogical standpoint it seems to me that the other languages must be considered side by side with the French.'[147] Recognizing that there was a third force in Canada led Woodsworth to resist embracing a binational, bicultural conception of the country.

After his election to the Commons Woodsworth maintained more direct contact with Quebec although he probably ventured little beyond holidaying on Meech Lake and giving periodic speeches to mainly English-speaking audiences. His eldest child, Grace, did eventually study at the Sorbonne, and in one of his last letters he revealed how much he wanted someone in the family to 'get to know the Quebec French people.'[148] One of his most direct bridges to Quebec after 1925 was his renewed friendship with Henri Bourassa, the member for Labelle and Woodsworth's desk-mate for a while. In foreign-policy questions involving Canadian independence of Britain, anti-imperialism, and even isolationism, they were brothers-in-arms. They shared one point of view of crucial importance to French-Canadian nationalists of all stripes – opposition to conscription in 1917 – though of course Woodsworth had arrived at this position for mainly pacifist reasons. But on domestic matters concerning French-English divisions, Woodsworth remained cautious and conditional in his support of French Canada. To nationalists in Quebec his commitments would always be too little and beside the point.

Woodsworth spoke at length in the Commons on bilingualism on at least two occasions in the inter-war period. The first was in the 1927 debate on the proposal to give preference in hiring to civil servants who knew both official languages. He argued that such a policy would be divisive. It had relevance in some parts of the country but not everywhere:

I am equally prepared to say that there may be some sections in this country where the first language would be French and the second language would be some other language than English. There are somewhere between three and four hundred thousand Ukrainians, for instance, in this country, and if the matter is to be placed on the basis of efficiency I can quite readily understand that a great many officials who have to do with that large group of immigrants possibly ought to have a working knowledge of the Ukrainian language.

AN HON. MEMBER: The Chinese language.

MR. WOODSWORTH: There are other languages in the west besides the Ukrainian. There are the Scandinavian languages, there is the German language. Somebody suggests the Chinese language on the west coast. That is true. If we have to deal with the Chinese we ought to have officials on the west coast who have a thorough knowledge of both English and Chinese. I will go so far even with regard to an oriental language.

He continued that for some positions in the civil service – the speaker of the House, for example – it was appropriate to insist on an ability to speak French and English, but there was more to public service than language and, in any event, the aggressive assertion of new language rights might trigger a reaction that would make it difficult to sustain respect for existing ones.[149]

Woodsworth's second major speech was in 1936 on the question of bilingual bank notes. Once again he lectured French-Canadian members against a 'too aggressive' assertion of francophone rights; he also pleaded with English Canadians to be more tolerant of the French: 'For my part it is a matter of indifference whether we have bills printed in both languages or not; it is not important at all from my standpoint. I say, however, that if we are going to carry out the spirit for which the Minister of Justice pleads we shall have to recognize a little more clearly than we do the point of view of others in Canada, and not to press too aggressively our own viewpoint.'[150] Later he spoke out against erecting a statue of Joan of Arc in a national battlefields park in Quebec. Joan of Arc, he said, had no connection with Canadian history and was someone who had direct interest 'only to some particular section or group of the population.'[151]

Whatever his desire to accommodate French Canada, the cruel truth was that Woodsworth was – to use Walter Young's phrase – a 'foreign element' in Quebec.[152] In his earliest theoretical speculations he had shown little appreciation of the advantages of traditional, intermediate identities and 'communities of character' and so could never make much sense of Quebec and French Canada as somehow a culture or a nation within the larger bounds of Confederation. His early Protestantism, as much as his later secularism and socialism, whether expressed in support of a divorce court for Ontario or the disallowance of Duplessis's Padlock law, struck a dissonant note in a society that was still deeply Catholic, ultramontane, and conservative. The conflict between his views and those of French Canada was officially confirmed by the ecclesiastical prohibitions against the CCF by Archbishops Georges Gauthier and Jean Marie Roderigue Villeneuve in 1934 and 1935.[153] No matter how much Woodsworth remonstrated that his socialism was British and not Marxist in character and consistent with papal encyclicals such as *Rerum novarum* (1891) and *Quadragesima anno* (1931), his message in French Canada fell on stony ground and deaf ears.[154]

Another factor contributing to Woodsworth's foreignness in Quebec was, of course, his constitutional centralism. As we have seen, he advocated an extensive redistribution of powers in Ottawa's favour; he disputed the view of Confederation as a compact of the provinces; and he implied that amendments to the constitution need be implemented by no other method than a simple address of the Canadian Parliament to its British counterpart. Yet a recognition of Quebec's concerns about provincial and minority rights brought him to adjust this position. As early as 1925 he argued for not just provincial consent in constitutional amendments affecting minority rights but indeed provincial unanimity.[155] Two years later he called for a bill of rights of some kind to protect minorities in matters to do with language, culture, and religion.[156]

It was in his important 1931 speech on the constitution that Woodsworth wrestled most manfully with the knotty problems of provincial and minority rights and federal power. He observed that modern life had made redundant a water-tight compartmental view of the division of powers; change had made traditional judicial stipulations invalid; and, therefore the BNA Act and conventional judicial practice should be significantly altered. He went on, as we know, to reduce to historical absurdity the account of Confederation as a compact of all the provinces and to claim that subsequent constitutional change in Canada had not in fact involved the consent of provincial governments and legislatures. After asserting that a general provision for provincial unanimity for constitutional amendments would lead to an unacceptable degree of 'rigidity,' he changed his tack to catch more provincialist winds. He suggested that consideration be given to Ernest Lapointe's position in 1927 at the federal-provincial conference, a position which distinguished between classes of subjects to be amended by different formulae. 'Ordinary' amendments would require a simple majority of the provinces and 'vital and fundamental' ones, such as those affecting provincial and minority rights especially in regard to language and religion, would require unanimous consent. Woodsworth also proposed protecting minority rights by an entrenched bill of rights from which existing rights could not be subtracted but to which new ones could be added.[157]

Quebec's insistence on its minority rights abutted onto two other general constitutional issues: the Senate and the patriation of the constitution. On both Woodsworth was thoroughly radical though not agreeably so to Quebec, which viewed the status quo in these matters as protective of its particular interests. Woodsworth proposed that the Senate be abolished. And the same should occur with Canada's lingering constitutional ties to Britain. His motion in the Commons in 1924 contained a simple formula for Canada's complete sovereignty: 'The governing powers of Canada as constituted by the BNA Act ... ought to possess under the British Crown the same powers with regard to Canada ... as the Parliament of Great Britain possesses in regard to Great Britain, its affairs and its people.'[158] Thus the constitution should be amendable only in Canada and appeals to the Judicial Committee of the Privy Council abolished.[159] One of Woodsworth's special concerns, even after the passing of the Statute of Westminster in 1931, was that the Canadian executive still was dependent on the British Crown and government, particularly in foreign policy-making. His prescriptions for the office of governor general would have made Canada into an undisguised republic. Of course, Woodsworth wanted a Canadian-born governor general and one appointed on the advice of the Canadian Privy Council.[160] Though he never called for the outright abolition of the monarchy he was at heart a republican. He disliked the pretentious and aristocratic accoutrements of the governor general's office and would have happily settled for an arrangement whereby the chief justice of the Supreme Court would become, *ipso facto*, governor general.[161] The same could obtain for provincial chief justices and lieutenant governors. Woodsworth's position in the 1926 constitutional crisis disclosed his belief that the governor general's function was simply to do the bidding of the prime minister of the day; that is, he no longer retained the power of dissolution.[162] He also claimed, in a complete break with established British and Canadian constitutional theory, that all authority resided in the people.[163] His view was that, if there was to be a king, at least let him be chosen by the Canadian Parliament. He did not believe that the government should have accepted George VI as the new king after the abdication of Edward VIII without the prior approval of the Canadian Parliament.[164] All in all, Woodsworth would not have been out of place in the home-rule and republican circles of Ireland, South Africa, and India of the time.

His most specific anxiety in the 1930s regarding the powers of the governor general involved the extent to which the office was sufficiently independent of the British Crown to allow the Canadian Parliament complete independence in foreign affairs, especially the declaring of war:

Since the passing of the Statute of Westminster the dominion may make any laws it likes, regardless of whether they conflict with British laws or have effect outside the borders of Canada, provided only that they do not conflict with any limitations imposed by the British North America Act. The conduct of foreign relations, being a matter governed by royal prerogative and not by statute, was unaffected by the statute of Westminster. The governor general in Canada represents the king and exercises the royal prerogative by delegation for the purposes of the dominion government. His powers are set out in the letters patent and instructions which govern his office, to which have been added certain other powers by constitutional usage. The conduct of foreign relations, however, is not included in these powers. Every Canadian treaty above the level of a mere convention or trade treaty must be ratified personally by the king in London. To put the matter in a nutshell, Canada has now full control over her own legislation, but not full control over the executive functions of her government. What is needed is to round out her control over the executive function in the same way that the statute of Westminster rounded it out over the legislative function.[165]

Woodsworth offered two proposals. In one the king would, on his own initiative, decree that the governor general enjoy every power in relation to the Dominion as the king did in relation to Britain, such powers being exercised, however, on the advice of the Canadian cabinet. To represent the symbolic import of this constitutional provision, the governor general would possess a great seal to attach to treaties and other documents relating to external affairs, as existed already in South Africa and the Irish Free State. Another possibility was to have the Canadian Parliament declare that the royal prerogative in foreign affairs was vested in the governor general. Woodsworth's detailed suggestions attest to the lengths he was prepared to go to attain for his country a status of complete constitutional independence; they also confirm that he possessed a fine mind for technical detail.

VII

And that, indeed, was no small part of the tragedy of Woodsworth's stand on the declaration of war in 1939. Looked at in its completeness, his assessment of international and constitutional matters between the wars, while sometimes naive and often contradictory, was multi-faceted, richly textured, and replete with informed and technically adroit arguments. None of these qualities were evident in his response to the issue of war. Whether it was a religious impulse, as Socknat argues,[166] or had its origins, as McNaught claims, in his theory of imperialism[167] – the two were probably inextricable – Woodsworth's pacifism was absolute and fundamental; war was never justified. Thus took place the final rejection of 'politics', realism, practicality, the idea of lesser evils, and gradualism. Woodsworth had said in 1914 that Christianity was an 'impossible idealism' and in 1939 his pacifism turned out to be exactly that.

The extraordinary meeting of the National Council of the CCF called in response to the British declaration of war and the summons of Parliament into emergency session took place in Ottawa on 6 September. The CCF had already qualified its outright opposition to war at its 1937 convention when it had decided to oppose 'imperialist' wars, thereby leaving open the possibility that Canadian participation in non-imperialist ones might be countenanced. At the meeting in Ottawa Woodsworth attempted to pre-empt support for any policy of participation by moving that the council refuse to discuss any measure that would involve committing Canada to war. The mood of the meeting did not run with him and the council decided against putting the motion to a vote. What eventually prevailed was a mixed policy: to support the involvement of Canada in the war but to oppose the sending of an expeditionary force; Canada could give economic aid and the CCF would not enter a national government. In essentials, though, on the matter of opposition to the declaration of war, Woodsworth had been defeated at the highest levels of his own party.

Conclusion

After the torchlight red on sweaty faces
After the frosty silence in the gardens
After the agony in stony places
The shouting and the crying
Prison and palace and reverberation
Of thunder of spring over distant mountains
He who was living is now dead
We who are living are now dying
With a little patience

T.S. Eliot

I

September 1939 was the end. At the CCF National Council meeting Woodsworth offered his resignation as council president, parliamentary house leader, and member of the party. It was not accepted. But he had ceased to be the *de facto* leader of the party; certainly that was how he saw it. He soldiered on, however. Never in especially good health, he had driven his body as though it were a beast of burden for all his working life. In his later years he was subject to high blood pressure and in the late 1930s he suffered a small stroke. T.C. Douglas recalled Woodsworth's difficulty seeing his notes even as he gave his defiant speech in September 1939.[1] There was now the personal sadness of defeat and the horror of a new war, and by early 1940 the prospect of a federal election. David Lewis, the CCF's national secretary, arranged for Woodsworth to travel across the country in a little comfort. When he sent him a first-class ticket and a voucher for a compartment of his own, Woodsworth replied:

You must not think me lacking in appreciation of your great kindness in arranging this mode of transportation for me but when I told you that such arrangements were unnecessary I meant what I said. Perhaps you will permit me to explain more fully. 1) Whenever possible I travel CN because this is at least an approach to a government-owned R.R. 2) As to a compartment, a) as you know I cannot read and to sit in a compartment for almost two days would be like sitting in a solitary cell. I sleep well on the train and incidentally pick up a quite a bit of information from my fellow passengers; b) the expense is quite unnecessary. Some of our men out here find it very difficult to raise the election deposit fund. My whole committee in the comparatively poor constituency is working away trying to collect 25 cent subscriptions. Some of these cannot be paid until the next pay-day. c) I have usually travelled tourist, this not merely to save expense both in berth and meals but also because I meet the class of people with which our movement is most clearly identified. Even in the tourist I often feel a bit uppish when compared with those sitting up all night in the day coach or the colonist.[2]

Despite the war, Woodsworth remained with his party. Yet his enthusiasm could not have been intense. In speeches during the 1940 election campaign he called for the nationalization of war industries and increased taxes on the wealthy to pay for the military effort; he also sought revisions to the recently promulgated emergency regulations in order better to protect personal freedoms.[3] The CCF survived the election but only barely. It polled 8.5 per cent of the vote and elected eight Members of Parliament, one of whom was Woodsworth, who held Winnipeg North Centre by less than 100 votes.

At a meeting of the National Council in Ottawa in May 1940 Woodsworth suffered a major stroke that paralyzed his right arm and leg. It was so serious that he was now physically incapable of any political activity. By August he was well enough to return to Winnipeg where he disposed of the contents of his home on Maryland Street, and travelled to Vancouver to recuperate. In November 1941 he made a concentrated effort to return to the Commons. He was strong enough to get to his seat, but became so sick that he returned to the west coast lying in a berth. Lucy nursed him devotedly, relieved occasionally by Grace (who had married CCF MP Angus MacInnis) and Charles, now a journalist on the *Vancouver Province*. One of his last letters was to

Howard, the youngest of the six children and the one who took the longest to find a professional niche in life. By January 1942 Howard was working as a clerk with a gold-mining company in Quebec. Woodsworth wrote:

As you know I am not very enthusiastic over these Company Towns and gold mining in a remote district is apt to show some of the evils of private enterprise in the raw to use your own expression. However you can do your specific work and keep your eyes and ears open without saying very much ... We are now located in the suite of Grace and Angus in the Montrose on the ground floor and there are only a half a dozen steps upward from the level of the sidewalk so it ought to be of advantage to me since I now have to be careful re my heart. It is very warm and comfortable. I cannot say that I am feeling much better. My doctor's advice seems to be 'wait and see' which isn't altogether the easiest to take. Vancouver is on the whole a much easier climate for me. You will be awaiting news of the draft. It is indeed difficult for a young man to know just what to do. You know pretty much my ideas on war. Perhaps you do not altogether share these and yet I think several of our children understand how little war really gets our country further forward. Perhaps this is one reason why they are not so enthusiastic as some of those who call themselves patriotic. You will have to think your way through such problems. In the meantime remember we are tremendously interested in your welfare.[4]

Later in 1942 Howard joined the Canadian Tank Corps. Charles remained a journalist until 1944 when, through the good offices of the Department of External Affairs, he went to New Delhi to work with the British Ministry of Information in the Japanese-occupied territories. Ralph, a qualified doctor, thought of joining the army, particularly the medical corps, but stayed in civilian life and practised medicine. Grace, like her husband, supported the war. Bruce, the second youngest of the children, would have enlisted had he not been sent on an engineering survey in northern Canada in 1942. All of this proves perhaps that Woodsworth's parental authority was never so overbearing that it compelled obedience from his children. It is a sobering truth that, on the question of the war, Woodsworth's family was as unwilling as his party to follow his example.

Woodsworth died on 21 March 1942. After a small private funeral service, his remains were cremated and scattered on the waves of English Bay. The night before, Charles, exhausted from nights sitting up with his father, had taken his small cruiser from False Creek on an all-night card-playing cruise up the coast with his journalist friends. On the way back it rammed a coast-guard cutter and was holed. Next day, as the family and friends proceeded into the bay, it was only with Charles and the others bailing assiduously that the boat was prevented from sinking.[5]

II

The public memorial service in Vancouver was held eight days after his death, not in a church but in the Orpheum Theatre, and included such hymns as 'When Wilt Thou Save the People' and William Blake's 'Jerusalem.' The times seemed far removed from the days almost fifty year earlier when the young Methodist probationer had wandered along lonely prairie trails from church to church; but, again, maybe they were not so far removed at all. Woodsworth lived in an age of tempestuous change: the coming of the railroad, the telegraph, the airplane; two world wars; the incursion of new forms of thought, from Darwinism to eugenics to Bolshevism. The old certainties were crumbling but Woodsworth showed little regret. His *métier* was as a provider of new meanings and new truths. In most respects he was not just unimpressed by tradition and the past, he positively disliked them. One thinks of the depths of his rejection of established forms of life in his dismissive judgment on the Russian church in 1931: 'The death of the church may prove no great loss.' Yet he himself never quite lost his own Christian identity so that, all in all, the general shape of his thought derived from the facts that he was born and raised a Methodist in a time of change. In effect he lost his Christian faith but throughout his political life he saw himself as a pilgrim and crusader, albeit on behalf of a churchless 'Christian' progressivism.

The social gospel was the stimulus to Woodsworth's socialism. It provided that indefinable moral impetus that must lie at the back of any life of moral conviction. But in presenting himself as Christ's disciple, Woodsworth rejected not just traditional Christian institutions but also much of conventional Christian theology. He knew only too well that established forms and ideas were not infinitely amendable; words and symbols meant certain things; what they signified may not be absolutely fixed but they could not mean whatever one chose to make them mean. Yet Woodsworth believed that Christian theology should be turned away from a preoccupation with the spiritual and the hereafter and made to concern itself with life in this world. Christians were enjoined to build children's playgrounds, design therapeutic environments for the mentally sick, and redistribute purchasing power to the poor. The knowledge suitable to these tasks was not that of the Bible or the writings of the church fathers but that of sociology, psychology, and administrative-planning theory. It may well be that, when all the contending views of the social and political message of the Christian religion have been resolved, the revolutionary-pacifist Christ of the Sermon on the Mount will be seen as the one closest to the truth. But social change is not all that Christianity stands for, and Woodsworth failed to confront this fact. When he did address traditional christological and eschatological subjects, his thought was shallow and imprecise, tailing off into a kind of mystical, personal deism or pantheism. In normal Christian terms his theology was, in the final analysis, atheistic.

Woodsworth was, then, very much a religious figure in a transitional time. He abandoned much of Christianity but not all of it. To many of his followers he embodied the appeal of the Christian saint; to King Gordon he seemed like an Amos or Isaiah; to Frank Scott he was aesthetic, quiet, soft-spoken, of 'indomitable courage ... and largeness of vision.'[6] Marian Scott told of Woodsworth gazing out upon Montreal and his recollection of standing on the Mount of Olives looking down on Jerusalem.[7] Woodsworth lived in an era when church-going and Christian thought-forms were an important, if declining, part of Canadian society. While he popularized newer ways of thinking, the basis of his appeal was often a traditional Christian one. Many of his disciples, after all, were sons and daughters of the manse, certainly raised in the church. They too were caught betwixt the old and the new. With the passage of time we can now see that, as Ramsay Cook persuasively argues, the social gospel in effect brought legitimacy to ideas that grew up outside the Christian world view and that were in the end inimical to and subversive of it.[8] Woodsworth helped promote the secularization of his world. In his day he did not see this consequence clearly; neither did his supporters. He talked of the origin of species, of the environmental causes of crime, of social engineering, and the perfectibility of man. But he himself was in his private life almost a complete puritan and in public, while he talked the language of sociology, biology, and the new management theories, he also seemed to his supporters to speak the biblical language of justice and salvation. Fifty years later Woodsworth's successors no longer strike us as being Christian or prophetic figures, yet the other part of his intellectual legacy, the message of secularism, thrives. Woodsworth did not live to hear of the Holocaust and the dropping of the atomic bombs on Hiroshima and Nagasaki and all that these events revealed about the moral void at the heart of the modern project. If he had he might have become convinced that the sunny optimism of the social gospel's account of human nature was misplaced.

While Woodsworth's thought was tied together by the social gospel, its mature texture of expression was socialism. Of course, the two were inseparable in him. Woodsworth may never have said, like Salem Bland, that to rail against public ownership was to sin against the Holy Ghost, but it was a sentiment that no doubt he shared.[9] The dominant shape of his idea of socialism was conveyed by his notion of cooperation, which emphasized centralization, hierarchy, and planning – in a word, it was statist. There was a relentless technological determinism to all this. The logic of monopolies went as follows: when scientific and managerial ingenuity was applied to larger and larger production units, efficiency was maximized. A theory of 'giantism' emerged from such thinking. If larger was better, then the largest was the best. National monopolies must give place to international ones and, ultimately, the greatest end of the human race was to create a universal monopoly, a monopoly of monopolies, a unitary world order, politically, economically, and socially. Even in his early years, when his account of monopolies was still undeveloped, Woodsworth emphasized social coherence and totality in his discussion of the Canadian identity; social unity must undergird any state. Here he was mainly talking of 'racial' or cultural attributes. But what he also revealed was his profound misgivings about intermediate, regional and local identities. In later life some of his nativism fell away. Even so, he continued to have trouble with intermediate communities – for example, provinces in his constitutional prescriptions, and participatory and voluntaristic groups in his version of cooperation and planning. His ideal society offered little room for pluralism. In his own life Woodsworth was a dissenter who knew directly of the pressing reality of antagonism and diversity. Yet his own vision of society saw little virtue in these.

Woodsworth's position on intermediate identities contributed to the emphatic centralism of his constitutional doctrine. National jurisdictional authority was to be enhanced although he also believed in the importance of protecting minority rights, partly by an entrenched bill of rights or by an amending formula requiring either majority consent by the provinces or unanimity. This centralist policy found its way into the Regina Manifesto and some variant of it remained dominant in the

CCF until the end of the party's existence. In part Woodsworth had helped educate a generation of English-Canadian socialists; in part he had simply expressed their natural inclinations. Centralist doctrine did not fare well in Quebec, where the CCF's vote in federal elections never rose above 2.4 per cent. After the founding of the CCF's successor, the New Democratic Party (NDP), in 1961, unfamiliar constitutional ideas surfaced within it. Recruits to the party from Quebec injected policies based on two-nations theory and binational and even associate-states images of the country. These co-existed, sometimes abrasively, with more conventional accounts of federalism. Another emergent view, particularly in the 1970s, was a provincialist one which – Saskatchewan under Allan Blakeney comes particularly in mind – maintained that socialism could be successfully built at the provincial level and that, in any case, most Canadians drew their sense of identity from either the locality, the region, or the province. Both newer strains of thought undercut the NDP's traditional emphasis on the centre and, belatedly, made much of the virtues of those intermediate identities that Woodsworth had found such difficulty in embracing.

The NDP were faithful supporters of Trudeau's policies of bilingualism and the 1982 constitutional arrangements. What opposition there was within the party came from those influenced by Quebec nationalism and western provincialism. It is worth noting that Woodsworth had helped lay the foundations for the three arches of the Constitution Act of 1982 – patriation, a Charter of Rights and an amending formula requiring the consent of the majority of the provinces (the first two more than the last). If Frank Scott gave Pierre Trudeau his idea of an entrenched charter, Woodsworth was instrumental in giving it to Scott. And in his day no English Canadian politician exceeded Woodsworth in his determination that Canada should in every respect be constitutionally independent of Britain.

Five years after the patriation of the constitution an agreement was reached to amend the terms of the 1982 Constitution Act. The Meech Lake Accord resulted from an alliance of two-nations federalists from Quebec and English Canadian provincial-rights exponents. By 1987 support within the NDP for these newly ascendant constitutional perspectives was strong enough to incline the federal parliamentary caucus and the premier of Manitoba, Howard Pawley, to consent to the accord. Critics of the accord on the Canadian Left were unwitting bearers of Woodsworth's and the CCF's main constitutional legacy: they rejected the binational, special-status implications of the distinct-society clause; they supported the charter as a pan-Canadian constitutional fixture to which Quebec's jurisdictional powers should be firmly subject; they opposed the accord's limits on the federal-spending power; and they worried that the amending formula governing the Senate was too inflexible. Woodsworth, who all his life was a frustrated sailor, had spent many hours sailing the waters of Meech Lake. Evidently his spirit was little present on that fateful night in April 1987 when the accord was first agreed to. But then, he never had much acceptance in Quebec when he was alive either.

In his public life Woodsworth sought to master the difficult art of pursuing a scheme of change that was coherent, democratic, and hegemonic while at the same time being immediate, partial, and practical. Since the history of parliamentary socialism in this century proves that such a model of change is not easily attained, it should come as no surprise that Woodsworth's task was not an easy one and that he should largely have failed. In many respects his problem, as he admitted in the early 1930s, was that he was torn and buffeted between competing intellectual and moral constraints, from the utopian to the practical, from the long-term to the immediate, from the absolutely right to the lesser of two evils, from what his conscience dictated to what his constituents demanded. Reconciling all these was unlikely and attempting to do so led him into contradictions: the same thing was both possible and impossible; it was both supportive of capitalism and subversive of it; it would make matters worse and make them better.

But, if Woodsworth's political thought was many-sided, we should at least do him the justice of not overlooking one of its predominant sides, namely its persistent immediacy and practicality. He was, for the most part, a gradualist, a reformer, and a pragmatist who, given half a chance, preferred to get something done. We have to lay to rest the received opinion of him as unrealistic, impractical, and other-worldly, a conception popularized, for example by Walter Young's argument that Woodsworth and the CCF were governed by a 'movement' orientation rather than a 'party' one.[10] The grand exception was his pacifism, which helped confound and confuse his responses to the international order, particularly in the 1930s, and led to the lonely impracticality of his stance in 1939. But his pacifism was only one part of his political life and should not be viewed as embodying all of it. He was, we may say, for good or ill, predominantly a hard-nosed gradualist and realist.

Woodsworth's political career has to be seen as a limited success at best. His achievements were not inconsiderable – an independent party of the Left, a major role in the founding of the welfare state and the managed, Keynesian economy – yet they somehow are overshadowed by his unrealized goals. He left the CCF a decidedly minority party and deeply divided over the issue of the war. The progressive tide of history that was to sweep over the tidal plains of capitalism and lift Canada on to the sunny, temperate uplands of a corporate, collective future failed to materialize, as it has failed ever since. Might there have been a different outcome? Probably not, but perhaps Woodsworth's strategic judgements hadn't helped matters. Admittedly, a united-front strategy would not necessarily have been more electorally successful. It would have foundered, as the CCF did, on the rocks of Canadian conservatism, and, as well, would have fatally compromised the CCF's independence and made it party to the CPC's submissiveness to Stalin and the Comintern. Maybe there would have been a somewhat different outcome if Woodsworth had employed less traditional, more dramatic, parliamentary tactics, applying to the whole range of legislation the sort of creative behaviour he exhibited in the debates on divorce reform in the late 1920s. But this was not his general political disposition. His typical parliamentary stance was to act as a conventional leader of an opposition party, opposing strenuously but in a reasonable way while at the same time seeking immediate improvements. He rejected the proposition that inadequate, incomplete, immediate changes were necessarily inferior to larger, more complete, later ones and should be rejected. This was his attitude towards everything, except war.

In sum, the actual outcome of Woodsworth's efforts was to establish the CCF as a minority, independent political force that pressed for immediate improvements from the governing party. If anything, he was far too 'cooperative' in his politics, only too willing to agree, to compromise, and to mediate. Perhaps greater independence and disaffiliation – in a word, greater 'impossibilism' – would have given his cause an enlarged clarity and electoral impetus, although it is doubtful that anything would have been sufficient to overcome the combined forces that militated against him and the CCF. For the simple truth is that there were a myriad of cultural and historical factors that vitiated the appeal of socialism in the 1920s and 1930s. By 1940 support for Woodsworth and the CCF was limited and regionally specific. What successes they had, legislatively, took the form of amendments to the principally liberal and capitalist character of Canada's political culture and economy. Under pressure from the Left Canada obtained an old-age-pension program, unemployment insurance, the Canadian Broadcasting Corporation, the Bank of Canada, and greater respect for individual and worker's rights; in time there would come a fuller welfare state and more extensive economic management. But there was little of Woodsworth's ideal of socialism in all this.

The fate of the Left has not greatly changed since 1940. In the 1960s the NDP climbed to a new plateau of national support at around 15 per cent and in the 1980s it struggled to a slightly higher level of about 20 per cent. It remains a minority party whose voting base is regionally concentrated; and it exudes an ethos of political practicality that is not out of character with that of Woodsworth, although its leaders are less likely, if at all, to preach the sort of socialist ideals that he expressed. Purged of his theoretical ideals, which in his own political practice he was often willing to set aside anyway, Woodsworth would not have been out of place in the NDP of David Lewis, Ed Broadbent, or Audrey McLaughlin. His gradualism blends agreeably with the NDP's later penchant for revisionist liberalism and social democracy. The problem is that this is not enough to distinguish it from the Liberal Party, at least when the latter is on its best behaviour. A logical national party system might postulate the pressing necessity of an inclusive, national, social-democratic party, an amalgam perhaps of the NDP and the Liberals. As an independent force, however, the federal NDP is stalled, frozen in the mould of a third party with its support limited to Ontario and parts of the West. It confronts an impasse that Woodsworth himself would recognize immediately and which he, too, found impossible to resolve.

Of course, a similar pessimism existed on the eve of the NDP's triumph in Ontario in September 1990. In principle, an equivalent breakthrough could occur nationally, the result of profound disenchantment with the Progressive Conservatives and Liberals and an advantageous division of the popular vote. We need to recall Woodsworth's sense of the indeterminacy of history. The political party he helped, indirectly, to establish may one day be victorious; equally, the country he dearly loved may, soon, be no more.

Notes

Fuller details of works cited in short form in the notes can be found in the bibliography.

PREFACE

1 Ziegler, *Woodsworth*, 201
2 *Manitoba Commonwealth*, 4 January 1935
3 William Irvine, 'Tribute to Mr. J.S. Woodsworth' (Vancouver 1942), Young Papers
4 Underhill, *James Shaver Woodsworth*, 3
5 McNaught, *Prophet*, 91, 165, 299, 316–17
6 Michael Holroyd, *Bernard Shaw: 1856–1898*, 1 (London 1988), 4

CHAPTER 1   Son of the Church, 1874–1909

1 James Woodsworth, *Thirty Years*, 77–8
2 McNaught, *Prophet*, 5
3 Benjamin Smillie, 'The Woodsworths: James and J.S. – Father and Son,' in Butcher et al., eds., *Prairie Spirit*, 100–21
4 Grace MacInnis, interview with the author, Vancouver, 22 October 1983. In contrast to McNaught, MacInnis tends to diminish James's influence on his son's theological radicalism.
5 A.G. Bedford, *The University of Winnipeg: A History of the Founding Colleges* (Toronto 1976), 26, 428
6 J.S. Woodsworth to C.B. Sissons, 26 January 1917, Sissons Papers
7 Friesen, *The Canadian Prairies*, 129–241
8 Woodsworth, *Thirty Years*, 85

9 Ibid., 12
10 Ibid., xii
11 Ibid., 191–2
12 Ibid., 124
13 Ibid., 228–32
14 Ibid., 80–97
15 Ibid., 83
16 Ibid., 86
17 Ibid., 91–2
18 Ibid., 94
19 MacInnis, *Woodsworth*, 13; Charles Woodsworth, 'A Prophet at Home,' 4. C.B. Sissons considered him 'bossy' after he had spent time with him in 1890–91. See C.B. Sissons, *Memoirs*, 46
20 On the Canadian social gospel, see Allen, *The Social Passion*; Cook, *The Regenerators*; and Butcher et al., *Prairie Spirit*.
21 Morton Paterson, 'The Mind of a Methodist: The Personalist Theology of George John Blewett in Its Historical Context,' *The Bulletin* 1978, 5–41
22 Gordon Harland, 'John Mark King: First Principal of Manitoba College,' in Butcher et al., *Prairie Spirit*, 171–83
23 J.S. Woodsworth to his mother, 23 October 1895(?), Woodsworth Papers, I
24 Ibid., 26 January 1896
25 Ibid., 1 February 1896
26 Ibid.
27 MacInnis, *Woodsworth*, 11
28 J.S. Woodsworth to his mother, 1 February 1896, Woodsworth Papers, I
29 C.B. Sissons to Frank Underhill, 10 December 1944, Underhill Papers, VIII
30 J.S. Woodsworth to his mother, 25 October 1899, Woodsworth Papers, I
31 Generally Woodsworth felt much closer to the Scots than to the English. He believed that Canadians had absorbed many of the exemplary characteristics of Scottish people. See J.S. Woodsworth to his mother, 23 March 1900 (?), ibid.
32 Ibid., 15 January 1900
33 Ibid., 25 October 1899
34 J.S. Woodsworth to Mary, 28 January 1900(?), ibid.
35 Francis, *Frank H. Underhill*, 26; Granatstein, *The Ottawa Men*, 35, 193
36 J.S. Woodsworth to his father, 22 January 1900, Woodsworth Papers, I
37 J.S. Woodsworth to Harold, 28 January 1900, ibid.
38 Ibid.
39 See Trigger, *Natives and Newcomers*, 3–49.
40 Woodsworth, *Thirty Years*, 86

41 He remained a teetotaller all his life and his opposition to smoking was extreme. Judge Roy St. George Stubbs remembers his father telling him that Woodsworth believed that anyone who smoked was unqualified to represent the body politic, since, as Woodsworth put it, how could anyone who abused his own body care for the wider world of society? Interview with the author, 24 February 1978

42 J.S. Woodsworth to his mother, n.d., Woodsworth Papers, I

43 Ibid., 19 May 1900

44 J.S. Woodsworth to C.B. Sissons, 2 March 1900, Sissons Papers

45 J.S. Woodsworth to his mother, 26 February 1900, Woodsworth Papers, I

46 Ibid., 22, 24, 26 June 1900

47 J.S. Woodsworth to his father, 15 February 1900, ibid.

48 On this matter of Woodsworth's encouraging his father to influence the Wesley board to obtain a job for him, Grace MacInnis's defence of her father is simply not consistent with the evidence. See MacInnis, *Woodsworth*, 43

49 On Woodsworth's Arminianism, see Smillie, 'The Woodsworths,' 116.

50 J.S. Woodsworth to his mother, 17 May 1900, Woodsworth Papers, I

51 J.S. Woodsworth to C.B. Sissons 8 May, 18 June, 24 July, 9 October 1901; 16 January, 17 February, 27 March, 12 April, 26 May 1902, Sissons Papers

52 Ibid., 9 October 1901

53 Ibid., 16 January 1902

54 Ibid., 27 March 1902

55 Ibid., 17 June 1902

56 Sissons, *Memoirs*, 44

57 I am indebted to Bruce Woodsworth for his many recollections of his mother.

58 J.S. Woodsworth to C.B. Sissons, 27 February 1902, Sissons Papers

59 Ibid., 21 August 1902

60 Ibid., 15 January 1903

61 Ibid., 14 November 1903

62 Sissons, *Memoirs*, 67

63 J.S. Woodsworth to C.B. Sissons, 14 November 1903, Sissons Papers

64 Ibid.

65 Ibid., 3 October 1903

66 Ibid., 14 November 1903

67 Sissons, *Memoirs*, 73. Clara married Blewett in 1906.

68 J.S. Woodsworth to C.B. Sissons, 24 April 1909, Sissons Papers

69 'Sermons and Addresses,' Woodsworth Papers, XV

70 Ibid., 70–2

71 Ibid., 261
72 Ibid., 199–200
73 Ibid., 261
74 Ibid., 33
75 Ibid., 16–33
76 Ibid., 20–1
77 Ibid., 103
78 J.S. Woodsworth to C.B. Sissons, 22 May 1905, Sissons Papers; Paterson, 'Blewett,' 12–13
79 'Sermons and Addresses,' Woodsworth Papers, XV, 216–31
80 Ibid., 224, 226
81 Ibid., 229
82 Ibid., 290–2
83 J.S. Woodsworth to C.B. Sissons, 21 July 1904, Sissons Papers
84 'Sermons and Addresses,' Woodsworth Papers XV, 292
85 J.S. Woodsworth to C.B. Sissons, 23 September 1905, Sissons Papers
86 Ibid., 22 December 1905
87 Ibid.
88 Woodsworth, *Following the Gleam*, 8
89 Ibid., 18
90 J.S. Woodsworth to C.B. Sissons, 25 April, 20 May 1912, Sissons Papers
91 Ibid., 11 October 1906
92 Woodsworth, *Following the Gleam*, 5–8
93 Ibid., 6
94 J.S. Woodsworth to C.B. Sissons, 13 June 1907, Sissons Papers
95 McNaught, *Prophet*, 35
96 J.S. Woodsworth to C.B. Sissons, 13 June 1907, Sissons Papers
97 Ibid., 12 July 1907
98 Ibid., 28 August 1907
99 Ibid., 28 October 1907
100 Ibid., 10 April 1908

CHAPTER 2: Setting Sail, 1909–1921

1 MacInnis, *Woodsworth*, 60
2 Allen, *The Social Passion*, 49
3 Minutes of the Winnipeg and District Branch of the Dominion Labour Party, 13 August 1919, Russell Papers
4 J.S. Woodsworth to C.B. Sissons, 20 July 1921, Sissons Papers

5 J.S. Woodsworth to Lucy Woodsworth, 20 November 1915; MacInnis, *Woodsworth*, 95

6 Woodsworth, *Strangers*, x, xii

7 *Hansard*, 18 June 1936, 3875. Dr Ralph Woodsworth described his father as 'much more like an Englishman than a Canadian.' Another son, Bruce, recalled his father saying of the problem of sibling rivalry: 'If you *must* fight physically (and I hope you and Howard are getting over this phase), then do it in the British way, with your fists; not the Italian or Spanish way, with a knife.' Interviews with the author, British Columbia, 21 August 1984

8 Woodsworth, *Strangers*, 158

9 Ibid.

10 Ibid., 92

11 Ibid., 239–40

12 Ibid., 208

13 Ibid., 16

14 Ibid., 42

15 Ibid., 240

16 Ibid., 248

17 Ibid., 240–1. My emphasis

18 *Manitoba Free Press*, 29 May 1913. Woodsworth himself was not especially tall, being about five feet, seven inches. C.B. Sissons estimated that he weighed about 140 pounds. See Sissons, *Memoirs*, 194.

19 Ibid., 30 May 1913

20 Ibid., 3 June 1913

21 Ibid., 4 June 1913. See also *The Voice*, 10 January 1913; 2 January 1914; Woodsworth, 'Nation-Building,' 85–99; *Studies in Rural Citizenship*, 58; *Labor Church*, 2.

22 *Manitoba Free Press*, 4 June 1913

23 See F.M. Barnard, 'Metaphors, Laments and the Organic Community,' *Canadian Journal of Economics and Political Science*, 22, no. 2 (1966), 281–301.

24 *The Voice*, 10 January 1913; *Manitoba Free Press*, 6, 11 June 1913; J.S. Woodsworth, 'How to Make True Canadians,' *Canadian Municipal Journal* 12, no. 2 (February 1916), 49; 'The Immigrant Invasion after the War,' ibid., 12, no. 3 (March 1916), 87; 'Nation-building,' 87–94; 'Dauphin area,' *Ukrainian Rural Communities; Report of Investigation by Bureau of Social Research* (Winnipeg 1917), 34; *Western Labor News*, 23 August 1918

25 *Manitoba Free Press*, 11 June 1913

26 Ibid., 9 June 1913

27 *The Voice*, 10 January 1913; *Manitoba Free Press*, 6 June 1913; Woodsworth, 'How to Make True Canadians,' 49; *Grain Growers' Guide*, 10 May, 7 June, 29 November 1916; Woodsworth, 'Nation-Building,' 97–9; *Rural Citizenship*, 48–52

28 *The Voice*, 8 September 1911, 27 February 1914, 14 January 1916; Woodsworth, 'Nation-Building,' 97–9; 'The Immigrant Invasion after the War,' 124; *BC Federationist*, 14 February 1919; *Western Labor News*, 22 August 1919

29 Woodsworth, *My Neighbor*, 139–45; *Manitoba Free Press*, 31 May 1913; Woodsworth, 'Nation-Building,' 89

30 *Manitoba Free Press*, 31 May, 3, 5 June 1913; *Grain Growers' Guide*, 8 March 1916; Woodsworth, *Rural Citizenship*, 58; *BC Federationist*, 14 February, 2 May 1919; *Western Labor News*, 23 April 1920

31 Woodsworth, 'Nation-Building,' 93–6; 'How to Make True Canadians,' 49; 'The Immigrant Invasion after the War,' 124; *Grain Growers' Guide*, 7 June 1916

32 Woodsworth, 'Nation-Building,' 88

33 Ibid., 96

34 *The Voice*, 10 January 1913; *Manitoba Free Press*, 6, 11, 13 June 1913; Woodsworth, 'Nation-Building,' 91–9; *Ukrainian Rural Communities*, 6; 'How to Make True Canadians,' 49; 'The Cooperative Community,' *Grain Growers' Guide*, 29 November 1916; *Rural Citizenship*, 58

35 Woodsworth, 'The Immigrant Invasion after the War,' 124

36 Woodsworth, 'Nation-Building,' 94–5

37 Information in Fernald and Goddard can be found in Rudolph Pintner, *Intelligence Testing: Methods and Results* (New York 1923), and Leon J. Kamin, *The Science and Politics of I.Q.* (New York 1974).

38 H.H. Goddard, *The Kallikak Family* (New York 1914)

39 H.H. Goddard, 'The Binet Tests in Relation to Immigration,' *Journal of Psycho-Asthenics* 18 (1913), 105–7

40 *Manitoba Free Press*, 11 October 1916

41 Ibid.

42 *The Voice*, 14 April 1916. This is Woodsworth's use of Goddard's *The Kallikak Family*.

43 *Manitoba Free Press*, 25 October 1916

44 Ibid., 15 November 1916

45 Ibid., 8 November 1916

46 *The Voice*, 17 November 1916

47 J.S. Woodsworth, 'Why I Resigned from the Christian Ministry,' in *Following the Gleam*, 5–10

48 Dr Ralph and Bruce Woodsworth, interviews with the author, Gibson's Landing and Silver Sands, British Columbia, 21 August 1984
49 Woodsworth, *Strangers*, 245–51
50 *The Voice*, 21 May, 9 July 1909; 8 September 1911; *Manitoba Free Press*, 6 June 1913
51 *The Voice*, 11 September 1914; Woodsworth, 'Nation-Building,' 95–6; *Rural Citizenship*, 48–52; *Manitoba Free Press*, 6 June 1913; *BC Federationist*, 6 September 1918; *Western Labor News*, 19 September 1919
52 *The Voice*, 23 January 1914; *Grain Growers' Guide*, 14 June 1916; *BC Federationist*, 27 December 1918; *Western Labor News*, 25 July 1919, 7 May 1920
53 *Grain Growers' Guide*, 14 June 1916
54 Ibid.
55 *BC Federationist*, 6 September 1918. See also ibid., 11 April 1919; Woodsworth, *Labor Church*, 12; *The Voice*, 19 February 1915; MacInnis, *Woodsworth*, 95.
56 *The Voice*, 18 June 1909
57 Ibid., 1 December 1911, 19 February 1915; *BC Federationist*, 7 March 1919; *Western Labor News*, 15 August 1919
58 *The Voice*, 17 November 1916; Woodsworth, *Labor Church*, 11–16; *Western Labor News*, 15 April 1919
59 *The Voice*, 27 February 1914; *Grain Growers' Guide*, 14 June 1916; *BC Federationist*, 11 April 1919; *Western Labor News*, 1 August, 19 September 1919; 7 May, 30 September 1920; J.S. Woodsworth, 'The Spirit of the New World,' *Canadian Municipal Journal* 13, no. 3 (March 1917), 87
60 *The Voice*, 17 November 1916. See also Woodsworth, 'The Spirit of the New World,' 87.
61 Woodsworth, *Rural Citizenship*, 50–2; *Grain Growers' Guide*, 14 June 1916; *BC Federationist*, 6 September 1918; *Strike Bulletin*, 15 June 1919; *Western Labor News*, 19 September 1919
62 *Manitoba Free Press*, 6 June 1913; *Western Labor News*, 16 April, 22 August 1919; *BC Federationist*, 29 October 1920
63 Ibid., 6 September 1918
64 *Manitoba Free Press*, 6 June 1913
65 Woodsworth, *Labor Church*, 10–14
66 Ibid., 12, 14
67 *Manitoba Free Press*, 6 June 1913; *BC Federationist*, 6 September 1918; Woodsworth, 'My Religion'; *Labor Church*, 11
68 *Western Labor News*, 16 April 1919; see also Woodsworth, 'My Religion.'
69 Michael Walzer, in *Spheres of Justice* (New York 1983), defines the term as:

'Historically stable, ongoing associations of men and women with some special commitment to one another and some special sense of their common life' (62).

70 .*Manitoba Free Press*, 7 June 1913

71 Woodsworth may have been a modernist in most things but clearly not in poetic taste. Then again, modern poetic idioms did not reach English Canada until the 1920s.

72 J.S. Woodsworth, 'Does Our Democracy "Democ",' *Canadian Municipal Journal* 12, no. 11 (November 1916), 583

73 *Western Labor News*, 1 August 1919

74 Woodsworth, *My Neighbor*, passim; *The Voice*, 16 November 1916; Woodsworth, *Rural Citizenship*, 22–3, 40–1; *Labor Church*, 11–13; 'The Spirit of the New World,' 87; *BC Federationist*, 25 October 1918; 1, 22 November 1918; 21 March 1919; 4 February 1921; *Western Labor News*, 16 April, 15 August 1919

75 *BC Federationist*, 22 November 1918

76 Woodsworth, *My Neighbor*, 17–123; *Grain Growers' Guide*, 14 June 1916; *BC Federationist*, 18 October, 8 November 1918

77 Woodsworth, *My Neighbor*, 78–9

78 Ibid., 100–1

79 Ibid., 115, 119–20

80 *Manitoba Free Press*, 29 May, 7, 9, 10 June 1913; Woodsworth, *Rural Citizenship*, 36–7; 'The Spirit of the New World,' 87; *BC Federationist*, 4 October 1918, 10 January 1919

81 *BC Federationist*, 10 January 1919

82 *Manitoba Free Press*, 30 May 1913; Woodsworth *Rural Citizenship*, 9; 'Does Our Democracy "Democ",' 583; *Western Labor News*, 22 April 1919; *BC Federationist*, 14 June 1918

83 Woodsworth, *Rural Citizenship*, 11

84 Ibid., 11–12

85 Woodsworth, *My Neighbor*, 17–123; *Rural Citizenship*, passim; *Manitoba Free Press*, 9 June 1913; *BC Federationist*, 18 October 1918, 21 March 1919; *Strike Bulletin*, 10 June 1919; *Western Labor News*, 15 August 1919

86 Woodsworth, *My Neighbor*, 45–6

87 *The Voice*, 9 July 1909

88 *Western Labor News*, 15 August 1919

89 Woodsworth, *My Neighbor*, 81; *Rural Citizenship*, 5–7, 18–19; *The Voice*, 9 July 1909; *Manitoba Free Press*, 9 June 1913; *Grain Growers' Guide*, 14 June 1916; *BC Federationist*, 8 November 1918, 7 February 1919; *Western Labor News*, 7 May 1920

90 Woodsworth, *My Neighbor*, 79–86; *Rural Citizenship*, 22–7; 'Does Our Democracy "Democ",' 583; *Strike Bulletin*, 10 June 1919; *BC Federationist*, 24 January 1919

91 *Manitoba Free Press*, 11 June 1913; Woodsworth, 'Nation-Building,' 88, 93; 'Does Our Democracy "Democ",' 583

92 Woodsworth, 'Does Our Democracy "Democ",' 583

93 F.M. Barnard, *Herder's Social and Political Thought: from Enlightenment to Nationalism* (Oxford 1965); 'Metaphors, Laments and the Organic Community,' 281–301; F.M. Barnard and Richard Vernon, 'Recovering Politics for Socialism: Two Responses to the Language of Community,' *Canadian Journal of Political Science* 16, no. 4 (December 1983), 717–37

94 *BC Federationist*, 1 February 1918

95 Ibid., 8 March 1918

96 Bercuson, *Fools and Wise Men*, 123; Phillips, *No Power Greater*, 73; McCormack, *Reformers, Rebels, and Revolutionaries*, 157–61

97 *BC Federationist*, 4 July 1919

98 J.S. Woodsworth to C.B. Sissons, 1 December 1918, Sissons Papers

99 Steeves, *The Compassionate Rebel*, 42

100 *BC Federationist*, 30 August 1918; 3, 10, 24 January 1919; *Western Labor News*, 8 October 1920

101 *BC Federationist*, 30 August 1918; 10 January, 16 May 1919; *Western Labor News*, 5 September 1919

102 Woodsworth, *My Neighbor*, 78; *Waterfront*, 16, 20, 24; *BC Federationist*, 27 December 1918; *Western Labor News*, 25 July 1919

103 *Manitoba Free Press*, 7 June 1913

104 *Western Labor News*, 23 August 1918

105 *The Voice*, 1 March 1912; Woodsworth, *Rural Citizenship*, 27; *Waterfront*, 16, 17; *BC Federationist*, 30 August 1918, 24 January 1919

106 *BC Federationist*, 21 June, 30 August 1918; 17 January, 17 February, 23 May 1919; *Western Labor News*, 25 July 1919

107 *BC Federationist*, 30 August 1918

108 Ibid., 30 August 1918, 24 January 1919

109 Ibid., 30 August 1918

110 *The Voice*, 1 March 1912; *Grain Growers' Guide*, 8 November 1916; *BC Federationist*, 30 August 1918, 24 January 1919; *Western Labor News*, 23 August 1918

111 Woodsworth, *My Neighbor*, 88; *Rural Citizenship*, 57; 'Does Our Democracy "Democ",' 583; *Labor Church*, 2; *BC Federationist*, 1 November 1918, 7 February 1919, 4 March 1921

112 Woodsworth, *My Neighbor*, 88

113 Woodsworth, *Labor Church*, 2
114 *The Strike Bulletin*, 12, 23 June 1919
115 *The Voice*, 1 March 1912; *BC Federationist*, 30 August, 6 September, 1 November 1918; 7 February 1919
116 In writing of his time on the docks in Vancouver, Woodsworth claimed that he felt at one not only with the workers but with all of humanity.
117 *BC Federationist*, 30 August, 1 November, 13 December 1918; *Western Labor News*, 25 July, 29 August, 26 September 1919
118 *BC Federationist*, 3 January 1919
119 Ibid., 4 March 1921
120 Ibid.
121 Ibid., 30 August 1918
122 Woodsworth, *My Neighbor*, 88
123 *Western Labor News*, 25 July 1919
124 Ibid., 8 October 1920
125 *BC Federationist*, 3 January 1919; See also J.S. Woodsworth, 'The British Way,' in *Following the Gleam*, 13–15; *Western Labor News*, 8 August 1919
126 McNaught, *Prophet*, 90–7
127 *BC Federationist*, 7 February 1919
128 *Western Labor News*, 25 July, 8 August 1919
129 *BC Federationist*, 27 December 1918
130 Ibid., 3 January 1919
131 *The Voice*, 9 July 1909, 4 February 1910, 31 March 1911; Woodsworth, *Rural Citizenship*, 53
132 *BC Federationist*, 3 January 1919
133 Ibid.
134 Ibid. See also ibid., 20 September 1918.
135 Henry Pelling, *A Short History of the Labour Party* (London 1965), 44–5; Norman Mackenzie, ed., *The Letters of Sidney and Beatrice Webb*, 3 (Cambridge 1978), 90–1; A.M. McBriar, *Fabian Socialism and English Politics, 1884–1918* (Cambridge 1962), 343
136 Ross McKibbin, *The Evolution of the Labour Party, 1910–1924* (Oxford 1974), 91–106
137 *BC Federationist*, 30 August 1918; 7 February 1919; 9 July, 19 November 1920; *Strike Bulletin*, 10 June 1919; *Western Labor News*, 25 July 1919
138 *BC Federationist*, 7 February 1919
139 Ibid.
140 Ibid., 30 May, 13 June 1919
141 MacInnis, *Woodsworth*, 137–8
142 *Strike Bulletin*, 10 June 1919

143 Ibid., 12 June 1919
144 Ibid.
145 Ibid., 23 June 1919. In 1921, Woodsworth acknowledged that his reaction to the strike had been to seek a settlement. See MacInnis, *Woodsworth*, 135, 146. And in 1928 he stated that his article was written in a conciliatory tone 'after consultation with some of the leading business men in Winnipeg.' See *Hansard*, 9 June 1928, 4099.
146 *Strike Bulletin*, 23 June 1919
147 *BC Federationist*, 27 December 1918
148 I disagree with Penner's argument that these *Western Labor News* articles 'seem to represent a shift from the position of his 1918 article in which he favoured moderation of working class demands in order to appeal to the natural allies of the working class.' See Penner, *The Canadian Left*, 184.
149 *Western Labor News*, 1 August 1919
150 *BC Federationist*, 21 March 1919
151 Ibid. Woodsworth also spoke out for a frank and scientific approach to the sexual education of children. See ibid., 14 March 1919.
152 *Western Labor News*, 22 August 1919
153 Ibid., 23 August 1918
154 Ibid., 6 August 1920
155 Interview with the author, Ottawa, 21 October 1984

CHAPTER 3   Politics, Parliament, and Revolution, 1922–1940

1 J.S. Woodsworth to David Lewis, 6 March 1940, CCF Papers, CVII; *Weekly News*, 27 July 1928, 29 July 1932; Arthur Lower referred to Woodsworth's 'inevitable charts' in his *My First Seventy-Five Years*, 176.
2 Woodsworth, 'My Religion'
3 J.S. Woodsworth, 'Mobilizing Progressive Opinion in Canada,' *The Canadian Forum* 5, no. 50 (November 1924), 41
4 *Hansard*, 10 April 1922, 843; 8 January 1926, 28; *Weekly News*, 5 February 1926
5 Ibid., 11 September 1925, 5 February 1926, 25 March 1927, 4 March 1932
6 *Hansard*, 23 June 1926, 4926–32
7 Ibid., 9 March 1932, 963
8 Ibid., 14 May 1923, 2721; *Weekly News* 11 September 1925; 21 May, 10 September 1926; 25 March 1927; 29 March 1929
9 *Hansard*, 20 March 1924, 509; 18 July 1924; 10 February, 18 June 1925; 12 September 1930; *Weekly News*, 11, 18 September 1925; 25 March 1927

10 *Weekly News*, 12 August 1932, 11 May 1934, 8 June 1936; *Hansard*, 19 April 1934, 2328–9
11 *Weekly News*, 12 August 1932, 11 May 1934; *Hansard*, 17 September 1930, 302; 26 May 1931, 1969; 19 June 1935, 3811; 27 February 1936, 583
12 *Hansard*, 19 May 1936, 2975
13 Ibid., 14 May 1923, 2721; 16 May 1934, 3105; *Weekly News*, 4 April 1930
14 The state of working-class organizations and politics in the 1920s is discussed in Palmer, *Working-Class Experience*
15 *Weekly News*, 21 October 1927
16 Ibid., 11, 18 September 1925
17 Independent Labor Party Minutes, The Pas Branch, 25 September 1925
18 Neatby, *King, 1924–1932*, 165
19 *Weekly News*, 17 September 1926
20 Robin, *Radical Politics*, 266–7
21 Ibid., 273
22 *Weekly News*, 1 November 1929
23 Ibid., 12 July 1930
24 W.L. Morton, *Progressive Party*, 190–1; McNaught, *Prophet*, 209
25 *Weekly News*, 24 May 1934
26 Horn, *League for Social Reconstruction*, 19
27 Francis, *Frank H. Underhill*, 89
28 Gerald L. Caplan, *Dilemma of Canadian Socialism*, 14
29 Ibid., 55–6
30 J.S. Woodsworth to R. Lambert, 5 February 1935, Woodsworth Papers, III
31 J.S. Woodsworth to John Mitchell, 14 May 1935, ibid.
32 David Lewis, *The Good Fight*, 80
33 *Hansard*, 7 May 1923, 2551–4; J.S. Woodsworth, 'Political Democracy,' 310–2
34 *Hansard*, 4 March 1934, 1077
35 Woodsworth, 'Political Democracy,' 310–11
36 J.S. Woodsworth, 'Co-operative Government in Canada,' 648–55; 'Political Democracy,' passim; *Weekly News*, 4 June 1926; 19 April 1929; 13 June 1930; 30 January, 27 February 1931
37 Woodsworth, 'Co-operative Government', 650–2
38 *Hansard*, 1 March 1934, 1077; 19 April 1934, 2332; 22 January 1935, 86–7; Woodsworth, 'Political Democracy,' 310–14
39 Woodsworth, 'Co-operative Government,' 648; *Hansard*, 31 March 1927, 1765; 9 February 1932, 75; 1 March 1934, 1077; 11 February 1935, 694
40 Woodsworth, 'Co-operative Government,' 648
41 *Hansard*, 1 March 1934, 1077

42 Ibid., 9 February 1932, 75

43 According to McNaught, the constitutional crisis of 1926 was a watershed in Woodsworth's thinking about party politics. He claims that after the crisis Woodsworth abandoned group-government theory, embraced the party system, and moved to establish a new party of the Left (*Prophet*, 228). He also argues (275) that 'the most striking aspect of the article ["Political Democracy"] was the absence of any reference to group government.' Group government theory meant many things: anti-partyism, direct democracy, cooperative government, and vocational representation. Certainly after 1926 Woodsworth came to reject direct democracy. But the other parts of the theory can still be found in his thinking in the later 1920s and 1930s. This is not to say that Woodsworth did not also think in fairly traditional terms when envisaging a new party. It is my claim that, for him, the assertion of one view did not preclude the assertion of an apparently contradictory, alternative one. Finally, Woodsworth in 'Political Democracy' may not have advocated the complete panoply of group government, but it is of interest that he did in fact advocate vocational representation just as he also expressed a militantly anti-party criticism of Canadian political organization.

44 *Weekly News*, 27 August 1926, 20 April 1928, 30 January 1931; *Hansard*, 14 December 1926, 65; 14 March 1929, 956–7; 21 April 1931, 764

45 *Weekly News*, 27 August 1926

46 *Hansard*, 21 April 1931, 764

47 Woodsworth, 'Political Democracy,' passim; *Weekly News*, 28 July 1933

48 J.S. Woodsworth to F.H. Underhill, 27 February 1934, Woodsworth Papers, III

49 This is almost the only occasion when Woodsworth advocated anything other than a centralized federation for Canada.

50 Woodsworth, 'Political Democracy,' 313–14

51 W.F. Dawson's *Procedure in the Canadian House of Commons* is indispensable on the subject of the evolution of parliamentary rules.

52 Conor Cruise O'Brien, *Parnell and His Party, 1880–90* (Oxford 1957)

53 *Hansard*, 23 June 1926, 4920–8, 4932–3; 30 June 1926, 5186–7

54 *Weekly News*, 5 February 1926. See also 4 June 1926; 24 February 1928; 4 April, 16 May 1930; *Manitoba Commonwealth*, 26 July 1935.

55 MacInnis, *Woodsworth* 274

56 *Weekly News*, 5 February 1926

57 Ibid., 24 February 1928

58 *Manitoba Commonwealth*, 6 September 1935

59 *Weekly News*, 19 December 1930

60 Ibid., 27 February 1931

61 Ibid., 4 June 1926

62 In calculating the extent of Woodsworth's alignment with party blocs, I have taken it as proven that he was in alliance with a party bloc if he voted in the company of 60 per cent or more of a given party's caucus membership.

63 *Hansard*, 7 February 1936, 25–6

64 Ibid., 8 January 1926, 28; 1 April 1935, 2292; 18 June 1936, 3875

65 Ibid., 1 April 1935, 2292; 18 June 1936, 3875

66 Ibid., 26 June 1923, 4380–1; 29 January 1926, 561

67 Ibid., 14 May 1923, 2728; 24 April 1924, 1459; 29 January 1926, 560–1; 13 February 1929, 89–90; 9 September 1930, 49–50; 27 April 1931, 1011; 23 February 1932, 449; 11 February 1935, 694

68 Ibid., 14 March 1929, 955–61; 27 April 1931, 1011–2; 29 April 1931, 1111; 11 February 1932, 114; 11 February 1935, 694

69 Ibid., 13 February 1928, 367; 26 March 1928, 1708; 17 September 1930, 300–1; 28 June 1934, 4383; *Weekly News*, 26 March, 27 August 1926; 6 July 1928; 11 May, 8 June 1934

70 *Hansard*, 2 March 1932, 732

71 *Weekly News*, 8 June 1934

72 *Hansard*, 29 January 1926, 560–1

73 Ibid., 18 February 1927

74 *Weekly News*, 25 September 1925; *Hansard*, 11 April 1927, 2236–8; 19 April 1934, 2328–9; 22 January 1935, 89; 11 February 1935, 695–7

75 *Weekly News*, 4 June 1926

76 *Hansard*, 11 February 1935, 697

77 *Weekly News*, 4 November 1932

78 *Hansard*, 9 March 1934, 1324

79 Ibid., 28 June 1934, 4383

80 Jock Brown, interview with the author, Winnipeg, 31 May 1985

81 G.H. Williams to J.S. Woodsworth, 11 June 1937, Young Papers

82 J.S. Woodsworth to G.H. Williams, 15 June 1937, ibid.

83 J. King Gordon, 'A Christian Socialist in the 1930s,' in Richard Allen, ed., *The Social Gospel in Canada* (Ottawa 1975), 148–9

84 George Eliot, *Felix Holt, the Radical* (Boston 1908 [1866]), 163

85 *Hansard*, 11 April 1927, 2267; 30 April 1928, 2528–30; 9 June 1928, 4095–8; 23 February 1933, 2407–9; Woodsworth, 'What Does Radical Labor Want?' 12; J.S. Woodsworth, 'The Labour Movement in the West,' *The Canadian Forum* 2, no. 19 (April 1922), 585–7

86 *Hansard*, 9 June 1928, 4097

87 Woodsworth, 'What Does Radical Labor Want?' 12
88 *Hansard*, 30 April 1928, 2529
89 Ibid., 23 February 1933, 2408, 2413
90 *The Independent*, 2 September 1921
91 McNaught, *Prophet*, 148; Robin, *Radical Politics*, 212
92 S.J. Farmer, 'The Canadian Labor Party,' *The Independent*, 2 September 1921
93 Woodsworth, 'The Labour Movement in the West,' 587
94 Independent Labor Party of Manitoba Minutes, Center Branch, 5 April 1923
95 *Weekly News*, 5 September 1925
96 Ibid., 10 December 1926
97 Woodsworth, 'The Labour Movement in the West,' 587
98 *Weekly News*, 21 October 1927
99 *Hansard*, 21 April 1931, 765
100 Ibid., 3 July 1934, 4603
101 Ibid., 23 April 1928, 2307–10; 30 April 1928, 2526–31; 8 May 1929, 2352–8; 14 July 1931, 3751–3; 14 February 1933, 2098–2100; 3 July 1934, 4602–5; 30 March 1937, 2290–2
102 Frank R. Scott, *Essays on the Constitution*, 49–75
103 *Hansard*, 30 April 1928, 2526–8; 8 May 1929, 2357–8; 14 February 1933, 2100
104 Ibid., 2 July 1935, 4128
105 Ibid., 8 May 1929, 2353
106 J.S. Woodsworth to Herbert Orliffe, 8 October 1937, Young Papers
107 Ibid.
108 *Manitoba Commonwealth*, 7 August 1936
109 *Hansard*, 28 May 1928, 3461–3; 17 March 1931, 77–8; 4 May 1931, 1245–9; 11 February 1932, 114–20; 17 February 1936, 260–1
110 Woodsworth constantly emphasized that force was the inevitable consequence of the unreleased, pent-up energy of deprived and exploited classes, and that those who refused concessions to the exploited were themselves ultimately responsible for any resort to violence. Woodsworth's use of this argument was sometimes so indiscriminate that it was as if the rhetoric of violence was, for him, a handy stick with which to beat the authorities and the established classes. Equally, Woodsworth was willing to use the threat of violent change as a means of winning over the establishment to his avowedly more moderate course.
111 *Hansard*, 15 April 1931, 622; 11 February 1932, 115

112 Woodsworth's admiration of the British parliamentary Left continued through the 1920s. Ramsay MacDonald's and Philip Snowdon's 'betrayal' of the Labour Party in 1931 was extensively noticed by the *Weekly News* but Woodsworth was largely silent on this matter. Through the 1930s he often recommended Sweden as an example to the Canadian Left.

113 *Hansard*, 19 September 1930, 479–80; 17 March 1931, 77–8; 1 April 1935, 2295–6

114 Ibid., 28 May 1928, 3461–2. The editorialists of the *Weekly News* were a good deal more circumspect in their comments on the Soviet Union than Woodsworth. Compare, for example, what Woodsworth said on the French and Russian revolutions with what an editorial on 26 May 1933 had to say: 'There are undoubtedly many fine ideals being put forward in Russia as there were unquestionably 150 years ago in France. But the evidence that the Russian Revolution has launched humanity on a new period of progress is so far decidedly weak. And if after another 150 years the evidence that Russia helped us onward toward the millenium is no stronger than that the butcheries of the French Revolution did the same thing, then the case for bloody revolution remains far from proved.'

115 *Hansard*, 28 May 1928, 3462

116 David Caute, in *The Fellow-Travellers: A Postscript to the Enlightenment* (London 1973), argues that three principal ideas marked fellow-travellers' attitudes towards the Soviet Union: that Russia gave up nothing in adopting a one-party government, although the liberal democracies must continue to cleave to ancient liberties; that, in the era of the Five-Year Plan, scientific planning must be extolled; and that, in essence, communism was desirable for others but not for themselves. Woodsworth certainly met the first two criteria, and came close to meeting the third.

117 *Weekly News*, 31 May 1929

118 *Hansard*, 19 September 1930, 479

119 Ibid., 17 March 1931, 77–8

120 Ibid., 11 February 1932, 117–18

121 J.S. Woodsworth, 'Europe – 1931,' Woodsworth Papers, xv

122 *Weekly News*, 6 November 1931

123 *Toronto Star Weekly*, 5, 12 December 1931

124 Ibid., 5 December 1931

125 Ibid.

126 Ibid.

127 Ibid., 12 December 1931
128 *Hansard*, 11 February 1932, 114–20
129 Ibid., 117
130 J.S. Woodsworth to Mrs. J. Penner, 29 July 1940, Woodsworth Papers, IV

CHAPTER 4   Economics, Cooperation, and Socialism, 1922–1940

1 M.C. Urquhart and K.A.H. Buckley, eds., *Historical Statistics of Canada* (Toronto 1965), 61, 84, 130, 173, 304
2 A.J.P. Taylor, *Beaverbrook* (New York 1972), 24–42
3 *Hansard*, 13 February 1928, 388
4 J.C. Weldon, 'Consolidations in Canadian Industry,' in L.A. Skeoch, ed., *Restrictive Trade Practices in Canada* (Toronto 1966), 234
5 Marr and Paterson, *Canada: An Economic History*, 413
6 On mergers and the new management doctrines, see Craven, '*An Impartial Umpire*,' 90–110.
7 Easterbrook and Aitken, *Canadian Economic History*, 449–70
8 Urquhart and Buckley, eds., *Historical Statistics*, 246
9 Marr and Paterson, *Canada: An Economic History*, 253–4
10 Ibid., 254
11 Laxer, *Open For Business*, 13
12 *Hansard*, 9 June 1931, 2549
13 Marr and Paterson, *Canada: An Economic History*, 295, 296
14 Safarian, *Foreign Ownership*, 10
15 Urquhart and Buckley, eds, *Historical Statistics*, 169
16 Ibid., 197
17 Ibid., 202
18 *Hansard*, 24 April 1922, 1070; 29 May 1922, 2245; 14 May 1923, 2723–4; 15 June 1925, 4299–300; 17 June 1931, 2751; 29 July 1931, 4290–1; 15 February 1934, 604–5
19 Ibid., 29 May 1922, 2245–6; 24 February 1928, 766; 31 July 1931, 4391–2; 2 March 1932, 732; 22 January 1935, 87; 12 March, 1937, 1748
20 Ibid., 14 March 1922, 89; 30 March 1922, 518–20; 16 June 1922, 3076; 24 April 1924, 1459; 2 June 1924, 2709; 19 April 1926, 2565; 24 February 1928, 766; 31 May 1929, 3105–6; 21 April 1931, 768; 4 May 1931, 1244–9; 17 June 1931, 2751; 2 March 1932, 732; 11 October 1932, 64; 16 May 1934, 3105–6; 27 February 1936, 581–3; 12 March 1937, 1748; *Weekly News*, 25 March 1927
21 *Hansard*, 14 May 1923, 2724, 2727
22 Ibid., 22 March 1923, 1344; 14 May 1923, 2723–4; 5 February 1934, 268;

11 June 1935, 3544; 27 February 1936, 579–80; *Weekly News*, 25 August 1933

23 *Hansard*, 11 February 1935, 691

24 Ibid., 24 April 1924, 1459; 13 February 1929, 87; 1 February 1933, 1692; 16 May 1934, 3105

25 Ibid., 24 April 1922, 1128; 29 May 1922, 2250; 20 March 1923, 1344; 14 December 1926, 66–7; 14 March 1929, 955–61; 20 September 1930, 504; 1 August 1931, 4454; 2 March 1932, 728; 19 April 1934, 2331–2

26 Woodsworth, *Distribution of Personal Income*, passim; *Hansard*, 14 May 1923, 2725–9; 13 February 1929, 87; 14 March 1929, 958–60; 9 September 1930, 50; 21 April 1931, 767; 18 February 1935, 914

27 Ibid., 14 May 1923, 2724. See also 11 June 1935, 3545

28 Ibid., 11 June 1935, 3543

29 F.A. Hayek, *Studies in Philosophy, Politics and Economics* (Chicago 1967), 82–95

30 *Hansard*, 1 April 1930, 1149

31 Ibid., 10 May 1926, 3262–3

32 Ibid., 7 May 1923, 2551–2

33 *Weekly News*, 10 September 1926. See also *Hansard*, 9 September 1930, 50.

34 *Weekly News*, 5 October 1928

35 Ibid., 10 September 1926

36 *Hansard*, 16 June 1922, 3076; 14 May 1923, 2729; 24 April 1924, 1459; 17 June 1931, 2751; 1 February 1933, 1692

37 Ibid., 31 July 1931, 4392. The Beauharnois scandal broke in 1931. It involved a syndicate of successful businessmen, notably Senator W.L. McDougald, who received approval by the Quebec and federal governments to develop hydro stations on the St Lawrence. An investigation by a Commons committee found that McDougald and Liberal Senator Andrew Haydon, both advisers to Mackenzie King, had been in a conflict of interest because they had used their relationship to the federal cabinet to influence the 1929 order in council which allowed the project to go ahead and had received subsequent financial advantage. The testimony of R.O. Sweezey, an engineer with the syndicate, was particularly damning. He admitted to having given between $600,000 and $700,000 to the Liberal Party in 1931, out of 'gratefulness.' See Neatby, *King, 1924–1932* and Whitaker, *The Government Party*.

38 *Hansard*, 1 February 1933, 1692

39 Ibid., 30 March 1922, 520; 29 May 1922, 2245; 2 February 1923, 44; 14 May 1923, 2725–7; 24 April 1924, 1458–9; 31 May 1929, 3105–6

40 Ibid., 5 February 1934, 267
41 Ibid., 4 May 1931, 1245–8; 11 February 1932, 114–20; 5 February 1934, 267–8; 9 March 1934, 1329–30; 27 February 1936, 581–2
42 Ibid., 21 April 1925, 2316–17; 17 June 1925, 4420–3; 20 May 1932, 3137–8; 10 March 1933, 2909–15; 9 May 1933, 4731–4
43 Ibid., 18 September 1930, 397
44 Ibid., 29 May 1922, 2242; 14 May 1923, 2723–4; 21 April 1925, 2304; 18 September 1930, 397; 4 May 1931, 1248; 16 May 1934, 3105; 22 January 1935, 86–7; 11 February 1935, 692
45 Ibid., 1 February 1933, 1690; 16 May 1934, 3103. See also 21 April 1931, 764; 29 April 1931, 1112; 4 May 1931, 1248; 11 February 1932, 114.
46 Ibid., 7 May 1923, 2552–4
47 *Weekly News*, 23 May 1930
48 *Hansard*, 2 March 1932, 727–8
49 Ibid., 9 September 1930, 47
50 Ibid., 4 May 1931, 1249
51 Ibid., 19 April 1934, 2329, 2332
52 Ibid., 16 May 1934, 3105
53 Ibid., 2 February 1923, 41; 14 May 1923, 2721; 23 March 1925, 2301; 17 September 1930, 302; 2 April 1936, 1749
54 Ibid., 18 May 1925, 3302
55 Ibid., 11 February 1929, 50; 7 May 1930, 1863; 9 September 1930, 47; 17 September 1930, 302
56 Ibid., 21 April 1925, 2304
57 Ibid., 14 May 1923, 2728; 24 April 1924, 1454–5; 10 May 1926, 3262; 13 April 1932, 1997; 23 April 1934, 2448
58 Ibid., 18 September 1930, 399. See also 21 April 1925, 2302; 22 March 1928, 1619; 14 March 1929, 955–6; 22 November 1932, 1445; 22 June 1938, 126–7.
59 Ibid., 21 October 1932, 430
60 Ibid., 11 February 1929, 50
61 Ibid., 19 September 1930, 479–80; 18 March 1931, 74–7
62 Ibid., 12 June 1924, 3149; 18 September 1930, 400–1; 17 March 1931, 75–6; 5 February 1934, 269; *Weekly News*, 10 April 1931
63 *Hansard*, 21 April 1925, 2304–8. See also ibid., 15 March 1926, 1562–4.
64 Ibid., 29 May 1922, 2243–4; 24 April 1924, 1455–6; 22 March 1926, 1770; 21 February 1927, 526; 31 January 1928, 71; 11 February 1929, 49; 9 June 1931, 2459–60; 5 April 1933, 3739; 28 May 1936, 3193
65 Ibid., 11 February 1929, 49–50
66 Ibid., 21 February 1927, 526

67 Ibid., 19 April 1926, 2566
68 Ibid., 24 April 1924, 1454–5; 24 February 1928, 766; 9 September 1930, 47–8; 9 June 1931, 2459; 21 October 1932, 431
69 Ibid., 24 February 1928, 766
70 Ibid., 9 September 1930, 47–8
71 Ibid., 9 June 1931, 2459
72 Ibid., 24 April 1924, 1457
73 J.S. Woodsworth, 'Notes on the Banking Committee,' *The Canadian Forum* 3, no. 35 (August 1923), 333
74 Carl Berger, *The Writing of Canadian History* (Toronto 1976), 25; S.E.D. Shortt, *The Search for an Ideal: Six Canadian Intellectuals and Their Convictions in an Age of Transition 1890–1930* (Toronto 1976), 108–10; Mardiros, *William Irvine*, 158; J.H. Dales, 'Canadian Scholarship in Economics,' in R. Hubbard, ed., *Scholarship in Canada* (Toronto 1968), 83–4
75 *Hansard*, 24 April 1924, 1455–7; 15 March 1926, 1568; 1 April 1930, 1149; 31 March 1931, 474; 2 March 1932, 727–8; 21 October 1932, 429; 22 January 1935, 89; 12 March 1937, 1748
76 Ibid., 4 March 1925, 754; 15 March 1926, 1569; 4 May 1932, 2643–4; 4 February 1935, 460; 9 June 1936, 3566
77 Ibid., 2 February 1923, 44; 18 June 1923, 4020–1; 4 March 1925, 753–9; 14 April 1926, 2416–19; 13 February 1928, 387–93; 1 March 1934, 1081; Woodsworth, 'Notes on the Banking Committee,' 333–4
78 *Hansard*, 18 June 1923, 4021–5; 13 February 1928, 389; 22 February 1934, 833–5; 1 March 1934, 1076–7; 11 June 1935, 3546
79 Ibid., 13 February 1928, 391
80 Ibid., 13 April 1932, 1996–7; 5 April 1933, 3740; 15 February 1934, 599
81 Ibid., 13 April 1932, 1996; 1 February 1933, 1690
82 Ibid., 10 May 1926, 3264; 14 February 1934, 597–9
83 Ibid., 4 March 1925, 754; 14 April 1926, 2416; 13 February 1928, 391–2
84 Ibid., 2 February 1923, 44; 18 June 1923, 4020–1; 4 March 1925, 754; 14 April 1926, 2416; 13 February 1928, 391–2; 1 March 1934, 1079–81; 9 March 1934, 1327–9; 4 February 1935, 460–1
85 Ibid., 9 September 1930, 48–9; 17 June 1931, 2749; 17 February 1936, 261; *Manitoba Commonwealth*, 1 January 1937
86 *Hansard*, 4 March 1925, 759
87 Ibid., 13 February 1928
88 Neatby, *King, 1932–1939*, 34–9
89 Fullerton, *Graham Towers*, 41–4
90 *Hansard*, 9 March 1934, 1324

91 Ibid., 9 March 1934, 1328–30
92 Ibid., 28 June 1934, 4383
93 Ibid., 21 April 1931, 764
94 Ibid., 28 March 1935, 2184
95 Ibid., 4 May 1932, 2643–4
96 Ibid., 17 March 1931, 72; 31 March 469–74; 9 March 1932, 964;
   15 February 1934, 601; 22 January 1935, 89; 11 February 1935, 692;
   26 February 1935, 1208
97 Ibid., 16 June 1922, 3076; 5 February 1934, 266; 11 February 1935, 696;
   27 February 1936, 582
98 Ibid., 2 March 1932, 732; 1 February 1933, 1688; 5 February 1934, 266;
   19 April 1934, 2330; 11 February 1935, 695–6; 27 February 1936, 582–3
99 Ibid., 14 May 1923, 2723–4; 2 March 1932, 730; 5 February 1934, 268;
   11 June 1935, 3544; 27 February 1936, 579–81; *Weekly News*, 25 August 1933
100 *Hansard*, 27 February 1936, 580
101 Ibid., 580–1
102 Ibid., 16 May 1934, 3104

CHAPTER 5   Canada and the World: Peace and Security, 1918–1939

1 The following figures are from Urquhart and Buckley, eds., *Historical Statistics*, 61, 197–202.
2 Eayrs, *In Defence of Canada*, 270–1
3 Socknat, *Witness*, 11–42, 65–8
4 MacInnis, *J.S. Woodsworth*, 209
5 George Woodcock and Ivan Avakumovic, *The Doukhobors* (London 1968), 223
6 Socknat, *Witness*, 71
7 *Hansard*, 22 March 1926, 1772; 25 January 1937, 240; Woodsworth, 'My Convictions about War' *Vox* 13.no. 1 (December 1939), 4; *Following the Gleam*, 9
8 Woodsworth, 'My Convictions,' 4
9 Woodsworth, *Following the Gleam*, 9
10 *Hansard*, 21 March 1929, 2686
11 *The Voice*, 1 December 1911
12 J.S. Woodsworth, 'Out of the Night, the Angels' Song,' in *Hours That Stand Apart*, 9
13 Woodsworth, *Following the Gleam*, 9
14 *Hansard*, 26 May 1930, 2593
15 Ibid., 24 July 1931, 4144

16 Woodsworth, 'Out of the Night,' 7
17 *Hansard*, 30 March 1939, 2448
18 Ibid., 8 September 1939, 46–7
19 Ibid., 1 April 1935, 2292
20 Ibid.
21 *Hansard*, 2 Feb. 1923, 46; 26 June 1925, 5046; 22 March 1926, 1772; 8 May 1931, 1404; 1 April 1935, 2296; 19 June 1936, 3878; 24 May 1938, 3220; 8 September 1939, 44–5; *Weekly News*, 10 July 1931
22 *Hansard*, 8 May 1931, 1404
23 *Manitoba Commonwealth*, 30 September 1938
24 *Hansard*, 2 February 1923, 45; 24 April 1924, 1457; 22 March 1926, 1770–2; 28 May 1928, 3462–3; 25 January 1937, 240–1
25 Ibid., 25 January 1937, 240–2
26 Ibid., 25 April 1922, 1143; 9 April 1927, 2208; 4 June 1929, 3215; 16 May 1932, 2975–8; 19 May 1936, 2988; 24 May 1938, 3221
27 Ibid., 1 April 1935, 2294
28 Ibid., 24 May 1938, 3221
29 Ibid., 4 June 1929, 3215–16
30 Ibid., 3221
31 Ibid., 28 May 1936, 3194
32 Ibid., 29 June 1923, 4654
33 Ibid., 25 June 1937, 237–8
34 Ibid., 2 February 1923, 47; 18 May 1925, 3302; 31 March 1927, 1764–5; 26 March 1928, 1707; 2 March 1936, 675; *Manitoba Commonwealth*, 26 December 1936
35 *Hansard*, 26 March 1928, 1707
36 Ibid., 12 February 1934, 492
37 Ibid., 5 March 1923, 845; 4 June 1929, 3217; 7 May 1930, 1862
38 Ibid., 5 March 1923, 845
39 Ibid., 24 April 1924, 1454–6; 22 March 1926, 1770; 11 February 1929, 49–50; 9 June 1931, 2459
40 Ibid., 11 February 1929, 49
41 Ibid., 25 April 1922, 1143; 18 May 1922, 1974–7; 9 April 1927, 2207–9; 26 March 1928, 1704–8; 4 June 1929, 3215–21; 6 March 1930, 345; 22 June 1931, 2900–2; 21 March 1934, 1690–7; 24 May 1938, 3213, 3221
42 Ibid., 4 June 1929, 3217; 28 May 1936, 3197; 18 June 1936, 3875; 25 January 1937, 241
43 Ibid., 25 April 1922, 1143; 24 May 1938, 3212
44 Ibid., 28 May 1936, 3192–3; 18 June 1936, 3875; 25 January 1937, 241; *Manitoba Commonwealth*, 25 December 1936

45 *Hansard*, 18 June 1936, 3875
46 *Manitoba Commonwealth*, 25 December 1936
47 *Hansard*, 8 May 1929, 2358
48 Ibid., 4 June 1929, 3217
49 Ibid., 28 May 1936, 3193
50 Ibid., 19 February 1929, 249–50; 4 June 1929, 3216–17; 1 April 1935, 2293
51 Ibid., 28 May 1928, 3461; 11 February 1929, 51; 1 April 1935, 2293; 24 May 1938, 3221; 8 September 1939, 46
52 Ibid., 28 May 1928, 3458–61; 11 February 1929, 50–3; 12 February 1934, 494
53 Ibid., 2 February 1923, 41–7; 11 February 1929, 51
54 Ibid., 28 May 1936, 3194
55 Ibid., 26 May 1930, 2591
56 Ibid., 18 June 1936, 3875
57 Ibid., 22 March 1926, 1770
58 Ibid., 29 June 1923, 4652; 22 March 1926, 1769–73; 31 March 1927, 1759–65; 12 February 1934, 490–2; 15 March 1934, 1534; 1 April 1935, 2293–4; 28 May 1936, 3194–7; 25 January 1937, 238–41
59 Ibid., 1 April 1935, 2294
60 Ibid., 15 March 1934, 1534
61 Ibid., 24 May 1938, 3220
62 Ibid., 26 June 1925, 5048
63 For Ewart's influence on King, see Stacey, *Age of Conflict*, 6, 40, 80.
64 *Hansard*, 31 March 1927, 1764; 11 February 1929, 51; 8 April 1930, 1391–2
65 Ibid., 15 January 1937, 15
66 Ibid., 12 February 1934, 494
67 Ibid., 15 June 1923, 3993–7; 26 June 1925, 5045–8
68 Ibid., 21 April 1925, 2305; 15 March 1926, 1563; 28 May 1928, 3458–62
69 Ibid., 8 April 1930, 1393
70 Ibid., 25 May 1932, 3437
71 Ibid., 12 February 1934, 491–2
72 Ibid., 1 April 1935, 2292
73 Ibid., 15 March 1934, 1535
74 Veatch, *Canada and the League of Nations*, 163
75 Minutes of National Council, Winnipeg, 30 November 1935, CCF Papers, 1
76 *Hansard*, 2 March 1936, 676; 18 June 1936, 3876; 25 January 1937, 241; 24 May 1938, 3215–16; *Manitoba Commonwealth*, 22 December 1939
77 *Hansard*, 2 March 1936, 676, 678; 18 June 1936, 3876–8; 25 January 1937, 239–40; *Manitoba Commonwealth*, 30 September 1938
78 *Hansard*, 25 January 1937, 239

79 Douglas, *Making of a Socialist*, 101
80 *Hansard*, 2 March 1936, 675–8
81 Ibid., 18 June 1936, 3873–9
82 Ibid., 3877
83 Ibid.
84 Ibid., 25 January 1937, 239
85 See Hoar, *Mackenzie-Papineau Battalion*.
86 Djwa, *Politics of the Imagination*, 170–4
87 *Hansard*, 19 March 1937, 1942–5; *Manitoba Commonwealth*, 25 March 1937
88 *Manitoba Commonwealth*, 4 February 1938
89 *Hansard*, 28 February 1939, 2610
90 J.S. Woodsworth to D. Portlance, 27 February 1939, CCF Papers, CVII
91 *Manitoba Commonwealth*, 30 September 1938
92 *Hansard*, 8 September 1939, 46–7
93 Urquhart and Buckley, eds., *Historical Statistics*, 23, 27–8
94 Ward, *White Canada Forever*, passim
95 *Hansard*, 4 May 1923, 2485
96 *Manitoba Commonwealth*, 6 September 1935
97 *Hansard*, 20 March 1923, 1338–45; 29 January 1926, 569–74; 7 June 1928, 3904; 8 May 1931, 1402–3
98 Ibid., 20 March 1923, 1341; 20 March 1924, 512; 16 April 1924, 1425; 6 April 1927, 2012; 8 May 1931, 1402; 3 May 1932, 2595
99 Ibid., 20 March 1923, 1336–45; 24 April 1924, 1457–60; 29 January 1926, 570–4; 6 April 1927, 2011–3; 7 June 1928, 3898–904; 5 March 1934, 1173
100 *Weekly News*, 14 August 1925
101 *Hansard*, 16 April 1924, 1424–5
102 Ibid., 1 May 1928, 2573
103 Ibid., 18 March 1925, 1274; 3 July 1934, 4601
104 Ibid., 20 March 1923, 1340
105 Ibid., 24 April 1924, 1457
106 Ibid., 20 March 1923, 1341
107 Ibid., 29 January 1926, 570–1
108 Ibid., 570
109 Ibid., 8 May 1931, 1402
110 Ibid., 29 January 1926, 573
111 *Weekly News*, 7 December 1928
112 *Hansard*, 7 June 1928, 3903–4
113 Ibid., 7 May 1930, 1862
114 Ibid., 6 June 1928, 3825–6; 13 July 1931, 3674–8; 20 March 1936, 1289–96; 30 May 1938, 3352–3
115 Ibid., 17 June 1925, 4420–1

116 Ibid., 3 July 1934, 4604
117 Ibid., 7 June 1928, 3899
118 Ibid., 2485
119 Ibid., 11 July 1924, 4357; 25 June 1925, 4907; 24 July 1931, 4143–5; 20 February 1936, 388–91
120 Ibid., 12 February 1934, 494
121 Charles J. Woodsworth, *Canada and the Orient*
122 *Hansard*, 11 February 1938, 381; 24 May 1938, 3203
123 Ibid., 25 June 1925, 4907
124 J.S. Woodsworth to Mackenzie King, 3 March 1926, Woodsworth Papers, II
125 Ibid.
126 *Hansard*, 20 February 1936, 388
127 Ibid., 389
128 Ibid., 2 May 1928, 2617–18; 24 May 1938, 3203
129 Ibid., 20 February 1936, 390
130 *Manitoba Commonwealth*, 10 December 1937
131 *Hansard*, 24 May 1938, 3203
132 Abella and Troper, *None Is Too Many*, 25, 65
133 *Hansard*, 20 March 1924, 508–9
134 Ibid., 5 March 1923, 845; 18 July 1924, 4750–3; 19 April 1926, 2563–6; 18 February 1927, 448–9; 14 March 1929, 959–61; 23 May 1929, 2783–5; 27 May 1930, 2690–2; 12 September 1930, 166–7; 26 May 1931, 1969–70; 4 May 1932, 2643–5; 19 April 1934, 2332; 13 March 1935, 1672–3
135 Ibid., 15 February 1929, 166
136 Ibid., 23 April 1934, 2447
137 Ibid., 19 April 1926, 2567
138 Ibid., 7 March 1938, 1080
139 Ibid., 20 March 1924, 512; 18 February 1925, 302–3; 11 May 1931, 1467–73; 28 January 1935, 219–21; 1 February 1937, 441
140 Ibid., 11 May 1931, 1471–2
141 Woodsworth, *Strangers*, 90, 245–7
142 Ibid., 90
143 Ibid., 245–7
144 *Manitoba Free Press*, 30 May 1913
145 J.S. Woodsworth to C.B. Sissons, 1 March 1916, Sissons Papers
146 Ibid., 13 September 1916
147 Ibid., 21 November 1916
148 J.S. Woodsworth to Howard Woodsworth, 21 January 1942, copy in possession of the author.
149 *Hansard* 2 March 1927, 817

150 Ibid., 11 June 1936, 3632
151 Ibid., 26 April 1938, 2262
152 Young, *Anatomy of a Party*, 215
153 Gregory Baum, *Catholics and Canadian Socialism* (Toronto 1980), 124–5
154 *Hansard*, 17 June 1931, 2750; 2 March 1932, 729; *Weekly News*, 26 October 1928
155 *Hansard*, 18 February 1925, 303
156 Ibid., 9 March 1927, 1039
157 Ibid., 11 May 1931, 1466–73.
158 Ibid., 20 March 1924, 508
159 Ibid., 20 March 1924, 508–13; 18 February 1925, 302–3; 11 May 1931, 1466–73
160 Ibid., 15 June 1925, 4299–300; 4 May 1928, 2708
161 Ibid., 26 May 1930, 2592
162 Ibid., 8 January 1926, 25–9; 30 June 1926, 5187
163 Ibid., 20 March 1924, 510
164 Ibid., 14 January 1937, 4–5; 15 January 1937, 13–16
165 Ibid., 28 May 1936, 3195
166 Socknat, *Witness*, 195–6
167 McNaught, *Prophet*, 298

CONCLUSION

1 Douglas, *Making of a Socialist*, 124
2 J.S. Woodsworth to David Lewis, 6 March 1940, CCF Papers, CVII
3 *Manitoba Commonwealth*, 1 March 1940
4 J.S. Woodsworth to Howard Woodsworth, 21 January 1942, copy in possession of the author
5 Charles Woodsworth, interview with the author, Old Chelsea, Quebec, 21 October 1984
6 Djwa, *Politics of the Imagination*, 109–10
7 Ibid., 109
8 Cook, *The Regenerators*, 213–23, 228–32; '"Madame Bovary's Problem,"' unpublished paper, delivered at University of Winnipeg, October 1988, 4–5
9 Salem Bland, *The New Christianity* (Toronto 1920), 49
10 Young, *Anatomy of a Party*, 12–101

Select Bibliography

I. PRIMARY SOURCES

A. *Archive material*

National Archives of Canada, Ottawa
MG 28, IVI   CCF Papers
MM 63/W868   Sissons Papers
MG 30, D204   Underhill Papers
MG 27   Woodsworth Papers

Provincial Archives of Manitoba, Winnipeg
MG 14/B25   Dixon Papers
MG 14/B64, D4   Independent Labor Party of Manitoba Papers
MG 14/B31   Ivens Papers
MG 10/A14–1   Russell Papers

Special Collections, University of British Columbia Library, Vancouver
MacInnis Papers
Young Papers

University of Winnipeg Library
Wesley College Calendars

B. *Newspapers*

BC Federationist
Canadian Forum

Canadian Municipal Journal
Grain Growers' Guide
Independent
Manitoba Commonwealth
Manitoba Free Press
Strike Bulletin
Voice
Weekly News
Western Labor News

C. *Interviews*

Brown, Jock, Winnipeg, 31 May 1985
MacInnis, Grace, Vancouver, 22 October 1983
Stubbs, Roy St. George, Winnipeg, 24 February 1978
Woodsworth, Bruce, Silver Sands, BC, 21 August 1984
Woodsworth, Charles, Old Chelsea, Quebec, 21 October 1984
Woodsworth, Howard, Scarborough, Ontario, 27 October 1984

D. *Contemporary Sources*

Douglas, T.C. *The Making of a Socialist: The Recollections of T.C. Douglas.*
    Edited by Lewis H. Thomas. Edmonton 1982
Hansard: Debates of the Canadian House of Commons; Official Report
Irvine, William. *The Farmers in Politics.* Toronto 1920
– *Co-operative Government.* N.p. 1929
Lewis, David. *The Good Fight: Political Memoirs, 1909–1958.* Toronto 1981
Lower, Arthur R.M. *My First Seventy-Five Years.* Toronto 1967
Sissons, C.B. *Nil Alienum: The Memoirs of C.B. Sissons.* Toronto 1964
– *Bi-lingual Schools in Canada.* Toronto 1917
Underhill, Frank H. *James Shaver Woodsworth: Untypical Canadian.* Toronto
    1944
Votes and Proceedings of the Canadian House of Commons
Woodsworth, Bruce. 'Unpublished Recollections'
Woodsworth, Charles. *Canada and the Orient: A Study in International
    Relations.* Toronto 1941
– 'A Prophet at Home: An Intimate Memoir of the Late J.S. Woodsworth,
    M.P.' Unpublished
Woodsworth, J.S. *Studies in Rural Citizenship.* Winnipeg n.d.
– *Strangers within Our Gates.* Toronto 1972 [1909]

- *My Neighbor.* Toronto 1911
- 'Nation-Building,' *University Magazine* 16, no. 1 (February 1917), 85–99
- *On the Waterfront.* Ottawa n.d.
- *The First Story of the Labor Church.* Winnipeg 1920
- 'What Does Radical Labor Want?' *Maclean's Magazine*, April 1922
- 'My Religion,' in *Following the Gleam*, 15–18. Ottawa 1926
- *Hours That Stand Apart.* N.p. 1929
- 'Co-operative Government in Canada,' *Queen's Quarterly* 37, no. 4 (Autumn 1930), 648–55
- 'So this is Russia,' *Toronto Star Weekly* 5, 12 December 1931
- *The Distribution of Personal Income.* N.p. 1934
- 'Political Democracy,' *University of Toronto Quarterly* 4, no. 3 (April 1935), 296–314
- 'My Convictions about War,' *Vox* 13, no. 1 (December 1939), 4–7
- ed., *Ukrainian Rural Communities: Report of Investigation by Bureau of Social Research.* Winnipeg 1917
Woodsworth, James. *Thirty Years in the Canadian North-West.* Toronto 1917

II. SECONDARY SOURCES

Abella, Irving, and Harold Troper. *None is Too Many: Canada and the Jews of Europe, 1933–1948.* Toronto 1982
Allen, Richard. *The Social Passion: Religion and Social Reform in Canada, 1914–28.* Toronto 1971
- ed. *The Social Gospel in Canada.* Ottawa 1975
Bedford, A.G. *The University of Winnipeg: A History of the Founding Colleges.* Toronto 1976
Bercuson, David J. *Fools and Wise Men.* Toronto 1978
Bercuson, David J., and Kenneth McNaught. *Confrontation at Winnipeg: Labour, Industrial Relations, and the General Strike.* Montreal 1974
Butcher, Dennis L., et al., eds. *Prairie Spirit: Perspectives on the Heritage of the United Church of Canada in the West.* Winnipeg 1985
Caplan, Gerald L. *The Dilemma of Canadian Socialism: The CCF in Ontario.* Toronto 1973
Cook, Ramsay. *The Regenerators: Social Criticism in Late Victorian English Canada.* Toronto 1985
- '"Madame Bovary's Problem."' Unpublished paper, delivered at University of Winnipeg, October 1988
Craven, Paul. *'An Impartial Umpire': Industrial Relations and the Canadian State, 1900–1911.* Toronto 1980

Dawson, W.F. *Procedure in the Canadian House of Commons.* Toronto 1962

Djwa, Sandra. *The Politics of the Imagination: A Life of F.R. Scott.* Toronto 1987

Easterbrook, W.T., and Hugh G. Aitken. *Canadian Economic History.* Toronto 1965

Eayrs, James. *In Defence of Canada: From the Great War to the Great Depression.* Toronto 1964

Francis, R. Douglas. *Frank H. Underhill: Intellectual Provocateur.* Toronto 1986

Friesen, Gerald. *The Canadian Prairies: A History.* Toronto 1984

Fullerton, Douglas H. *Graham Towers and His Times.* Toronto 1986

Glazebrook G.P. de T. *A History of Canadian External Relations.* Toronto 1950

Graham, Roger. *Arthur Meighen* 3 vols., 2: *And Fortune Fled.* Toronto 1963

Granatstein, J.L. *The Ottawa Men.* Toronto 1982

Hoar, Victor. *The Mackenzie-Papineau Battalion.* Toronto 1969

Horn, Michiel. *The League for Social Reconstruction: Intellectual Origins of the Democratic Left in Canada 1930–1942.* Toronto 1980

Horowitz, Gad. *Canadian Labour in Politics.* Toronto 1968

Laxer, Gordon. *Open for Business: The Roots of Foreign Ownership in Canada.* Toronto 1989

Levitt, Joseph. *Henri Bourassa and the Golden Calf.* Ottawa 1969

Lipset, S.M. *Agrarian Socialism.* New York 1968

MacInnis, Grace. *J.S. Woodsworth: A Man to Remember.* Toronto 1953

MacPherson, Ian. *Each for All: A History of the Co-operative Movement in English Canada, 1900–1945.* Toronto 1979

McCormack, A. Ross. *Reformers, Rebels and Revolutionaries: The Western Canadian Radical Movement 1899–1919.* Toronto 1977

McNaught, Kenneth. *A Prophet in Politics.* Toronto 1959

Mardiros, Anthony. *William Irvine: The Life of a Prairie Radical.* Toronto 1979

Marr, William L., and Donald G. Paterson. *Canada: An Economic History.* Toronto 1980

Mills, Allen. 'The Later Thought of J.S. Woodsworth, 1918–1942,' *Journal of Canadian Studies* 17, no. 3 (Fall 1982), 75–95

– 'Cooperation and Community in the Thought of J.S. Woodsworth,' *Labour/Le Travail* 14 (Fall 1984), 103–20

Morley, J.T. *Secular Socialists: The CCF/NDP in Ontario, A Biography.* Kingston and Montreal 1984

Morton, W.L. *The Progressive Party in Canada.* Toronto 1950

Neatby, H. Blair. *William Lyon Mackenzie King, 1924–1932.* Toronto 1963

– *William Lyon Mackenzie King: 1932–1939.* Toronto 1976

Owram, Doug. *The Government Generation: Canadian Intellectuals and the State 1900–1945.* Toronto 1986

Palmer, Bryan D. *Working-Class Experience: The Rise and Reconstitution of Canadian Labour, 1800–1980*. Toronto 1983

Penner, Norman. *The Canadian Left: A Critical Analysis*. Scarborough 1977
– *Canadian Communism: The Stalin Years and Beyond*. Toronto 1988

Philipps, Paul A. *No Power Greater: A Century of Labour in British Columbia*. Vancouver 1967

Robin, Martin. *Radical Politics and Canadian Labour, 1880–1930*. Kingston 1968

Safarian, A.E. *Foreign Ownership of Canadian Industry*. Toronto 1966

Scott, Frank R. *Essays on the Constitution: Aspects of Canadian Law and Politics*. Toronto 1977

Skeoch, L.A., ed. *Restrictive Trade Practices in Canada*. Toronto 1966

Socknat, Thomas P. *Witness against War: Pacifism in Canada, 1900–1945*. Toronto 1987

Stacey, C.P. *Canada and the Age of Conflict: A History of Canadian External Policies, 1921–48*. Toronto 1981

Steeves, Dorothy. *The Compassionate Rebel: Ernest Winch and His Times*. Vancouver 1960

Teeple, Gary, ed. *Capitalism and the National Question*. Toronto 1972

Trigger, Bruce G. *Natives and Newcomers: Canada's Heroic Age Reconsidered*. Kingston and Montreal 1985

Trofimenkoff, Susan Mann. *The Dream of Nation*. Toronto 1985

Urquhart, M.C., and K.A.H. Buckley, eds. *Historical Statistics of Canada*. Toronto 1965

Veatch, Richard. *Canada and the League of Nations*. Toronto 1975

Wade, Mason. *The French Canadians, 1760–1967*, 2 vols. Toronto 1968

Ward, W. Peter. *White Canada Forever: Popular Attitudes and Public Policy towards Orientals in British Columbia*. Montreal 1978

Whitaker, Reginald. *The Government Party: Organizing and Financing the Liberal Party of Canada, 1930–58*. Toronto 1977

Wiseman, Nelson. *Social Democracy in Manitoba: A History of the CCF-NDP*. Winnipeg 1983

Young, Walter, D. *The Anatomy of a Party: The National CCF, 1932–61*. Toronto 1969

Ziegler, Olive. *Woodsworth: Social Pioneer*. Toronto 1934

Credits

National Archives of Canada: All Peoples' Mission picnic (c66636); Woodsworth family before leaving Winnipeg for British Columbia (c80128); Woodsworth in front of the Centre Block, Ottawa (c66639); delivering a speech at the YMCA (c55451)

Bruce Woodsworth: delegates to the 1934 CCF convention

Western Canada Pictorial Index (University of Winnipeg): Senior Stick (763–22957); J.S. and Lucy Woodsworth (763–22961); Woodsworth in the late 1930s (804–24068)

Winnipeg Free Press: cartoons by Ardrie Dale, 20 and 25 July 1933

The epigraphs are drawn from the following: 'The Journey of the Magi' and 'The Waste Land' in *Collected Poems 1909–1962* by T.S. Eliot, copyright 1936 by Harcourt Brace Jovanovich, Inc., copyright 1964, 1963 by T.S. Eliot, reprinted by permission of Harcourt Brace Jovanovich, Inc., and Faber and Faber, Ltd.; 'Efficiency. Social Notes II' from *The Collected Poems of F.R. Scott*, used by permission of the Canadian Publishers, McClelland and Stewart, Toronto; 'Bottleneck' from *The Collected Poems of Louis MacNeice*, reprinted with permission of Faber and Faber, Ltd.

Index